TELL ME HOW THIS
ENDS

TELL ME HOW THIS
ENDS

GENERAL DAVID PETRAEUS AND
THE SEARCH FOR A WAY OUT OF IRAQ

LINDA ROBINSON

PublicAffairs
New York

Published in the United States by PublicAffairs™, a member of the Perseus Books Group.

PublicAffairs books are available at special discounts for bulk purchases in the U.S. by corporations, institutions, and other organizations. For more information, please contact the Special Markets Department at the Perseus Books Group, 2300 Chestnut Street, Suite 200, Philadelphia, PA 19103, call (800) 810-4145, ext. 5000, or e-mail special.markets@perseusbooks.com.

Designed by Linda Harper
Text set in 11.25 Minion

Library of Congress Cataloging-in-Publication Data

Robinson, Linda
Tell me how this ends : General David Petraeus and the search for a way out of Iraq /
Linda Robinson. — 1st ed.
    p. cm.
Includes bibliographical references and index.
ISBN 978-1-58648-528-3
1. Iraq War, 2003– —Campaigns. 2. Petraeus, David Howell—Interviews.
3. Postwar reconstruction—Iraq. 4. United States—Politics and government—
2001– 5. Iraq—Politics and government—2003– I. Title.

DS79.76.R63885 2008
956.7044'3—dc22
                                                                    2008021517

First Edition
10 9 8 7 6 5 4 3 2 1

FOR THOSE WHO GAVE
THEIR LIVES TO HELP IRAQ

THE SHIA ARE AFRAID OF THE PAST,
THE SUNNIS ARE AFRAID OF THE FUTURE,
AND THE KURDS ARE AFRAID OF
BOTH THE PAST AND THE FUTURE.

—HOSHYAR ZEBARI

Contents

Principal Cast of Characters
(as of February 2007)

Gen. David Petraeus, Commanding General (CG), Multi-National Force-Iraq (MNF-I)

Lt. Gen. Graeme Lamb (UK), Deputy CG, MNF-I

Lt. Gen. Raymond Odierno, CG, Multi-National Corps-Iraq (MNC-I)

Lt. Gen. Martin Dempsey, CG, Multi-National Security Transition Command-Iraq (MNSTC-I)

Lt. Gen. Stanley McChrystal, CG, Joint Special Operations Command Task Force

Maj. Gen. William Caldwell, Deputy Chief of Staff (DCS), Strategic Effects, MNF-I

Maj. Gen. David Fastabend, DCS, Strategic Operations, MNF-I

Col. Peter Mansoor, Executive Officer to MNF-I CG

Col. William Rapp, Commander's Initiatives Group, MNF-I CG

Col. Steve Boylan, Public Affairs Officer to MNF-I CG

Dr. Derek Harvey, Senior Intelligence Adviser to MNF-I CG

Dr. David Kilcullen, Senior Counterinsurgency Adviser to MNF-I CG

Col. (Ret.) John Martin, Senior Adviser to MNF-I CG

Col. Mark Martins, Staff Judge Advocate, MNF-I

Sadi Othman, Senior Adviser to MNF-I CG
Col. H. R. McMaster, Co-leader, Joint Strategic Assessment Team
Maj. Everett Spain, aide de camp

MULTI-NATIONAL DIVISION-BAGHDAD (MND-B)

Maj. Gen. Joseph Fil, CG, 1st Cavalry Division
Brig. Gen. John Campbell, DCG for Maneuver
Lt. Col. Doug Ollivant, Chief of Plans
Lt. Col. Steve North, Chief of Intelligence
Col. Steve Townsend, Commanding Officer, 3rd Brigade (Stryker), 2nd
    Infantry Division
Lt. Col. Van Smiley, Commander, 1st Battalion, 23rd Infantry Regiment
    (Stryker)

BAGHDAD OPERATIONS COMMAND (IRAQI)

Lt. Gen. Abboud Qanbar, CG

KARKH AREA COMMAND (IRAQI)

Maj. Gen. Abdul Ameer Yaralla, CG, 6th Iraqi Division
Col. Ghassan Khalid, Commanding Officer, 1st Brigade, 6th Iraqi
    Division

WEST BAGHDAD (MANSOUR AND KADHIMIYA SECURITY DISTRICTS)

Col. J. B. Burton, Commanding Officer, 2nd Brigade, 1st Infantry
    Division
Lt. Col. Dale Kuehl, Commander, 1st Battalion, 5th Cavalry Regiment,
    1st Cavalry Division
Maj. Chris Rogers, Maj. Chip Daniels, battalion executive and
    operations officers
Cpt. Mike Ernst, Cpt. Brendan Gallagher, Cpt. Eric Cosper, company
    commanders
Sgt. First Class Joseph Frye, platoon sergeant

Northeast Baghdad (Adhamiya and Sadr City Security Districts)

Col. Billy Don Farris, Commanding Officer, 2nd Brigade, 82nd Airborne Division

Lt. Col. Eric Schacht, Commander, 1st Battalion, 26th Infantry Regiment, 1st Infantry Division

Maj. Clay Padgett, Maj. John Meyer, battalion executive and operations officers

Cpt. John Nakata, battalion intelligence officer

Cpt. Mike Baka, Cpt. Scott Gilman, company commanders

Lt. Matthew Martinez, Sgt. Tim Ybay, platoon leaders

Sgt. Widmark Quashie, platoon sergeant

South Baghdad (East and West Rashid Security Districts)

Col. Ricky Gibbs, Commanding Officer, 4th Brigade, 1st Infantry Division

Lt. Col. George Glaze, Commander, 1st Battalion, 18th Infantry Regiment, 1st Infantry Division

Lt. Col. Jim Crider, Commander, 4th Squadron, 1st Cavalry Regiment, 1st Infantry Division

Lt. Col. Pat Frank, Commander, 1st Battalion, 28th Infantry Regiment, 1st Infantry Division

Combined Joint Special Operations Task Force-Arabian Peninsula

Col. Ken Tovo, Commanding Officer, 10th Special Forces Group (Airborne)

Lt. Col. Sean Swindell, Commander, Special Operations Task Force-Central

U.S. Embassy

Amb. Ryan Crocker (arrived March 2007)

Amb. Pat Butenis, Deputy Chief of Mission

Amb. Charles Ries, Minister for Economic Affairs

Amb. Marcie B. Ries, Counselor for Political-Military Affairs
Matthew Tueller, Counselor for Political Affairs
Philip Reeker, Counselor for Public Affairs
Phyllis Powers, Director, Provincial Reconstruction Teams

GOVERNMENT OF IRAQ

Prime Minister Nouri al-Maliki
President Jalal Talabani
Vice President Adil Abd al-Mahdi
Vice President Tariq al-Hashimi
Deputy Prime Minister Barham Salih
National Security Adviser Mowaffak al-Rubaie
Amb. Sadiq al-Rikabi, Political Adviser to the Prime Minister
Bassima al-Jaidri, Dr. Safa Hussein, Office of the Commander in
    Chief/National Reconciliation Committee
Foreign Minister Hoshyar Zebari
Amb. Samir Sumaidaie

OTHER IRAQIS

Muqtada al-Sadr, Shia political leader
Abdul Aziz al-Hakim, leader of the Shia party Islamic Supreme Council
    of Iraq (ISCI)
Sheikh Humam Hamoudi, ISCI legislator
Sheikh Khaled Muhamed Ahmad Mizwid al-Ubaydi
Abu Abid, nom de guerre of Saif Sa'ad Ahmed al-Ubaydi

WHITE HOUSE OFFICIALS

Meghan O'Sullivan, Special Assistant to the President and Deputy
    National Security Adviser for Iraq and Afghanistan

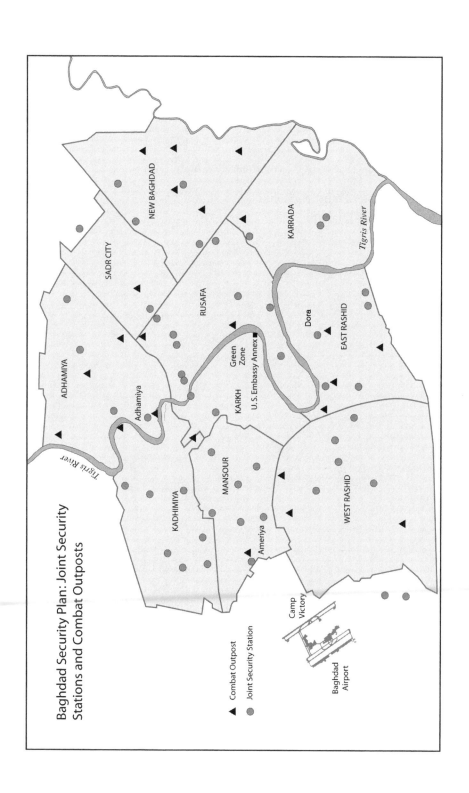

Baghdad Security Plan: Joint Security Stations and Combat Outposts

▲ Combat Outpost
● Joint Security Station

Preface

During a jog around the manmade lakes of Camp Victory at dusk, not far from the runways of Baghdad Airport, a siren sounded and a recorded voice came over speakers mounted at intervals along the paved road of Saddam's former pleasure palace complex. "Take cover. Take cover," the metallic voice said. I had not yet turned onto the exposed back stretch of road that sat atop a berm between Saddam's Walleye Lake and the airport fence. I glanced behind me and saw two soldiers, a female and a male, duck between two cargo containers beside the road and ran over to crouch beside them. No incoming rockets landed within earshot. A few minutes later, the voice proclaimed "all clear." Although most of the mortars and rockets aimed at Victory fell harmlessly short, two soldiers had been killed a few months earlier so no one was complacent. It was a far cry in lethality from the hell that had reigned in Baghdad neighborhoods twelve months earlier. The fighting had not ended by any means, but by June 2008, Iraq was as calm as it had ever been.

THE IRAQ WAR has been a seminal event in American history. It deeply divided and discouraged the American public, and it certainly did not turn out to be as short and cheap as the relatively bloodless interventions, proxy wars, and peacekeeping missions that the United States undertook in the quarter-century between the Vietnam War and Operation Iraqi Freedom. The Iraq war has more closely resembled Vietnam in terms of the cost, duration, and irregular nature of the combat than any other military action in recent memory. Its signature weapon is the homemade bomb, the guerrilla weapon of choice of America's adversaries, which appeared in a dizzying array of ever-more lethal configurations.

This book is the story of a war turned around. The book's opening chapters trace the crucial decisions, missteps and trendlines between 2003 and 2006, viewed with the benefit of hindsight and new reportage. Having covered the war from its inception, I wanted to provide readers with a perspective of the conflict's entire dynamic, since much of what was done in the latter years was an attempt to undo earlier mistakes.

The deepening war in 2006 led the Bush administration to seek a change in course and a new general to lead what was widely viewed as America's last best effort. David Petraeus had served two tours in Iraq and then overseen the writing of a new Army-Marine Corps counterinsurgency manual, as the military grappled with the failures in Iraq and more generally the challenges of irregular warfare. Well aware that Americans' patience was ebbing, Petraeus returned to Iraq to develop a political-military strategy that would integrate civilian and military efforts in a simultaneous "bottom-up" and "top-down" campaign. His leadership of the so-called surge of 2007–2008 is recounted from the strategic and operational level to its implementation throughout Baghdad, which was declared to be the main effort since most violence was occurring there. The Baghdad security plan's design and execution by U.S. and Iraqi units is chronicled in detail, including the experiences of 1st Battalion, 26th Infantry Regiment, and 1st Battalion, 5th Cavalry Regiment, in two of Baghdad's most violent neighborhoods.

Petraeus and his strategists believed the political causes of the conflict had to be addressed to end the war, which meant focusing all "lines of operation" on this goal. This concept applied to all military units down to the tactical units on the ground, but also to the diplomats and other civilians involved in the effort. Ambassador Ryan Crocker and the embassy team were central actors in developing the strategy and carrying it out.

Iraq's political leaders, parties, and ordinary citizens are fighting over how their country is to be governed and, indeed, whether it will continue to exist at all. The book aims to provide insight into the motivations and interactions among the political parties and leaders who have found it so very difficult to decide whether and how they will lead their country into the future.

The reason for adopting such a broad approach is to pay more than lip service to the notion that war is a profoundly political phenomenon, especially wars such as this one. To understand the war it is necessary to understand the issues at stake. To succeed, a strategy must address those causes with appropriate measures and adequate resources. The book examines how military and nonmilitary resources and influence have been applied, are being applied, and might be applied to produce the "political solution" that is widely considered to be the war's only true exit strategy.

The war in Iraq is not yet over, and even when the fighting does finally end the political situation is likely to remain fluid for some time. Iran and other outside actors remain involved in the contest. If war, according to Prussian military strategist Carl von Clausewitz, is the conduct of politics by other means, then the best hope for Iraq is for politics to become the preferred means of fighting the war's final battles.

1

The Genesis of a Civil War

Two days after the fall of Baghdad on April 9, 2003, the head of the CIA's Middle East Division, Rob Richer, was on the ground, driving around the sprawling, dun-colored city in an armored car with the station chief. Iron rebar jutted from bombed government buildings, and looters moved over the landscape like locusts. Over "near beer" and hot dogs with Gen. John Abizaid and other generals, Richer was surprised to hear the war-fighters talking of going home. Central Command chief Tommy Franks had announced his retirement, and the army land forces commander based in Kuwait, David McKiernan, would soon pack up. Jay Garner, the Pentagon-appointed head of the Office of Reconstruction and Humanitarian Assistance, showed up, only to be replaced within days by Paul Bremer and the Coalition Provisional Authority (CPA).

On subsequent trips over the coming months, Richer saw and heard why the CPA acquired the nickname "Can't Provide Anything." Richer saw schools without teachers, the creeping influence of Iran in southern Iraq, and little electricity anywhere. The CPA's outpost in Hilla, a city south of Baghdad, had to buy its own generators on the black market.

Back in Washington, no one really knew what Bremer was doing. His counterpart would call from the State Department and ask Richer, "Have you seen anything?" Bremer rarely sent cables, maybe one every ten days, and the ones he did send, Richer recalled, "were not substantive, and unbelievably positive."

With the lid popped off of the Iraqi dictatorship, the centrifugal forces were destined to grow among the country's fractured and oppressed population. Saddam Hussein's regime had disproportionately empowered the roughly 20 percent of the Sunni Arab population, most of all his own kin, although the secular socialist Baath Party apparatus contained many Shia as well. He had viciously repressed the Shia Arab majority, particularly after the 1991 uprising that followed the first Gulf war. Saddam had also waged a genocidal campaign against the Kurds, Iraq's third major population group, who had long agitated for their own state. The remaining Iraqis were a kaleidoscopic array of Turkomans, Assyrians, Chaldeans, Yezidis, and others.

Iraq was not only the cradle of civilization, Mesopotamia, as schoolchildren the world around were taught to call the area between the Euphrates and Tigris rivers. It was also the cradle of Shia Islam and one of the few Arab countries where Shia Islam was the dominant religion. Majority rule in the post-Saddam Iraq would inevitably bring the Shia majority into power for the first time in the Arab world. What was unknown, since the secular Baathist rule had lasted for thirty-five years, was how potent a political force Shia Islam would become. All the parties together polled less than 10 percent support in 2003. Historically, the two main Shia Islamist parties had been outlawed, driven underground, and persecuted, along with all other rivals to the Baath Party. Also, the Shia religious hierarchy had espoused a different vision from the theocratic state, in which mullahs ruled, that the Iranian revolution had implanted next door in Shia Persia.

Some believed that modern Iraq was fundamentally an unworkable construct destined to fragment. In this view, the rancor among its principal groups was too deep and the historical foundation of a country fashioned by the British from the Ottoman Empire was too weak to sustain a state without a dictator to hold it together. Since 1991 the United

States had protected an autonomous Kurdish region in northern Iraq with a no-fly zone that kept Saddam's military largely at bay, and the Kurds hoped to preserve and increase that autonomy. There was a sense of national identity, at least among Arab Iraqis, which had been forged by years of statehood, however poorly ruled, and pride in a rich ancient history that was shared across many of Iraq's subgroups. But without a concerted effort to forge a political condominium among Iraq's main groups, the chance of the country holding together after 2003 was nonetheless slim.

Instead of declaring such a pact his goal and enshrining its primacy, Bremer's first two decisions fatally complicated the chances of reaching it. The Coalition Provisional Authority enacted Decrees 1 and 2 under Bremer's signature on May 16 and 23, respectively, in 2003. The first decree denied jobs to the top four tiers of Saddam's Baath Party, thereby throwing out of work thousands of professionals at state-run institutions, from universities to hospitals to every government office, as well as much of the managerial class. Because the economy was largely state-run, that meant that not only government offices but also hospitals, schools, food depots, water works, electrical plants, oil refineries, and virtually every other institution ceased to function. The second decree abolished the security and intelligence services, which had scattered during and after the invasion. Although most of Iraq's million-man armed forces had already deserted, little effort was made to recall officers or soldiers or to otherwise mollify them.

With two strokes of a pen in the space of a week, hundreds of thousands of former members of a thirty-five-year regime were fired and told they did not have a place in the new order in Iraq. The Sunni insurgency was born. This central fact was obscured over the coming years by repeated references to the Al-Qaeda-affiliated radicals who came to fish for converts and allies in these troubled waters. Had there been a concerted outreach to the Sunni population early on, tolerance for the activities of the Al-Qaeda jihadists among the mostly secular Sunni might very likely have evaporated.

These original central errors were thereafter compounded by decisions that favored the Shia Islamist parties. Bremer's memoir, *My Year in Iraq,* documents in detail the various stratagems and maneuvers the Islamist Shia parties used to blackmail and dragoon him into decisions that favored their interests. The Sunnis viewed all these developments as evidence that the United States was turning over the keys of the country to the Islamist Shiites, so they boycotted elections. The next fateful decision, to proceed with elections without Sunni participation in January 2005, gave the Islamist Shia coalition control of the government, and it proceeded to write a constitution that favored its agenda and that of the Kurds. Enshrined in power, and under attack from the outcast Sunnis and former regime members, the Shia Islamists used their militias and the instruments of the state to counterattack. The stage was set for civil war.

The State Department was completely shut out from the administration of a postwar Iraq. One of its most senior career Arabists, Ambassador Ryan Crocker, had been sent over temporarily in May 2003 to help Bremer form the Iraqi Governing Council—an advisory body that replaced the original plan of convening an assembly to select a temporary Iraqi government. When Crocker suggested bringing his whole team of some one hundred Arabists, friends at CPA told him: "Better not. The fewer folks from State the better." The neoconservatives in the White House and the Pentagon looked upon the State Department's Arabists as supporters of the region's Sunni regimes; some of the neocons saw themselves as the liberators of the Shia and promoters of democracy, and in other cases they merely distrusted the State Department.

Matters came to a head in November when the CIA station chief in Baghdad sent a lengthy cable known as an AARDWOLF back to Washington describing the deteriorating situation in Iraq. The CIA's basic analysis was that the United States was facing a largely homegrown insurgency of Iraqis who did not see any benefit for themselves in the emerging political and economic order.

At 1 p.m. November 11, 2003, the National Security Council (NSC) convened to discuss the CIA's report. In addition to President Bush, others attending included Vice President Dick Cheney; Secretary of Defense Donald Rumsfeld and his deputy, Paul Wolfowitz; National Security Adviser Condoleezza Rice and her deputy, Stephen Hadley; CIA head George Tenet; and Rob Richer. Bremer and Gen. Abizaid were linked in via video. The meeting had barely begun when Rumsfeld interrupted, insisting that there was no insurgency. A White House military aide bravely offered the Pentagon's official definition of insurgency as a group seeking the overthrow of a government. Bremer did not dispute the CIA report. Bush cut short the substantive discussion. He was angry that the AARDWOLF had been leaked to the media. "I don't want to see anyone commenting in the press about an insurgency," he said. "We have an election to win."

It was a moment of revelation for Richer. "We finally got an NSC session to talk about the insurgency, and instead it was all about the spin," he fumed, still angry as he discussed it four years later. The 2004 U.S. election was a year away, but the president's message was that electoral considerations would trump substantive concerns about the direction Iraq was taking. Richer took issue with the administration's constant harping on Al-Qaeda in Iraq and its terrorist leader, Abu Musab al-Zarqawi. In Richer's view, it distracted attention from the larger number of non-Al-Qaeda Sunni insurgents and why they were fighting, and pushed the administration toward a kill-and-capture strategy, which would not work as an overall approach to the insurgency.

Although Bremer was certainly Washington's proverbial man in Baghdad, there was plenty of blame to go around for the mounting chaos. Richer believed that Rice bore an enormous amount of responsibility for the positions she took and the influence she exercised behind closed doors. "Rice insisted on democracy, on elections. Democracy had to be put in place immediately," he recalled. "The president is a realist, but he listened to her and was swayed. . . . Rice's vision that Iraq had to look like us overnight was catastrophic."

ONE OF THE IRAQIS WHO WITNESSED the unfolding Iraq drama from the inside from its earliest days was Samir Sumaidaie, the only secular Sunni who participated in each incarnation of the Iraqi government from 2003 on. He agreed to become a member of the Iraqi Governing Council in 2003 and then served as interior minister in 2004. An urbane and gracious man, Sumaidaie offered Bremer advice but grew frustrated and offended by the American's dismissiveness. He longed to return to his work in computer science and graphic design but he could not bear to see his country slide into the abyss again as its long-denied opportunity for a fresh start was squandered.

Sumaidaie was born to a middle-class family in Fadl, in the old quarter of Baghdad, attended the Mustansiriya prep school, and then won a scholarship to study computer science in England. Graduating in 1965, he returned to Baghdad to computerize some of the government's public works. But after the Baathist regime came to power in a 1968 coup, Sumaidaie began to feel uncomfortable at his workplace. "You were scrutinized if you were not of their ilk," he recalled. "Over time, the environment grew more restrictive and oppressive. I felt in danger." Sumaidaie feared he was being targeted after he was denied permission to travel abroad.

The breaking point was a school performance at his four-year-old son's kindergarten in 1973, where Sumaidaie and his wife arrived to find the front row occupied by Baath Party operatives, all wearing moustaches, packing pistols, and looking menacing. The children took the stage, and to Sumaidaie's consternation, began to shout slogans praising the government leaders. As they finished, the Baathist officials took out their pistols and fired them into the air. "Why did you do that?" Sumaidaie, furious, asked the men. "To harden the children," one said. That night Sumaidaie made up his mind to take his family to England.

In London, Sumaidaie found a thriving exile community of Iraqis. He launched his computer design business and landed a large and prestigious commission to take part in the restoration of Mecca in Saudi Arabia. He designed the steel-and-polymer *mukarnas,* two giant goldleaf praying hands holding the Koran that stand at the shrine's gate. After Saddam's invasion of Kuwait in 1990, Sumaidaie was drawn into Iraqi exile politics as Iraqis began to sense the opportunity to rid their country of its scourge. He attended various exile gatherings and helped form a small party, the secular liberal Iraqi Democratic Association.

In 2003 Emad Dhia, another expatriate, contacted Sumaidaie to see if he would participate in the Iraqi Reconstruction and Development Council, a Pentagon-sponsored group that was rounding up technocrats and professionals to return to help rebuild Iraq. Sumaidaie agreed. Eager to return to Iraq and see his relatives, he flew to Amman in May 2003, where his cousin met him to drive him across the desert province of Anbar to Baghdad. Between Ramadi and Fallujah, their Mercedes was stopped by armed, masked men in a pickup truck who demanded their money. Sumaidaie's plucky cousin rebuked the men. "You should be ashamed of yourself. You are attacking Samir Sumaidaie, a *sayyid* [documented descendant of the prophet Muhammad] from your own area." Sumaidaie's family had come from Anbar, and some of his relatives lived near Fallujah. The men recognized his name. Apologizing profusely, they shut the car door and took off in their truck. It was a daunting welcome home. Things soon got worse.

The original plan had been for Bremer to transfer responsibility for Iraq to the Governing Council, but he decided against it. Sumaidaie believed that any provisional government by Iraqis, whether technocrats or expatriates, would have been preferable to an occupation authority. "It was a fatal mistake. We were branded as collaborators," he said of the council members and others who worked alongside Bremer. "The insurgents won the mantle of patriots by fighting the occupier."

Sumaidaie cringed as the CPA's missteps continued. He could not believe Bremer disbanded the ministry of information. "We need some organ or channel to put out our message. We kept asking for a channel," he said. The Pentagon hired large defense contractors, first Science Applications International Corporation and then Harris, which spent more on security than TV programming, which was wildly inappropriate. "They bought cheap, old programs from Lebanon and Cairo just to fill the air time. There was a cooking show with ingredients that no one in Iraq had," he said in disgust. "It made us look foolish." Bremer also used the channel as an outlet for his weekly speeches, which cemented his image as proconsul among Iraqis.

Well aware that opposition among Sunnis was growing, Sumaidaie met with many of his clan relatives in Anbar. Their demands were not especially outrageous. He presented Bremer with an eight-point proposal. He suggested that all non-Iraqis be registered and that they be required to have local sponsors. Such a program was in effect in other Persian Gulf states where imported labor was common. He proposed reviving the trucking businesses that had sustained most Anbar families, who transported goods from Amman. The United States should stop relying on Jordanian companies and give their business to the Iraqis. The Iraqis would also provide security for the routes across Anbar. Bremer agreed to discuss the ideas with Anbaris, and Sumaidaie booked a restaurant for the occasion. Bremer never showed up and none of the eight points was ever implemented by the CPA. Bremer also denied the Anbaris' request that detainees be released in exchange for the families' pledge to not take up arms.

In Sumaidaie's view, the way in which the January 2005 elections were held fatally cast the die for what was to follow. There was no time to create electoral districts, and the closed-list system favored parties over individuals with local standing. The Islamist Shia and Kurdish parties thus dominated the assembly that would write the constitution, which provided for a weak central government and potentially powerful regions and set the stage for deadlock. As the new government was formed, hundreds of cronies and militia members began filling the ministries, their security forces, and the police.

Sumaidaie moved to New York City to become Iraq's ambassador to the United Nations. He hoped that from that position he could enlist support for Iraq from other countries. In June 2005, one of his relatives, a twenty-five-year-old cousin, was killed by marines in Anbar, in a small village called al-Sheikh Hadid. He had been killed answering the door at his home. Breaking with protocol, Sumaidaie gave an interview on CNN to say he knew his cousin Mohammed personally and that he was not an insurgent.

In 2006 Sumaidaie moved to the orange brick embassy on Washington's Dupont Circle as ambassador to the United States. The deaths continued to mount, and his aide Osama Altayi interrupted his meetings regularly with grim news. One morning he came in to tell Sumaidaie that the son of their office administrator had been killed. The following week, the nephew of the embassy's first secretary was killed. The silver-haired diplomat's brown eyes held a perpetually sad expression. These deaths were not statistics, they were relatives and friends and countrymen.

WHEN VETERAN DIPLOMAT John Negroponte became U.S. ambassador to Iraq following Bremer's disastrous year, Rob Richer said he pulled his punches rather than frankly convey the peril of Iraq's situation. "Negroponte didn't call it like it is. He wants to be secretary of state." He tried at times to use Richer as a foil for bad news. "No one would give a dissenting view. If you do, you are ostracized," Richer said of the top-level interactions. Negroponte arrived in the summer of 2004 and within six months was clamoring to get out of Baghdad. When tapped to become the first director of national intelligence in early 2005, he left Iraq to prepare for his confirmation hearings. The embassy was without an ambassador for five months at a critical juncture: the new government was busily packing its ministries with Shia militiamen and writing a constitution that would enshrine Islamic law and increase the centrifugal forces in Iraq.

Just weeks before the constitution was to be completed and submitted to a referendum, White House insider and longtime Cheney associate Zalmay Khalilzad became ambassador. He went into overdrive to head off the impending train wreck. Khalilzad had served as the U.S. liaison to the Iraqi exiles in the runup to the Iraq war and had been expected to play a major role when Bremer was suddenly named instead. That fateful change of plans came about for two reasons. Senior State officials opposed creating an interim government of Iraqi exiles, which they believed was Khalilzad's plan. In fact, he intended to include Iraqis from inside the country, as had been done in Afghanistan. The president wanted two envoys, but Bremer then insisted that there be only one— him—and the president acquiesced. It is almost certain that 2003–2005 would have turned out quite differently if Khalilzad, who understood Iraq's complex dynamics, had gone instead.

At any rate, when Khalilzad arrived in Iraq in the summer of 2005, he worked against the clock because Washington would not hear of delaying the referendum or subsequent elections. Khalilzad strove mightily to convince the majority Shia to offer an olive branch to the minority Sunni. He won concessions that diluted the influence of Islamic law, postponed the creation of powerful regions that would carve up Iraq, and promised constitutional revisions within four months of the new parliament's convening. Largely on the strength of those commitments, the constitution was narrowly ratified and Sunnis came out to vote in the December 2005 elections.

Khalilzad then tried to ensure that the new Iraqi government would be a national unity government that excluded the noxious sectarians who had run the interim government. The negotiations to form the government were excruciating and protracted. The Islamic coalition had won a plurality, 128 of 275 seats in parliament, and wanted the sitting prime minister, Ibrahim al-Jaafari, to continue, but he could not muster enough votes from other parties. Jaafari was not only ineffective but also sectarian. He refused to impose a curfew to stop the retaliatory killing after the Shia mosque in Samarra was bombed in February; he said the Shia needed to "let off steam." Khalilzad had also clashed with him the previous fall, when secret interior ministry prisons were found holding tortured Iraqis.

Jaafari held out for three months. Finally he agreed to step aside for one of two successors from his Dawa party. The choices were Ali Adeed, whose Iranian father and close ties to Iran would cause a storm among Sunnis, or Nouri al-Maliki, who was not pro-Iranian and explicitly disavowed the Iranian model of rule by mullahs.

After Maliki was chosen as prime minister in April, Khalilzad brokered hard-won agreements on two nonsectarian security ministers, a broad-based political council for national security, and a national reconciliation agenda with a timetable for implementing it. By then it was October 2006. Amid the raging violence, the rival politicians openly called each other "enemy." Khalilzad managed to eke out agreement on a foreign investment law, but drafts of an oil framework law and a new de-Baathification law ran aground.

It was hard, perhaps impossible, to make more headway when the country was exploding in violence. But the White House also undercut Khalilzad, denying him the latitude to undo the many errors that had preceded his arrival and, in particular, to deliver credible ultimatums to the Shia Islamists. Khalilzad's efforts were complicated by the competing view, and backdoor maneuvers, of some officials at the White House and State, who believed the United States should throw in its lot with the Shia against the Sunni. The Shia leaders would call their friends in the White House and play them off against Khalilzad whenever he sought to extract concessions from them. Iraqi leaders accused the Sunni Afghan American of being partial to the Iraqi Sunnis, and White House officials suggested that he lower his profile.

Khalilzad's clout was also diminished by the regular videoconferences the president granted to Maliki, who loved the attention. When a senior U.S. official tried to explain how Bush's rhetoric about standing with the Iraqis no matter what didn't help move Maliki to compromise, the president replied, "Are you saying I'm the problem?" The White House opposed attempts to penalize the Iraqi government's behavior, much to the consternation of American officials in Iraq. "In order to pressure these guys, we are trying to shape behavior by saying there will be costs," a senior U.S. official said.

Many observers concluded that if Khalilzad could not bring about an agreement among the Iraqis, there was none to be had. The sectarian fires would simply have to burn themselves out. But civil war may not have been inevitable. Khalilzad might have achieved a national compact if he had been unambiguously supported from the top instead of opposed by those who viewed the Shia as the rightful rulers of Iraq and the Sunni as the enemy, rather than the relative few who were allied with Al-Qaeda. The Shia had indeed suffered horribly at the hands of the old regime, but many in Iraq now feared that the Shia were becoming the new oppressors. U.S. officials who witnessed the behavior and comments of top Shia officials came to believe that they were bent on playing "winner take all." That was, after all, the traditional rule of politics in the Middle East, and a thousand years of underclass status had stoked the Shia's desire for revenge.

RICHER DID NOT LET THE MILITARY duck responsibility for its mistakes. "They fought the war tactically," he said. "They did not have a vision. They had no endgame." The military was too focused on troop levels and troop movements and not enough on the reasons why the Iraqis were fighting them. "Because Sunnis didn't embrace us, it became personal," he said. Richer did not think the accumulation of errors could be undone. "We're two years too late," he said in 2007.

Richer readily conceded that the lack of intelligence crippled the military's postwar effort. The Pentagon wanted tactical intelligence to go after the resistance that was mushrooming in the summer of 2003, but U.S. intelligence resources were being sucked up by the ongoing search for weapons of mass destruction, which were never found. Richer said Condoleezza Rice played an important role in this matter as well by steadfastly opposing the creation of an Iraqi intelligence service. "Our policy was to stand down as the Iraqis stood up, but the Iraqis did not stand up because we did not give them intelligence, heavy brigades, a pay system," Richer said. "Their military had no nationwide communications until 2006."

One of the enduring questions of the war was whether the U.S. uniformed military had asserted itself strongly enough in challenging civilian officials' views that it felt were ill-considered or downright risky. Retired army chief of staff Gordon Sullivan acknowledged that the army establishment did not want to go into Iraq in 2003 with so few forces. Only Army Chief of Staff Gen. Eric Shinseki had voiced concern publicly, however, and this was under duress during questioning by Congress. More forces were needed for the postcombat phase rather than the invasion itself; the troops could have been either American or Iraqi, but the failure to provide enough boots on the ground ranked as the most egregious military error of the war's early years. The war's commander, Tommy Franks, acceded in the decisions on troop levels. Some inside the military felt the institution was chronically prone to a relentless optimism. As one retired colonel put it, "Our can-do attitude is killing us."

Too often, the war's strategic decision-makers concerned themselves with a tactical level of operations: how many Iraqi soldiers were trained, equipped, and deemed more or less proficient. The metric of soldiers produced was held out as the determining factor of when to send U.S. troops home and declare the job finished. Even the president repeated the phrase "as they stand up, we will stand down." But it betrayed a mechanistic thinking about the problem. Iraq did not lack security because it lacked an army. It lacked a consensus over who would wield power and how. Iraq's Shias, Sunnis, and Kurds would continue fighting unless they reached agreement over how political and military power and economic resources were to be shared and used.

Leaders failed to see that holding elections and writing a constitution did not accomplish that central, substantive objective. This was the key strategic failure from which all others flowed. All points of leverage were not applied to produce the needed agreement. Instead, the U.S. military became a shield for the Shia-dominant government. It supported a political situation that was creating the violence.

That is not to say that there weren't dozens of thoughtful officers who saw that the war was heading over the cliff and tried to inject profound critiques and constructive recommendations into the planning and assessment process of the military apparatuses in Iraq and stateside. One of the enduring mysteries of the war, and a testament to its shape-shifting complexity, was that so many intelligent officers of all ranks made superhuman efforts to grapple with the task of analysis and prescription to relatively little effect. The long hours and press of battle and the proximity to the daily minutiae made it hard for many to see the forest for the trees. Those not in Iraq often lacked sufficient grasp of the evolving conflict and the cultural realities that governed what was and was not possible. And even equally intelligent officers who were immersed in Iraq's reality came up with very different diagnoses and prescriptions.

Most heartrending of all, local and tactical successes were scored again and again all over the country, sometimes more than once in the same area, which then unraveled. One officer came close to tears upon returning to Baquba in 2006 to see that his unit's progress had come undone. Samarra, Rutba, Tal Afar, Mosul, Saba al Bor, Sadr City—it happened in more places than not. New commanders brought new approaches. Enemy forces were cleared but then returned. Iraqi units were trained and mentored and then went AWOL. Iraqi allies switched sides or, more often, were killed or left the country. And, most frustrating of all, Iraq's leaders made commitments but never fulfilled them, without penalty.

The fault lay at the strategic level, with the military and civilian leadership. These islands of progress could not be sustained without a strategic approach that knit them together and addressed the underlying cause of the conflict. No one at the top of the totem pole grappled effectively with what was happening to America's first major war since Vietnam. Many a straight-talking American sergeant knew the Iraq project wouldn't be fast or easy, but after four years the trajectory was deeply discouraging.

BY THE SUMMER OF 2006, Baghdad was on fire. Sectarian violence was spilling into all-out civil war, and it swept up hundreds of thousands of Iraqis. An Iraqi sergeant named Omran Hamad was kidnapped when he went home to Baghdad in July 2006. Like all Iraqi soldiers, the strapping Iraqi with a wide moon face and close-cropped hair left his unit and went home every month or two to take money to his family because there was no direct deposit or electronic banking system. When he reached his neighborhood, he was stopped at a checkpoint guarded by masked men carrying AK-47s. They demanded to see his ID and then threw him into the back of a van. They captured him because his name was similar to Omar, a common Sunni name. But Omran was Shiite, like his captors, who belonged to a militia called the Jaish al-Mahdi (JAM). He tried to convince them by reciting Shia Islamic prayers, showing them the Shia songs on his cell phone, anything he could think of to win his freedom. For three weeks they held him until a militia member who came from the south heard Omran's description of his hometown of Shatrah and knew he was telling the truth. Only Shia lived there.

Omran was distraught. He pondered bringing his family to Kirkuk, where he was posted, but that city was also a powder keg as Kurds sought to reclaim it from Sunnis. Omran had Sunni relatives but the war had driven the family apart. He had joined the army because Sunni insurgents had killed his brother in front of their house, but now he feared going home to Baghdad because of the Shia militia. "Jaish al-Mahdi is taking over the city," he said.

Every day, more Iraqis fell victim to the growing maelstrom of sectarian violence between Sunnis and Shia. Corpses with bound hands and gunshots to the head littered the streets, which were barricaded with torn-up concrete, barbed wire, and vehicles. Police either fell in with the militias or deserted their stations. Iraqi and U.S. soldiers conducted sweeps by day but returned to their bases at night. Sunni insurgents fought back with their favored tactics—car bombs and buried, remotely detonated bombs. Sectarian violence had been building since the interim Shia-led government was formed in February 2005, but it went through the roof in 2006, when the United Nations estimated that 34,452 Iraqis died. Baghdad was the epicenter of the violence, but it was not the only crisis zone. According to the *Washington Post*, the marines' intelligence chief in Anbar province considered it all but lost to the Sunni insurgents.

The year had started off on a hopeful note. U.S. officials expected a new prime minister to be selected any day. They planned for him to sit in the balcony for President Bush's State of the Union address on January 31, 2006. Gen. George Casey, the four-star commander of the U.S.-led coalition, the Multi-National Force-Iraq (MNF-I), directed his staff to write a plan to draw down U.S. forces from the fifteen combat brigades then in Iraq to ten brigades by October or November 2006, and to five brigades by December 2007. Casey went to Washington and briefed his plan to the Joint Chiefs of Staff—the chiefs of the army, navy, air force, and marines—in their secure briefing room known as the "tank."

Then the Iraqi government's formation was delayed for one, two, three, then five months as Khalilzad and the parties argued over its composition. The embryonic governing institutions ground to a halt. Casey still intended to carry out his drawdown plan, but his new subordinate commander, Lt. Gen. Peter Chiarelli, grew concerned as the indecision and chaos continued. Chiarelli had taken the helm of the three-star command that directed daily military operations, the Multi-National Corps-Iraq, in January 2006. It was his second tour: he had been the two-star chief of the Baghdad division in 2004.

The time came for 2nd Brigade, 10th Mountain Division, the first brigade, to leave, but the Iraqis had not even formed a government. The Baghdad division commander, Maj. Gen. J. D. Thurman, had the same feeling. "Boss, I just don't know," he told Chiarelli, who went to Casey's planners to share their concerns. "Listen, the conditions that we predicated are not the conditions that we have in place," he said. Chiarelli had also been implementing Casey's orders to lessen the U.S. footprint by drawing troops back onto fifty of the forward operating bases, the U.S. bases scattered around the country, and shutting the rest down or turning them over to Iraqi forces by 2007. All this was supposed to be "conditions-based," i.e., as conditions permitted, but when Chiarelli formally recommended to Casey that they delay 2/10 Mountain's departure or bring up the strategic reserve from Kuwait, he was overruled.

Finally, on May 28, 2006, Prime Minister Nouri al-Maliki's government was inaugurated. Within days, a joint U.S.-Iraqi operation, Operation Forward Together, was launched to rein in Baghdad's violence. But the two Iraqi brigades promised for it never showed up. Maliki presented a twenty-four-point national reconciliation plan, but he did not act on that either. Thurman did not have enough troops to tamp down the violence. The strategic reserve was brought up from Kuwait one battalion at a time, but the sectarian violence in Baghdad continued to grow. When 2/10 Mountain pulled out of the Baghdad neighborhoods Ghazaliya and Kadhimiya, Sunni insurgents and JAM filled the vacuum. The one bit of good news in June—the death of the Jordanian-born leader of the Al-Qaeda-affiliated insurgents, Abu Musab al-Zarqawi, in an air strike—proved to be a mere blip on the radar in what had become an all-out Shia versus Sunni conflict, with both sides aiming at civilians.

The next unit, the 172nd Stryker Brigade Combat Team, was scheduled to depart by August. The decision to let the troops go had to be made weeks before, since they would be loading their nineteen-ton armored vehicles onto trailers and trucking them to Kuwait. Chiarelli recommended delaying their departure, but again Casey was adamant the brigade would leave.

"Nobody was willing to call a spade a spade," said one of Casey's staff officers. "We were still going down to five brigades, by God." Casey went to Washington, D.C., to brief administration officials in July. He reiterated his view that drawing down would force the Iraqi army to do more and the Iraqi politicians to reconcile and rein in their militias. Some at the White House were concerned, but there was no countermandate.

Baghdad's killing spree went off the charts. "We started seeing the number of bodies executed in Baghdad go up, up, up," Chiarelli said. He and Thurman visited Ameriya, once an upper-middle-class neighborhood. Chiarelli knew the city's neighborhoods intimately from his year as Baghdad division commander, when he had devoted much of his first tour to improving city services and infrastructure, especially in Sadr City, in a bid to win the slum away from Jaish al-Mahdi. He was shocked by what he saw in Ameriya. "It was worse than Sadr City," Chiarelli said.

Up to 150 bodies were appearing on Baghdad's streets each night. Alarmed, the deputy MNF-I commander and other top officials met with Maliki in Casey's absence and laid out for him what was occurring. The prime minister shrugged. "It was far worse under Saddam Hussein," he told shocked British and American officials.

Casey returned on Sunday, July 23. In the small group meeting after the next morning's briefing, Chiarelli appealed to him: "The 172nd is our last chance. We can't let them go." They had no other forces to call upon; the reserve in Kuwait would not be replenished for four months. "We reach the tipping point on Wednesday," Chiarelli warned. By then half of the 172nd would have left the country. The first troops were already back at their base in Alaska. "I agree," Casey said finally. He called Rumsfeld, and within forty-eight hours the decision had been made to bring all of the 172nd back and move them into Baghdad.

Looking back on this critical period, a senior military official assessed why the breaking point came in the summer of 2006. "I will tell you everybody points to Samarra as the pivotal point. I don't. I don't at all," he said. "We had been successful, we thought, in clamping down the sectarian killing after Samarra. . . . The real accelerant was that what we were looking for was a government of national reconciliation. That became our mantra. The delay in seating the government was to get a government of national reconciliation. And this government sat—and I'm not going to draw conclusions one way or another, but I will tell you that within thirty days of that government's seating when we saw JAM come out of their holes and everything else, the Iraqi Sunni realized that this was not a government of national reconciliation, that this government was going to follow certain policies that they believed were sectarian in nature, specifically aimed against the Sunni population. I'm not making a value judgment, I'm just telling you what the Sunni felt. And we were held responsible for this blight on their house. To me, from May 28 into early July was when we saw the wheels come off."

IN LATE AUGUST, CHIARELLI SAT on the back patio of his house overlooking the man-made lake at the Al Faw palace complex, having an after-dinner smoke that his wife most certainly would not have approved of. He furrowed his bushy black eyebrows as he brooded over the dire state of affairs. He knew that extending the 172nd for four months was merely a Band-Aid—and an inadequate one at that—not a solution. The U.S.-Iraqi operation to quell the violence was failing.

Chiarelli had clashed with Casey on more than one occasion. He was as vocal and passionate as Casey was terse and contained. After his first tour in Baghdad, Chiarelli had advocated in a *Military Review* article that U.S. troops could and should conduct counterinsurgency missions. He had become famous for his persistent, public championing of providing jobs and rebuilding infrastructure, especially in troubled areas, to employ youths and draw them away from the lure of insurgency. He believed that most of the armed youths would stop fighting if there were jobs and that the population would reject the instigators if they saw improvements in their daily lives. He had even sent his troops to learn from city administrators in Austin, Texas, before deploying, and had attached a team of development experts to each of his Baghdad brigades. When he left in February 2005, he felt that the vast Shia slum of Sadr City was winnable through his approach, but the next commander did not adopt it.

All over Iraq, neither the money nor the civilians to oversee such projects was forthcoming. At least a fifth of the $18.6 billion in reconstruction funds was diverted to security needs. As corps commander, Chiarelli fought the administration's ambitious attempt to convert Saddam's socialist economy to a free-enterprise system in the middle of a war. He argued instead for a pragmatic approach that generated employment. Such was his zeal that he personally visited state-owned factories and lobbied for aid to restart them. He knew precisely how many water, sewage, and power projects languished uncompleted. "We've built the world's largest water fountain," he said bitterly, referring to a water plant on Sadr City's outskirts that had been completed but not connected to any homes. He felt that too little was being done on this front as well as other noncombat "lines of operation," which led to frictions with Casey. Reacting to the criticism, one Casey staffer said that Chiarelli was seen as unwilling to take action and never satisfied with the resources he received. It was a comment indicative of George Casey's stiff-upper-lip philosophy.

No one cabinet member assumed responsibility for the conduct of the war, and the military leadership did not alert the administration that the war was heading over the cliff. It became clear in the fall of 2006 to even the most die-hard optimist that the United States was in danger of losing, but the many competing views of Iraq's situation complicated the effort to decide what to do next. When the Democratic Party reclaimed control of both houses of Congress in the midterm elections on November 7, 2006, it was clear that if the administration did not change course in Iraq, the Congress would. The Democratic majority interpreted its mandate quite simply: get out of Iraq.

History would render a severe judgment on the Bush White House for its management of the war. It had not even published a public strategy for the war until November 2005, when the war effort was already in trouble. The "National Strategy for Victory in Iraq" was encapsulated in two slogans. The first was "clear, hold and build": clear Iraq of insurgents, hold territory, and build government institutions and the economy. The second was "as the Iraqi forces stand up, we will stand down": the creation of competent Iraqi security forces would allow U.S. forces to go home. The first slogan was only sporadically implemented with inadequate resources, and the second (and possibly the first) was a decade-long endeavor. But even more important, these were *military* strategies that did not address the conflict's underlying cause—the lack of a political entente between the Shia and Sunni. The Shia had been progressively empowered, while the Sunni were left with no hope and no reason not to pick up guns. There was no *political* strategy to address that reality, and absent one the war would continue until the Sunni were dead, gone, or defeated.

Casey's boss, Gen. John Abizaid, was chief of Central Command, the regional combatant command for the entire Middle East. A Lebanese American and foreign area officer, he was considered one of the army's top regional experts. He had largely allowed Casey, his West Point classmate, to conduct the war in Iraq as he saw fit—much to the consternation of his CENTCOM staff—but Abizaid had a definite view of the cause and, therefore, the remedy for the conflict that had erupted after U.S. forces toppled Saddam Hussein's regime. As Abizaid repeatedly testified to Congress, he saw the United States' presence in Iraq as a primary aggravator of the conflict, which lent support to Casey's proposal for removing U.S. forces. The conflict among the Iraqis was one for Iraqis to settle, Abizaid believed, and the continuing violence in Iraq led many to believe that he was right.

The Sunni insurgency's relentless attacks on U.S. troops embittered Abizaid. On a visit to Jordan in October 2005, Abizaid even went so far as to tell Jordan's King Abdullah II, in a fit of pique, "I don't care if all the Sunnis die. We just want stability." The alarmed king relayed this conversation to Rob Richer, who had been a close friend since Richer's days as station chief in Amman. Abdullah had advised Abizaid to engage with the Sunni tribes. He was also concerned, as were the Saudis, about the geopolitical consequences of the rise of Shia Iraq. He gave a speech in Washington at Georgetown University warning about the rise of a "Shia crescent" between Iraq and Shia Iran. Such an alliance could pose a threat to his Sunni monarchy. Abdullah was certainly motivated by self-interest to give such counsel, but it was also true that, contrary to Abizaid's thesis, the violence in Iraq was increasingly Iraqis killing Iraqis.

Abizaid and Casey's boss, Defense Secretary Rumsfeld, had a characteristically impatient view of the matter: he wanted the Iraqis to solve their own problems now that the United States had removed their dictator for them. Rumsfeld had never wanted to be engaged in any nation-building exercise, let alone such a complex one. Therefore, he never grappled with the core issue of how Iraq's power struggle was to be resolved, even in his last memo as defense secretary on November 6, 2006. He outlined fifteen options, many purely tactical, without strongly endorsing any of them. The basic thrust of the first nine options was to draw down U.S. troops and shift to an advisory mission. Then he listed six options he labeled as "less attractive," including increasing U.S. forces in Iraq and in Baghdad, staging a Dayton-like peace process (such as used in the Balkans conflict in 1995), partitioning Iraq, and setting a fixed withdrawal date. Rumsfeld's influence at this stage was negligible, however, since the president had already decided to replace his most controversial cabinet member with former CIA Director Robert Gates.

IN MID-SEPTEMBER 2006 the White House launched a soup-to-nuts review to reexamine the assumptions of the current policy and figure out what needed to be done. It was led by the deputy national security adviser for Iraq and Afghanistan, Meghan O'Sullivan. As one of the few civilian officials who kept daily tabs on Iraq, she was in a key position to influence policy. She had spent 2003–2004 in Baghdad working in the Coalition Provisional Authority for Bremer on the governance team. During that time she developed especially close ties to the Supreme Council for Islamic Revolution in Iraq, one of the principal Shia Islamist groups that had been organized and based in Iran during Saddam's rule. O'Sullivan, who prepared a nightly memo of events in Iraq for the president, had grown concerned over the summer about the growing violence and Casey's troop withdrawal plan.

The White House review included discussions among a committee of deputies, which held lengthy discussions for three months. O'Sullivan had already formed her own ideas, but no one staked out positions immediately. Her boss, National Security Adviser Stephen Hadley, wanted to remain a neutral broker of alternatives in the traditional mold of his office. All options were examined, including the resources required to implement each one.

At the end of October, Hadley and O'Sullivan visited Baghdad and met with Maliki and other officials. It was Hadley's first trip to Iraq. On October 29, National Security Council officials first had breakfast with Casey, Chiarelli, and other officials. Chiarelli then accompanied the Washington officials to the Baghdad division headquarters at Camp Liberty to meet with Thurman in his conference room. Chiarelli and Thurman knew this was their chance to convey exactly what was happening in Baghdad and how dire the situation was. They did not know O'Sullivan, but the word within the U.S. military was that she favored the Shia side. It was critical that she understand how the Sunni felt and the reasons they felt that way.

The briefing laid out what had transpired over the summer. The JAM militia, with active or passive support from Iraqi government forces, had swept west from its Sadr City stronghold to entrench itself and attack Sunnis all over the city. Any attempt to rein in the Shia militias had prompted an outcry from the Iraqi government. The military was not allowed to target JAM without explicit approval from the prime minister or Casey. The officers saw that Hadley was surprised. One of the officials in the meeting remarked afterward, "They had never heard what we were telling them. This group from DC didn't seem to have any idea of what was actually happening here. It was crazy."

One of the officers tried to convey how important it was for the U.S. military to go after both Sunni *and* Shia "bad guys." The lack of even-handedness had created the impression among Iraqis that the United States not only approved of but was abetting the Shia campaign. "If I'm sitting over there as a frickin' Sunni," the officer said, "I'm seeing Stan McChrystal and his boys [from the Joint Special Operations Command] as the storm troopers for JAM. We're like their advance guard that goes in and takes out all the Sunni leaders so JAM can come over into an area and do their thing."

The meeting was interrupted by an urgent phone call from Casey. The officers left the room to take his call. Casey told them that Maliki had just demanded that they take down barriers Thurman's troops had erected along the canal around Sadr City to stop JAM from coming out of Sadr City and to aid the search for a kidnapped U.S. soldier. Casey ordered them to do it. The officers looked at each other, aghast. "This was a kick in the goddamned teeth," one of them said later. The barriers were an essential part of their effort to secure Baghdad. Without them, the military had no chance of stemming JAM's violence.

Upon their return from Baghdad, O'Sullivan drafted a memorandum for the president and the principals, which Hadley signed. It acknowledged the very serious questions about Maliki, but it also appeared to absolve him of responsibility for what was happening. It said: "We returned from Iraq convinced we need to determine if Prime Minister Maliki is both willing and able to rise above the sectarian agendas being promoted by others. Do we and Prime Minister Maliki share the same vision for Iraq?" The memo did not answer that central question, but hedged: "While there does seem to be an aggressive push to consolidate Shia power and influence, it is less clear whether Maliki is a witting participant."

That the administration still did not have a clear view of Maliki after nine months of dealing with him spoke volumes about both its reluctance to draw conclusions and the Iraqi's inscrutability. Behind thick glasses, his high forehead topped by a wisp of hair and a usually furrowed brow, Maliki kept his own counsel, his jaw often set with a pugnacious tilt. The memo outlined nine steps Maliki could take to rein in sectarian behavior, but it concluded that Maliki lacked the "capabilities to take such steps, which risk alienating his narrow Sadrist political base [legislators loyal to Muqtada al-Sadr, who supported Maliki for prime minister] and require a greater number of more reliable forces."

This way of framing the problem pointed to a continued embrace of Maliki to strengthen him against those perceived to be more sectarian. The interpretation of Maliki as a weak individual who needed to be bolstered, rather than a man who shared and deliberately pursued a sectarian agenda, had enormous consequences. President Bush would continue to embrace him and lend his prestige and support to him, which Sunnis would read as support for what they believed to be Maliki's agenda. It also reinforced a dangerous perception that Maliki and his advisers already held: that the president of the United States needed him more than Maliki needed President Bush.

Bush and Maliki were scheduled to meet in Amman on November 30; the memo was leaked the day before to the *New York Times,* presumably by someone who wished to create pressure on Maliki by publicly revealing the administration's doubts about his ability to deliver results. In another embarrassment, King Abdullah made his displeasure with Maliki known by declining to meet with the two leaders as originally planned.

At the meeting with President Bush in Amman, O'Sullivan was pleased to see the Iraqi government make its first PowerPoint presentation, to outline ideas for securing Baghdad with Iraqi forces. U.S. troops would remain on the city's perimeter. On the one hand, the Iraqi plan was a welcome demonstration of the Iraqis' determination to take responsibility for their own security, but the obvious question was whether the plan aimed to make Baghdad safe for Shias rather than the entire population. Secretary of State Condoleezza Rice was especially direct in conveying this concern to National Security Adviser Mowaffak al-Rubaie. She told him, "This is the perception that Americans have of your government—that it is sectarian." President Bush made the point as well, but he also sought to boost Maliki's confidence, telling him, "You are my man."

The Iraqis went away from the meeting believing that because they had presented their plan for Baghdad, the Americans had agreed to it. They had not. The president did ask Maliki to take the steps recommended in the November 8 memorandum, particularly to approve more aggressive action against the Sadr militia members who were engaging in violence. The administration had not yet concluded its policy review or framed its own plan for securing the city, but O'Sullivan had concluded that continuing on the current path was not a viable option. After three and a half years, it was manifestly clear to everyone that the administration's approach was not working.

2

A Failing War,
and the Decision to Surge

On Veterans Day weekend 2006, a group gathered at the White House to debate two options: change the conditions on the ground by increasing the resources to match the declared intent or conduct triage by pulling back forces from the cities and focusing on counterterrorism missions. Those attending were National Security Adviser Stephen Hadley; Secretary of State Condoleezza Rice and her counselor Philip Zelikow; Iraq specialist David Satterfield; Vice President Dick Cheney's national security adviser, John Hannah; and Deputy National Security Adviser for Iraq and Afghanistan Meghan O'Sullivan and her deputy, Brett McGurk. Rice argued that it was time for the United States to focus on its "core national interests," narrowly defined. She and the other State officials doubted that the United States had the ability to check the ascendance of the Shia Islamists. But White House officials argued that the United States could not ignore the sectarian violence.

As the final stage of the National Security Council (NSC) review, Hadley's deputy, J. D. Crouch, convened a formal interagency "strategic review" that included the intelligence agencies, the vice president's office, and all the relevant departments. The group met daily from November 2006 until the end of December. Crouch kept his cards close to his vest, but privately he, O'Sullivan, and McGurk called themselves the "surgios" —proponents of what would come to be known as the surge of U.S. troops, civilians, and resources. They believed that experience had shown Gen. John Abizaid's view to be wrong: whenever the United States had devoted more troops to an area, the population had come to their side. Troops had brought greater calm and not become a magnet for attacks in Tal Afar, Al Qaim, and parts of Baghdad where they had been reinforced. Each time they withdrew, however, the violence had resumed.

The White House review of Iraq strategy was not the only such review going on. In October, Peter Pace, the chairman of the Joint Chiefs of Staff, also initiated his own informal review by convening a group of sixteen colonels who had served in Iraq to deliberate in the Pentagon basement and to offer him a series of options he would use to inform his advice to President George W. Bush. Pace was frustrated that he was not getting any new thinking out of Gen. Casey's command in Iraq. In addition, a congressionally mandated review had been under way all year. The Iraq Study Group, an independent, bipartisan commission to examine and propose remedies for Iraq policy, was expected to announce its findings at year's end. The group had been briefed by senior officials in Iraq, and a large group of experts had helped write position papers. James Baker, former secretary of state for the George H. W. Bush administration, and Lee Hamilton, former chairman of the House Foreign Affairs Committee, led the commission, whose in-depth work was expected to carry some weight with the White House.

The colonels debating options for Pace met in the crisis action room of the National Command Center in the Pentagon basement. They would periodically troop into the "tank" for freewheeling discussions with the joint chiefs. The chiefs were careful not to squelch any ideas they disagreed with, lest the point of the exercise be undermined. After weeks of debate, the colonels developed four possible courses of action. Col. Peter

Mansoor, who had led a brigade of the 1st Armored Division in Baghdad in 2003–2004, summarized the options as the colonels prepared to deliver their final thoughts to the chiefs. Writing on a white board, he labeled the main options: Go Big, Go Home, Go Long. A fourth option was a hybrid of the first and third. Go Big envisioned a large increase in troops, which they eventually concluded was unfeasible because the United States lacked the available manpower. Go Home, total withdrawal, was discarded as likely to leave Iraq with a full-blown civil war. Deliberations then boiled down to two options: Go Long, shifting to a long-term advisory presence at lower troop levels, and the hybrid variation that would include a short-term increase in troops to try to get the sectarian violence under control, followed by a drawdown to some 60,000 troops from roughly 140,000. Mansoor favored the former, Go Long, while another colonel, H. R. McMaster, emerged as the proponent of the latter.

Perhaps sensing that the White House was leaning toward an increase, Pace decided to recommend the hybrid option to the president. The colonels did not know how many troops might be provided for a short-term increase, so they debated several scenarios. Pace had circumscribed his review to focus on troop levels and security missions rather than the key political question of the Iraqi government's intentions and how the employment of military resources might influence them. Counterinsurgency required grappling with the political aspects of a conflict, but Pace considered that to be "outside his lane." This reinforced the tendency within the administration to focus on troop levels and missions rather than the political questions.

Army Chief of Staff Gen. Peter Schoomaker told the president privately that he opposed the surge. Publicly, Schoomaker expressed skepticism, saying any troop increase should have a "measurable purpose." Others on the joint staff, such as the chief of operations, Lt. Gen. Doug Lute, opposed the surge as well. Any troop increase would require lengthening the twelve-month tours of units in Iraq and/or shortening the twelve months stateside that units had between tours, or activating more reserve units. The strains of the four-year war were beginning to show on the ten-division army.

In early December, the administration's cabinet members gathered for a principals meeting of the NSC. The president made a critical decision that significantly narrowed the options. He decided that U.S. troops could not continue to operate in Iraq and ignore the raging sectarian violence. "We can't say we have no role," Bush told his staff, recalling the impact of the Srebrenica massacre in the Balkans, according to a senior administration official. The question for the remaining weeks of the review then became how the United States should aim to stop the sectarian violence and what would be required to do it.

On December 6, the bipartisan Iraq Study Group, led by Baker and Hamilton, presented its report with seventy-nine findings. The key military recommendations were to move away from combat missions and to focus on training and on advisory and counterterrorism missions while beginning a gradual drawdown of forces. The primary political recommendation was to introduce formal conditionality into U.S. support. If the Iraqi government did not meet its commitments on political reconciliation, U.S. support should be curtailed. The report said: "If the Iraqi government does not make substantial progress toward the achievement of milestones on national reconciliation, security and governance, the United States should reduce its political, military or economic support for the Iraqi government." A third set of recommendations called for more robust regional diplomacy, including initiating direct talks with Iran and Syria, which the administration had so far resisted, with the goal of reducing support to armed groups in Iraq.

The study group's internal deliberations over troop levels were heated. One member of the group, Bill Clinton's former secretary of defense, William J. Perry, had advocated setting a deadline for withdrawing troops, but the proposal was not endorsed by consensus, the agreed-upon procedure. Those opposed pointed out that a fixed withdrawal date would undermine the effect of conditions. If the United States was leaving by a certain date, Iraq would have no incentive to agree to any quid pro quo. Baker held out for inclusion of an opposite recommendation, a small short-term increase in troops if the ground commander deemed it necessary either for combat operations or to expand the number of advisory teams.

Unfortunately, the U.S. debate both in public and inside the administration centered overwhelmingly on the limited question of U.S. troop levels rather than the more fundamental political question of whether U.S. and Iraqi goals were aligned, and if not, how they might be brought into alignment. The NSC review had framed the choice as between increased support or reduced exposure. It did not develop a third option of placing formal conditions on further assistance to the Iraqi government. The administration rejected conditionality because it believed that limiting support to the Iraqi government would play into the hands of the Al-Qaeda and Sunni insurgents. That fact, coupled with the president's decision that the United States could not ignore the problem of sectarian violence, put him on a course toward a more aggressive security plan than either the Iraq Study Group or the joint staff envisioned, and very likely an increased combat mission.

A second NSC meeting in December brought the administration closer to that decision. Still to be resolved was how many brigades the United States could send, how many the Iraqis would accept, and just how they would be employed. Casey and his staff still favored a continued drawdown and a shift away from combat missions. Some pushed for more of the remaining manpower to be assigned to bigger advisory teams.

An advocate of more and larger advisory teams was Maj. Gen. Bill Caldwell, who was Casey's deputy for strategic effects. He believed very strongly that more combat troops were not the answer. "You can kill bad guys all day long and it won't make a difference," he said. He also believed the United States did not have enough forces to throw into the fight to make a difference. Some of the subordinate commanders in Iraq argued that the advisory mission could be accomplished by "partnering" combat units with Iraqi units, but Caldwell said there was no comparison in the intensity of mentoring provided. "You can't pretend that partnering would do the job via periodic contact versus being present every minute of the day." He said the effort invested in creating the Iraqi forces should be matched by more intensive advising of them once created. "We put them through all this training and education, and then we put them out there. They can go corrupt overnight," he said. "They need constant mentoring and guidance."

As the White House was nearing its decision, a group of outside experts was invited to the White House on December 11. Over the past year, the NSC staff had periodically arranged for the president to meet with academic experts, retired military officers, and others to hear their views about Iraq. Three retired four-star generals and two academics were invited to the meeting: Jack Keane, the former vice chief of staff of the army; Barry McCaffrey, another retired four-star general and former Clinton White House official; Wayne Downing, who had been counterterrorism adviser in the White House after 9/11 and had led the Special Operations Command; author and professor Eliot Cohen, who directed the Strategic Studies Program at the Paul H. Nitze School of Advanced International Studies at Johns Hopkins University; and Stephen Biddle of the Council on Foreign Relations.

Keane was a ruddy-faced, imposing giant of a man with a forceful personality to match. His thick New York accent advertised his hometown as clearly as his towering physique and upright bearing said "soldier." He had loved road-marching with his 10th Mountain troops in upstate New York and had driven the 101st Airborne Division just as hard. Before retiring in 2003 as vice chief, Keane had been publicly known as Defense Secretary Donald Rumsfeld's choice to replace Gen. Eric Shinseki as army chief of staff for over a year—the early announcement of which was one of many slights the secretary had delivered to the army. But when Shinseki retired, Keane had surprised everyone by declining the army's top job. His wife was ill, and he made the commitment to care for her rather than take on a position that, like every senior post in Washington, was virtually a round-the-clock obligation.

Keane had remained involved in military and national security affairs as a member of the Defense Policy Board and had stayed visible as an ABC News analyst. He continued to visit Iraq, as McCaffrey did, and provided advice both to the commanders on the ground and officials stateside.

In August, Keane's wife had walked into their living room and found Keane sitting on the couch in the dark as dusk settled around their Virginia home. "What are you doing, Jack?" she asked. "Thinking," he replied. He had come to face the fact that the United States was on the cusp of losing its first war since Vietnam. As the late-summer light faded away, he decided that the United States had to do more to stop the violence that was overwhelming Iraq. Security was a necessary precondition for any progress. It was manifestly clear that U.S. forces had failed to provide that security, but Keane believed they could do it and that sufficient forces were available. Since troop readiness was a principal responsibility of the vice chief, he knew where to go for current information on exactly how many troops could be made available.

Keane concluded that he had to speak out, even though it meant speaking out against his fellow officers and his friends, and taking on Rumsfeld. On September 19 he went to see the secretary of defense. Rumsfeld was taken aback when Keane told him that he needed to send five to eight more brigades to Iraq. "Your commanders have been applying a short-war strategy," Keane told him. The approach Casey and Abizaid had applied since 2004 was one of transition, the retired general said, though he might have added that it was Rumsfeld's preferred option too. "We did not adjust when it was obvious it was wrong," he said. The reason the failure was not recognized, Keane said, was that it was being camouflaged by the holding of two elections and a referendum. "That gave us the appearance of political progress," he said. The narrative the military and the administration had adopted, that everything was proceeding according to plan until the February 2006 attack on the Shia mosque in Samarra, was simply not true. He had been shaken, as O'Sullivan had been, when over the summer Casey had insisted on sticking to his plan. "You've got to escalate," Keane told Rumsfeld bluntly.

The secretary took notes, as he always did, and asked many questions. But Keane could tell that Rumsfeld did not agree. "There was a general resignation about him that I'd never seen," Keane recalled later. The main flaw in Rumsfeld's argument, the general told the secretary of defense, was that the United States had not provided the security for Iraqis to be able to come together. "This was a rebuke of his ideology," Keane said.

Keane also went to Pace with his arguments but found him no more receptive. He talked to former House Speaker Newt Gingrich and Deputy Secretary of Defense Paul Wolfowitz. On December 7, the White

House called and invited Keane to come the following Monday to present his views to the president. The next day the vice president's office called and asked him to brief Cheney on the same day, along with Fred Kagan of the American Enterprise Institute.

On Monday, Keane, McCaffrey, Downing, Cohen, and Biddle were led into the Oval Office. Hadley introduced them and explained the format of the meeting. The guests sat on the couches, Cheney and Bush in armchairs.

Each guest had ten minutes to present his views. "The current strategy has failed, and failed miserably," Keane said. "The United States needs a complete change in strategy. The only hope we have at this point—as the government of Iraq is going over the cliff—is to finally do the one thing we had never been able to do and never committed to do, which is to provide security, because it is a necessary precondition for political progress and economic development. It is a painful lesson, and it's tragic that we had to wait four years to learn it. But any other option on the table—anything that implies pulling back or just increasing advisers—will not change the security and stability situation. The Iraqis cannot handle the level of violence that's being inflicted upon them. The only way we can bring down the level of violence is, for the first time ever, finally to agree to conduct proven counterinsurgency practices by protecting the population."

He went on to describe the failure of the kill-and-capture approach and the "short-war strategy." Despite the rhetoric of victory, the strategy being pursued on the ground was one of transition to an Iraqi force that would then take on the insurgency. "Nowhere in the military strategy did we have the mission to defeat the insurgency," Keane concluded bluntly. The president's face registered surprise. Keane believed that Rumsfeld, Abizaid, and Casey had never made clear to him what U.S. forces were *not* doing. This gap between the declared policy and the way in which the military forces were being employed was the crux of the matter, and yet no one had explained it to the president. The strategy's ends and means did not match.

Keane went on to lay out the argument for sending five more brigades to Baghdad, which would be the main effort, and two more brigade-sized marine regimental combat teams to Anbar province for support. The troops, he explained, would also be employed differently. "The character of the operation would be different than what we've done in the past because the troops would protect the people, live in the neighborhoods with them, sleep there, eat there, spend most of their time on foot," he explained. This type of coverage was not required all over Baghdad, he continued. "To use a military term, Mr. President, there is such a thing as critical terrain, and the critical terrain in Baghdad is the Shia-Sunni mixed neighborhoods." The population in those areas was about 1.8 million. Keane argued that intensive manpower was needed in those areas; in others, economic assistance could be provided. He argued against entering Sadr City with its two million Shia and instead advocated seeking a political solution with the Shia militias.

This prompted some debate. The Shia militias, especially Sadr's, were ascendant all over Baghdad and were attacking U.S. forces. Keane's reasoning, which was shared by Hannah, Cheney's national security adviser, was that the Shia violence had erupted in reaction to the sustained attacks against their community. The Shia militias had held off for two to three years in the face of Sunni attacks and the coalition's failure to provide security. A strategy of population protection might induce Shia militias to stand down without taking them on frontally.

Aware that his time was up, Keane concluded his comments. "We *have* the capacity to do this," he concluded. "This is a military operation which is militarily feasible. Whether it is desirable, given where we are politically, is another matter. But if you are asking me as a military professional, can we provide security and stability, the answer is yes." He added that it was necessary to hold all those involved, including the Iraqis, responsible for executing their end of the bargain—and to increase the overall size of the army and marines to relieve the strain. He had made the case for the surge.

Each of the other invitees spoke. Generals McCaffrey and Downing disagreed with Keane and instead advocated a greater reliance on training Iraqi forces so they could take over the fight. McCaffrey sounded his main theme, that a drawdown of troops was imperative to avoid breaking the army. "You've got to tell the generals to be down to seven to ten brigades by next November," he counseled. If not, he warned, the administration would turn over a wrecked military to its successor. In advocating more emphasis on training and advising the Iraqi forces, Downing argued that greater use of special operations forces in the training and advisory mission would yield significant results. Over four thousand special operations forces were serving as combat advisers to specialized Iraqi units, but the embedded U.S. military and police transition teams were made up of conventional active-duty and reserve personnel.

Keane was not surprised that the two other generals disagreed with him, but he was surprised that both Cohen and Biddle agreed, although Biddle's view was somewhat mixed. He believed that the United States could not dawdle with half measures: it needed to either engage fully or get out.

Cohen had been as blunt as Keane. He said the president was not holding his generals accountable. He said the administration was too focused on the fact that they were "good guys" and not on the fact that they were not producing the desired results. President Bush had read Cohen's influential book, *Supreme Command,* which argued that a president should exercise his constitutional decision-making authority on military affairs and not defer to uniformed leaders' views in lieu of his own judgment. For most of the war, however, the president had deferred to the advice of others on key decisions about how to conduct the war. When he repeatedly was asked about troop levels over the past four years, his usual response had been that he provided what his commanders had asked for. His primary role had been to stand fast on the goal of a stable, democratic Iraq and to resist pressure to give up or seek a second-best outcome.

The president asked the other invitees if they thought Gen. Casey should be replaced. They all agreed he should. He then asked who should be named in his place. "David Petraeus," said Cohen, and the other four agreed. McCaffrey told Bush that Petraeus was the most talented person he had ever met. McCaffrey had argued for a phased withdrawal and vigorously opposed the surge, but whatever the strategy adopted, he strongly recommended that the three-star general with a reputation for both brains and toughness be the one to implement it.

Immediately after the meeting concluded, Hannah took Keane to Cheney's office, where the three men continued the discussion, joined by Fred Kagan. Cheney took copious notes as they talked. The vice president had spoken up several times to ask questions during the Oval Office meeting. Kagan presented a fat deck of slides that outlined his proposal, which would be released in January with Keane as the coauthor under the title "Choosing Victory in Iraq."

That night Hannah called Keane at home. "I just wanted to give you some feedback," he said. "I don't know if you've had any."

"No, I haven't," Keane said.

"The meeting in the Oval Office turned out to be decisive, in terms of your presentation," Hannah told him. "You did two things in there that I haven't seen. You gave them vision and a way ahead, and you gave them courage. You're going to hear from Hadley's people."

The White House officials were aware that a decision to increase troops would fly in the face of public and congressional expectations. In the wake of the Democratic victories in the House and Senate, the release of the Baker-Hamilton recommendations, and the views of the joint staff, which had been leaked to the press, the White House faced mounting pressure for a course adjustment that would include fewer, not more troops, and fewer in combat roles. There was certain to be a firestorm when the administration announced the results of its policy review.

Some White House officials downplayed Keane's role in the decision to increase troops and said he was most valuable in helping to shape public opinion. Another official disagreed. "We would not have had the surge without Gen. Keane's artful explanations and credibility," he said, adding that Keane had influenced both the vice president's and the president's staff. Within the defense community, Keane was one of the most vocal surge proponents, arguing at think tanks and to journalists for a troop increase. Keane's military peers were furious at him for breaking ranks and lending his stature to a policy they believed would not work and would, in their view, quite possibly break the army. Keane was bucking virtually the entire military establishment and most of the foreign-policy elite, who favored drawing down troops and shifting to an advisory mission.

The final round of the policy battle occurred just after Christmas. Gen. Pace went to the president's home in Crawford, Texas, to present his recommendation that two more brigades be sent to bolster those in Baghdad and two battalions to Anbar. Another three brigades would be prepared as an emergency reserve. One surge proponent countered that this "Casey-Pace plan" was a "minimized, face-saving token increase that wasn't going to have the capacity to do anything."

After the president rejected Pace's proposal in favor of the five-brigade surge proposal Keane and others advocated, Hadley asked Keane if he would be willing to put his uniform back on to assume Casey's job of commanding the Multi-National Force-Iraq. Keane replied that his family commitment prevented him from accepting, but he promised to stay heavily involved and provide advice.

The debate over military strategy was thus settled in favor of escalation, but that did not address the all-important question of the Iraqi government's intentions. The political strategy was essentially to keep trying to persuade Iraq Prime Minister Nouri al-Maliki to do the right thing. He had promised to provide more Iraqi troops to secure Baghdad and to allow the targeting of Shia outlaws, but there was no implicit or explicit "or else" should he fail to do so. The main hope, as Keane, Hannah, and others had argued, was that if Sunni attacks were blunted, Shias would rein in their own sectarian agenda. But there was no appetite for imposing conditions on the Shia-led government.

Chiarelli believed the political strategy was a paramount issue. When Sen. John McCain, a longtime proponent of sending more troops to Iraq, visited Iraq in late 2006, Chiarelli discussed the troop issue with him as well as the political aspects of the strategy. "The real issue here is end-states," he said. Chiarelli believed the U.S. and Iraqi governments had fundamentally different objectives and that it was critical to resolve this "endstate mismatch." He believed, moreover, that the United States had the necessary leverage to resolve it. "We've got to negotiate to get to a point where we could support [Maliki's] endstate and establish enforcable benchmarks that would ensure he was moving toward that endstate," Chiarelli said. But no such negotiation took place.

Keane said sectarianism could not be completely eliminated. "We have to understand that in the context of one thousand years of domination, revenge is a major ingredient in the political culture and compromise is a minor ingredient," he said. The question was how far the United States would go to rein it in. Steve Biddle argued that the Shia political leaders, as well as stonewalling Sunni politicians, needed to know that the administration would not tolerate sectarian behavior from either side. He dubbed the approach "Tony Soprano Goes to Baghdad." It would require using military troops and resources as leverage—denying assistance or applying force as a result of noncompliance or to induce compliance. "This model requires connecting political negotiations in Baghdad to military operations," Biddle noted. "That's going to require getting in the knickers of [U.S.] commanders in a way they won't like either."

Saddam Hussein's execution on December 30, 2006, convinced some Americans of the Maliki government's unbridled sectarian hatred. Saddam was handed over to Iraqi officials at a former military intelligence center in Kadhimiya that was part of a joint military base Americans called FOB Justice. The Americans helped search those coming into the intelligence building and then withdrew. Iraqi officials then let other Iraqis in the back door. One of them recorded the execution on his cell phone, and the video was posted on the Internet a few hours later. The atmosphere was that of a lynching. Spectators taunted Saddam as the noose was placed around his neck. One chanted Muqtada al-Sadr's name. Another told Saddam to go to hell. Just as the former dictator started to say a prayer, the trap door opened below his feet. The video confirmed many Sunnis' worst suspicions, that the Maliki government was out for vengeance. One U.S. official who had been present held Maliki's national security adviser personally responsible for the circus atmosphere.

The day after CIA Director Robert Gates was confirmed as secretary of defense, he went to Iraq. Even before Gates arrived in Baghdad, it was obvious to Gen. Casey that he was losing the argument. His views had not prevailed in the policy review, and the "surgios" had won, although this was not yet public knowledge. Gates made clear that a new commander would be coming in to oversee the new strategy.

Casey, a taciturn, almost dour man who trusted few in the press corps and liked even fewer, was personally exhausted after two and a half years in Iraq. The four-star general, fifty-eight years old, had stayed longer than any other senior official serving in Iraq. He had the support of Abizaid, Schoomaker, and until recently the president. He had endured an untold amount of micromanaging by Rumsfeld and, as the war went badly, a fair amount of whispered criticism from colleagues who said he was not up to the job intellectually. But none of his peers had spoken out with a better idea. Rumsfeld had cowed almost everyone. It was very likely a point of honor for Casey to soldier on grimly in Iraq until he was told to go. Few Americans knew his family's poignant history: his father had been the highest-ranking army officer to die in Vietnam, in a helicopter crash.

A steely-eyed man who often gave the impression of glaring at people from behind his glasses, Casey was the portrait of duty and determination, but also a kind of dogged defensiveness. The way he crossed his arms high across his chest when speaking telegraphed a "keep away" message. His sternness increased over time, as if to ward off anyone's pity for the ignominious end to his long tour in Iraq. He led the war, but he did not win it. He was unwilling to admit that Iraq had outfoxed him, beaten him, defied his every attempt to clobber the insurgency into submission. He had not been able to seal the borders, clean out the western desert, stop the insurgents from exploding car bombs, or prevent the latest disaster of untrammeled sectarian killing that threatened to plunge the country into full-scale civil war.

He would most likely be remembered for fighting the war with too few troops, accepting the constraints Rumsfeld placed on him, and banking on the ramp-up of Iraqi forces that in the end proved insufficient. But many other aspects of the military's strategy, operations, and tactics from 2004 to 2006 also deserved in-depth scrutiny. The way in which forces were employed often did not match the declared strategy and very often the effects canceled out one another. New commanders and units undid the gains of their predecessors. Troops were quartered on large bases, away from the population. When they sallied forth, it was in full kit and armored vehicles and very often to conduct some type of combat operation. Most effort and resources were expended in sweeps and search operations for "bad guys," and too little attention was paid to the feelings engendered in Iraqis. The troops did not know the people, the culture, or the neighborhood, and hasty counterinsurgency training for a few weeks could not remedy this deficit. Most were highly dependent on the talent and empathy of their interpreters.

Casey had twice proposed and attempted to draw down U.S. troop levels. In pursuit of that goal, he had relentlessly turned over territory and more than half the U.S. bases to Iraqi troops in the face of clear evidence that they were not capable of doing the job. He believed that doing more of the same would force them to step up to the task of securing Iraq. However, the evidence suggested that Iraqi militias with the tolerance or active connivance of some of the security forces were chasing Sunnis from Baghdad and the other three central provinces where much of the population lived in order to consolidate Shia control. It was also unclear whether Iraqis could deal with sporadic intra-Shia violence in the south and multiethnic Kirkuk and Mosul.

In recognition of his loyal service, the White House nominated Casey to be chief of staff of the army, setting off howls of protest from Congress and from those among the lower ranks of army officers who were frustrated with the way the war had been conducted. It was the administration's habit to reward senior officials whose accomplishments were debatable: Tommy Franks, George Tenet, and Paul Bremer had all received the Medal of Freedom. One officer who believed Casey should have retired instead of accepting the nomination to lead the army speculated that the White House had offered him the job so he would not become a high-profile critic of his civilian bosses' policy decisions, as had a passel of lower-ranking retirees in the past year and a half. Casey would endure a bruising nomination hearing as senators from both parties challenged his record, but in the end he was confirmed for the post.

As he took up his new duties, Casey found further support for his belief that the best course for the United States was to draw down its troops. Subordinates at bases around the country and in the army staff showed him evidence of the toll that repeated deployments were taking on soldiers and equipment. Casey's predecessor as army chief, Gen. Peter Schoomaker, had repeatedly warned the Congress and the public that the cost for resetting the force would be at least $17 billion a year for several years after the war ended, and the monthly cost for the war continued to climb to $12 billion.

A prominent voice in the debate over whether the army was breaking under the strain of war was Gordon Sullivan, who had retired as army chief of staff in 1995 and thereafter headed the Association of the U.S. Army, the institution's main lobby and policy advocate. "I worry that the institution is not capable of refreshing itself over time," he said. "The army is not big enough to sustain this kind of commitment over time." Sullivan was a Vietnam veteran who had lived through the postwar nadir of the army, its rebuilding as an all-volunteer force, and then its downsizing after the cold war. He did not oppose the surge publicly, but after its announcement he wrote an editorial declaring that the "army is all in," meaning there was no more money in the bank.

Gates was quick to address the army's concerns as well as to make Iraq his top priority. Whereas Rumsfeld had steadfastly opposed increasing the army's size, one of Gates's first acts was to announce a further increase in the army, from an additional 30,000 to 74,000. The growth was planned to occur over three years, so it would not relieve the immediate stress Iraq caused. Just how long it would take depended on reenlistment rates. They had stayed surprisingly high, but retention in the critical ranks of captains and noncommissioned officers was slipping. To attain the required numbers, new soldiers who fell in the lower end of the acceptable range were being recruited. Gates wanted to reverse that practice, so the job of growing the army would be that much more difficult.

On January 5, 2007, the president announced that he was nominating Lt. Gen. David Petraeus, commander of the Combined Arms Center at Fort Leavenworth, Kansas, as Casey's successor. At the same time, Bush announced that he was nominating Adm. William "Fox" Fallon, the combatant commander of Pacific Command, to fill the vacancy at Central Command that Gen. Abizaid's retirement had created.

Petraeus's nomination was greeted with enormous publicity—he had been a high-profile general since Pulitzer-winning historian Rick Atkinson had accompanied him in the first month of Operation Iraqi Freedom in 2003 as commander of the 101st Airborne Division. In the run-up to the war, during a roundtable with *U.S. News & World Report*, Barry McCaffrey had touted him as the brightest general in the current generation of army officers.

McCaffrey was quite aware that Petraeus's promotion to four-star general would fuel the criticism that Petraeus engendered from his own army colleagues. President Bush was not unaware of this, and he asked another general why the army did not like Petraeus. "Part of it is sheer jealousy," McCaffrey said. "The army culture does that to you if you want to be famous." The army preferred the good-old-boy general who was unpretentious and didn't talk too much or too well. "How could the army dream of not advancing its most talented, effective officer? Why does the army do that to its best and brightest?" McCaffrey lamented. He had suffered similar hazing as the son of a general, as a graduate of Andover prep school, and most of all for his outspokenness and unabashed ambition. He had seen the same phenomenon with Gen. Wesley Clark, an ambitious Rhodes scholar and two-time combatant commander who antagonized his peers, found favor with the White House, and then ran into a buzz saw of criticism over his handling of the Kosovo conflict in the mid-1990s. "I nurtured him along," McCaffrey recalled. "I think I was the only friend he had in the army." Clark retired, wrote his memoirs, and went on to campaign unsuccessfully for the Democratic Party's presidential nomination.

This hazing of officers who had basked in or, worse yet, sought the limelight was a longstanding part of the army's culture. Even Norman Schwarzkopf, the victorious general of Operation Desert Storm who gave daily war briefings, felt the sting of criticism for his visibility. Angered, he refused to give speeches for the army, a typical duty performed by retired generals, for five years. The prohibition on standing out had ripple effects throughout the institution. The top army commanders set the tone: when they did not engage the press, their subordinates clammed up as well. The previous two army chiefs had shied away from the media. The same was true in Iraq. Under both Casey and his predecessor, Ricardo

Sanchez, there had been no authoritative army voice giving the military's side of the story. Casey's aversion to the press and infrequent briefings left the field open to the war's ever more numerous and vociferous critics.

Although he supported Petraeus as an iconoclast and considered him an ideal commander for Iraq, McCaffrey would continue to play the role of critic and opponent of the surge. He would continue to travel to Iraq and offer his unvarnished assessments to the ground commanders as well as on television as an NBC analyst. Rumsfeld had gone to great lengths to try to prevent McCaffrey's tours of the war zone, but the military continued to host his trips to Iraq. McCaffrey's strident criticism carried weight because he was a decorated war hero of Desert Storm and Vietnam. His own son was on his third combat tour. McCaffrey believed the United States would be largely out of Iraq within thirty-six months. He derided halfway measures that had been proposed, such as drawing back into a few bases in Iraq or on the perimeter. Hunkering down in a base in the middle of a raging sectarian war was a defensive posture that invited attack. And Kuwait, the primary location mentioned for over-the-horizon forces, would never tolerate more than one brigade of U.S. troops camped out on its soil, he said.

Petraeus's nomination stole the headlines, but Fallon's nomination came as a complete surprise. Central Command (CENTCOM) was traditionally a billet for a commander from the ground services. Now an admiral would be overseeing not one but two land wars in Iraq and Afghanistan. Fallon was a gruff and straightforward officer who had challenged Rumsfeld's global plan for changing the forward basing of U.S. troops, to make the footprint lighter and the forces more expeditionary. If Abizaid had been too hands-off, Fallon came with a reputation as a micromanager. It would be up to the president to preserve Petraeus's room for maneuver, if indeed he wished to maintain the precedent established under Casey, in which the lines of communication ran directly from Washington to Baghdad.

The story of how Fox Fallon came to be nominated as the next CENTCOM chief was instructive. In November President Bush was on his way home from the Asia-Pacific Economic Cooperation summit in Vietnam and stopped in Hawaii for a briefing on Pacific Command issues from Fallon. Instead of briefing the president on his own area of responsibility, the utterly confident Fallon told Bush what he should do about Iraq. "Iraq is all screwed up," he told him. "Here are the six things that need to be done." Such forthrightness appealed to Bush, whose staff had been mired in indecision and the torturous months-long policy review. Those who had been wrestling with the complexities of Iraq often bogged down in arguments that opponents would simply turn on their heads. If there ever was a hall of mirrors, it was Iraq. No one could decide what the key problem was, much less the solution. So the clarity of Fallon's remarks came as a breath of fresh air to the president. It did not matter that the admiral had not set foot in Iraq.

Joint Chiefs Chairman Pace saw that Fallon had made an impression on the president, and when the admiral visited the Pentagon a few weeks later, he ushered him in to see the new secretary of defense, Gates. Fallon, previously at the bottom of the list of possible replacements for Abizaid, was now moved to the top. After the meeting, Gates said he found Fallon an acceptable candidate, and Pace acted quickly to send the recommendation over to the White House. Confirmation hearings for Petraeus were scheduled for January 23, and for Fallon on January 30.

On January 10, President Bush announced the New Way Forward in Iraq in a televised address. "It is clear," he said, "that we need to change our strategy in Iraq." He said he was ordering an additional five army brigades and two marine battalions into Iraq—some 21,500 troops—to help stabilize the country. "These troops," he said, "will work alongside Iraqi units and be embedded in their formations. Our troops will have a well-defined mission: to help Iraqis clear and secure neighborhoods, to help them protect the local population, and to help ensure that the Iraqi forces left behind are capable of providing the security that Baghdad needs." The president acknowledged the failure of the past summer's attempt to rein in violence: "This time, we'll have the force levels we need to hold the areas that have been cleared. In earlier operations, political and sectarian interference prevented Iraqi and American forces from going into neighborhoods that are home to those fueling the sectarian violence. This time, Iraqi and American forces will have a green light to enter those neighborhoods—and Prime Minister Maliki has pledged that political or sectarian interference will not be tolerated." In addition to this military surge, he announced a surge of economic and political measures. The number of U.S. provincial reconstruction teams of development and governance experts would be doubled, accompanied by an economic aid package. For its part, the Iraqi government had promised additional forces for Baghdad and a $10 billion capital expenditure to support reconstruction and development out of its own healthy stock of oil revenues.

It had taken six months for the White House to produce a change in course and a new leadership, which Meghan O'Sullivan and others had recognized was necessary since the previous summer. Baghdad had continued to burn while the gears of government turned in Washington. There was, of course, no guarantee that the New Way Forward would meet with any greater success than the old way, but there was a distinct sense that this was a last-ditch effort to bring the war to some tenable conclusion. If it failed, the United States likely would be forced into outright withdrawal and a policy of triage aimed at preventing or containing a regional war.

In truth, no one knew whether the war could be turned around at this stage. It might not be possible to rectify or mitigate the errors made in the past four years. The geopolitical counterargument to withdrawal from Iraq was that the entire region could be destabilized by the escalating violence. It was a large country with the third-largest proven oil reserves, and the largest Arab country with a Shia majority. Sunni regimes on its borders felt threatened enough to undermine a Shia-led Iraq, and Iran next door saw a chance to extend its bid for regional hegemony. Syria was serving as an outpost for both the Sunni Baathist and jihadist insurgency. It was not difficult to imagine a regional war erupting if the United States departed.

The moral counterargument to leaving Iraq was a version of the oft-quoted Colin Powell "Pottery Barn" comment that if the United States invaded Iraq "it would break it, and it would own it." Tens of thousands of Iraqis had been killed and the rest were living in chaos and misery.

Americans wanted out, but they had not yet come to grips with what it would mean for America to lose its first war since Vietnam. The president's warning that Islamic extremism would spread sounded to many like the shrill hyperbole of a desperate politician. Yet there was a range of possibly dire consequences: The Middle East would almost certainly witness more turmoil, and many more Iraqis would die. Americans might react to losing a war with a retreat from global leadership and efforts to solve the many problems besetting the world. And, on balance, losers of wars could expect to experience diminished influence.

Like most of the Army graybeards, Gordon Sullivan dearly wanted to keep the army from breaking. He also knew the war had to be brought to as satisfactory a conclusion as possible, but it was not clear what "good enough" meant. Sullivan said the initial invasion plan of 2003 had been ill-advised and that the army had wanted to go in full-bore. "We went in with a knitting needle," he said. He rejected the surgical-force argument Rumsfeld had propounded, saying, "We can't go at things half-heartedly." But he was also philosophical about the mistakes. War, he said, is an iterative process. He cited the observation of Sir Michael Howard, a British military historian, that whatever doctrine an army goes to war with usually turns out to be wrong for that war, and that then the army adjusts. "What history may show is that our doctrine may not have been 100 percent correct, but the troops have adapted," Sullivan said. Given the rising vitriol over the war, he commented that Petraeus did not have much time to show results. "How much time does he need? Will the country give him that time?" he fretted.

3

David Howell Petraeus

On January 4, 2007, David Petraeus's cell phone rang. He, his wife, Holly, and their son, Stephen, were driving down the Los Angeles freeway on the way to visit his father, Sixtus, who lived one valley west of Los Angeles. Holly was behind the wheel, as she often was, since she was a less distracted driver than her husband. The car rental company had given them a gigantic brand-new Chevy Suburban. Petraeus answered the call. It was Defense Secretary Robert Gates. The signal was bouncing in and out. "Pull over, pull over," Petraeus said. "Where?" Holly said, scanning the traffic-choked lanes. She dove off the next exit, in a bad part of town, and parked in the lot of a convenience store. There Gates formally offered Petraeus the job as commander of the Multi-National Force-Iraq and the promotion to four-star general that went with it. "I want to make sure you will accept the job before we announce it publicly," he said. Within minutes after the secretary hung up, all the cell phones in the car began ringing. Gen. Peter Pace, chairman of the Joint Chiefs of Staff, could not get through on Petraeus's phone, so he called Stephen's.

It was hard to overstate the manifest downsides of replacing Gen. George Casey as MNF-I commander. Taking charge of a failing war the American public had soured on was as bad an assignment as a general could get. "I wasn't sitting in Leavenworth saying, 'I'd love to go back and be MNF-I commander,'" Petraeus said. The Central Command job was a far more attractive prize; the combatant commanders had real power, and in this case one could advise on and oversee the war effort without becoming entirely tarred with what might well be America's first lost war since Vietnam. He and Holly had talked at length, and tossed and turned at night. "We both realized that there were going to be plenty of opportunities for failure, to be pilloried in the press and by armchair generals," Holly said. "He was putting his neck on the line and probably it was going to get chopped off."

On the other hand, one could argue that his entire career had been a preparation for this assignment. He had just spent a year revamping the army's manual on counterinsurgency to help those in Iraq. His two tours in Iraq had given him a good feel for the country and relevant experience in the challenges of stabilizing its second-largest city and in raising the armed forces on which that country's stability would rest. Before that, he had served in peacekeeping operations in Bosnia and Haiti. Turning down the offer would have been an unusual abdication for a man who was motivated by challenge more than any other single impulse.

One young officer hoped he would take the opportunity to stand up and say no as a protest to the war, or at least to the terms on which he was being offered the job, which made the war unwinnable. "It will take 300,000 soldiers and 20 years," this officer said. "To say anything else is happy talk, and the generals are complicit." What some of the soldiers, including young officers who believed in Petraeus, wanted was for a senior officer in uniform to exhibit the type of backbone and leadership they felt had been sorely lacking in the previous six years while the pugnacious and overbearing Donald Rumsfeld had been secretary of defense. But generals traditionally gave their advice and then followed orders. Besides, it was not at all clear that any general would be able to convince President Bush that the Iraq war was unwinnable and that a troop drawdown and exit strategy was the best course. Other four-star generals had attempted to sway him during the policy review of the previous months without success.

The emotional debate over the wisdom and conduct of the war was bound to merge with reactions to the nomination of Gen. Petraeus, who also tended to provoke strong sentiments. Some supporters believed Petraeus accepted the job because his ambition had gotten the better of him and he wanted to advance his career. According to this view, Petraeus would be credited with trying to turn around the failing war and not blamed for its ultimate failure because the die had already been cast. He would be compared to Creighton Abrams, who succeeded Gen. William Westmoreland in Vietnam and was considered, at least by war historian Lewis Sorley, to have adopted the right approach there but too late to turn it around.

Petraeus sat in the convenience store parking lot in a ghetto and had one of the most serious conversations of his life. "Look, my obligation is to give you my best professional advice, and you need to know that's what you're going to get," he told Secretary Gates, who assured him that candor was what he wanted. Petraeus went on to outline exactly what that entailed. First he would be given a mission. From that he would derive the tasks to accomplish the mission, and then he would determine and request the forces needed to carry it out. "If for some reason, they're not available, [I will] explain the level of risk incurred," he said. "If the risk is too great [that might entail] at some point saying, you might be better off continuing this with somebody else in charge." Petraeus wanted to make crystal clear that he would not get wrapped around the axle as many suspected Casey had been.

Gates accepted the terms, and Petraeus said yes. He could have said that three tours abroad since 2001 was enough already; that would have been an acceptable answer. But now that he had agreed to shoulder the burden of a failing war and to be gone from home for another year or two, he set about doing everything possible to win. He would have to define what winning in Iraq meant. First, however, he had to win confirmation from a restless Senate dominated by Democrats who were angry that Bush had decided to send more troops instead of bringing them home.

The next few days were a thrill for ninety-year-old Sixtus Petraeus, as he experienced a taste of what his son's life would now be like. The calls flooded in at all hours. David Petraeus's e-mail in-box exploded with messages. As they went from one place to another, Petraeus would man the phones and answer e-mails while Holly drove. As soon as he returned from visiting his father, Petraeus began to plot his confirmation strategy. He flew to Washington and, in the days before his confirmation hearing, assiduously courted senators who were brought into a senator's office to meet with him. Worried that Petraeus was overdoing the glad-handing, the office of the army chief reined him in and warned against too many high-profile meetings. It was common practice to meet with senators before confirmation hearings, but the intense media glare made the army nervous. The army's usual approach was to shun the spotlight, directly opposite of Petraeus's inclination. Hearings shaped perceptions of the war, and therefore the latitude for its conduct, and judgments as to its course. They were arguably more important than any single military operation or other event that occurred on the physical battlefield in Iraq. But the army was uncomfortable with the massive head of publicity that was building up behind the combined phenomenon of the war and a man many of them viewed as a gifted but grandstanding general.

DAVID HOWELL PETRAEUS WAS BORN November 7, 1952, in Cornwall on Hudson, New York, a small town of some three thousand inhabitants located seven miles north of the U.S. Military Academy at West Point. Petraeus's father, Sixtus, was a Dutch merchant marine captain during World War II who then emigrated to the United States. His mother, an Oberlin College graduate, loved education and books, and Dickens in particular. A part-time librarian, she filled their home with thousands of books. At dinner she played a version of *Jeopardy!* at the dinner table with her two children. Petraeus's father, who coached some of his sports teams, encouraged his athleticism and competitive streak.

Cornwall was insulated from the raging anti–Vietnam War furor that gripped much of the country in the 1970s. As a bedroom community of West Point, it was a place where a young man could easily choose to join the army. The town was full of retired military men, and the West Point prep school was two blocks from Petraeus's house. His high school soccer coach was a retired colonel who had led the West Point team to a national championship. Young Dave's imagination was especially fired by Bill Carpenter, the famous "Lonely End" football star, West Point's All-American player who went to Vietnam and earned the Distinguished Service Cross before coming back to West Point and marrying a local girl. He would be one of Petraeus's teachers at West Point. "He was a real hero, and he looked the part too," Petraeus recalled. "A great-looking guy." He was, in short, all that Petraeus hoped to be. "A lot of life, I think, is about trying to be like people you think highly of," Petraeus reflected. He was also drawn to "the idea of service to something larger than oneself."

At West Point, Petraeus's personality as a striver came into full bloom. He graduated in the top 5 percent, which made him a "star man," so named for the stars the summa cum laude students wore on their collars, and was on the brigade staff, which entitled him to wear chevrons on his sleeve. He and his roommate chose to go into the pre-med program; he excelled at the difficult course of study, but in the end he decided against the years-long commitment of medical school, internship, and residency. Looking back, he said, "The reason I did it was it was just hard. Academically, it was like running up the highest mountain."

His classmates captured this trait in the Class of 1974 *Howitzer* yearbook, using the nickname that had followed him to West Point. His Little League baseball teammates had called him Peaches, because pronouncing the name Petraeus stumped many of them. Beneath a photo of a handsome young man with a toothy grin, the description reads: "Peaches came to the Mil Acad with high ambitions, but unlike most, he accomplished his goals. A striver to the Max, Dave was always 'going for it' in sport, academics, leadership, and even his social life. This attitude will surely lead to success in the future, Army or otherwise."

The yearbook reference to his social life was an enduring part of the story. By the time he graduated, he was engaged to the daughter of the West Point superintendent, Maj. Gen. William A. Knowlton, who had been secretary of the army general staff under Westmoreland and would go on to successive NATO posts before retiring as a four-star general.

Petraeus's classmates teased him mercilessly. Years later, many still wondered how on earth had a cadet managed to meet, let alone become engaged to, the daughter of the top general on campus.

In October 1973, Hollister Knowlton was headed home for a visit from Carlisle, Pennsylvania, where she had begun her senior year at Dickinson College. A friend of her mother's suggested that she might like to go to the football game. When the cadet the woman had in mind for a date turned out to be otherwise committed, she called the cadet office to find someone who was free that night. Young Petraeus, the assistant brigade adjutant, was on duty and accepted the invitation. When Holly arrived home and found out that her blind date was someone neither her mother nor her mother's friend had ever met, she was appalled.

The two youths went to the sold-out game. David turned to Holly and asked her for the tickets. "What tickets?" Holly asked. The woman who arranged the date had forgotten to arrange for tickets, so he wheedled the gate guards into letting them in and took her to the cadets section, where they could sit without tickets. It did not take long for word to circulate as to Holly's identity. The other cadets kept giving David the thumbs-up and shouting and calling out to him. "It was just ridiculous, really," Holly recalled with a laugh, adding that it was one of those rare blind dates with a happy ending.

Holly and David were married on July 6, 1974, at the West Point chapel. The whirlwind courtship and engagement occurred as both students raced through their final studies to graduation. Holly was busy writing her honors dissertation in French on Nobel laureate novelist François Mauriac. She would forever disdain those who assumed Petraeus had married her because she was the super's daughter. "It's very insulting to me," she said. "I'm not stupid. I wouldn't have married someone who was on the make. We got married because we fell in love." For his part, Petraeus said of his witty, intelligent wife, "She could have done anything, but instead she married me."

Holly's mother, Peggy, was fond of young Dave from the day he started coming around to the back door to call on Holly. "I call him my fourth son," she said. Petraeus could count on Holly and her family to understand everything he was going through, down to the intricacies of career assignments and the army's most obscure acronyms. Holly's three brothers were in the national service, and all three served in Vietnam along with their father. Her oldest brother had graduated from West Point in 1970 and her youngest had enlisted in an airborne infantry unit and later became a drill sergeant.

Gen. Knowlton was a somewhat formidable figure: one of his tasks as superintendent was to restore discipline and enforce the school's honor code at a time when the hippie era, black power, Vietnam, and draft-dodging were all reaching their height. Knowlton proposed that officers spend a year in combat before being allowed to go to graduate school. This, he felt, would inoculate them from the leftist ideas then popular in academia and temper the influence of the wives they were likely to meet and marry there.

The Vietnam War was not far from the minds of the cadets at West Point. Conrad Crane, who was also in the Class of 1974, recalled sitting next to Petraeus in their Advanced Military History course. Their instructor, Capt. Rod Paschall, was on his way to Cambodia two weeks after the course ended, Crane recalled, wondering if he would return. "Vietnam permeated everything we did," Crane said. They were beginning their careers in the shadow of the lost war in Vietnam. Their class included a South Vietnamese cadet at West Point, Phan Min Tam, who was nicknamed "Phantom." He returned to his country and was sentenced to ten years in a reeducation camp after the war, but his former classmates successfully petitioned to get him out.

Knowlton would be an important influence on and role model for Petraeus. From a prominent and well-off Massachusetts family, Knowlton graduated from St. Marks prep school but was set on a military career and received an appointment to West Point. He married Peggy Downey, daughter of the noted author Fairfax Downey. Knowlton was an articulate, breezily self-confident man who spoke seven languages fluently, including Vietnamese, Arabic, Russian, Turkish, and romance languages. His successful army career set a standard that Petraeus would seek to meet: Knowlton became a four-star general, held prestigious commands in Europe and the army staff, and distinguished himself in battle in both World War II and in Vietnam.

Knowlton was a gifted raconteur of his wartime exploits, for which he had been decorated with the highest medals: three Silver Stars, the Distinguished Flying Cross, and others. He earned his first Silver Star as a twenty-four-year-old lieutenant who led sixty-five soldiers through German lines to link up with the Russians at the end of World War II. His witty account was published in *Reader's Digest* with help from his father-in-law. As a top official in the Civil Operations and Revolutionary Development Support (CORDS) program, Knowlton visited every hamlet in the country. To his delight, he then received a command in the Mekong Delta, where Creighton Abrams ordered him to dismantle the Vietcong network. During that tour, he received two Silver Stars for his ingenuity and gallantry under fire. Back at the Pentagon, he was an early champion of investigating the My Lai massacre.

Petraeus saw how Knowlton's deep grasp of world history—and his crackling sense of humor—made him an effective military ambassador. Knowlton's advice tended to be practical. He counseled Petraeus to round out his education by attending armor school, and he urged him not to procrastinate in writing his dissertation. He did not weigh in on Petraeus's topic—Vietnam's influence on the next generation of officers—but he had been dismayed by the aid cut-off to Vietnam in 1975. The two men kept score of their respective achievements in a lighthearted competition, but Petraeus would not get the chance to prove himself in combat, as young Knowlton had, until he went to Iraq as a two-star general.

AFTER RECEIVING HIS COMMISSION as a second lieutenant, Petraeus served first in the 509th Airborne Infantry Battalion in Italy and then the 24th Infantry Division. Petraeus's drive to compete and win in difficult contests led him to Ranger School, the most physically grueling training in the army. He won all three top awards there: Distinguished Honor Graduate, the Darby Award, which includes the highest peer ratings, and the Merrill's Marauder Award for land navigation and high peer ratings. The latter two awards were especially important to Petraeus. He wanted to win but also to be seen as a team player—and he recognized the tension between the two. "The challenge is how do you do your best," he said. "How do you try to win and still be a good team player? And that's difficult, candidly . . . because it is hard to be both a great team player *and* to excel." That was an ongoing dilemma for Petraeus. Officers compete intensely at every stage of their careers, and his drive to be the best would lead many peers to believe he was not a team player. That perception became his chief obstacle since both qualities are required to succeed in an institution that is both a hierarchy and a fraternity.

As a junior captain, he was chosen along with seven others to attend the Command and General Staff College at Fort Leavenworth, Kansas, two years ahead of time. It was a one-time experiment to include younger officers in a class that was normally for captains who had been selected for major. The younger officers were housed separately, and Petraeus recalled feeling a little bit intimidated, as the youngest in a class of some one thousand officers. He put his head down and worked, and the young captains gradually became more accepted. In the last week of the school year Petraeus learned that he would graduate at the head of the class of 1983 and receive the George C. Marshall Award. After receiving the phone call, the ecstatic captain was about to burst from happiness. He laced up his running shoes and went for a run along the scenic wooded Leavenworth Ridge overlooking the Missouri River to savor his triumph. He may not have graduated first at West Point, but he was at the head of the class this time.

The deepest and most important professional relationship Petraeus would form in his career began when he served for a year as the aide de camp to the 24th Division's incoming commander, Maj. Gen. John R. "Jack" Galvin. Galvin's assistant division commander offered to pick out the best captain he could find. Galvin immediately clicked with his young aide. "In a very short time—a few days—I realized that this young man was really organized," Galvin recalled. "He was always a step ahead of everything that was going on. He sensed priorities."

Galvin, one of the most intellectual officers of his generation, took the education of his young aide very seriously. Aides de camp were to be used for substantive purposes. "I've always felt that the aide is not someone who lights your cigarettes," he said. Petraeus was fortunate to find, this early in his career, a mentor who saw thinking and teaching as integral to leadership. Petraeus had just finished commanding a company and was full of ideas he was eager to try out. Galvin encouraged him. When they traveled, he would send Petraeus off to gather his own impressions.

"He was just as impressive as could be," Galvin recalled. "He was the best aide I ever had, out of fourteen. . . . For all the time I've known him he has been in high gear; he doesn't know what low gear is. We would run with the troops in the morning at dawn. He would have already run five or six miles by himself. Just to prove the point that he could. Then after we stopped, and everyone was puffing, we would take our departure—running."

Galvin ribbed the young captain about his perfectionist tendencies. "He does not like to make a mistake. He would say he has never made one," Galvin said with a laugh. "He would do something that I would call a mistake, and I would try to get him to admit it, but he would always talk his way around it."

The year began an extended tutorial on leadership, which remained Galvin's abiding interest throughout his career. "We had lots of discussions about decision-making, the problems of command. We were always discussing leadership, what to do in what kind of circumstances," he said. "We used to talk about the fact that there is no book that tells you how to lead in battle." The two men would choose a topic to discuss, such as communication, teamwork, education. In one such conversation, Galvin said, they agreed that one mark of a good communicator was someone who listened 50 percent of the time. Both acknowledged, however, that they rarely did that.

Despite the great gap in their age, rank, and experience, Galvin said, "I listened to him very often." Although some of his staff thought the captain overstepped his bounds, he had his mentor's full support. "He would challenge people's view of the situation," Galvin said. "He was a can-do kind of person, not one who would just wait for you to tell him what to do next. He would show you that he is already doing that."

One day the chief of staff remarked to Galvin, "This aide of yours wants to be the division commander."

"What's wrong with that?" Galvin replied.

Jack Galvin's influence was a major factor in Petraeus's decision to go to graduate school. As Holly put it, it was Galvin who encouraged her husband to "get his head out of the foxhole and begin thinking and writing about his profession." So the couple moved to New Jersey with their first child, Anne, while Petraeus attended Princeton University's Woodrow Wilson School of Public and International Affairs, where he obtained a master's degree in public administration in 1985 and a doctorate in international relations in 1987. While completing his doctoral dissertation, Petraeus taught at West Point in the social sciences department. Their second child, son Stephen, was born during this educational hiatus in his career.

Some career-minded peers warned Petraeus that spending so much time on the academic track, rather than out in the field with troops, would jeopardize his upward mobility. Petraeus found the academic environment stimulating, and his studies bore directly on the national security issues of the day. His research focused on leadership and decision-making as they pertained to the major conflicts of his time, and his doctoral dissertation, "The American Military and the Lessons of Vietnam: A Study of Military Influence and the Use of Force in the Post-Vietnam Era," examined whether the Vietnam War had made the current generation of senior military leaders overly cautious regarding the use of force. The answer was a carefully nuanced yes. He did not seek to publish his thesis as a book, partly because he felt it needed one more scrub, but also out of a wish not to gouge the current senior leadership in public.

The dissertation examined the posture of military leaders after the Vietnam War, noting the parallels between the post–Vietnam War generation and the "Never Again" club after the Korean War. Vietnam had deeply marked the officers who rose to lead the army in the mid-1980s. A new thesis emerged that became known as the Weinberger Doctrine and later the Powell Doctrine. In essence it held that the country should not go to war unless vital national interests are threatened, and then the use of force must be overwhelming and accompanied by manifest public support and a clear exit strategy. If such conditions were rigorously applied, military force might never again be employed.

In opposition to that view, Petraeus quoted Secretary of Defense James Schlesinger, who testified to the Senate in February 1985 that "the role of the United States in the world is such that it must be prepared for, be prepared to threaten, and even be prepared to fight those intermediate conflicts—that are likely to fare poorly on television." Petraeus cited as well the judgment of Eliot Cohen, a young professor who would later become a friend, that "American participation in small wars remains an inevitable concomitant of America's world role."

Petraeus believed that the wars of his era were likely to be such wars and that America would have to calibrate its response rather than take refuge in all-or-nothing formulas. Those haunted by Vietnam feared that any military engagement could constitute a slippery slope inevitably leading to combat. Those who were willing to countenance engagement would have to define how far U.S. interests extended and whether, if U.S. aims were not achieved, disengagement from a failing enterprise would be preferable to escalation.

The issue was far from an academic one in the mid-1980s when Petraeus was at work on his dissertation. Most contentiously in Central America but in much of the Third World, the Soviet Union and the United States were engaged in a contest for control and influence. The Reagan administration chose to support the Salvadoran government against a Marxist insurgency and to create the Nicaraguan contras (or counterrevolutionaries) to fight the Marxist Sandinista government. The United States also fought a proxy war against the Soviets in Afghanistan and opposed Soviet- and Cuban-backed regimes in Africa and elsewhere. The policies, especially in Central America, generated enormous controversy and fears that the United States would intervene directly and become bogged down in "another Vietnam." Petraeus traveled with Galvin, then combatant commander in Latin America, as he sought to thread the needle between support for allies and the quicksand of combat.

Petraeus's early thinking about these dilemmas of small wars and insurgency provided an intellectual foundation for his later assignments in Haiti, the Balkans, and Iraq, as well as his work on revising the army's counterinsurgency manual. Although the cold war was about to end, the contests of the future would include many small, messy conflicts that would require decisions about whether and how to intervene. While working on his thesis and teaching at West Point, Petraeus co-authored an article with Galvin on this topic, titled "Uncomfortable Wars: Toward a New Paradigm," which was published in the military journal *Parameters*. He was also quoted in a 1986 *Wall Street Journal* article as an adviser to Galvin, using the euphemism the military had adopted for small wars and insurgencies, "low intensity conflict (LIC)." He said, "LIC is a growth industry."

During Petraeus's sojourn in the civilian world of graduate school, he left the military bubble in which many officers live for most or all of their careers. He later credited this experience with helping him to navigate another completely foreign world, the post-invasion Iraqi city of Mosul. Speakers with provocative views are routinely invited to military colleges, but it was another matter to be transplanted entirely out of one's comfort zone and constantly engaged in debates where one might be the distinct minority. Petraeus recalled going from staff college, where a fierce debate raged about the appropriate number of MX nuclear missiles, to the Ivy League graduate school where deeply debated positions ranged from the MX to doing away with the multiple independently targeted reentry vehicle missiles or even all land-based missiles, to pledging no first use of nuclear missiles, to total disarmament.

After finishing his teaching tour at West Point, Petraeus again went to work for Gen. Galvin, who had become the supreme allied commander in Europe. The following year, 1988, Petraeus moved to Schweinfurt, Germany, to begin a three-year tour with the 3rd Infantry Division. After one year as a battalion operations officer, Petraeus became assistant operations officer for the brigade, which was a high-level assignment for a major. He had just started the job when he received a call telling him to fly to Washington to interview with the army chief of staff, Gen. Carl Vuono, to be his aide. Petraeus went reluctantly. At the end of the interview, Vuono asked him if he wanted the job, and he said no. "Good," Vuono replied. "I wouldn't want you if you wanted it, so go back and pack."

Petraeus's stint as aide to Vuono fed his image as an officer on the fast track, but Vuono was a different sort of boss than Galvin. He chewed out his staff and vented frustrations that he could not express to others. As the United States was girded for its largest military operation since Vietnam, Desert Storm, to push Saddam Hussein's military out of Kuwait, the army's task was to marshal the vast quantities of troops and equipment that Gen. Norman Schwartzkopf would need. In addition to the pressures of impending war, Gen. Vuono was in pain much of the time, as he went through a hip replacement that year. Nonetheless, he recognized Maj. Petraeus's talents and made use of his skills to draft papers and help him with speeches.

As Vuono's aide, Petraeus had a front-row seat to the inner workings of the top echelons of the U.S. military and daily contact with its top officers. Army Vice Chief of Staff Gordon Sullivan was in constant contact with Petraeus and found him "bright, innovative and indefatigable. . . . He knew where he fit, but was a man with substantive ideas." Sullivan succeeded Vuono on his retirement in 1991 and remained until 1995 to oversee the army's post–cold war transition. Petraeus also met Gen. Barry McCaffrey, then SOUTHCOM commander, when he accompanied Vuono to Latin America. McCaffrey recalled going to Petraeus's hotel room early one morning because Vuono had gone to bed the previous night without clearing the next day's speeches for their meetings with foreign officials. It was well before dawn, but he found the young officer already up, having taken his morning run and eating breakfast with his uniform on, not a hair out of place.

As Petraeus acquired the reputation of an officer on the fast track—with an Ivy League PhD to boot—he also acquired detractors. Galvin was distressed at the perception that his protégé had engineered a series of jobs. "Because he's articulate and a good writer, he's had jobs with higher-level staffs and leaders," the general said. "Dave is always trying to learn, you can sense that with him. It is not really a technique, it is his self." The two men had stayed in close touch even after Galvin retired, became the dean of the Fletcher School of Diplomacy at Tufts University, and then envoy to the Balkans. If Petraeus had cared only about improving his chances of promotion, Galvin said, "he should not have spent so much time in airborne infantry units. But he'd probably say, 'I'm having fun jumping out of airplanes at 4:30 a.m.'"

PETRAEUS DID SPEND THE NEXT YEARS jumping out of airplanes at 4:30 a.m. He moved his family to Fort Campbell, Kentucky, and as a lieutenant colonel commanded the 3rd Battalion, 187th Infantry Regiment of the 101st Airborne Division from 1991 to 1993. He was delighted to serve in the Iron Rakkasans, a storied unit that had fought in every U.S. war since World War II. When the Japanese saw the soldiers jumping out of the sky with their parachutes open, they nicknamed them Rakkasans, or "falling-down umbrellas."

While in the Rakkasans, Petraeus suffered a near-death experience. A fellow soldier shot him in the chest during a live-fire training exercise soon after Petraeus assumed command. The 101st's assistant division commander, Jack Keane, was standing next to him on the range. A soldier threw a grenade into a bunker and was running back when he tripped. His finger was on the trigger of his M-16 rifle—contrary to standard procedure—and the gun discharged when he hit the ground. The bullet hit Petraeus, who was standing less than twenty-five feet away. The high-velocity 5.56 round entered cleanly just above his right nipple, but it left a gaping exit wound in his back. Part of his lung was blown away. Kneeling over the fallen soldier, Keane quickly called for a medevac helicopter to fly them to Nashville. Luckily, the high-velocity bullet had not ricocheted inside Petraeus's body to damage other organs. Before wheeling him into surgery, the trauma medic jammed a tube into his chest, using the full force of his shoulder and upper body, to suck out debris and bacteria. No anesthesia was used for the procedure, as it would delay the surgery. Patients normally rise up from the gurney and scream in agony, but Petraeus merely grunted. The medic was so astounded that he later relayed this to Keane and said, "That may be the toughest person I've ever had my hands on." He marveled at the absence of body fat on the thirty-nine-year-old Petraeus's sinewy, five-foot-nine-inch, 150-pound frame. Thanks to his superb physical fitness, he led his battalion on a training exercise one month after the shooting.

As Petraeus rose through the ranks of command, he sought to balance his drive to be first with the skills of team building. One of his captains in the Iron Rakkasans, Fred Johnson, said that contrary to the reputation that developed, Petraeus was very collegial with his subordinates and peers. At their major training exercise in Fort Irwin, California, Petraeus quickly dropped his staff's plan of attack in favor of one suggested by his company commanders when he saw they had doubts. After the battalion's assault fell short, Petraeus went on ahead, during a lull in the action, to cheer on his fellow battalion commander.

Forging strong bonds is not a nicety but a necessity for units to hold together in life-or-death situations. From his earliest days in the army, an officer is taught to grant any request for help from the platoon, company, or battalion to his right or left. "No one thinks Petraeus will do it," one peer said, noting that such concerns were reflected in his peer evaluations. Petraeus recounted many examples to the contrary, including how he gave his star captain to a fellow brigade commander and his artillery section to the 3rd Infantry Division on the march to Baghdad. Despite his efforts to dispel the perception that he was not a team player, it continued no matter what the actual reality. His penchant for tart comments, coupled with his rising profile, did not help on this front. It boiled down to "who do you want on your flank?" on officer said, even if most of his peers recognized his extreme ability. Petraeus might succeed despite this perceived flaw, but the kudos he won were always mixed with the antipathy of others.

Petraeus's identification with the battalion and the 101st Airborne Division would remain his strongest unit bond throughout his career. Johnson decided to tweak his commander when he arrived at the storied Rakkasans after his stint with Vuono in the Pentagon. He told Petraeus that his soldiers thought he looked a little wimpy with his hair so long. "Wimpy?" Petraeus said, looking even more shocked than the day he was shot on the training range. Holly liked him with his hair a little longer, but this unit's style was the traditional "high and tight," so Petraeus immediately went to get the sides of his head shaved. No event was too trivial to instill esprit de corps. Johnson recalled a chili cookoff at Fort Campbell in which Petraeus carried bowls of their admittedly bad chili around to every person in attendance, winning a "best try" award for the battalion.

The next year, Keane tapped him to work on the division staff, where Keane was ramping up the training regimen to increase the division's level of readiness. He had found Petraeus to be a kindred spirit. "We're both change agents," the general said, acknowledging that they were demanding bosses who kept their subordinates hopping. "It's hard to work for us," he admitted. "We have a good idea every day."

In 1995 Petraeus got a taste of a messy Third World stability operation in Haiti, after the United States had intervened a few months earlier to reinstate President Jean-Bertrand Aristide, who had been overthrown in a military coup. Petraeus had begun a fellowship at Georgetown University —newly minted colonels who are selected for command typically spend a year at a college—but was tapped in early 1995 to serve a brief stint on the United Nations peacekeeping force in Haiti as its chief of military operations. He could readily see that there was no quick fix for this poor, chaotic Caribbean nation.

For the all-important brigade command, Col. Petraeus moved to Fort Bragg, North Carolina, to command the 1st Brigade of the 82nd Airborne Division from 1995 to 1997. Every military unit has its mystique and traditions, none more than the 82nd, the army's on-call unit for emergencies. But one of Petraeus's company captains, Kevin Petit, recalled that "he forced us to challenge every assumption, ask why, question everything. He never accepted 'that's the way we have always done it' and empowered his subordinates to do so as well." Petraeus and the "Devil Brigade" changed many of the standard practices at Fort Bragg: a live-fire mock village was built for training in urban combat, training scenarios were changed from cold-war to humanitarian crisis situations, they hung mortars and fired artillery in new ways, and the unit increased physical fitness training by 50 percent and put sergeants in charge of it. Petraeus eagerly embraced the new information technology being developed.

Petit, a self-declared "Petraophile," called his commander "Doc" or "Professor Petraeus" in deference to his PhD. Other subordinates thought Petraeus's hard-charging ways and constant competition went overboard. Petraeus arranged transfers for those who could not keep up with his grueling physical training regimen, and officers invited to his home found glowing performance reviews written by Petraeus's superiors laid out for subordinates to read. The message was clear: here is the standard you are expected to meet. Petraeus the striver wanted those who worked for him to do the same. But to some soldiers, he was just showing off.

After brigade command, Petraeus returned to the world of high-level staff aide from 1997 to 1999 as the executive assistant to the chairman of the Joint Chiefs of Staff, Gen. Hugh Shelton, a private man whose closest friend was his wife. The job gave Petraeus another chance to meet and observe the top leaders in the U.S. government and throughout the world. Serving as the chairman's executive officer also virtually guaranteed promotion to brigadier general, provided one did not screw up. In 1999, Petraeus returned to Fort Bragg as a one-star general to serve as the 82nd Airborne's assistant division commander for operations.

The next year his career hit a significant speed bump that might well have ended it. Almost every weekend, Petraeus went to the nearby town of Raeford to parachute with the army's Golden Knights skydiving team. It was like playing with the L.A. Lakers. Petraeus could not resist the chance to play with the best in the world. Late one day, on the last jump, Petraeus made a hook turn too low. His chute lost its air and he crashed into the ground. One of the Knights phoned Holly, telling her that Petraeus had had "a little accident." When she arrived at Womack Army Medical Center's intensive care unit, she heard him groan even before she saw him. As they wheeled him around, he felt every crack in the floor. The X-ray showed a severely displaced broken pelvis. The doctor gave him two choices: to recover by lying flat on his back for weeks or to undergo surgery. Petraeus immediately opted for the surgery to bolt the two halves back together. He was ordered to stay on crutches for three months and not to climb more than one flight of stairs a day. Holly set up a bed on the first floor of their home so he could save his stair quota for the single flight into his office at the XVIII Airborne Corps headquarters, where he had just been named chief of staff.

For the first few weeks, his boss, Lt. Gen. Dan McNeill, instructed his staff judge advocate to fill in for Petraeus and let him work half days, thus saving Petraeus's job and his career. The general did not have to do this, since the accident had occurred on Petraeus's leisure time rather than as part of official duties. He could have been medically retired at that point.

Petraeus, grateful for the break, began working at home and did all he could to speed his recovery. By the next fall he was back in form: he ran the army's annual ten-mile race in under sixty-four minutes.

Those who thought Petraeus might fall off the fast track were wrong. Petraeus had reached the point in his career where the funnel narrowed dramatically. Few colonels make general and even fewer earn each successive star. Petraeus had a network of important mentors and "Petraophile" subordinates, but he also had a serious set of competitors for those next slots. One friend and skydiving partner from his days working for the chairman was Mike "Ranger" Jones, who retired as the chairman's sergeant major. Jones, who went on to a successful business career and active philanthropy for the military services, recalled the atmosphere of intense competition as Petraeus scaled the general officer flagpole. "When Gen. Petraeus had that accident, there were other people who wanted to decapitate him," Jones said. "Some are petrified of him because he sets such a high example for others to follow."

Most generals are political animals, and have to be to win the competition, but the unwritten rule is to keep one's ambition under wraps. More than most, Petraeus was dogged by charges of careerism, and indeed, a civilian friend described him as "insanely ambitious." He had chosen a career that very much resembled a mountain, with its strict hierarchy and guiding rule of "up or out." Few generals from each year group or cohort reach four-star status, and only one four-star officer becomes chief of staff of the army or chairman of the joint chiefs.

Petraeus's zeal to rise to the top of his profession was not the only force propelling him, however. He sought to learn the soldiering profession well and become the best leader he could be, since the officer profession is essentially about leadership. This quest for excellence appealed to his intellectual side, and he respected competence wherever he found it. The other strand of his personality that developed over the years was that of change agent: Petraeus sought new and better ways of doing things. He liked to break the mold and try different approaches, even if experimenting meant failing—temporarily. The impulses to rise, to excel, and to improve could be complementary forces, but in Shakespearean terms the contest was whether ambition would outstrip the other two traits.

Petraeus deployed to the Balkans in 2001 as part of the NATO peace-keeping force. His first position was assistant chief of staff for operations. After the 9/11 attacks, attention immediately shifted to the threat of global terrorism. The Balkans were not the front lines, but Saudi-funded Islamic radicals were helping the Muslim Bosniacs fight the Serbs. The internal Balkan conflict between Serbs, Croats, and Bosniacs was not only a by-product of the Soviet empire's dissolution but also a playing field for a new struggle between Islamic radicals and secular regimes. So Petraeus donned another hat as deputy head of a joint interagency counterterrorism task force, which sought to track not only Balkan war criminals accused of ethnic cleansing but also Islamic terrorist suspects.

While sitting at an outdoor café in Sarajevo one day with his chief of staff, Col. Michael Meese, Petraeus spotted one of their subordinates, 1st Lt. Jeanne Hull, walking by. Calling her over, the general informed her, only half in jest, that they had decided she should be the army's next PhD candidate at Princeton's Woodrow Wilson school, where both Meese and he had received their doctorates. Hull was one of many young officers Petraeus would push toward grad school, and toward Princeton in particular.

She had become another of Petraeus's protégés after his aide, Dave Fivecoat, had seen her running one day with a distinct hobble in her stride. She too had broken her pelvis in a skydiving jump, four months after Petraeus. On Fivecoat's suggestion, Petraeus met her. He quizzed Hull about her class rank at West Point (fifth) and her staff position (assistant brigade commander), noting that both were higher than his own. Hull, a military intelligence officer, was a very junior officer in the task force's intelligence fusion cell, but Petraeus liked her briefing style and made her the main briefer for the full staff. Hull knew the database backward and forward and as an amateur thespian was confident and sure-footed on stage in front of the generals.

When the general invited her on a run, Fivecoat advised her not to try to beat him, because he would only speed up. He had never seen the general finish second. "Just stay slightly behind," the aide said. "But don't fall out unless you are hurt." The general sometimes chided those who fell out by saying, "You're a leader. You have to set an example." Other times he said nothing. But he always remembered who fell out.

Soldiering is a physical profession, and Petraeus was a great believer in exercise as a stress buster. He believed a leader's job was literally to set the pace, demonstrate the standards, and overcome obstacles. At home station he normally ran eight to ten miles, and five to six on deployment. Hull did not fall out, despite her pelvis injury. She was tempted to have T-shirts made that said, "I survived a run with Gen. Petraeus." He did help her get to Princeton four years and two combat tours later. When her personnel manager refused Hull's petition to go to graduate school, Petraeus made it happen with a single phone call.

While in Bosnia, Petraeus was overjoyed to learn that he would be promoted to major general and become commander of the 101st Airborne Division. It meant he would be going to war in Iraq, if the president made the final decision to go. He asked Hull if she was ready to go to war with him. Iraq would be the first combat tour of Petraeus's career.

AFTER MONTHS OF DELAY AND THEN feverish preparation, the 101st Airborne Division deployed to Kuwait on the eve of the March 2003 invasion, with the seventeen thousand paratroopers and Apache attack helicopters that gave the division its air-assault capability. The division ended up playing a supporting role in the major-combat phase of operations while the 3rd Infantry Division and the marines raced to Baghdad. The 101st's mission was to secure the V Corps flanks from Iraqi attacks and conduct reconnaissance probes for the western invasion force as it swept north from Kuwait toward Baghdad. The 101st also liberated the southern cities of Karbala and Najaf, where irregular forces came out to challenge U.S. troops guerrilla-style. There was discussion of the 101st seizing the Baghdad airport, but in the end the division did not take part in the capture of Baghdad. Instead in mid-April it leapfrogged north in the longest air assault in the army's history to Mosul and Ninewa province in northern Iraq.

During the major-combat phase in March, Petraeus executed his assigned combat missions with proficiency and foresight. Although some of his staff grumbled, he exercised notable restraint in calling in air strikes and making frontal forays into Iraq's cities. He lost his first soldiers in battle, including seventeen soldiers when two helicopters collided. Given the awesome machinery and prowess of America's highly trained armed forces, there was little doubt that the United States could win a frontal military contest with Saddam Hussein's regime. Baghdad fell on April 9, less than a month after the initiation of hostilities. But Petraeus understood that the conflict did not end with the major-combat phase, even though news organizations withdrew many of their reporters in April on the assumption that the main story was over. The prevailing view was that a quick victory would be followed by an equally quick withdrawal, but Petraeus voiced no such certainty. Instead, he posed a prescient query that he would repeat often in the years ahead. In conversation with journalist and historian Rick Atkinson, who covered Petraeus as an embedded reporter in March and early April 2003, he prodded, "Tell me how this ends."

Petraeus foresaw that the most challenging phase of the war would begin after the battlefield victory. His ability, and that of the entire U.S. military and government, to conduct postcombat stability operations would be tested from the day Baghdad fell. Petraeus's personal challenge began when he arrived in Mosul, Iraq's second-largest city and the cradle of Saddam's Baathist army. Mosul, the ancient capital of Mesopotamia, was a melting pot of Iraq's many ethnic and religious groups—and the largest city where Sunnis were the majority. If there was a place to give birth to a serious resistance movement, it was Mosul.

This was the murky low-intensity conflict he had studied, written about, and seen firsthand in Central America, Haiti, and the Balkans. Petraeus quickly established his top two priorities: reestablish government and economic functions. He spoke to Jay Garner, head of the Office of Reconstruction and Humanitarian Assistance, and received permission to hold elections. A month later, Ninewa province had a governor and a governing council. He made sure all the province's many ethnic and religious groups, as well as women, were represented on the twenty-four-member council. The 2nd Brigade of the 101st Division, commanded by Col. Joe Anderson, was responsible for operations in Mosul proper and for encouraging local participation in the vote.

All of Petraeus's colonels benefited from his activist leadership style, even if it wearied them. No one, it seemed, was neutral about Petraeus. His operations officer in Mosul, William Hickman, described their typical day. Work began during their 6 a.m. runs, when Hickman would update Petraeus, offer ideas, and receive instructions. Then Petraeus would be off to meet with Iraqis and visit the battalions scattered around the four northern provinces by helicopter or Humvee. His overarching message to the troops was "What have you done for Iraqis today?" Hickman said, adding that the only way Iraqis would know that they were an army of liberation, not occupation, was through the troops' actions.

To jump-start the economy, Petraeus reopened the border with Syria so trade could resume and struck a deal to supply Iraqi oil in exchange for Syrian electricity. Then he persuaded Paul Bremer to release funds captured during the invasion. He challenged his brigades to outspend each other on schools, clinics, irrigation projects, and other local economic, infrastructure, and governance projects. The division even began a televised talent show featuring local Ninewa citizens. By the end of its twelve-month tour, Hickman's records showed, the unit had spent over $57 million on 5,026 projects, about one-third of the total spent nationwide. The 3rd Brigade outspent the other two brigades handily, but Petraeus won the contest by spending twice that much.

This program was then formalized as the Commander's Emergency Response Program (CERP), funded by the United States to give military commanders money that could be disbursed quickly on small-scale economic or political projects that would immediately help the community. The program was designed to avoid the volumes of bureaucratic red tape most large-scale U.S. civilian and military aid projects required. While the massive and ambitious projects to build power plants, water plants, and other major infrastructure became bogged down and were often subject to graft or mismanagement by contractors and subcontractors, the CERP projects were judged by the U.S. special inspector general for Iraq to be the most effective aid the United States provided in the postwar period. Petraeus also helped Barham Salih, governor of the adjacent semiautonomous Kurdish region of Iraq, transport computers the Kurds had purchased in Turkey for the university in Sulaimaniya. Troops from the 101st provided a security convoy and unloaded the boxes at the school.

Petraeus was able to accomplish as much as he did in part because Mosul was far from the bureaucratic and political turf battles that were developing in Baghdad. But he did butt heads with Bremer over the two disastrous decrees on de-Baathification and the dissolution of the Iraqi security services. Decree 1 had put every professor at Mosul University out of a job, which also meant that none of the students would graduate that spring. Under the old regime, professors, lawyers, doctors, and other high-level professionals had to be Baath Party members to obtain or keep their jobs. Bremer granted Petraeus's request to rehire the university professors temporarily so the students could graduate and to try a local reconciliation effort. "We held Baath Party renunciation ceremonies to which thousands of people came and tore up their party cards or swore allegiance to the new Iraq and renounced the use of violence," Petraeus recalled.

The success was short-lived. Bremer then turned implementation of Decree 1 over to an Iraqi de-Baathification committee, which refused to approve the recommendations of the Mosul reconciliation committee Petraeus had formed to vet former Baathists. Petraeus conveyed his strong objections to sweeping de-Baathification to the Pentagon's deputy secretary, Paul Wolfowitz, who called him frequently to get field reports. The general told him the decree was depriving Iraq of much of the expertise that would be needed to get the country running again. Those arguing for a de-Nazification-type campaign included the Pentagon's undersecretary for policy, Doug Feith; White House aides; and Ahmed Chalabi, a Shia exile politician and neoconservative darling who became the head of the de-Baathification commission.

Chalabi's commission blocked all the local reconciliation committee's recommendations. "Unfortunately, at a certain point it became clear that there were not going to be any exceptions to de-Baathification," Petraeus recalled. "That led to a loss of hope among the Sunni Arabs in Mosul and Ninewa, and eventually to a feeling of many Sunni Arabs (especially former Baath Party members, of which there were thousands in Ninewa alone) that there was no place for them in the new Iraq. That obviously made for fertile ground for AQI [Al-Qaeda in Iraq]."

Petraeus was equally concerned about Decree 2. He met a couple of times with a retired officers' association in Mosul, which the 10th Special

Forces Group had helped form and Joe Anderson's brigade had been dealing with. Petraeus knew they needed to devise a way to deal with these severely disgruntled Iraqi army officers. Iraqis regarded serving in the military as an honorable profession, and these men had been disgraced by the preemptory Bremer decree. Petraeus argued for holding a big ceremony to retire the officers honorably, present them with medals for their service, and then invite them to rejoin a new entity. The Coalition Provisional Authority rejected the proposal. There were mass demonstrations in Mosul, and some 101st soldiers were killed. Petraeus was furious. He had told the CPA what would happen and it did.

Petraeus was focused on embracing and helping the population, but the division did its share of targeting insurgents as well. One day an Iraqi walked up to the gate of their base at the airport and said he knew where Saddam's two sons, Uday and Qusay, were hiding. The sons were killed in the subsequent raid, when they remained holed up in the house and refused to surrender. The $30 million reward was paid to those who helped finger the hideout, and the Iraqi tipsters were resettled abroad for their safety.

Brig. Gen. Frank Helmick joined Petraeus in Mosul as one of his assistant division commanders. The brigadier general recalled that his very first day, Petraeus took him out to a traditional gathering featuring roasted kid in the hinterlands near the Syrian border. Helmick already knew Petraeus well; he had served under him as a battalion commander. "This was one man who understood [the war] wasn't about going out and shooting things up," Helmick said, noting that Petraeus had assigned his aviation brigade to rebuild Mosul University. "He was open to learning about the culture. The Iraqis loved him because he would eat all the food and go around talking to people. We had *iftars* [meal to break the fast during the Islamic holy month of Ramadan] at night for different groups. That makes all the difference."

As they prepared to leave Iraq at the end of their tour in February 2004, some officers in the 101st Division had qualms about the impending transfer of the province to a smaller task force organized around a Stryker brigade. Anderson, the brigade commander in Mosul, said the division's assessment was that the transition to a smaller unit could be successfully carried out. At the time, the level of violence was low, and the economy and government had been revived. Another officer noted that as they conducted the transition with members of Task Force Olympia, the new unit seemed inclined to take a much more aggressive approach to Mosul. There were two opposing views within the U.S. military regarding northern Iraq. One view was that the area could be pacified with a minimum of combat and a lot of reconstruction and political outreach to Sunnis. The other view was that not enough of Saddam's military had been destroyed in the initial operations, leaving open the possibility that his troops would come back to cause trouble.

A serious debate would erupt over the wisdom of the decision to replace the 101st Division of seventeen thousand troops with a task force of ten thousand. The decision was made at the corps level, but with Petraeus's blessing. Petraeus was concerned that Task Force Olympia would have a much less robust intelligence capacity than his division had, and he recommended that it be assigned a military intelligence battalion. That recommendation was not acted upon.

The successes of Mosul would come unglued in the latter half of 2004 as a chain of events roiled the entire country. The killing of American security contractors in Fallujah in April 2004 coincided with the uprising of Shia followers of cleric Muqtada al-Sadr in Baghdad and the south. Between April and November, when a massive U.S. assault on Fallujah was launched, many insurgents fled north into Ninewa province and Mosul. The governor of Ninewa was assassinated in July, and Mosul's police force collapsed in November after large numbers were executed and left on the roads as a warning. Task Force Olympia was not able to handle the combined effects of this upsurge in violence.

The question of whether Petraeus had oversold the successes of the 101st Division was perhaps more appropriately a question of whether he had anticipated and given enough weight to the worst possible scenarios that might ensue and included that in his recommendations as he finished his tour. The question nipped at his heels because the division received a great deal of press coverage of its accomplishments in Mosul. The biggest problem was that Petraeus had been overruled on de-Baathification, which created fertile ground for insurgents.

After a few short months at home in 2004, Gen. Petraeus was tapped to return to Iraq in June to lead a new command that was formed to train and equip the new Iraqi army. In the first year of the war, a hodge-podge of security forces had been created in helter-skelter fashion with varying degrees of oversight and control by the U.S. military. Many American division commanders did as little as possible with the Iraqi civil defense (later National Guard) units they were ordered to form. They were not prepared to train, equip, and mentor these Iraqi units, and in most cases they regarded them as security threats to their own troops. In 2005 these units would eventually be incorporated into the Iraqi army as the even-numbered divisions.

The new command Petraeus was tasked to head was named Multi-National Security Transition Command-Iraq, and its acronym, MNSTC-I, quickly replaced the unwieldy name. Petraeus hated the name "mint-sticky," but it stuck as the only pronounceable option. His mission was to train and equip ten divisions of Iraqi soldiers as quickly as possible; nine battalions had been created thus far. This was the road home: to create a force to which the U.S. military could turn over the country and depart. The faster it was done, the sooner the U.S. military could leave. This was the most urgent message being sent to U.S. officers in Iraq from the four-star Central Command regional combatant commander, Gen. John Abizaid, and Secretary of Defense Rumsfeld.

Petraeus also took over the police training program. A private U.S. security company, DynCorp, had originally been in charge of it and used mostly retired American policemen and sheriffs as trainers. Petraeus immediately realized that his job would entail not only churning out more troops but also creating the entire infrastructure of a func-tioning military: higher echelons of command, an officer corps, and a cadre to handle the staff functions to pay, feed, clothe, house, train, and equip the army. That meant, in turn, overseeing a massive $2 billion construction project to rebuild the looted and destroyed barracks and training facilities. Equipping a force two and a half times the size of the British army with uniforms, body armor, vehicles, arms, radios, and ammunition would become a major headache and a source of graft within the new defense ministry. Petraeus's successor would be assigned the job of advising the ministries of defense and interior, but during his tenure Petraeus regularly met with ministry officials and assigned liaison officers to attempt to keep tabs on what was happening.

Capt. Jeanne Hull had accepted Petraeus's invitation to join him on a second Iraq tour. She became his note-taker at most senior meetings and his liaison to the embassy and national intelligence assets in the country. The MNSTC-I job was an overwhelmingly tall order, in Hull's view. There was little recognition back in the United States, she said, "that it takes two years to destroy an army and twenty years to rebuild it."

In her view, and in Petraeus's view, successes later became fodder for critics who rarely placed events in context. For example, during the uprising in Najaf in the spring of 2004, the Iraqi Intervention Force, the best unit at the time, was deployed to the battle without sufficient arms. MNTSC-I airlifted arms to them and strove to supply other Iraqi units waging fierce battles in Fallujah, Mosul, Baghdad, and elsewhere. Chronic problems existed, however. When soldiers deserted, they often took their arms with them, and despite efforts to get Iraqis to adopt accounting systems, there was in fact little accountability. American sergeants assigned to train Iraqi units said the *jundis* ("soldiers" in Arabic) routinely took bullets downtown to sell them for a little extra cash. Graft was a cultural problem that would not go away.

The challenge of building an entire military institution in the middle of a rapidly worsening insurgency was staggering, as Petraeus quickly came to appreciate. "It was one of those times when sheer force of will comes into play," he recalled of the dark days in the late summer and fall of 2004. "We were always pushing—and AQI [Al-Qaeda in Iraq] was murderous in pushing back." Sunni Arabs were leaving the Iraqi security forces due to intimidation of their families, kidnapping, and murder. Busloads of recruits were killed by improvised explosive devices and ambushes. Officials in the defense ministry and upper echelons of the army were killed. At the same time, Petraeus was under constant pressure to build more units faster. At night he read T. E. Lawrence's account of his tribulations in building a force of Arab fighters during World War I, for both insight and consolation. By day, he drove himself and the loyal subordinates he had asked to join him: Hull, J. R. Martin, Charlie Miller, Bill Hickman, and many others.

Many of Petraeus's early decisions would later come under a congressional microscope. One of the most vexing problems developed from the Iraqi interior ministry's formation of the Special Police Commandos. The regular police were hapless and no match for the burgeoning insurgency, which was fully equipped with an arsenal that included machine guns, rocket-propelled grenades, and other munitions that had been looted from the vast unsecured stocks of Saddam's army. There was a clamor for a more robust paramilitary type of police force; Petraeus argued for and formed Public Order Brigades, but the interior minister at the time insisted on forming the commandos, who were highly trained former regime soldiers who were willing to fight on the new government's side. When Petraeus went to see them, he was impressed and dropped his opposition. But under the subsequent interior minister, Bayan Jabr, the original ranks of the commandos were purged and Shia militia members took their place. In another case, Petraeus had a showdown with the ministry and cut off funding for the major-crimes investigative unit. But sectarian behavior and abuse pervaded the ministry, whose commandos were found, in late 2005, to have detained and tortured many former regime members in secret prisons around Baghdad.

Petraeus had accomplished his main mandate of creating more Iraqi security forces by the time he handed over the job to his successor, Lt. Gen. Martin Dempsey, in September 2005. But there were ongoing disputes over just how many troops had been trained and equipped, how capable they were, and how many were in fact present for duty. The largest single downward adjustment in the number of Iraqi security forces occurred in late 2004 when the Facilities Protection Services (FPS) personnel were taken out of the count. These forces, which Dempsey had created when he was the 1st Armored Division commander charged with securing Baghdad from 2003 to 2004, were intended to help secure key infrastructure since there were not enough U.S. troops. The FPS subsequently came under the control of Bremer, who parceled them out to the various ministries. The ministries then filled their ranks with militia members. The FPS became rogue armed bands accused of criminal and sectarian violence and kidnappings.

In sum, the job was enormous and fraught with problems. MNSTC-I had to compete for resources and manpower for its own staff—which was largely reservists and individuals plucked from other units—with the much larger three- and four-star "war-fighting commands" in Iraq. This organizational friction was compounded by a certain antagonism toward the high-profile and newly minted three-star general, which his actions helped generate. A glowing *Newsweek* cover story titled "Can This Man Save Iraq?" with a cover photo of Petraeus in a Patton-like pose did not help internal military relations, particularly with those generals who outranked him, as he arrived to take up the job. A few months later, Petraeus wrote an op-ed that appeared in the *Washington Post* in September 2004, little more than a month before the U.S. presidential election, which cited the growth and progress in building the security forces. Larry Di Rita, Rumsfeld's assistant secretary for public affairs, chastised him for not clearing it with him, but Di Rita's deputy *had* cleared it. The article was criticized as an overly optimistic portrait, but even more for the timing of its appearance. Petraeus staunchly defended its accuracy— and noted that the article also acknowledged problems—but he reluctantly came to regret publishing it due to the controversy it generated.

IN SEPTEMBER 2005, WHEN PETRAEUS returned from Iraq, Army Chief of Staff Gen. Peter Schoomaker named him commander of the Combined Arms Center (CAC) at Fort Leavenworth, which was the Training and Doctrine Command's major subordinate organization for training and educating soldiers. Partly as a result of the tensions with the other generals in Iraq, and some grumbling in the Pentagon about self-promotion, the assignment was perceived by some as exile. Petraeus would oversee the Command and General Staff College and seventeen other schools and training programs as well as doctrinal development. Petraeus turned it into an academic sabbatical with a purpose: to reshape the army to fight Iraq and similar irregular wars more successfully. He retooled the system to quickly feed lessons from the battlefield into the army's training and education system.

Petraeus processed his own experiences in Iraq for lessons that could be used to help turn around what was obviously a struggling war effort. His abiding career interest had been whether and how the military should fight such wars, which the institution had finally, over the defense secretary's objection, come around to calling insurgency and counterinsurgency. He was a strong advocate of reinvigorating U.S. civilian agencies, such as the Agency for International Development, to help in such wars. Petraeus gave numerous speeches and wrote an article in the January/February 2006 issue of Fort Leavenworth's journal, *Military Review,* titled "Learning Counterinsurgency: Observations from Soldiering in Iraq."

The most important project Petraeus undertook during his fifteen months at Fort Leavenworth was writing a new counterinsurgency manual. He invited the Marine Corps to collaborate to provide a common foundation for U.S. ground forces in conducting counterinsurgency. The army had not revised its counterinsurgency manual in twenty years, since the early years of its counterinsurgency in Latin America. An interim field manual had been hastily produced after 9/11, but Petraeus felt that a more in-depth overhaul of the manual was needed to address Iraq and the irregular wars of the twenty-first century.

Eliot Cohen, professor at the Nitze School of Advanced International Studies at Johns Hopkins University in Washington and a noted military author, thought the interim manual was terrible and urged Petraeus to mount a full-bore effort to rewrite it. Cohen suggested Conrad Crane, a historian at the Army War College and Petraeus's West Point classmate, as the primary author. Cohen had been impressed by a monograph Crane had cowritten for the Strategic Studies Institute on challenges for the military in reconstructing Iraq. Crane's principal coauthor would be Lt. Col. John Nagl, who had served in Iraq and written his dissertation at Oxford University on the lessons of counterinsurgency in Vietnam and Malaya. While a cadet at West Point, Nagl had met Petraeus, who was an instructor at the time, and then worked for him at NATO under Gen. Galvin. Nagl was extremely bright and an avid networker—another up-and-comer cut from the same cloth as Petraeus. Nagl published his dissertation under the title *Learning to Eat*

Soup with a Knife, with a foreword by army chief Gen. Schoomaker, and then went to work as military aide to Deputy Defense Secretary Wolfowitz.

With Petraeus's approval, the coauthors assembled a group of experts to help draft each chapter. The manual's core propositions were developed and published in a *Military Review* article by Cohen, Crane, Nagl, and others. Crediting the work of Max Manwaring, a longtime scholar on insurgency and irregular war, they identified legitimacy as the cornerstone for any successful counterinsurgency. If a government was not or could not be made legitimate in the eyes of its population, there was little chance of defeating a determined insurgency. The article formulated nineteen other principles, imperatives, and paradoxes for conducting counterinsurgency, including the primacy of political over military goals and means and the importance of providing security for the populace and of separating them from the insurgents. The paradoxes included warnings that use of force can generate more insurgents than it vanquishes, that perceptions can be more important than the actions themselves, and that tactical successes do not guarantee victory.

The committee of writers, including some dozen contributors in all, produced a draft in January. In February Petraeus convened a workshop to critique it. A diverse group of about one hundred people with deep knowledge of counterinsurgency-related topics were invited for an intensive two-day discussion. Sarah Sewall, deputy assistant secretary of defense for peacekeeping in the Clinton administration, director of a human-rights think tank at Harvard University, and organizer of a series of conferences on Iraq, offered to cosponsor the event. After Crane assured Petraeus that her input and that of human rights activists she proposed to include would be valuable and constructive, he agreed. Sewall's insights were as useful as Crane had anticipated, and the human-rights lawyers' critiques led to major revisions of the sections on interrogation and detention.

The two-day workshop was as intensive and freewheeling as a graduate seminar. Discussions spilled out into the hallway of the conference center and into the night over drinks at Petraeus's red brick house. He participated in every session, questioning, rebutting, or adding to interlocutors' comments. Attendees included British Brig. Nigel Aylwin-Foster, a sharp critic of the U.S. campaign in Iraq who had spent a year in the south; anthropologists Montgomery McFate and David Kilcullen; Kalev Sepp and other professors from U.S. war colleges; Central Intelligence Agency officials; members of the Special Forces; a few journalists; and a wide variety of think-tank denizens.

Petraeus went over the draft manual with a fine-tooth comb, particularly the first chapter and chapters three, four, and five, which were the heart of the guide for conducting counterinsurgency operations. After an article by Ralph Peters appeared criticizing the draft for taking too soft an approach to fighting insurgents, and Petraeus's four-star superior advocated qualifying the stark language of the paradoxes, Petraeus ordered modifications over Crane's strenuous objections. Thus, the final paradoxes read: "*Sometimes,* the more force is used, the less effective it is" and "*Some* of the best weapons for counterinsurgents do not shoot," which was a less elegant rendering than the unqualified originals. Petraeus's favorite aphorism "Money is ammunition," which he had coined in Mosul, remained untouched. T. E. Lawrence's maxim "Do not try to do too much with your own hands" was reformulated as "The host nation doing something tolerably is normally better than us doing it well."

Field Manual 3-24, *Counterinsurgency,* was published in December 2006. Like all field manuals, it was intended as a general guide for officers conducting operations in the field. It recommended a multifaceted approach to counterinsurgency rather than relying only or even principally on military operations. These "logical lines of operations" all aimed to increase the legitimacy of and support for the host nation government. They included not only combat or security operations but improvement of host-nation security forces, essential services, governance, and economic development, as well as information operations. Enhancing a government's legitimacy required above all an understanding of the population's sentiment and the culture. One of the key exhortations of the manual had not been followed in Iraq: the need to have a clear view of the cause of a conflict. "Knowing why an insurgent movement has gained support . . . is essential in designing a counterinsurgency campaign." The manual cited Napoleon's six-year occupation of Spain as an example of a failure to understand how that country would react to an invasion, which sparked a resistance that wound up requiring three-fifths of his force to combat and sapped his empire's strength.

The manual did not provide an alternative policy or strategy for Iraq, but its general precepts would help identify shortfalls. Iraq was not a textbook insurgency. The textbook cases were those in which the United States or Britain had assisted a host-nation government in combating an indigenous, Marxist, and possibly secessionist-inspired insurgency. In the case of Iraq, the insurgency had sprung up in response to a U.S. invasion that implanted a government that most Sunnis mistrusted and rejected. The Iraqi government had technically been legitimized through the elections and a ratified constitution, but its legitimacy was disputed by the large and educated Sunni minority.

Crane, the principal drafter of the manual, recognized that in Iraq, the U.S. challenge was not only to support the government but also to change its attitude and behavior. "Most of these internal wars are concluded by some kind of political compromise that addresses to at least some extent the grievances that caused the conflict," he said. Throughout history the United States had supported allies while also exerting pressure on them. "In such a situation . . . we have to find a way to somehow alter that local concept of legitimacy, [but] it is usually difficult for American advisers to get sovereign allies to do all that we think they should do." Difficult allies have been more the rule than the exception, the historian added, citing the examples of Greece in the 1940s, Korea in the 1950s, and Vietnam in the 1960s and 1970s.

With his nomination to succeed Casey as the commander in Iraq, Petraeus would now have a chance to test-drive the manual. As he prepared to take on the new job, his family girded for another separation. Since 2001 he had been deployed abroad three and a half years, to Bosnia and twice to Iraq. He had been home for very little of his son's high-school years. Stephen had graduated at the top of his class despite attending three different schools. He and his sister were used to military life, but they were not ready for the overwhelming publicity that was about to engulf their father's life and, by extension, theirs. The wave of publicity that had greeted the counterinsurgency (COIN) manual had caused the army headquarters to feel that once again Petraeus was overexposed in the media. The media crush would escalate throughout 2007.

IN HIS CONFIRMATION HEARINGS on January 23, Petraeus endorsed the "surge" of additional U.S. troops. But he noted that there was only a political, not a military solution to the conflict, and that military force was necessary but not sufficient to that end. He promised to provide his "bosses" and Congress with "forthright, professional military advice" and specifically pledged "that should I determine that the new strategy cannot succeed, I will provide such an assessment." He tried not to sugarcoat what lay ahead. "The situation in Iraq is dire," he said in closing. "The way ahead will be very hard. . . . But hard is not hopeless."

The senators grilled Petraeus, but not too hard. The Senate committee chairman, Democrat Carl Levin, voiced his doubt that "more military presence and involvement promotes that goal of Iraqis achieving political settlement." He advocated the opposite approach of withdrawing military support to the Iraqi government to force it to make political compromises. Petraeus agreed with him that the United States should exercise leverage over the Iraqi government by "providing assistance or withholding assistance in various forms" if it failed to meet its commitments. That conditionality was not embraced by the White House, however.

The Senate confirmed Gen. Petraeus unanimously, 81–0, for the position and for promotion to full general. Before he left Washington, Petraeus was summoned to the White House for a meeting with Bush. After a brief introduction, Stephen Hadley and the other officials left the two men alone in the Oval Office for about twenty minutes. Petraeus had already met the president on several occasions, including just before the confirmation hearings. When he returned from his MNSTC-I tour in September 2005 he had also visited the White House. Bush had peppered him with questions about the Iraqi security forces, the prospects for the impending elections, the security situation, the personalities of the various Iraqi leaders. And in 2004 he and Holly had hosted the president and Laura Bush at Fort Campbell for a welcome-home ceremony with the

101st Airborne when it returned from Iraq. In this latest conversation, Petraeus thought Bush realized the strain on the U.S. military and the difficulty of the challenge facing them in Iraq.

As he said good-bye to his family and colleagues at Fort Leavenworth, Petraeus looked back on his tenure there with satisfaction. The writing and publication of FM 3-24 had been the high point, of course, but the entire assignment had gratified the academic in him. Fort Leavenworth's military historian, Glenn Robertson, gave him a copy of Bruce Catton's book *Grant Takes Command,* in hopes that it would offer him some useful perspective on the command he was about to assume. He inscribed it:

Sir,

On the days when casualties mount, subordinates fail, politicians waver, and victory seems utterly unattainable, it may be of some small comfort to consider how another great commander successfully surmounted similar challenges.

Best wishes in your new command. God bless you—and God bless the American soldier.

WILLIAM GLENN ROBERTSON
Command Historian
USACAC

Petraeus was touched by the gift and read it during his first weeks in Iraq. Reading about Ulysses S. Grant's effort to turn around the foundering Union effort gave him inspiration. Gen. Galvin also sent him a little book by J. F. C. Fuller titled *Generalship: Its Diseases and Their Cure.* Its basic theme, Galvin said, "is that if you are the leader, be where the point of action is."

In the last conversation Con Crane had with Petraeus in his office at Fort Leavenworth, they talked about the circumstances under which the general would tell his bosses that what they wanted could not be done. Petraeus thought it was vital that there be a surge in four areas: not just the military, but also the civilian side of the U.S. government, the Iraqi forces, and Iraqi political will. He was fairly sure he could create a window of perceived security, but whether the Iraqis could take advantage of it was much less certain. As Crane left the old yellow-painted building on the bluff above the winding Missouri River, he thought it was an unfair situation for one of the army's brightest generals to be in. His concern was that both Petraeus and the doctrine they had labored over together would take the fall for how things turned out in Iraq.

As a historian Crane couldn't help but think of historical parallels. In every American war, he said, a general had taken command at a critical time in which the war's outcome depended on his leadership, and each one had contributed to victory. He cited Nathanael Greene in the Revolutionary War, Winfield Scott in Mexico, Grant in the American Civil War, John J. Pershing in World War I, Dwight D. Eisenhower in World War II, and Matthew Ridgway in Korea. He shied away from the parallel of Creighton Abrams in Vietnam.

Petraeus, an avid reader of generals' autobiographies, knew all their stories. Grant's memoirs were his favorite, and he had often dipped into Forrest C. Pogue's four-volume biography of George C. Marshall, who had not written his own account. Ridgway's *Soldier* was simple and direct. The fellow paratrooper had been a particular hero, whom Petraeus had been thrilled to interview for his dissertation and later meet while serving as Gen. Vuono's aide. At fifty-six, Ridgway had taken command of the Eighth Army in Korea at a similarly bleak moment. To Petraeus, fifty-four, even the prospect of wearing a fourth star was still something of an "out of body experience," he said. But he was on his way back to Iraq, and the president had asked him to rescue a failing war. To his own question, "Tell me how this ends," Petraeus now was being invited to provide an answer.

4

The Petraeus Team Launches

The smell of Iraq was the smell of smoke. The sulfuric smell of cooking fires, propane heaters, and neighborhood generators pervaded the city and country alike, and in poor neighborhoods and towns it was mixed with the smell of excrement. Iraq's other unforgettable sensation was of the ubiquitous dirt as fine as talcum powder, which coated the skin, filled the eyes, ears, and nose, and, during storms, turned the skies brown for days on end. Iraq was a wealthy land, but its wealth had been poorly spent. The landscape of bland and blocky modern buildings was studded with Saddam Hussein's monumental palaces, outsized mosques, ceremonial arches, and grandiose memorials in strange shapes—a spiraling dome, an egg, and massive crossed swords. An ancient land decorated with a dictator's garish taste, it was being ravaged by war for the third time in a quarter-century.

Underneath a mammoth crystal chandelier in the cavernous atrium of the Al Faw palace, Gen. David Petraeus took command of the

Multi-National Force-Iraq (MNF-I) on February 10, 2007. Before a seated crowd, Gen. John Abizaid performed the time-honored change-of-command ritual. He took the MNF-I colors from Gen. George Casey and handed them to Petraeus, who then made a short speech.

His transition to full general was in all an unceremonious affair. Holly had wanted to pin her own father's four stars on her husband and throw him a party at Fort Myer, Virginia, to celebrate reaching that pinnacle. Instead, just before the change of command, Abizaid ripped the Velcro three-star patch off the center placket of Petraeus's combat fatigues and slapped on a four-star patch.

Petraeus had been told to get to Iraq as soon as possible. In early January he had called Steve Boylan, his press aide at Fort Leavenworth, who had headed the coalition press information center in Baghdad during 2004–2005. "Are you ready to saddle up?" he asked. Boylan's wife, Michelle, had predicted the call. Boylan phoned her and said, "I hate it when you're right." Like many officers' wives who adjust to the life of the always-deployed husband, Michelle was enormously capable and self-sufficient. As an army nurse, she had earned two master's degrees and had completed the course work for her PhD. Now a senior health-care executive, she traveled, raised their teenagers, and in her spare time managed their fifty-five-acre ranch and six horses. The three children were upset to hear the news, but when their father made a farewell speech at their school assembly and the close-knit Tonganoxie, Kansas, community gave him a rousing send-off, they felt proud in spite of everything.

As Petraeus's plane banked over the Baghdad airport, Boylan looked out the window and marveled at how many lights were on in the city. "That's a good sign," he thought. He soon found out that the extra electricity reflected a huge expansion in the number of private and neighborhood generators, not because the government had made a great leap forward in its own generating capacity since he had left Iraq in the summer of 2005. Iraq's orgy of violence was claiming two thousand to three thousand lives a month. The announcement of the surge had prompted the insurgents to react with a wave of bombings that drenched the country in blood. On February 3, a bombing at Baghdad's Sadriya *souk,* or market, killed 135 Iraqis and wounded 339. Two days after Petraeus arrived, the capital's largest *souk*, Shorja, was hit by a car bomb and eighty people were killed. A female suicide bomber blew herself up nearby at Mustansiriya University, killing three dozen people. And in a killing that sent alarms through the U.S. military, Shia militiamen in stolen SUVs infiltrated a joint compound in Karbala and kidnapped and killed five American soldiers.

The insurgents had also stepped up attacks against U.S. aircraft. Four U.S. helicopters had been shot down in the previous month. The coalition depended heavily on helicopters for transport, fire support, and surveillance. Use of army helicopters had increased from 240,000 to 334,000 flight hours between 2005 and 2006. The helicopters averaged about one hundred exchanges of fire per month and were struck by fire about seventeen times a month. Pilots nicknamed Balad, the giant logistics base north of Baghdad, "the duck pond" because they were normally shot at during takeoffs and landings. All told, since the war began, twenty-nine helicopters had been shot down, some of them by SA-7, SA-14, and SA-16 surface-to-air missiles. After four years of war, Saddam's arsenals still were not depleted.

Petraeus took in Iraq's current reality with fresh eyes. Many of those who had been in Iraq while the violence ratcheted up were inured to the growing mayhem, like frogs in a pot of slowly warming water. On his first night in Iraq, Zalmay Khalilzad hosted a dinner for Petraeus at the ambassador's residence. Defense Minister Abdul Qadir Jassim joined them, as did Mahmoud Mashadani, speaker of parliament. Both men were Sunnis, but before the main course was served, they began to argue. "You should be doing more for Sunnis," shouted Mashadani at the defense minister as the situation escalated. Petraeus knew Jassim well from his previous tour. He had performed well as head of the armed forces before becoming defense minister. Jassim retorted that he was not a Sunni Arab but an Iraqi. He was supposed to be nonsectarian, a minister for all Iraqis. The two men were on their feet, pointing at each other and yelling. Infuriated, Mashadani tried to go around the table to punch Jassim, but the others restrained him. A pediatrician, Mashadani was something of a loose cannon, but Petraeus was sobered by the raw display of tempers. The fissures in the country were even deeper than he had realized and they reached into the top levels of the government.

The next day, he toured some of Baghdad and was shocked by what he saw. Dora, a Sunni neighborhood in southern Baghdad, was a ghost town. Not a single shop in the market was open. Trash and pools of sewage lay everywhere. Bombs were often hidden in potholes, broken curbs, and mounds of trash. Residents told him they were afraid to cross the bridge into central Baghdad to go to the hospital. Sunnis had been kidnapped and killed in the Shia-controlled hospitals, but, the Iraqis told him, that was not the only problem. They could be killed en route at police or militia checkpoints, many of which sprang up overnight as militias moved into new areas.

"I had this unbelievable sinking feeling," Petraeus said, as he realized what sectarian violence had done to the city. In west Baghdad, Petraeus found that the once-vibrant streets of Ghazaliya, a mixed but heavily Sunni middle-class neighborhood, were also deserted. When he left Iraq in September 2005, the city was plagued by violence but stores were open, cars packed the roads, and people were out and about. Now the violence had grown exponentially and the city was under siege. He had been reading the classified briefing updates daily on his secure computer at Fort Leavenworth, but nothing had prepared him for what he found.

"What in the world have I done?" he wondered. "Why did I ever agree to sign up for this thing?" For months afterward, he referred to Iraq's "torn social fabric," and pondered whether it was too late to repair it.

Petraeus had urged the Pentagon to send the five combat brigades as soon as possible, but the units were scrambling to get ready and conduct their predeployment training. They would arrive over five months. The first, the 2nd Brigade of the 82nd Airborne Division, had already moved into Baghdad and another was on its way, but it would be June before all five were in place. The additional Iraqi units that had been promised were flowing into Baghdad, albeit at less than full strength.

Petraeus would need other types of units to support the five U.S. brigades, such as military police to guard the enemy forces the surge would round up, but he still had to work out the details with the force providers in the Pentagon. Their deployment would take weeks or months as well. Prying the additional forces out of the army was not easy. It was his job as theater commander to request the forces he needed to execute his mission, and the army chief of staff's job to mind the army's health. Petraeus was resolved to ask for the forces he felt he needed, and if the answer was no, he would explain the risks and, if necessary, suggest a corresponding change in mission if he judged that he could not accomplish his mission with the assigned forces.

He had told Defense Secretary Robert Gates when he was interviewed for the job that he felt the war effort had suffered from what he euphemistically called "troop-leading"—commanders telling their superiors what they wanted to hear. He was not going to do that. Over the course of the war, the military had made do with less. This likely was the last big push the U.S. military would make, so Petraeus was determined to do all he could to succeed. As he told Boylan after his confirmation, "They're stuck with me now." If they did not like his recommendations, they could find another general to run the war. In the end, he asked for and received the military police, a combat aviation brigade, a division headquarters, and other enablers that would bring the surge force closer to 31,000 than the originally announced 21,500.

It was inevitable, however, that Petraeus would fight the war against the backdrop of acrimonious debate at home. The majority in Congress as well as the army leadership opposed the surge or were at least very skeptical that it would succeed. His unanimous confirmation for the job did not change that fact, and, indeed, soon after he left town Congress began debating legislative proposals to set a date for withdrawing troops from Iraq.

Among those watching was Gordon Sullivan, the retired army chief of staff who had known Petraeus for two decades. Sullivan knew he tended to think quickly and act quickly and that the pressures on him would reinforce that tendency. He hoped the commander would make his decisions deliberately. "I know he's at his best when he can reflect on the challenges he's been given," Sullivan said, "and think about it, and then issue guidance."

Petraeus sought to balance the need for speed with the need for deliberation. From his first days on the ground he injected a climate of urgency and expectation into the Multi-National Force command and every echelon below it. His activist leadership style was immediately felt. The operational level of war required constant decisions and there, too, he made his mark early. But he also moved deliberately to assess what changes would be needed in the strategy and the campaign plan. While the MNF-I general staff focused on current matters, he put his own brain trust to work on a wide-ranging strategic assessment. He was well aware that he had not been in Iraq for sixteen months and needed to understand the current situation and the new government that had been elected since he left. To enable him to run the vast enterprise the war had become and to move all the levers at his disposal, he counted on a handpicked inner circle of aides.

Boylan had predicted that Petraeus would step on the gas pedal and not let up, and that's what happened. The change in the command climate and in the top commander's management style was most readily apparent each morning in the battlefield update assessment, a classified, highly orchestrated event attended by dozens of staff officers of both the MNF-I and the three-star Multi-National Corps-Iraq (MNC-I), which oversaw daily operations. Most mornings Petraeus would fly from his quarters at Camp Victory, the main U.S. military base by the airport, to the Republican Guard palace downtown in the Green Zone, where he would preside over the briefing. The palace was officially the U.S. embassy, but MNF-I officers shared the space to be near Iraq's senior officials. The Green Zone enclave by the Tigris River was home to U.S. diplomatic personnel, soldiers, aid workers, and contractors, as well as senior Iraqi officials and other fortunate few who lived inside its heavily guarded concrete barriers. It also contained the Council of Ministers' offices, the convention center where the parliament met, the intelligence service, the Rashid Hotel, and the U.S.-led coalition military press center. Across from the embassy sat a PX (post exchange), and pizza and other fast food could be bought at a small, sun-baked plaza. Concrete duck-and-cover blast shelters dotted the Green Zone, but it was vastly safer than the rest of the city—the Red Zone.

The business of commanding a war, at the top echelons, occurred largely in meetings. At 8 a.m. each day MNF-I officers filed into the cramped briefing amphitheater in the embassy, with thermal mugs of steaming coffee that propelled them through the string of presentations and the series of meetings that followed. At the same time, MNC-I staff officers would file into their enormous amphitheater at Camp Victory. The two locations were video teleconferenced and giant plasma screens in both amphitheaters displayed the same classified PowerPoint slides. One screen displayed a head shot of Petraeus as he conducted the briefing. Another camera normally was trained on the MNC-I commander, but the current one, Lt. Gen. Raymond Odierno, declined to have his face broadcast. He chose to sip his coffee behind a screen displaying the MNC-I logo. If Odierno spoke, the logo would disappear and his large shaven head would appear in its place. When told that this made him seem like the Wizard of Oz, the towering general hooted with laughter.

Each staff section reported on the previous twenty-four hours' military operations, intelligence, and logistics, as well as political and economic events and the full gamut of Iraqi government activities in extraordinary detail. For example, each day the assessment documented just how much oil had been pumped, refined, and exported throughout Iraq. A detailed graphic depicted the status of the entire oil infrastructure, which pipelines and pump stations had been attacked or were out of service, and what the production trends were over the previous week, month, and year. Since oil accounted for over 90 percent of Iraq's revenues, it was literally the economy's lifeblood. Attacks on exposed pipelines had been a chronic problem, and theft continued even though meters had been installed at the pumping stations. The goal was to restore production to the 2.5 million barrels produced before the war. With further capital investment and a secure environment, experts estimated that Iraq's production could be increased to 4 million barrels a day in a few years. But since 2003 the United States had struggled to get oil production to 2 million barrels a day on a regular basis.

Petraeus used the morning assessments not only to receive a complete picture of what was happening in the country, but just as much to transmit directives, ask questions, and issue guidance to the entire organization. He requested reports on specific areas he did not understand or he wanted more attention paid to, such as the status of the Iraqi banking system and the regulations governing it. Petraeus used the battlefield update as a much more aggressive management tool than Casey had. Petraeus held dialogues with the other generals and poked, prodded, and queried his staff officers. As one officer put it, "he says what he thinks and stirs things up."

Petraeus's staff soon realized that he would stay locked onto a problem until it was solved. He would follow up for weeks or even months. One such issue was the egregious state of power generation in Iraq. The United States had plowed $4 billion into electrical production since 2003 to increase capacity by 2,000 megawatts, but overall production remained around 4,000 megawatts due to the decrepit infrastructure, poor maintenance, and frequent attacks on the power grid. Power generation had fallen steadily in Iraq from 9,000 megawatts in 1991 to 4,400 at the start of the 2003 war. The U.S. decision to redistribute the available supply of electricity to the rest of the country at Baghdad's expense also created discontent in the capital. As of spring 2007, Baghdad received government-produced power on average 8.4 hours a day, and the rest of the country about 14.5 hours.

Petraeus, like Lt. Gen. Peter Chiarelli before him, knew Iraqis complained about the lack of electricity more than anything but security. Every morning when Petraeus flew to the Green Zone he would peer out the window of his Black Hawk helicopter to see how many of the Dora power plant's four smokestacks had smoke coming out of them.

Petraeus latched onto the case of Tower 57, a high-voltage power pylon in a rural area just south of Baghdad, which had been damaged in a recent attack. He asked the staff to find out why no one had fixed it. The answer came back a day later: the workers were afraid to go to the tower, which was on a dirt road in a known insurgent area. After further inquiries, the Iraqi security forces said they were willing to provide security, but even then no action was taken. The staff reported that the threat appeared to come from the Shia JAM militia. Petraeus told Sadi Othman, his longtime friend, cultural adviser, interpreter, and principal intermediary to the Iraqis, to phone a Sadr leader with whom they were in touch and ask him to send the miscreants a message. "Tell him that if they do not stay away from that tower, we will send the ISOF [Iraqi special operations forces] after them," Petraeus said. Still the workers balked at fixing the tower. Petraeus finally wrote a letter to the prime minister, suggesting that the electricity ministry was not doing its job. Letters, Petraeus had learned, had the forceful impact of a formal démarche in Iraqi culture. That night, Sadi received a call from the electricity minister, who was worried he would be fired, promising to fix the tower. In September, months after it was first brought to Petraeus's attention, it finally came back online.

The morning briefings were only one of the tools Petraeus used to oversee the complex political-military battlefield of Iraq. He also managed the implementation of his strategy through battlefield circulations twice a week or more to chosen locations around Iraq, by hundreds of e-mails daily, and by weekly five-mile runs with selected officers, during which Petraeus asked questions and gave instructions to battalion commanders and to their staff officers. He had a finger in every pie, but he also gave subordinates room to implement and improvise on his orders. During battlefield circulations he ate lunch with company commanders of whatever unit he visited—without their superiors present—to ask the captains what was on their minds, what was working, and what was not.

Many senior officers repeated the mantra that this was a battalion and company commander's war, but Petraeus sought to convey to these youngest officers that they *did* have the authority, and indeed the responsibility, to produce the intended results as quickly as possible. Petraeus ran a flat organization. "He is more accessible than any general in the army," said Boylan, his press aide and spokesman. "He will respond to anyone from an E-2 [a private] to a three-star." Of course, Boylan noted, such accessibility could be a double-edged sword in that it also provided an opportunity for the soldier to show his lack of good sense, which the general would duly note. In one such moment, a lieutenant colonel asked Petraeus for one of his commander's coins. The general replied evenly, "You have to earn it first."

At times Petraeus would jump to the wrong conclusions, misinterpret data, or upbraid subordinates unjustly, but usually his formidable ability to process data and reach conclusions outstripped most of those around him. His basic intellectual approach was pragmatic—if someone had a good idea that promised the desired results, he was inclined to embrace it. Expediency could sometimes pose its own pitfalls, but Petraeus was determined to energize both the cautious military bureaucracy and the Iraqi government. By his own admission, he was focused on results and would "use any available means of persuasion—legal ones, of course."

PETRAEUS INHERITED A COMMAND structure of three-star and two-star generals, most of whom he knew very well. After the battlefield update assessment (BUA) ended at 9 a.m. each day, the senior staff would convene in a cramped room behind the amphitheater. This was the "small group," which was in turn followed by the "small small group," where the day's most urgent, sensitive, and highly classified issues would be discussed in greater detail. Odierno was conferenced into the meeting from Camp Victory. The men around this table were the highest ranking and most experienced officers in Iraq, who had been on the ground most of the past year and, for some, much longer.

The MNF-I deputy commanding general, British Lt. Gen. Graeme Lamb, jokingly referred to the five most senior generals in this group as alumni of the "class of 2003," since they all had participated in the first year of Operation Iraqi Freedom. In addition to Lamb, Petraeus, and Odierno, Lt. Gen. Stanley McChrystal of the Joint Special Operations Command had come in midway through the first year of the war to replace Lt. Gen. Dell Dailey. The fifth member of the "class of 2003" was Lt. Gen. Martin Dempsey, Petraeus's successor as head of MNSTC-I. The MNF-I general staff also included two-star generals who were the deputy chiefs for strategic operations, Maj. Gen. David Fastabend; strategic effects, Maj. Gen. Bill Caldwell; and strategic plans and assessments, Maj. Gen. Kurt Cichowski.

These generals provided Petraeus with an important reservoir of institutional memory and knowledge of recent events in Iraq. They had been in Iraq since the middle of 2006 or longer, so they had a close-up view of what had transpired from the painful and protracted formation of the new Maliki government through the months of Iraq's unraveling. Petraeus heard out their views even when he ultimately did not agree with them. The predominant view among the senior MNF-I staff who had served under Casey during 2006 was that it was necessary to transform the U.S. occupation into a smaller and more benign presence.

Some of the generals in the MNF-I command argued for using additional U.S. manpower to create more and larger advisory teams to embed in the Iraqi forces. Even though the surge had been announced, these generals hoped to persuade Petraeus to modify the approach to shift the U.S.-led coalition away from combat and expand its advisory role. For the first couple of months of Petraeus's tenure, these proponents argued for using some of the additional troops to create more robust Military Transition Teams, or Super MiTTs. There were only some 4,000 Iraqi advisers at the end of 2006—far too few to adequately mentor and keep tabs on a 300,000-strong military and police force. A strong advocate of this approach was Maj. Gen. Caldwell, the MNF-I deputy for strategic effects. He would be leaving in the summer to take Petraeus's old job at Fort Leavenworth and receive a third star. Caldwell had known Petraeus for years: he had been an aide to Joint Chiefs Chairman Hugh Shelton when Petraeus was his executive officer, and had succeeded him in that job.

Lt. Gen. Marty Dempsey had been Petraeus's peer and competitor since they had been classmates at West Point. Dempsey had been an obvious contender for Casey's job, and when Petraeus was selected, Dempsey was slated to go to Central Command as the deputy commander, where their professional rivalry would continue from afar. In 2003–2004 Dempsey had commanded the 1st Armored Division for an extended first tour, first in Baghdad and then in Najaf, where Old Ironsides was sent to deal with the Sadr uprising in the spring of 2004. Dempsey had arrived in Iraq with more knowledge of Arab culture than any other division commander, having spent the previous two years overseeing the U.S. training of the Saudi Arabian National Guard. In Baghdad, he had sought out sheikhs, including Muqtada al-Sadr's uncle, to understand Iraqi political dynamics. The wry Irishman was adored by his troops, whom he was known to regale with "Danny Boy" in a fine singing voice. A precise, thoughtful man who had once taught English at West Point, Dempsey had adapted his Germany-based tank division for counterinsurgency on the fly in 2008. Now Dempsey believed the top U.S. priority should be to position itself for a long-term relationship with Iraq.

Dempsey and Graeme Lamb had spent a great deal of time talking about what needed to be done. Lamb was on his fourth tour in Iraq, having participated in the 1991 Gulf war as a member of the Special Air Services (SAS), the British army's special operations unit, led them in 2003–2004 in Iraq, and then served as the Multi-National Division-Southeast commander based in Basra, where he too had butted heads with Paul Bremer. Lamb's departure in July 2007 would leave a tremendous gap in the command's institutional memory. The British general avoided the limelight, but he was one of the war's most unusual characters. Working behind the scenes, he had developed relations with Iraqis and exercised enormous influence over the past year. Lamb, a Scot, was a boisterous combination of profanity and intellect. An avid snowboarder, he told colorful stories about SAS exploits and complained that the bloated command was full of "shitters and eaters" instead of doers.

The swashbuckling special operator was also steeped in the most esoteric doctrinal concepts. Before returning to Iraq in the summer of 2006, he had played a lead role in the U.S. Army's annual war game, which for the first time was based on an unconventional warfare scenario. The army was refining its systemic design concept, which placed enormous emphasis on analyzing a conflict in depth and then continuously adjusting the plan in response to ongoing assessments. Had it been employed in the Iraq war, that type of feedback process would almost certainly have produced course corrections far earlier than 2007. The premise was that irregular warfare was so amorphous that it could be fought only through constant adaptation as or before the adversary also adapted. Putting these esoteric concepts into practice required patience, subtlety, and a willingness to accept that Iraqis' own proclivities were going to drive much of the war's outcome. The coalition could not dictate the outcome by brute force, but merely try to facilitate the best possible outcome with ingenuity, patience, and guile.

This concept of limited war would draw shudders from the Vietnam generation of officers, but Lamb accepted it as the norm. His experiences in Northern Ireland as an SAS soldier had prepared him to accept war as a fight-and-talk proposition. Ireland had been a protracted police action to counter a mostly terrorist campaign, and a protracted negotiation that seemed to go nowhere for thirty-eight years. That led Lamb to talk about Iraq from a historical perspective that sounded strangely optimistic in light of the current dismal situation. Leaning over a cup of tea at a small table in his office, he talked about "an emerging series of opportunities" that could make 2007 a turning point. He emphasized the need to give Iraq a genuine lead internally even though it seemed little prepared to assume it. Lamb believed Iraq would claim its place as a significant player in the Middle East. "Iraq has the potential to establish itself as a formidable economic force and a force for good in the region," he said. No sooner were those optimistic words out of his mouth than a car bomb explosion, the second of four that would go off that day, rattled the windows of his palace office.

Lamb took a much longer perspective than most other officials, who keenly felt the pressure to call Iraq a win or loss during the course of 2007. That such wars are long-term affairs was the basic lesson he learned in Ireland. He did not draw explicit parallels between the nature of the Iraqi and Irish conflicts, but the latter had driven home the point that the same people his "lads" had been trading brickbats with were the very ones with whom reconciliation would have to occur. With these experiences firmly in mind he proposed, when he arrived in 2006, to quietly reach out to antagonists. This proposal, his main contribution to this phase of the Iraq war, was called the strategic engagement initiative. Khalilzad was of like mind and it would become a major part of the Petraeus strategy. Petraeus and Lamb discussed it during a 2006 trip Petraeus made to England while he was still commander at Fort Leavenworth and before Lamb went back to Iraq. The two men had met in Bosnia, where Lamb had been director of the British Special Forces, and both were involved in the hunt for Balkan war criminals.

Although Iraqis and many Americans opposed dealing with those with "blood on their hands," Petraeus said, "the big idea is that you can't kill your way out of an insurgency." When Petraeus arrived in Iraq, he, Lamb, McChrystal, Odierno, the U.S. and British ambassadors, and a few others, discussed reconciliation schemes over monthly dinners at

Maud House, the British gathering place in the Green Zone. They decided to form an ad hoc organization of special ops and intelligence personnel called the Force Engagement Cell to reach out to insurgents. Petraeus said, "the institution isn't set up to deal with this stuff. We were sort of intellectually low-crawling, trying to find the right path."

Meanwhile, to help him think through his overall strategy, Petraeus employed the same method he had in writing the counterinsurgency manual. He assembled a brain trust that was formally called the Joint Strategic Assessment Team (JSAT). This outside group would examine the war, its causes, and the current juncture with fresh eyes. The JSAT had three months to produce its findings, which would then be used to revise Casey's campaign plan. This in-depth study paralleled one ordered by Creighton Abrams when he arrived in Vietnam in 1968, which helped pave the way for a shift from Gen. William Westmoreland's large-scale search-and-destroy combat missions to a clear-and-hold strategy aimed at securing the population.

The JSAT was headed by Col. H. R. McMaster and included two dozen participants, some of whom had participated in drafting or critiquing the counterinsurgency manual. McMaster was an articulate, bold man whose clean-shaven head advertised his headstrong personality. As a captain, he had earned a Silver Star for his leadership in the Battle of 73 Easting in the first Gulf war. In 2005 he had conducted what was considered one of the most successful counterinsurgency operations in the northwest city of Tal Afar as commander of the 3rd Armored Cavalry Regiment. He partnered with Iraqi army units and their Special Forces combat advisers to conduct a sophisticated campaign to clear the city of insurgents and resuscitate its political and economic life.

McMaster was also the author of an important and provocative book about the failure of the Joint Chiefs of Staff to effectively render their best professional military advice during Vietnam. His *Dereliction of Duty: Lyndon Johnson, Robert McNamara, the Joint Chiefs of Staff, and the Lies that Led to Vietnam*, written in 1997, carried enormous resonance in the current war. He was unusually willing to challenge the military's bureaucratic, consensus-seeking culture, which tended to blunt the hard edges of disagreement and foster a can-do spirit that made admission of failure taboo. "Do you notice we always tend to say 'challenges' instead of 'problems'?" he noted, skewering the military's penchant for euphemism. McMaster's outspokenness may have delayed or cost him promotion to general, but he was perfectly suited to head the Petraeus brain trust, having served in a similar advisory capacity to Central Command Gen. John Abizaid.

Another member of the team was David Kilcullen, Petraeus's senior counterinsurgency adviser. He was an equally outspoken and probing character, a cheery Australian who had been advising the U.S. government in various capacities since the 9/11 attacks. Kilcullen first worked in the Pentagon as a second lieutenant colonel from the Australian army, then as chief strategist for the State Department's counterterrorism coordinator. During his twenty-one-year military career, Kilcullen had practiced counterinsurgency in East Timor as a company commander and advised other militaries engaged in irregular wars. He obtained a doctorate in political anthropology for his work on Indonesia's insurgent and terrorist groups, and developed ideas for combating Islamic radicalism as a global insurgency. In Iraq he translated theoretical insights into practical tactics soldiers could apply in the field, some of which he distilled in "Twenty-Eight Articles: Fundamentals of Company-level Counterinsurgency." Kilcullen was also an early advocate of conducting "population-centric" rather than "enemy-centric" counterinsurgency.

Most of the JSAT could be characterized as realists or even skeptics who agreed that the war was not going well and admitted the possibility that it was too late to change the outcome. Another key feature of the group was the number of civilian experts, including co-leader David Pearce, and Robert Ford, and Molly Phee, all from the State Department; Richard Waddell, an oil expert; and Toby Dodge from the International Institute for Strategic Studies. The JSAT process served a critical "red-team" function to challenge established policy and offer up contrary ideas. The group also served an important function: to counterbalance Petraeus's thinking and his urge to race ahead to conclusions. His tart manner was refreshing to some but intimidating to others. Not infrequently subordinates or colleagues felt the sting of a dismissive or challenging reply. Sometimes, however, after discarding a suggestion he later would come back and adopt it—without necessarily acknowledging the course correction. One of the academics who participated in the counterinsurgency manual process was crushed by Petraeus's rejection of a central recommendation and then taken aback a few months later when he made the same recommendation in a speech.

WHILE JSAT CONDUCTED ITS ANALYSIS, Petraeus made his initial decisions on how to use the available military forces to best effect. This task, which he called the "battlefield geometry," was done in conjunction with Lt. Gen. Raymond Odierno, commander of the MNC-I, the subordinate organization in charge of daily military operations throughout Iraq. MNC-I was headquartered at Camp Victory, the sprawling U.S. military base next to the Baghdad International Airport on the city's western outskirts.

First-time visitors were shocked by the vast military complex that had grown up to run the war in Iraq. A series of bases ringed three sides of the Baghdad airport, the largest of which was Camp Victory along the northeast side. The huge physical installation housed thousands of staff officers, enlisted soldiers, and civilian contractors. The two-tiered command structure had been created in May 2004, which in turn spawned huge and in many cases duplicate staff apparatuses. The rationale for two separate war-fighting commands was that a four-star general was needed to command the "strategic" level of the war and coordinate with civilian and host-nation entities, and a three-star general was needed to direct the day-to-day military operations of 130,000 or so coalition forces all over Iraq. A passel of other generals served in MNC-I: every significant coalition partner wanted to be represented by a deputy commanding general. Granting that Lt. Gen. Ricardo Sanchez, who had been a two-star division commander and had been promoted to three stars to take over the postwar command in May 2003, was widely considered to have been overwhelmed, ill-prepared, and poorly staffed to take on the postwar stabilization mission, the next iteration swung far in the direction of overkill. Once it was created, the twin command structure was never revisited.

With duplicate headquarters came enormous administrative tasks and thousands of bodies to oversee, house, feed, entertain, and move around. To be sure, overseeing daily operations of twelve divisions involved numerous tasks. However, only six were territory-owning units, such as the Baghdad division command; others included the Corps of Engineers' Gulf Region Division and the logistics command based in Balad.

Although most of the palaces occupied by coalition forces had been turned over to the Iraqi government, the continuing occupation of Saddam's Al Faw palace, the MNF-I and MNC-I headquarters, was another sore point. The airport was the logical place for the U.S. military headquarters, but its proximity reinforced the dependence on air travel instead of making the roads safe. The airport's runways were used for both commercial and military traffic. American military C-130 planes arrived several times a day from Kuwait and Jordan, and a constant stream of helicopters and planes ferried military personnel, diplomats, contractors, and journalists to a dozen bases around the country. Another circular route flew to a dozen Baghdad sites.

In addition to Camp Victory, the other bases ringing the airport were Camp Liberty, which housed the Baghdad division and units under its command; Camp Cropper, the main U.S. detention facility; Camp Striker, a tent camp and way station for those traveling on official orders; Camp Slayer, which included another of Saddam's ubiquitous palaces and guest quarters, used by civilian government agencies; and the Radwaniya Palace Complex, which was used by Iraqi and U.S. special operations forces.

For travelers with official travel orders, another way to reach the Green Zone in downtown Baghdad was aboard ungainly armored buses called Rhinos. They traveled down the hazardous airport road to the Green Zone in the dead of night at an unspecified hour to avoid being targeted. A convoy of armored Humvees would escort each run, and unmanned aerial vehicles flew overhead to conduct surveillance. As the road became safer, the Rhinos began to make daytime runs as well.

A fleet of minibuses circled the complex of bases surrounding the airport. Sometimes traffic was so congested with military Humvees, semitrailers hauling supplies, armored SUVs carrying officers, and an assortment of armored trucks, tanks, and route-clearance vehicles arriving at or leaving Camp Liberty that a trip from one side of the airport to the other could take an hour. At night the traffic was even worse, as long lines of semitrailers would form convoys to make the dash back to Kuwait. A man who worked for KBR, the American company that provided logistics support to the U.S. military, said managers switched drivers on routes frequently so they would not mourn the loss of fellow drivers who had been killed. But for many on the large U.S. bases, life could seem far removed from the war and chaos of Iraq. The daily rhythm was dictated by staff meetings and by the meal hours at the dining halls, which were the size of football fields. The main threat to Camp Victory came from poorly aimed rockets launched from the neighborhood of Rashid to the east and the countryside to the west and north. Most often the rockets and mortars would fall harmlessly into the man-made lakes that dotted the camp. But the insurgents knew that when the big white aerostat balloons used for surveillance over the sprawling bases were aloft, American eyes could see, so they would time their attacks accordingly.

Petraeus lived at Camp Victory and had an office there, but he spent most of his days in the Republican Guard palace complex downtown. The MNF-I commander's residence was a large dun-colored stone villa like others at the Al Faw complex. It was of the uninspired modern design that had been common under Saddam's rule. The villa fronted on a man-made lake facing the Al Faw palace. Outside the house, a temporary helipad, a tarp just large enough for three Black Hawks to land on, had been staked to the ground. Between the residence and the palace sat an ornate conference center used as a guest house for distinguished visitors and the one mansion in all of Camp Victory that had its own pool, which the fun-loving Australian officers had immediately claimed for their quarters in 2003 and held on to ever since. When off-duty, one general fished for carp in the lake's algae-infested waters from a folding chair on the deck of the guest house. In the early years, soldiers occasionally could be seen cruising about the lake in a pedal boat.

Directing the war was easily a seventeen-hour-a-day job, seven days a week. The time difference conspired to lengthen the days, since at 5 p.m. in Baghdad it was only 9 a.m. in Washington. Nights in Iraq were often busy: most raids took place at night, and Iraqi politicians favored meetings that began late and went into the wee hours. Petraeus had learned during his Mosul tour how to escape from the latter by pleading urgent business and turning over an extended gabfest with tribal sheikhs to a subordinate so he could get a decent night's rest. He did not give out his personal phone number, although the cell phone of his cultural adviser, a kind and patient, white-haired Palestinian American named Sadi Othman, never stopped ringing.

Petraeus and Odierno forged an effective partnership, despite the history of frictions between the two commands. Odierno had taken the reins of MNC-I in December from Lt. Gen. Peter Chiarelli. As with the decision to split the military command structure in Iraq into two parts, the practice of rotating in a new MNC-I commander every year had been adopted in 2004 and never reconsidered. The division commanders who brought along the troops for their regions perhaps were forced by the nature of the all-volunteer force to come and go on twelve-month tours. But applying the same rotational scheme to MNC-I meant that every year a new personality with a new view of the conflict came in. Time was lost in establishing a new relationship with the "other" general in town, and the tour usually ended before the kinks had been worked out. This turnover was further complicated by the fact that every MNC-I commander had chafed at Casey's leadership.

The Petraeus and Odierno duo was a study in contrasts: the small, intense Petraeus wore the mantle of intellectual counterinsurgent, while the massive six-foot-five-inch, 285-pound Odierno was considered by many fellow officers to have taken an overly militaristic approach to his part of northern Iraq during his first tour. His 4th Infantry Division had come late to the war since Turkey had barred its entrance into northern Iraq, so he had arrived in Saddam's hometown of Tikrit to take over the Sunni Triangle after Baghdad fell. Odierno's supporters pointed to many reconstruction projects his troops undertook along with the many detentions of military-age males. He was harshly criticized in a book by *Washington Post* reporter Tom Ricks, *Fiasco*, for tactics that worsened the insurgency. Odierno was not the only commander in 2004, when the insurgency was blooming, who believed that not enough of the regime's troops, leaders, and infrastructure had been destroyed at the outset, especially in the Sunni Triangle, which enabled an essentially undefeated force to mount such a strong rearguard battle to regain power. But Petraeus, in Mosul, had pursued a distinctly less "kinetic" approach.

The immediate issues involving the "battlefield geometry" that Petraeus had to decide with Odierno's input were the size and nature of the supporting effort in the areas surrounding Baghdad, the fight against Al-Qaeda in Iraq, and the measures to stop the cross-border flow of weapons and fighters primarily from Iran and Syria. The basic choice that had to be made was how much of the available force to devote to attacking Al-Qaeda and other armed adversaries, and their bomb factories, sanctuaries, and supply lines for arms and fighters—namely, how much enemy-centric counterinsurgency to wage—and how much to the population-centric approach, which would focus on providing security, services, and political rapprochement as a means to win Iraqis' help in targeting insurgents.

Securing Baghdad had been declared the main effort, but Odierno argued that it could not be done without securing the surrounding areas. He cited intelligence showing that the "belts" around Baghdad contained safe havens for insurgents and bomb factories. He wanted to secure the major approaches to Baghdad from the south, north, and east. Two additional marine battalions and a Marine Expeditionary Unit were already headed to Anbar to pacify the insurgent safe haven west of the capital. The other area of concern was Diyala province and its capital, Baquba, just north of Baghdad, which had become the declared capital of Al-Qaeda's Islamic State of Iraq since the group was being chased out of Ramadi and much of western Anbar province. In one of the very few bright spots of 2006, the tribal sheikhs of Ramadi, led by Sheikh Abdul Sattar Bezia al-Rishawi, had revolted against the bloody, draconian, and alienating tactics of the jihadists and their foreign cohorts and had joined with U.S. forces to fight them. Other tribal chieftains had attempted to do so previously but had been killed. By the end of 2006, fourteen tribes had joined the growing Anbar Awakening movement.

The upsurge in car bombs and other insurgent attacks helped persuade Petraeus that some of the additional "surge" manpower had to be dedicated to rooting out insurgent safe havens and bomb factories outside Baghdad itself. He chose to divide his forces between Baghdad, where commanders emphasized the more population-centric approach, and the belts around Baghdad, where they initially adopted an enemy-centric approach to go after Al-Qaeda insurgents.

Petraeus also agreed to Odierno's request for another division command to handle the southern and eastern belts of Baghdad, creating the Multi-National Division-Center (MND-C). Baghdad's southern and eastern perimeter had long been an insurgent stronghold with little U.S. presence. In particular, the MND-C would focus its efforts on the hotbed of Sunni insurgency around Yusufiyah called the Triangle of Death, Arab Jabour, and Salman Pak to the east. A very intensive campaign of force was waged there in the first months, and many bombs were dropped.

Petraeus and Odierno would decide exactly how many troops to send to Diyala, the belts, and Baghdad as each of the surge brigades arrived. Petraeus sent one battalion to Diyala right away to help the brigade in that mixed Sunni-Shia province. Ultimately Petraeus devoted roughly equal forces to the belts (twenty-six battalions) and inside Baghdad (twenty-eight battalions).

Petraeus decided that in the face of the Sunni insurgents' onslaught he had to try to take down its key leaders, facilitators, and bomb-making networks. Although this approach had been pursued vigorously throughout the war to little apparent result—the killing of Al-Qaeda in Iraq's leader, Abu Musab al-Zarqawi, in June 2006 had not had the hoped-for effect—new tactics promised greater results. Over the course of the war the various components of the Sunni insurgency had collaborated and in some cases merged. The main components were the former regime members, Sunnis who felt disenfranchised by the new order, and radical Islamist groups, such as Al-Qaeda in Iraq and Ansar al-Islam, later renamed Ansar al-Sunna. Although Al-Qaeda in Iraq (AQI) was a small part of the total insurgency, it was responsible for the most spectacular and lethal attacks, such as car bombs.

Lt. Gen. Stanley McChrystal led the special operations fight against Al-Qaeda and spent much of his time in Iraq at the helm of a classified task force drawn from the Joint Special Operations Command (JSOC) based at Fort Bragg, North Carolina. When he was not there, one of his deputies, Brig. Gen. John Mulholland, was. The task force charter was to go after the "high-value targets" of the terrorist organization, but that definition sometimes extended to car-bomb networks or even bomb emplacers. They adopted new tactics, whereby the classified JSOC forces often operated in tandem with U.S. conventional forces. Previously, JSOC, which had received a massive infusion of intelligence assets and high-tech surveillance tools since 9/11, had operated unilaterally in secrecy, but in Iraq the "black" special operations units often partnered with U.S. conventional forces to flush out terrorists. When a conventional unit entered a neighborhood, the insurgents' electronic networks would light up as they began using their cell phones, which led the operators to them. JSOC also used Iraqi and Arab partners, who were essential in the successful raid on Zarqawi. The conventional forces also played a critical follow-on role of staying to secure the area with Iraqi security forces.

MNC-I's part of the strategy for dealing with Iran and Syria aimed at blocking the influx of weapons and fighters. A number of former regime officials known to be funding or directing insurgent attacks were hiding out in Syria, and the country was a way station for foreign fighters coming to join the jihadist movement. Most of the suicide bomb attacks, U.S. intelligence officials believed, were conducted by foreign fighters rather than Iraqis. Up to ninety fighters a month were arriving via Syria, so Petraeus and Odierno decided to position a joint U.S.-Iraqi force on the border to stop the influx.

Iran was a much more complicated problem. The Iranian government was ostensibly friendly toward the Iraqi government, since the defeat of its mortal enemy Saddam and the advent of a Shia-led Iraq represented an enormous geopolitical gain for Iran. Many Shia and Kurdish Iraqis had lived in exile in Iran, which had helped form and underwrite anti-Saddam militias and activities. But Iran was also supplying weapons and training for militias to attack U.S. troops. It appeared to be hedging its bets by backing a variety of Shia groups, not knowing which would emerge victorious in the intra-Shia power struggle. The number and type of weapons Iran supplied had proliferated, and more Iraqis appeared to be going to Iran for training in their use. To try to stem this flow, the military beefed up border checkpoints with Iraqis and Americans. Interdiction was a difficult task, however, given the large commercial, religious, and civilian traffic between the two countries.

U.S. officials also believed that a growing number of Iran's Revolutionary Guard al-Quds Force operatives were in Iraq to build intelligence and resistance networks. The U.S. military detained five Iranians in January in Irbil, claiming they were Quds officers. The Kurdish regional government protested their detention and said the officials were working in an un-official but longtime consulate office. Two other Iranian officials had been detained in the home of a prominent Shia leader with deep ties to Iran.

A major diplomatic component was added to the strategy in late February 2007 when Secretary of State Condoleezza Rice announced that the United States would participate in talks with Syria and Iran over Iraq-related issues. This was a significant change in the administration's stance and an embrace of one of the key recommendations the Iraq Study Group made in 2006. It signaled the administration's new willingness to undertake a combined approach of military and diplomatic measures to stop the material aid the two countries were supplying to armed groups in Iraq.

In addition to decisions about where and how to focus U.S. troops' efforts, Petraeus and Odierno made a constant stream of decisions about the coalition forces, civilian reconstruction personnel, and Iraqi security forces, which all had to be integrated into the scheme of operations. As allies left Iraq, adjustments had to be made. Mounting public opposition to the war forced Britain to begin bringing home its five thousand troops, who were stationed mostly in the southern city of

Basra. The presence of Ukrainian, Polish, Italian, Korean, and other coalition partners even in small numbers saved the mission from being entirely a unilateral U.S. one, even though their numbers had dwindled to about half their original twenty-four thousand. Small countries such as Estonia and El Salvador sent contingents and, in the latter case, had played a notable combat role defending outposts in the 2004 uprisings in the south. In 2007 a new partner, Georgia, sent a brigade to help secure the eastern border with Iran.

By far, the biggest daily task was to coordinate operations with the growing Iraqi security forces and mentor Iraq's fledgling high command. Since the Iraqi security force had been rebuilt from the ground up, the emphasis for the first three years had been on churning out new soldiers and battalions, then the brigade and division commands. The high-command structures were the last to be formed. U.S. forces could not leave until Iraq's commanders were ready to plan and lead operations by themselves. The maturation of the commands would take time, and leadership development in general was the Iraqi military's biggest internal challenge. It was a constant struggle to find enough military officers who were both trusted by the new government and were capable professionals.

The Iraqi Ground Forces Command was to have assumed sole responsibility for all Iraqi divisions by the end of 2006, but that had not happened. Only one army division, the tiny air force and navy, had passed to sole Iraqi control by then. A confusing scheme had been adopted whereby Iraqi forces progressed from being formed to being led, to being in the lead, and then finally to assuming independent operations. Six of ten divisions were "in the lead" by the end of 2006. But the defining traits of "independent" operations were fully staffed and equipped units and a fully functioning superstructure of administration, logistics, and combat enablers—which were still years away.

Another transition that had been under way was the transfer of responsibility for security in provinces from coalition forces to provincial governments. Three of Iraq's eighteen provinces had assumed responsibility for security by the time of Casey's departure. A fourth, Maysan, along the Iranian border, passed to provincial control in April. The three Kurdish provinces were scheduled to assume responsibility in 2007, as well as Karbala. The provincial governor had the power to hire and fire the provincial police chief and force, and his job was to call on coalition forces if they were needed. Petraeus was inclined to continue turning provinces over to governors as the threat level permitted.

DIRECTING THIS VAST APPARATUS and multifaceted campaign was an enormous job. Petraeus's effectiveness as a leader depended in large measure on the efficiency of his personal staff, an inner circle that would function as extra arms, legs, eyes, ears, and brains. When he went to work each day, three people were always by his side: Col. Pete Mansoor, his executive officer; Col. Bill Rapp, head of the Commander's Initiatives Group; and his aide de camp, Maj. Everett Spain, a fleet-footed officer who could and did outrun his boss. They would go for a five- to six-mile run on weekends, and other unsuspecting souls would be invited to join the pack to see if they could keep up. Rapp also enjoyed participating in the physical fitness contests they would organize after the runs. A major function of Spain's job was to make sure the transport helicopters, gunships, cars, and security bubble were in place wherever the general went.

Mansoor, who held a PhD in military history from Ohio State University, had been hired by Petraeus as the first director of the counterinsurgency center at Fort Leavenworth. Like most of Petraeus's inner circle, Mansoor was an overachiever. He had graduated first in his West Point class and in 2003–2004 had commanded a brigade of the 1st Armored Division in east Baghdad. His job now as chief of staff was to serve as gatekeeper to the general and to make sure the MNF-I staff knew what he expected of them. Mansoor, who had a gift for succinct summation, also provided input on the strategy and assessment documents that flowed into Petraeus's in-box.

Their days did not end when they returned to Camp Victory. Petraeus had three identical office suites in the Green Zone, the Al Faw palace, and in his villa, where Mansoor also lived. Petraeus and Mansoor typically would go to the house about 7 p.m. and start working again. They made calls and answered e-mails until 10 or 11 p.m. Mansoor's one break came on Friday afternoons when Petraeus attended a standing meeting with Iraqi leaders. "It's pretty much a constant stream of Mondays," Mansoor observed of his life in Baghdad.

Mansoor prided himself on efficiency but could not fathom how his boss managed to get so much done. Most of Petraeus's staff was awed by the pace he maintained. Petraeus received hundreds of e-mails every day and answered many of them himself. Holly, his wife, lamented that some people were only encouraged to e-mail more often by his quick replies. While Petraeus attended meetings or flew around the country, Mansoor was tethered to the MNF-I commander's office suite in the Republican Guard palace, which was reached via a marble staircase to the second floor at one end of the palace. The door opened into a reception room decorated with flags, a wide-screen television, couches, and a globe made of semiprecious stones. To the left was Petraeus's suite and to the right was the ambassador's suite. This configuration of office space was intended to foster coordination and communication between the top military and civilian officials in Iraq, which had been sorely lacking in the first year of the war and thereafter had improved only somewhat. One of the guiding principles Petraeus brought with him to Iraq was that the mission's success would depend on the synergy between the military and political effort. Chapter two of the counterinsurgency manual was devoted to "unity of effort" for that very reason. Achieving it would be a top priority when Ambassador Ryan Crocker arrived in late March.

Bill Rapp described his job as head of the Commander's Initiatives Group (CIG) as serving as Petraeus's "extended memory." The tall, lean colonel shadowed Petraeus everywhere he went, took notes, and kept track of everything Petraeus saw, heard, and said. Rapp had been recommended to Petraeus by Col. Mike Meese, chairman of the West Point social sciences department, where Rapp had taught for two years. Rapp had all the attributes the general prized: he had graduated at the head of his officer advanced course, had gone to Ranger School, and was a master parachutist and an army strategist. He had a PhD from Stanford University and had been a fellow at the Council on Foreign Relations. An engineer, Rapp had commanded the 555th Combat Support

Brigade, attached to the 101st Airborne Division, in Iraq. His brigade's job was to find and counter the improvised explosive devices that caused most American casualties. He had been home for less than three months when Petraeus called him in early January.

"Hey, sir, I just left the theater," Rapp said when Petraeus offered him the job.

"So have we all," Petraeus replied, signaling that he was not going to take no for an answer.

"I'm still in command," Rapp said, trying again. He was really thinking of what it would mean for his wife, Debbie, who would be a single mother of their three children, ages eight, ten, and twelve, for another long year.

"I can fix that," Petraeus said. With a call he could shorten Rapp's brigade command with no detriment to his career. In fact, Rapp had already been selected for promotion to brigadier general and his next command would be held open for him until his return.

"I need a couple of hours to talk to my wife," Rapp said. It was his last try. He was on a training exercise, so he called Debbie.

"Absolutely," she said. "You need to do this." While he had been in Iraq last time, she had taken it upon herself to form a nonprofit, tax-exempt organization so that her husband's unit could legally receive donations to pay for funerals, wounded soldiers' needs, and homecoming parties. The Rapps lived on post at Fort Lewis, Washington, which meant that she would at least have a support network of families on the base. She could also get help from her parents, who were an eleven-hour drive away in Sacramento, California. Rapp called Petraeus back and accepted the job. Rapp's deputy, Lt. Col. Charlie Miller, had been Petraeus's chief of staff at MNSTC-I, the train-and-equip command, on his last tour. The general had bumped into him at the Pentagon in December. When he found out Miller was lounging in a joint staff job, he told him, "You're coming with me."

Among their many duties, Miller and the CIG prepared a daily press digest for Petraeus, who liked to see everything written about him and the war. While Steve Boylan managed the daily deluge of press requests for interviews, access, and information, they earmarked important stories and highlighted bits that might be of interest to help him digest the coverage more quickly. The CIG team also included Capt. Liz McNally, a Rhodes scholar who drafted speeches and articles for Petraeus. The team also helped him prepare for his weekly video teleconferences with President Bush, as well as television interviews and briefings, by laying out themes and arguments he could cite.

Rapp came to know more about Petraeus's thinking than anyone else because he spent so much time with him, worked with him on the full range of issues, and witnessed literally every encounter. Given his singular knowledge about where Petraeus stood on every issue, the principal MNF-I staff officers for plans, operations, and effects came to him regularly for information and to sound out whether their ideas or proposals might fly with the boss. Petraeus wanted Rapp to function like a second brain, to digest the same information he received and help him make sense of it. Rapp did this quietly and efficiently, in contrast to the fanfare and publicity that surrounded much of the Petraeus show. He was in a unique position to provide an independent reality check on virtually every individual and encounter the general had. He sat (off-camera) in the videoconferences with the president, he attended every meeting with the prime minister and other top Iraqi officials, he witnessed Petraeus's interactions with every U.S. general and enlisted soldier, and he saw every neighborhood and market Petraeus visited. Alone among Petraeus's staff, Rapp had no competing duties other than to help him see the bigger picture.

One member of Petraeus's inner circle was his Iraq expert: Derek Harvey, a retired military intelligence colonel. Harvey had spent his active-duty career in the Defense Intelligence Agency as an Arabist and held a PhD in Islamic political thought and jurisprudence. From the beginning of the war Harvey had been passed from one commander to the next as the "crown jewel" of the intelligence community, as one officer put it. He had advised MNC-I commander Lt. Gen. Tom Metz in 2004–2005 and had participated in talks with the Fallujah sheikhs and insurgents in the summer of 2004.

Like every good intelligence analyst, Harvey was scrappy, skeptical, and contrarian. He knew there were no easy answers in Iraq and fought the pressure to reduce the complex struggle to a clean and manageable formulaic policy prescription. The Sunni were leaderless, bent on fighting, and opposed to accepting their demoted status. The Shia, for their part, were starting to flex their power and were disinclined to make any concessions. That was the heart of the struggle that was playing out. Although he had argued for the surge because the stakes in the Middle East were too high to make leaving a responsible option, Harvey was no Pollyanna. In early 2007 before he left Washington for Iraq, he told Vice President Dick Cheney and Newt Gingrich that the odds of success were only one in six.

To complete his personal staff, Petraeus tapped another loyal, longtime friend, Col. Mark Martins, as his staff judge advocate. Martins, a Rhodes scholar, had served in Petraeus's battalion when Petraeus was shot in the chest. Martins recalled Petraeus's early focus on low-intensity conflict, the term in the 1980s and early 1990s for both postwar stabilization operations and counterinsurgency. The lawyer had helped him integrate media and civilian role-players into their exercises, as well as a battlefield unit to provide legal advice. Martins had provided legal advice on use of seized Iraqi funds to jump-start reconstruction funds. In early 2006, Petraeus asked Martins to write the legal appendix for the counterinsurgency manual. The taciturn, dependable man, who had come to Iraq in 2006 to serve as Casey's staff judge advocate, agreed to stay as long as Petraeus did.

Martins served as Petraeus's chief legal adviser, but his passion was implementing the ideas he had outlined in the manual appendix. Strengthening Iraq's justice system would provide a major boost to the government's legitimacy. That entailed strengthening its evidence-gathering capacity and reliance on evidence over confessions, which were frequently coerced. Open, transparent trials would also distinguish the government from an adversary that staged execution-style beheadings. The entire government would gain legitimacy from a visibly functioning court that prosecuted Shia and Sunni lawbreakers alike. American troops were also frustrated by what they viewed as the current "catch and release" practice: they would catch and Iraqis would release.

The focal point of this effort was the Rule of Law Complex, which brought together police, courts, and prison in one location in eastern Baghdad. A complex was built adjacent to the police college; it housed a new detention center, secure lodging for judges and officials of the major-crimes unit, and a state-of-the-art courtroom. There were 2,500 jail cells and eventually there would be 5,400. The law and order task force included 9 Iraqi judges, 12 investigators, and 63 U.S. personnel, and would grow to 125. Individual training and mentoring had already improved the quality of the investigations and resulted in a quantum leap in warrants. The first trial was held in March, of a Syrian who was convicted of terrorist attacks. A lieutenant colonel of the National Police was tried and convicted for the torture of prisoners at a secret interior ministry jail known as Site 4. Unfortunately, in one of the most-watched cases, the charges were dismissed against the deputy health minister and his chief of security despite substantial evidence of kidnaps and murders in Baghdad hospitals.

In early April 2007 the Joint Strategic Assessment Team completed its study, a hundred-page report with voluminous appendices. Team members had labored in a warren of makeshift cubicles with plywood walls in a ballroom at the back of the Republican Guard palace.

H. R. McMaster's team had spent weeks analyzing the conflict to come up with the most accurate definition possible. From this key step all of the prescriptions would flow. The JSAT boldly departed from U.S. government pronouncements by acknowledging that the conflict had evolved into a civil war. It concluded that the war had become primarily a "communal struggle" (by which the group meant a low-grade civil war) with elements of insurgency, jihadist terrorism, and failed-state syndrome. There were also foreign influences and criminal actors. Labeling the conflict a civil war carried enormous implications. It meant recognizing that the Iraqi government was a party to the conflict, not just a government to be supported against an insurgency. It did not mean that the counterinsurgency manual was inapplicable. "There is obviously an insurgency, to which the COIN tactics, techniques and procedures apply," said Mansoor, who gave his input to the JSAT. But additional measures would be needed.

The JSAT recognized the complexity of the conflict and that in fact many insurgencies had elements of civil war and vice versa. But it rejected the reductionist conclusion that there was no remedy for civil wars other than to let them burn themselves out. It also rejected the view that if the government was part of the problem, the United States ought to withdraw its support. The United States had frequently imposed conditions on allies or otherwise sought to modify their undesirable behavior.

The JSAT advocated a multifaceted approach to ending the conflict. "We do not believe that Iraqis want a country divided along sectarian lines," said one of the report's authors. The main recommendations were (1) to adopt a political strategy of seeking cease-fire agreements with individual groups or key actors, (2) to apply a military strategy of protecting the population and attacking those who would not come to the table, (3) to engage in active regional diplomacy, (4) to build government capacity, and most controversially, (5) to root sectarian actors out of the government, if necessary unilaterally using the authority vested in the coalition under the U.N. Security Council Resolution. The proposal to purge the government reflected the frustration and pessimism many group members felt over the sectarian violence the Maliki government had permitted, as well as its general failure to move forward notably in the past year. One of the highest-ranking officials who many felt should be removed was Bayan Jabr. As interior minister in 2005 he had packed the police and ministry with sectarian Shiites who rounded up and tortured former regime officials in secret cells that were discovered late in the year. Two of his notorious subordinates were still in the ministry. Now, as Maliki's finance minister, he had refused to disburse funds and had been starving Sunni areas of resources.

The team also concluded that much larger Iraqi security forces were needed. It said that the forces suffered from a dearth of leadership and expertise and had been insufficiently vetted. The report proposed a large expansion of the Iraqi army to replace, on a one-to-one basis, the 170,000 coalition troops expected to leave in the not-too-distant future. The assumption was that Iraq's conflict would not end quickly and that more security forces would be needed to fill the vacuum. Although the

Iraqis had recently accepted the U.S. recommendation to add 40,000 troops in 2007, the JSAT envisioned a substantially bigger increase.

The JSAT report also made a bold proposal to integrate the U.S. political and military effort. To achieve not only "unity of effort," as called for by the COIN manual, but also "unity of command," the team proposed formally fusing the embassy staff and the MNF-I command. Staffs would be integrated under the dual leadership of Petraeus and Crocker, the new ambassador. Many experts believed that unity of command was vital to success in counterinsurgencies. One model was the CORDS (Civil Operations and Revolutionary Development Support) program in Vietnam, which combined military and civilians in the same chain of command. If a conflict was truly a political-military one and the solution was deemed to be at least 80 percent nonmilitary, such an organizational structure made sense in theory. Petraeus decided against formal integration at the top, but two important advances in unity of command were made at lower echelons. The military advisory teams assigned to each Iraqi battalion were placed under the operational control of the U.S. brigade in charge of the area so the two elements would be more tightly coordinated. The new provincial reconstruction teams in Baghdad were also embedded at each brigade headquarters, where they reported to the brigade commander.

The next step was for Petraeus to decide how much of the JSAT report to adopt. The classified study was shared with a few senior officials, including Marty Dempsey. He had a distinctly different view and gave the team his recommendations of what a long-term sustainable strategy would look like. If the United States wanted Iraq as a long-term ally, in Dempsey's opinion, it needed to make a commitment to the Shia majority that now ruled Iraq. He proposed looking for ways to reassure the Shia so they would not feel it necessary to resort to extreme methods. The carrot of U.S. aid could be used to induce some of the desired changes, and as U.S. combat brigades were withdrawn, the money freed up from the cost of their operations could be applied to security assistance.

Dempsey argued that the United States needed to decide what kind of relationship it wanted with Iraq in 2010 and then find a way to get there through what he called a strategy of commitment. His views were obviously colored by his experience in Saudi Arabia, where the relationship was not an unambiguous client-state relationship and where the U.S. military had been training, advising, and equipping the security forces for almost half a century. The difference in the two approaches to Iraq boiled down to embracing the Shia government and trying to influence it at the margins, or trying to change it now to something more embraceable.

Petraeus asked John Martin, his former West Point classmate with a reputation for hard-boiled pragmatism, to help pull together the JSAT findings and feedback from the embassy and the MNF-I staff to revise the joint campaign plan. Petraeus and Crocker had the final word on the campaign plan redesign that was to guide and unify the U.S. effort. Martin leaned toward Dempsey's view that the goals of the JSAT report might be too ambitious. "The optimism regarding what we could do here was unrealistic," he said of the JSAT's sweeping recommendations.

Some senior embassy officials also strongly opposed the recommendation on purging officials with sectarian agendas, since Iraq was a sovereign country with a sovereign government. Evidence would need to be brought forward and due process followed. Petraeus decided against a full-scale purge approach. "I think we probably only need to do it with one or two officials to have the intended effect," Martin said. Thus, the approach eventually adopted was less confrontational than the JSAT recommended, but even so, its implementation would test the skills of the Petraeus-Crocker team.

5

Fardh al-Qanoon,
the Baghdad Security Plan

The Baghdad security plan was written and set in motion before Gen. Petraeus arrived in Iraq, even though it was not officially launched until February 14, 2007. In mid-December 2006, Gen. George Casey tasked the Multi-National Division-Baghdad (MND-B) with formulating a new plan to bring Baghdad under control. The 1st Cavalry Division of Fort Hood, Texas, had returned in the fall on its second tour in Iraq to take over MND-B. The soldiers of the 1st Cavalry moved back into the base at Camp Liberty that they had built two years earlier, when Peter Chiarelli was the division's commander. The division's mascot, a giant wooden horse, was moved back to its place of honor in the prefab division head-quarters so visitors could be photographed next to it, and the black and yellow emblem of the horse's head was repainted and rehung at every door. A black Stetson with silver tassels decorated most officers' cubicles, and soldiers walking to and from the giant prefab mess hall saluted their superiors and murmured the required slogan, "First Team."

Even though the war could seem very remote to staff officers at Camp Liberty, every day or two the sound of mortars or rockets reminded them of the dangers. When the giant Phalanx guns that protected the base went off, with a chilling *brrrp*, a metallic staccato riff, everyone took note.

When Casey tasked MND-B with coming up with a new plan for securing Baghdad in mid-December, that job fell to Lt. Col. Doug Ollivant, the division's chief of plans. In a war of mishaps and missteps, for once the right person was in the right place at the right time. Ollivant was a brilliant young officer with an acerbic wit whose talents had been noticed by senior officers and their advisers. He and the majors working for him framed the objectives of the plan: to secure the population, defeat the armed elements, and promote the government's legitimacy by supporting governance, economic, and communications programs. The primary goal of securing the population was the new emphasis, a change informed by the debate that had been going on within the military, by the new counterinsurgency manual, and by Ollivant's views drawn from his own combat experience of his first tour.

Soon after arriving in the summer of 2004, Ollivant had realized that he was enmeshed in a political struggle, rather than a military one, which affected every aspect of the strategy, operations, and tactics. He had just graduated from the School of Advanced Military Studies at Fort Leavenworth, whose rising-star students are nicknamed Jedi Knights, and had previously earned a PhD in political science from Indiana University. Now he found himself in the classroom of a ferocious battlefield. His unit was thrust into the middle of the uprising of Muqtada al-Sadr's Shiite militia, which had erupted in April and by the summer had occupied the main Shia mosque in Najaf and its adjacent vast cemetery of honeycombed tombs. The young officer grasped that the fight was a chess move, a power bid by the young Shiite cleric, who was leading a nationalist resistance campaign against the Americans and simultaneously challenging other, more established Shia players. Ollivant experienced how politics affected even the tactical operations, as he explained to a journalist reporting on the battle. His unit frequently received orders from the interim Iraqi government of Ayad Allawi, directing it to fire or withhold fire on given targets.

After the standoff in Najaf was resolved with what amounted to a cease-fire brokered by the country's preeminent Shia cleric, the Ayatollah Ali al-Sistani, Ollivant's battalion moved to the Shiite neighborhood of Kadhimiya in Baghdad. Here, power resided with another Shia militia, the Badr Corps. Ollivant strongly believed the correct approach was to conduct armed politics rather than conventional military operations to counter the Shia militia's moves. The battalion commander did not agree, preferring to fight rather than talk. Ollivant's performance review would suffer as a result of the argument, and with it his chance for battalion command.

After his tour ended in mid-2005 and he returned to home base at Fort Hood, Ollivant collaborated with the battalion's intelligence officer to write an article, "Producing Victory: Rethinking Conventional Forces in COIN Operations," published in mid-summer 2006 in *Military Review*. Officers of all ranks, including generals Petraeus, Chiarelli, and Tom Metz, distilled the experiences of their tours for publication in this journal, which under the editorship of Col. Bill Darley had become the leading venue for sophisticated, freewheeling debate about the Iraq war and counterinsurgency. By the time Ollivant's article was published, he and the 1st Cavalry Division were headed back to Baghdad.

The core concept of the Baghdad security plan was contained in Ollivant's article, the thesis of which was that "the combined arms maneuver battalion, partnering with indigenous security forces and living among the population it secures, should be the basic tactical unit of counterinsurgency (COIN) warfare." The article described the varied roles such a battalion would play each day alongside Iraqi policemen and soldiers to provide security and help local officials with governing, public services, and reconstruction. It argued for placing central responsibility at the battalion level, rather than at the corps, division, or brigade, and dispersing the troops among the population rather than fortified bases away from the people and the insurgents. This dispersion scheme was drawn from the work of French counterinsurgency expert David Galula.

Under this scheme, battalion commanders would delegate the initiative down to the company level, and captains and noncommissioned officers would be in daily contact with the population. These officers were now veterans with one or two previous tours' worth of experience in Iraq's culture. This formula for conducting networked operations against a highly networked adversary was a radical proposal for the army, a hierarchical institution in which decision-making authority was concentrated at the top. "While we cannot transform our hierarchical Army into a fully networked organization overnight, powering down to the lowest practical level will enable the most adaptive commanders to implement a Galula-like solution," wrote Ollivant and his co-author.

The Baghdad security plan, which was dubbed Operation Fardh al-Qanoon (Enforcing the Law), created a grid of embedded units as envisioned in Ollivant's article. Baghdad would be divided into ten security districts, and a U.S. battalion and an Iraqi brigade would be assigned to each district. The Iraqi brigade would be based at a district joint security station, where it would coordinate all Iraqi security forces. The U.S. battalions would be in combat outposts, many of them near or adjacent to their respective Iraqi partner brigade. The U.S. battalions would also send smaller elements of ten to fifty soldiers to other joint security stations throughout the district for periods of twenty-four hours to several days, depending on the threat level.

After initial shaping operations, the major phase of the plan would consist of operations to successively "clear," "control," and "retain" the city neighborhood by neighborhood. The operations to *clear* areas of armed antagonists were to be carried out by division-controlled forces, primarily Stryker brigade elements, partnered with Iraqi security forces. As areas were cleared, the battalions would move in to *control* the area, secure the population, and support governance and economic activity. Once Iraqis were capable of *retaining* the gains, U.S. forces would progressively back out, leaving enhanced embedded adviser teams and moving to tactical, then operational, and then strategic overwatch positions. This last phase was more or less what Casey and Chiarelli had attempted in 2005–2006, but without first establishing adequate security.

The "control and retain" part of the plan would be the key to achieving lasting success. MND-B commander Maj. Gen. Joseph Fil underscored one of the war's enduring lessons: "We are very good at clearing areas, but that does not count for anything unless you hold it afterward."

That could serve as the epitaph for much of 2003–2006. By denying the enemy access to the population on a continuing basis, and providing the population with security and basic services, the new plan to shift the population's allegiance to the host-nation government and induce them to identify and expel or neutralize the armed insurgents. Soldiers would continue to target armed insurgents, but the decisive effort would be to change the environment around them and the conditions that enabled the armed networks to continually regenerate. That meant working with Iraqi security forces, encouraging Iraqi officials, getting neighborhood and district councils to respond to local needs, and reaching out to influential citizens and the population.

Soon after Petraeus was tapped for the job of top commander in Iraq, he contacted Ollivant via e-mail to discuss his work on the plan. It was typical of Petraeus to reach out directly to a subordinate five echelons below. They discussed how Ollivant was applying the ideas in his *Military Review* article. He noted that the essential difference between a pure counterinsurgency mission, in which the primary task was supporting the host-nation government, and the current situation was that the government itself was a party to the sectarian conflict, which called for U.S. troops to act as well in a peace enforcement capacity to ensure that the government did not permit or endorse sectarian attacks. Ollivant cautioned, as the JSAT would, "We need to be constantly aware of actions that empower one belligerent over another, particularly within the government itself." Petraeus agreed and said he would ask Odierno to disseminate Ollivant's article and his caveats.

He encouraged Ollivant to continue to feed him ideas, writing: "You're a very bright guy and these are exceptional times (we're going to get one last shot at this and we need to make it really count—and you're the planner for the main effort). We're putting it all on the line and we need to be cognizant of that. It's not business as usual, as I'm sure you know." Ollivant was encouraged by Petraeus's maverick style and openness to new ideas. In Ollivant's view, the tradition-bound army was populated by "Cold War generals, Bosnia colonels, and Iraq captains." Incorporating the latter's insights might well entail revolutionary and painful changes, but if the army was not prepared to scoop up the knowledge its captains, majors, and lieutenant colonels had gained over the past six years on the front lines, it would lose that wisdom—and many of the officers—and probably the war.

Like most of those participating in the war at this stage, Ollivant did not make any predictions of success. Indeed, his *Military Review* article concluded with the sobering statement that "the war in Iraq may now have moved beyond this possible solution." His quick mind would be the first to critique his own plan, and only time would tell whether it would achieve its goals. The former Chicago resident's outlook was shaped by years of rooting for the Cubs. It was, he said, "good preparation for life in general (and I suppose Baghdad in particular). The ending will probably be tragic, but you still go out to the ballpark."

Although it would undergo some adaptations, over the coming months the Baghdad security plan would be implemented largely as designed by Ollivant's team. The battalion-based scheme was adopted and the troops spread out among Baghdad's neighborhoods and settled into buildings they called combat outposts. The battalions in turn sent one or two platoons to live, on rotating schedules, in the smaller joint security stations, most of which were blue-and-white painted cinder-block police stations, which the troops first worked to fortify by various means. The Ollivant scheme was eventually adopted by other divisions outside Baghdad.

Even though five additional brigades had been pledged to secure Baghdad, along with ten new provincial reconstruction teams, the manpower provided fell well short of the ratios prescribed by standard counterinsurgency doctrine. The newly released U.S. Army Field Manual 3-24, *Counterinsurgency,* for example, recommended a minimum of 20 counterinsurgents per 1,000 inhabitants. The planned forces would total roughly 91,500 rather than the 120,000 required under that formula for a population of 6 million. Petraeus chose to focus the available forces on the sectarian "fault lines" in the city. Nonetheless, there was an ongoing struggle for troops. Ollivant argued with Odierno for more, but Odierno, McChrystal, and Petraeus wanted to pursue Al-Qaeda-linked insurgents in their various sanctuaries around the country. Half of the surge forces would ultimately be deployed outside Baghdad. The additional forces eventually totaled over 31,000 servicemen and -women, including "combat enablers" such as an aviation brigade, military police to serve as prison guards for the expected increase in detainees, and the headquarters staff of the new division that the MNC-I commander, Lt. Gen. Raymond Odierno, created with Petraeus's approval.

Odierno felt there were too many brigades for one division headquarters to command and control, although MND-B disagreed, pointing out that Chiarelli had managed as many when he was division commander. The division argued that the brigades' missions were all essentially the same, unlike a maneuver campaign, so it would be possible and indeed desirable to coordinate all units from one headquarters. Odierno's decision to create another division had numerous implications. The new division, Multi-National Division-Center (MND-C), had to be supplied with brigades, so it became an instant competitor with MND-B for the incoming surge brigades. MND-C's area of operations would extend from the troubled Sunni area south of Baghdad nicknamed the Triangle of Death and east to Salman Pak, another area where resistance had found a safe haven and begun building car bombs. Aircraft, intelligence, and other assets would also be diverted from the main effort, running the danger that all might suffer from insufficiency. That had been one of the recurring problems of the war. As the surge evolved, Odierno and Petraeus would have to arbitrate the competing demands of the various division commanders. The tug of war would continue over which areas required more emphasis and resources, and between the population-centric approach and the enemy-centric approach of attacking Al-Qaeda hideouts.

The Baghdad security plan's chances of success depended, of course, on its implementation. One of the biggest challenges in the implementation was integrating the Iraqi and U.S. forces to achieve the desired effects. The commanders had to ensure that the Iraqi forces showed up on a daily basis in the required numbers and executed the plan rather than a sectarian or rogue agenda. It was a test for the still-green Iraqi command, planning, and support structures.

To oversee the Iraqi side of the plan, a new headquarters was created. Lt. Gen. Abboud Qanbar was chosen by Prime Minister Nouri al-Maliki in mid-January to be the Iraqi commander of all Baghdad operations. His appointment caused concern among U.S. officials because he was an unknown quantity. Abboud, a grandfatherly man with big, drooping cheeks like a basset hound's, had served as an inspector general in Saddam Hussein's army and had been an American prisoner of war in the 1991 Gulf war. He was also a Shia and a distant relative of Maliki's. At the Baghdad Operations Command, Lt. Gen. Abboud had a full-time U.S. adviser, Col. Bob Newman, one of the few Arabic-speaking foreign-area officers who had been involved in Iraq since the beginning of the war. Newman was an invaluable round-the-clock information node and something of a canary in the coal mine. If the Iraqi military commanders began receiving conflicting orders, he would be the first to detect it.

Formally, Lt. Gen. Abboud's counterpart was the U.S. commander of MND-B, Maj. Gen. Fil, but the job of making the Baghdad plan work fell to Fil's deputy commanding general for operations, Brig. Gen. John Campbell. Campbell was both forceful and friendly, and a soldier's soldier. Whenever he got into a Humvee he would invariably strike up a conversation with one of the enlisted men and ask him where he was from and how he was doing. Making his daily rounds through Baghdad, he made sure his personal security detachment—the soldiers who traveled with him—had time to get lunch before their reconnaissance of the afternoon routes. He helped solve his officers' problems and advance their careers. By taking care of them, Campbell earned his soldiers' devotion and best efforts in return.

Campbell spent as little time as possible at the MND-B headquarters at Camp Victory, where the twice-daily battlefield updates droned on for hours in the high-tech amphitheater with its giant plasma screens. To do his job, Campbell had to be out in the city. He was the eyes, ears, and voice of the division and, by extension, of Odierno and Petraeus. He was the most senior officer connecting the deciders with the doers, or those who were supposed to be doing things on the ground. He could make things happen only if he knew firsthand what was happening in Baghdad and then stayed by the Iraqis' side to make sure decisions were carried out.

Commanding his own brigade commanders in charge of the ten security districts was the least difficult part of Campbell's job. They were full colonels who sat atop the most well-trained, highly functioning military force in the world. Virtually every one had served a tour in Iraq already. Campbell's most difficult job was to nudge and maneuver the Iraqi military chain of command into doing what needed to be done. He had to take the measure of individual Iraqi commanders throughout the Baghdad chain of command, cultivate those most likely to get the job done, and try to neutralize others' detrimental effects.

Two subordinate commands were created to oversee operations on each side of the Tigris River, which divided Baghdad roughly in half. The Karkh Area Command (KAC) oversaw western Baghdad operations, and the Rusafa Area Command (RAC) oversaw those on the eastern side. Two-star generals with two-star deputies headed these commands. The KAC was led by a verbose national police general named Wajih Hameed with an effective army general, Maj. Gen. Abdul Ameer Yarella, as his deputy. On the east side the roles were reversed: army general Riyadh Jalal Tawfiq, with whom Campbell often argued, led the RAC with police general Abdul Karim as his number two.

The eastern and western commands each oversaw five of the city's new security districts. On the east side of the Tigris, the five districts were named for the principal neighborhood in that area: Adhamiya, Sadr City, Rusafa, New Baghdad, and Karrada. On the west side of the river were Kadhimiya, Mansour, Karkh, East Rashid, and West Rashid.

On February 14, 2007, the Baghdad security plan was formally launched. The first official clearing operations were carried out in Shaab and Ur, two neighborhoods bordering Sadr City in northeast Baghdad. The units of choice for the clearing phase were those equipped with the army's state-of-the-art Strykers, personnel carriers designed for low- and mid-intensity combat in urban terrain. They were more survivable than Humvees and more maneuverable and less damaging to streets and curbs than tanks or heavy armored vehicles. Although the actual clearing operations would involve targeted or house-to-house searches on foot, the Strykers were the best means of putting a lot of men into a neighborhood quickly.

The nineteen-ton, eight-wheeled armored vehicles possessed numerous advantages, including a top speed of over 60 mph, high-tech information systems that provided situational awareness, and room for soldiers in each unit. The Strykers looked ungainly: their trapezoidal body was surrounded by a slatted cage meant to repel rocket-propelled grenades. The armor itself protected against 14.5 mm rounds. To conceal the gunner and the soldiers when they rode standing up with the hatches open, their head and shoulders exposed, a camouflage net was draped over the top. Because their 350-horsepower engines made little noise, some Iraqis dubbed them the Ghost Riders. As the war went on, various modifications were added: extra armor was bolted onto the sides, and bulletproof drop-down windows were added in the rear so soldiers could fire from see-through portholes. The FBCB2 (Force XXI Battle Command Brigade and Below) command system allowed soldiers to share information via a secure wireless network. En route to a mission or battle, they received graphics, overlays, and new data on threats provided by unmanned aerial vehicles and other units. With the tap of a stylus, the sergeant at the onboard computer screen could add icons to show locations of friendly units as well as bombs. When they approached a marked threat, a warning beep would sound. The Strykers offered creature comforts as well. Unlike that of most of the armored vehicles, the air conditioning really worked, and built-in cookers heated canned meals without the mess or hazard of the chemical heaters in the standard Meals Ready to Eat. As much as the Stryker units appreciated their technologically advanced vehicles, they were even more grateful that being in the army's newest units gave them the chance to experiment with new operational concepts and tactics and serve with highly motivated peers. Competition to get into the units was stiff, and Rangers were disproportionately selected.

The Stryker unit that carried out the majority of the clearing operations was the 3rd Stryker Brigade Combat Team, 2nd Infantry Division (3-2), commanded by Col. Steve Townsend. Half of the soldiers had been on the first Stryker combat deployment in Mosul in 2004–2005. Now, on their second tour, elements of his brigade took part in the kick-off clearing operation in Shaab and Ur, along with the brigade that

would stay to oversee northeast Baghdad. The Stryker brigade was organized around three infantry battalions, with cavalry, artillery, and support units filling out the four thousand–member formation equipped
with 310 Stryker vehicles. The three maneuver battalions of the 3-2
would frequently be sent off to different parts of the city and surrounding provinces. When Townsend was not locked up in meetings to plan
the next operation, he and his headquarters unit would join one of the
battalions in the field or coordinate combined operations. Townsend
was a hard-charging Ranger, but he was very quick to assure his fellow
brigade commanders who were assigned to Baghdad's ten security districts that his job was to support them. Townsend's brigade was also the
MNC-I reserve force, so Lt. Gen. Odierno could, and did, order it to respond to emergencies outside Baghdad.

One of Townsend's battalion commanders, Lt. Col. Van Smiley, became well known to the media in Baghdad. For one thing, the relatively
safe Stryker vehicles were considered the best ride in town for embedded journalists. Smiley, an outgoing, telegenic soldier, had no fear of
journalists ruining his career. He looked straight into the cameras and
said what he thought. "I authorized the release of a Hellfire missile into
Sadr City," he said on one such occasion. Born in 1966 in an army hospital, Smiley upset his father when he decided to go ROTC in college
because he wanted a different life for his son. As a high school student,
Smiley had lived in Saudi Arabia, and the experience had given the
young Smiley a taste for life abroad and an appreciation of what Americans enjoyed at home. He served in the 75th Ranger Regiment and then
volunteered for the Stryker brigade. At home, he and his wife, Tamara,
were raising a son, Miles, twelve, and a daughter, Gracie Ann, seven.

Smiley's unit, 1st Battalion, 23rd Regiment, conducted clearing operations in Shaab and Ur and helped open Combat Outpost Callahan. Not
enough of the U.S. "surge" troops had yet arrived to secure the sprawling
area, which was largely controlled by the Shia militia JAM as it had
pushed outward from its base in next-door Sadr City. The battalion was
then sent to clear Route Pluto, a dangerous street where Shiite militiamen fired deadly projectiles called explosively formed penetrators (EFPs)
in the army's lingo, as well as mortars and rocket-propelled grenades,

daily at passing U.S. vehicles. The battalion also helped set up a joint security station on the edge of Sadr City. The plan was not to move troops into Sadr City initially, but for the Iraqi government to pump money and projects into it in hopes of winning over the population. After taking ferocious fire from Sadr City, Smiley called in an Apache helicopter to respond with a Hellfire missile.

Smiley and his men were then sent to the west side of Baghdad, to Mansour and Ameriya, for a monthlong clearing operation in March and April. Many of the homes in Mansour were unoccupied, as many of the upper-middle-class residents had fled. Troops collected tips from residents about who remained, as well as intelligence gleaned from other sources. Some areas were searched house-to-house. Near the end of the operation, one of Smiley's companies found a bunker full of boots and clothes, likely an air raid shelter left over from Saddam's era. Surveying the solid structure, its concrete exterior painted pastel blue and white, Smiley thought it would make a good location for a joint security station or combat outpost.

He had begun the day downtown, where two of his companies formed a convoy with Iraqi companies under the command of Col. Ghassan Khalid, one of the most able Iraqi officers. They met at the parade ground under the giant crossed swords where Saddam had presided over countless military reviews. Next to the plaza sat a huge park and modernistic monument dedicated to the soldiers who had fought and died in the Iran-Iraq war. An Iraqi platoon leader, Lt. Hassan Issa Faraj, explained to Smiley's company commander that many of his sergeants were not there because the American advisers assigned to their unit were holding a training course for noncommissioned officers. Lt. Hassan was grateful that the Americans were patrolling jointly. "There are a lot of areas that we cannot handle on our own," he said. "When they are with us and give us air support, that is a big incentive."

Smiley and the local U.S. brigade commander, Col. J. B. Burton, had had trouble with one of Ghassan's battalion commanders. The Shia officer would target only Sunnis and often conducted indiscriminate roundups based on little intelligence. A car bomb that blew up a bridge had come from his district, and the Americans believed he knew about it. After the officer attempted to put the blame on someone else, Burton requested that he be removed.

The Iraqis, in their armored Humvees, and Smiley's Stryker set off for Mansour, a few blocks away. While the Iraqis guarded the perimeter, the U.S. soldiers went to the iron gate of an empty house and began hitting it to open it. They had a tip that it was being used by insurgents. A middle-aged woman wearing a gold-tipped black veil came hurrying toward them, jangling a set of keys. The soldiers' Iraqi interpreter explained what the agitated woman was saying. "She says that she was left in charge of the house. The neighbors are gone. She is afraid you will break something." Smiley's men assured her they would search the premises carefully, but she trailed along behind them, unconvinced and still upset. When Smiley asked her about the neighborhood's composition she said, "We are from all different groups here. It doesn't matter. I'm Sunni, this couple who lives here are both Sunni and Shia. They went to Syria, and then came back to live in Karrada," a Shia neighborhood in east Baghdad. The soldiers found nothing suspicious and moved on. On their way out, they put the gate back on its hinges.

Out in the street, two schoolteachers, Ilham and Naham, their heads covered in colorful scarves, paused to talk. They were upset at the concrete barriers that had closed all but a few streets into and out of the neighborhood. But they were very happy the American troops were there. "We need the Americans here so they can find the bad people," said Ilham. "The children cannot attend school without the security. They have already missed so many weeks."

On another street, Smiley found Col. Ghassan, known by his first name in Iraqi custom, standing on a corner talking with several Iraqi men. They exchanged the traditional Iraqi greeting, three kisses on the cheeks. Ghassan held the American's hand as they stood there talking. Smiley's soldiers snickered, but they knew that his gregarious personality and willingness to adopt the local ways had paid off. Ghassan, at forty-one a twenty-year veteran of Saddam's army from Diyala, had been imprisoned on the ruler's orders for a year. His prominent, bulbous nose gave him a comical look, but the analytical Ghassan was one of the best the army had. Although there had been firefights in the area and many bodies had shown up on the northern edge of Mansour, the Sunni-Shia fault line, he believed they would get the area under control with enough U.S. and Iraqi troops. He said the key to success was his soldiers' behavior. "We have to treat the people well so we earn their respect. This is critical in order to gain their help," he said.

The depth of mutual suspicion in Mansour became evident a few blocks away, in Yarmouk, where U.S. troops were setting up a joint security station. As soldiers settled into a large mansion that had been the home of one of Saddam's closest cronies—and purportedly his procurer of prostitutes—neighborhood men in the traditional ankle-length cotton dishdashas stood around a car grumbling. They periodically looked up at soldiers sandbagging the rooftop parapet and setting up a machine gun at the corner. "They have come here to spy on us," the men said. "Our women cannot go out into their yards because they are looking at them." Another man said, "They are bringing in the Shia army and police to kill us." Capt. Jose Henderson, who was on duty inside the mansion, said they had not been attacked, but they were on guard. He knew the joint security station in Ghazaliya had been fired on and snipers had killed one soldier. The Iraqi soldiers tended a pot of boiling chai on the stove. The Iraqis outside who saw them as the enemy were very possibly members or supporters of the local insurgent cell. Cars rigged as bombs had been found nearby.

Distrust of the Iraqi police was even greater. A blue building behind two barricades was both the Mansour district headquarters and the local precinct. "They are *very* happy we are here," Smiley said with a laugh. The overwhelmingly Shia police force rarely left the building to patrol. Sitting in his office, the district police chief, who was the third one in four months, admitted that in his district "the main issue is the killings. We do not know who is committing them."

On the rooftop of the police station, Smiley's operations officer, Maj. Jesse Pearson, peered over the wall into the courtyard of the building next door. Several pickup trucks with machine guns mounted in the beds and flashing lights on the top of the cabs were parked there. Pillboxes, or watchtowers, topped each corner. Men in bulletproof vests carrying rifles came and went. It was a virtual armed camp. The compound was the Iraqi Islamic Party, of which the Sunni vice president was the head. "Ten or twenty parliamentarians live here," Pearson said. He described a visit he and another officer had paid them some weeks before. The guards pointed their weapons at them as they approached. "Take it easy. We're not your enemies," Pearson told them. But the Americans did confiscate their PKC machine guns and left them with the AK-47s permitted under Iraqi law. Every politician had a militia or at least a security detail, so clashes with regular army units were a constant danger.

As the operation to clear Mansour wound down in mid-April, Townsend decided to join Smiley and his sister battalion in Ameriya for a final sweep of the neighborhood. A few more locations had been identified that he wanted searched. About half the targets turned out to be dry holes, Townsend said, even though they tried to verify the tips they received. At 4 a.m. the Strykers revved their engines and set out from Camp Liberty. They rolled down the airport road to Ameriya, to a house that might be serving as a first aid station for insurgents.

The soldiers entered the home through the front metal gate across the driveway and found an entire family sleeping on the floor in the front room. In another room several men were asleep on couches. It looked like they were squatters. In another room they found medical supplies in boxes and on shelves. A sign advertising a pharmacy stood in a corner. The man of the house said that relatives had shut down a pharmacy business in a Shia neighborhood and moved the supplies here. One of Townsend's sergeants patiently questioned the men, looking for inconsistencies in their explanations. He also used a device called a HIIDE (Handheld Interagency Identification Detection Equipment), which took pictures, fingerprints, and biometric scans of the men's retinas. The new units were being used to create a registry of military-age males in insurgent areas. The information was dumped into the database, called Biometric Automated Toolset (BAT), which other units could access. Four years into the war, the soldiers finally had the technology to compile a reliable population registry to prevent multiple interrogations and searches and mistaken identities, and to track those who were found to engage in violent activities.

As the soldiers searched the house and questioned the men, Townsend and his security detail walked down the street. In the early dawn, he asked his interpreter, a Tunisian American woman, to translate graffiti painted on a wall. First she translated it as a pro-American statement but then corrected herself. "It says, 'We'll be here long after the Americans are gone. God is great.'" The message seemed to warn residents who might be thinking about collaborating with the American troops. Al-Qaeda-affiliated insurgents had used this area to hide car bombs, and they had also imposed strict Islamic practices and dress codes. At the end of the block, as if to underscore the message, two dead bodies lay in the street next to a mound of stinking, rotting garbage. Both men's hands were bound, and one was blindfolded as well. Both had been shot in the head. The bodies were bloated, indicating they had been there for some time.

As the soldiers approached, Townsend reminded them to use a grappling hook. One soldier tossed the hook and dragged it toward him until it caught on the corpse's clothes. He tugged on the body until it moved. They had adopted this tactic to determine whether a body had been booby-trapped. The soldiers had grown accustomed to finding bombs planted in the most unusual places. They had seen bombs stuffed in animals and corpses, and hung from trees and overpasses to be detonated as soldiers drove by in Strykers. Townsend went back into the house. The family was huddled in blankets, watching. The man told him he did not know the bodies were there, which Townsend found very strange. "How is it you have dead bodies outside your house and you don't even know it?" He urged them to report anything they saw. There were many unanswered questions about the bodies, the residents, and the medical supplies, but there were no grounds for detaining anyone. Townsend was not satisfied, but after searching a couple of homes on the block and questioning residents, the soldiers in the Strykers moved on.

When the Mansour clearing operation concluded, Townsend tallied the tangible results. Over thirty-six days, three insurgents had been killed in battle, forty-two had been detained, and two kidnap victims had been rescued. They had unearthed ninety-two weapons caches, destroyed 356 small arms, mortars, and rocket-propelled grenades, 147 explosive munitions, three car bombs, two suicide vests, and 143 completed or partial roadside bombs. They had blown up three abandoned houses where homemade explosives were being made and raided another home with thousands of electronic components for making roadside bombs.

Townsend did not claim to have achieved a sweeping or lasting success with one operation. The success of the plan depended on intelligence, which required local cooperation, and on sufficient forces to stay behind. The Baghdad security plan was still in its early days. "The Iraqi security forces were not even entering Ameriya thirty-six days ago," he said. The intangible results were, for Townsend and Smiley, far more important. "What is most important is that Iraqis see that we are out there with them and that we are working side by side with the Iraqi army and police," said Townsend. Inducing the army and police to start working together was one of their main goals. Smiley was concerned about Americans' impatience. "If they just give us time to keep doing what we're doing, we'll get the Iraqis over the hump," he said.

Just as the operation wound down, the news leaked from Washington that all units' tours would be extended to fifteen months. Soldiers' morale plummeted. They grumbled to total strangers, and sergeants expressed disgust at Iraqis' inability to get their act together. But the surge could not be sustained without lengthening the tours, and Defense Secretary Robert Gates had faced that fact. At a makeshift gazebo outside their drab brigade headquarters at Camp Liberty, Smiley held a hail and farewell for some of the contractors who kept their high-tech Strykers running and for new augmentees who were arriving. Except for those bound for the sergeant major academy, they had all been "stop-lossed"—prevented from leaving the unit for school, retirement, or other positions—for the duration of the tour. Nonalcoholic beer was in abundant supply (General Order 1 prohibited troops' consumption of alcohol in Iraq), and a ceremonial hookah was brought out and filled with Coca-Cola to initiate the newcomers to the "Tomahawks" battalion. A couple of soldiers gave funny speeches, and Smiley presented coins and ribbed a few of his men with jokes. He had just returned from leave, so he gave them a status report on wounded comrades he had visited at Walter Reed Army Medical Center in

Washington. The party was intended to boost spirits a bit. Knowing the Strykers were in such demand, Smiley had prepared his troops for a likely extension of their tour months before.

FOR THE GENERALS IN CHARGE of implementing the Baghdad security plan, every day brought a new headache. Chronic problems plagued the manning of the Iraqi side of the effort because the Iraqi security forces were still struggling to create new units to reach the size needed to secure the country. Nine additional Iraqi battalions had gone to Baghdad for the surge as promised, but they were scheduled to rotate out in ninety days. The nine battalions of additional troops were on loan from other regions, and their commanders wanted them back. Their departure was postponed, and Brig. Gen. Campbell urged the Iraqi generals to ensure that replacements would arrive before they released the current units. Some units were not fully manned, even allowing for the fact that 25 percent of the unit was allowed to be on leave at any one time. The first units had shown up with 40 percent missing, but that had gradually improved to about 30 percent. Campbell carried around a binder with encyclopedic information on each Iraqi army unit's readiness, including the numbers of soldiers present for duty. The U.S. military advisory teams embedded with each Iraqi unit provided him with updated information each day. One day he warned against the Iraqis' plan to send into combat a unit that was rated at the lowest level of readiness. The various Iraqi commanders bickered among themselves and competed for each new battalion that came off the production line. There simply were not enough to go around.

The commanders eventually arrived at a solution: to create the 11th Division, whose three brigades would be permanently assigned to Baghdad. One brigade was created out of new and existing units, the second was to be created by January 2008, and the third by spring 2008. The formal assessment was that Baghdad needed forty-two thousand Iraqi troops to secure it. In the meantime, even though the capital city had one-quarter of Iraq's population and had been formally designated the main effort, it would have to struggle for manpower. At Campbell's suggestion, Iraqi Lt. Gen. Abboud agreed to push back against a competing plan to move some troops from Baghdad to Basra, where rival Shia militias were battling each other as British troops prepared to pull back from the city to an overwatch position in the air station just to the north.

Every day brought new and strange problems. One of the trickiest was the prime minister's decision to put the Karrada peninsula, the heavily Shia area in downtown Baghdad, under the control of the presidential brigade. This five thousand–man brigade was composed primarily of a force of Kurdish *pesh merga* militiamen who had fought Saddam for years and were President Jalal Talabani's personal security guards. It also included members of the former Shia Badr Corps. Talabani had loaned some forces to guard a house of the prime minister, as he had the Sunni vice president's in Mansour. Maliki was eager to have forces directly under his control, but taking charge of Karrada would usurp the military's role and invite the possibility of inadvertent clashes between the two forces. Lt. Gen. Abboud said they had just received the government's written proposal and suggested they hold a meeting with Maliki to discuss alternatives. "You need to do it quickly," Campbell said. "I just learned that the prime minister's order is coming out in two days. This is already happening. They are already on the bridges. If you don't work this out, you are going to have fratricide."

Campbell frequently clashed with Gen. Riyadh over the big problem on the east side of Baghdad—the violence that emanated from Sadr City and New Baghdad, the principal sanctuaries of the JAM militia and especially its aggressive "special groups." The special groups were the most extreme elements of the militia and the ones responsible for the deadliest Shia violence against American forces. They were the ones who fired EFPs, which were killing the most U.S. soldiers on the east side. The EFPs contained a precisely milled concave copper disk that when fired turned into a molten slug of metal that could penetrate the most heavily armored U.S. military vehicles, including tanks and Bradley Fighting Vehicles. The U.S. military claimed that these disks were made in Iran and that the special groups were receiving training on their use in Iran. The JAM fighters also launched rockets, mortars, and rocket-propelled grenades from Sadr City into other areas of Baghdad, including the Green Zone on the other side of the Tigris.

At one of the weekly meetings of the Baghdad Operations Command, Riyadh was absent, so Campbell turned to Riyadh's deputy and said, "Abdul Karim, we are not getting HUMINT [human intelligence] on JAM and the special groups in New Baghdad and Sadr City, and we need that. You know how I feel about this. I need your help." He showed a slide with a map of all the locations where EFPs had been fired in the past week. "We are getting no intelligence from the Iraqi forces on EFPs," Campbell said, not letting up. He asked that it be made the main agenda item for the next day's meeting of the eastside Rusafa command. Campbell also noted that JAM was active in Kadhimiya on the west side, where Iraqi troops had stopped an ambulance and found that it was carrying a brand-new 107 mm rocket manufactured in Iran. Hospital employees, Sadr loyalists, were transporting it. Lt. Gen. Abboud then said he had ordered that all ambulances be inspected and had requested a meeting with the Ministry of Health to discuss steps to prevent ambulances from being used to transport arms.

Sunni insurgents were also conducting their share of mayhem: they had managed to blow up several bridges, despite the eleven Backscatter X-ray machines the United States had installed at their ramps.

The business of war was often enervating. Col. Stu Pollock, the American adviser to Maj. Gen. Abdul Ameer, sat through so many fractious meetings that every day seemed like the movie *Groundhog Day*. Significant decisions took weeks or even months. He had one of the better advisory jobs and knew it, since Maj. Gen. Abdul Ameer was smart and aggressive. Pollock had tried to encourage his best tendencies and rein in aspects that were less helpful. He knew the goal was to influence the general gradually over time. These daily meetings were the main avenue through which the Americans sought to professionalize and shape the Iraqi armed forces and, through them, the government.

In addition to the turgid, endless debating and dithering, there was a bombast to many of the Iraqi officers' presentation that no doubt derived from decades of speechifying to a dictator. One American general mimicked the rhetoric in a robotic voice. "'I say to you we will slay the enemies of our country. We have defeated the terrorists—Al-Qaeda is 75 percent defeated.' We say, 'Where did you get that from?' Of course, he doesn't know, but it sounded good. I mean, they almost make this stuff up," he said, noting the penchant for hyperbole.

Campbell kept going day after day like a bulldog. He did not win every argument, by any means. Even when they did not agree with him, the Iraqis respected his commitment and his down-to-earth manner. They knew he would be right back there with them the next day, trying to push the Baghdad plan forward one step at a time. "In his nine-word Arabic vocabulary, he manages to get the Iraqi commanders on board. They are terrified of letting him down," remarked one of Campbell's officers. "At the end of the day, they realize he cares more about Iraq's security than the Iraqi government does."

The clearing operations were deemed the essential preliminary before the control phase could begin. The goal was to remove enough enemy forces to permit U.S. troops to settle into their neighborhood outposts. In April, Townsend's and Smiley's Strykers rolled into southern Baghdad, the Rashid security district, for clearing operations with the Iraqis and the U.S. 4th Brigade, 1st Infantry Division, which was based there. This area included Dora, one of the toughest neighborhoods in Baghdad. The violelnce continued for the rest of the summer, and the 4th Brigade would lose a lot of men. Al-Qaeda had dug into the Sunni neighborhood, supported by several ratlines they used to move supplies and fighters into and out of the south.

The job was far from done in Rashid, but Odierno ordered the Strykers north to Diyala to reinforce the fight there against Al-Qaeda in Iraq and Iranian-supplied Shia militias. One of Townsend's battalions had been sent earlier to help the unit assigned to Baquba, the capital of Diyala province. The original plan had been to turn the province over to Iraqi control in 2007, but the place had gone to hell in a handbasket when the Al-Qaeda-linked Sunni insurgents rousted from Ramadi showed up in Baquba. Diyala was a mixed province and had been the scene of sectarian atrocities committed by both Sunnis and Shia, so it was a tinderbox waiting to be relit. On June 19, Smiley's battalion drove to Diyala under cover of night and began clearing operations at 3 in the morning. Gen. Odierno flew in to inaugurate Operation Phantom Thunder. Acknowledging the effect of advance publicity, the general said that 70 percent of the leadership targets had fled Baquba. Smiley was philosophical: the intent was to secure the population. They could pick off the estimated three hundred targets if they returned to fight. "The enemy can always move," he said.

The Diyala operation proved the costliest yet for Smiley's unit. He lost four men when insurgents detonated a house full of homemade explosives. Smiley's battalion had adopted dismounted tactics, patrolling on foot to defeat the bombs aimed at their vehicles, but they had not been prepared for this latest cruel invention, the house bomb. In the unit's twelfth month of fighting, the loss hit the soldiers hard. But they pressed on and in thirty days had taken control of western Baquba and set up combat outposts. Their sister unit, 5th Battalion, 20th Infantry, was assigned to the eastern side. After sixty days, they had persuaded the Diyala provincial police chief to start hiring Sunnis. The Shia-dominated provincial government had been playing sectarian politics with public services, but the provincial reconstruction team pushed ahead with joint projects to fix the water and electrical lines and institute trash collection. The local Iraqi army commander remarked to Smiley one day, "Look at the colors coming out, like spring." Women were dressing in colorful clothes again, and men were smoking. For the moment, at least, Diyala was calm again.

6

The Political Puzzle

As a humorous reminder that he had accepted the most difficult job on offer, Gen. David Petraeus kept a copy of the London-based Arab newspaper *Asharq Al-Awsat* on the table behind his desk at the palace downtown. Shortly after he was nominated for the job, the paper had published a cartoon that depicted Iraq as a menacing Goliath looming over a small, slightly stooped David. If the task of dampening the violence and providing security to the population was difficult, it was dwarfed by the challenge of bringing about political reconciliation among Iraq's warring factions. Over thirty thousand Iraqis had been killed in 2006. The magnitude of that bloodletting made peace a distant prospect. The basic theory of the surge as put forth by the White House was that population security would provide Iraqi leaders the breathing room to work out their differences, but the Petraeus-Crocker team did not have the luxury of proceeding sequentially. They had to try to make headway on both fronts simultaneously.

Petraeus knew, as he had said in his January testimony, that the real endgame for the Iraq war was a political solution. That meant delving into the intricacies of Iraq's religious, ethnic, and personalistic factions, much as he had done in Ninewa in 2003–2004, to see what kind of levers of persuasion and influence might be effective in bringing them together. The Joint Strategic Assessment Team's study had concluded that Iraq was now locked in a communal conflict, or low-grade civil war, which meant that the government that was the United States' ally was also a party to the conflict. That put Petraeus and Ambassador Ryan Crocker in the delicate position of both supporting and browbeating their Iraqi partner. Since the United States had been instrumental in bringing these Iraqi political factions and individual leaders into power, it would have to deal with them no matter what their flaws.

Iraqi politicians were locked in a power struggle in which they feared to trust each other and feared for their very lives. Iraqi leaders spent most of their time in the Green Zone, protected by American troops and private security guards, when they were not traveling abroad. Two weeks after Petraeus's arrival, the existential threat the Iraqi leaders lived under was driven home by a bomb that narrowly missed assassinating the Shiite vice president, Adil Abd al-Mahdi, who was considered one of the most moderate, educated Shia politicians. He had lost a bid to become prime minister in 2006 by one vote to Nouri al-Maliki and had been a contender for the transitional prime ministership in 2005. Minutes after Mahdi stepped away from the podium at a municipal building in Mansour, in western Baghdad, where he was speaking to public works employees, a bomb exploded in the room. His bodyguards leaped on top of him to shield him with their bodies. He was not killed, and recovered enough to visit President Bush the following month in the White House, but he still had shrapnel in his foot.

Petraeus and his staff spent a lot of time trying to keep the leaders alive and to calm their ever-frayed nerves. The Sunni vice president, Tariq al-Hashimi, wrote a letter to Petraeus almost daily to express a complaint, demand, or fear. Hashimi's Iraqi Islamic Party (IIP) was one of three members of the Iraqi Accordance Front (or Tawafuq), which had won forty-four seats in the Iraqi parliament—the most of any

Sunni bloc—so in the torturous negotiations brokered by Zalmay Khalilzad to form the new government Tawafuq had received the second vice presidency and six ministries. But participation in the Shia-led, U.S.-backed Iraqi government had placed Hashimi and Tawafuq squarely in the crosshairs of the Sunni insurgents for what they regarded as traitorous collaboration. At the same time, Tawafuq was targeted by the Jaish al-Mahdi (JAM) Shia extremists. Many Shia believed it had at least one foot in the insurgency against the government. Making matters even more complicated was that the Islamist Tawafuq did not enjoy the support of secular Sunnis.

Hashimi, a small, white-bearded man with dark circles under his eyes, had all these reasons to be paranoid. He had paid a high personal price for agreeing to be part of the Maliki government: three of his four siblings had been murdered in targeted killings in 2006. His brother Mahmoud was shot while driving on April 13. Two weeks later, just as the new government was formed, his sister Mayson was killed by gunmen as she backed her SUV out of her garage—the day after Hashimi publicly called for the Al-Qaeda insurgents to be crushed. Abu Musab al-Zarqawi, the Al-Qaeda leader in Iraq, had released a videotape that exhorted Sunnis to fight the new government and called those who cooperated with it "agents" of the Americans. At a news conference with President Jalal Talabani and Mahdi, Hashimi had retorted: "We are agents, agents for Islam, for the oppressed. We have to defend the future of our people." The three had just met with Condoleezza Rice and Donald Rumsfeld, who had made an unusual joint visit to Iraq at President Bush's request to meet the new government leaders. The next day Hashimi was scheduled to go with Mahdi to meet with Iraq's senior Shiite cleric, the Grand Ayatollah Ali al-Sistani. In October, Hashimi's brother Amir's home in northern Baghdad was broken into and he was killed.

The attacks continued in 2007. The Mansour home of his fellow Tawafuq leader, Adnan al-Dulaimi, was attacked in the spring, and a garbage truck full of explosives blew up at the IIP's television station, killing the deputy director and wounding a dozen others. Hashimi called Sadi Othman, Petraeus's cultural adviser and de facto liaison to the Iraqi leaders, in a panic. Hashimi believed the party headquarters would be attacked and wanted the Americans to do something about it. A dozen IIP legislators and officials lived there because it was more secure than their own homes.

Othman called the Multi-National Force-Iraq (MNF-I) duty officer for operations and reported Hashimi's plea for help. He also informed them that President Talabani had dispatched some of his presidential guard to protect them. The duty officer relayed this to the MNF-I Deputy Chief of Staff for Strategic Operations, Maj. Gen. David Fastabend, who sighed and picked up the phone. "Sadi, tell him they have got to coordinate this with the BOC," the Baghdad Operations Command. Talabani's five thousand–strong presidential guard was probably the most benign of the various armed groups running around Iraq, but it was not under the formal Iraqi military chain of command. The Baghdad security plan clearing operations were under way in the area, so there was a good chance of inadvertent fratricide if the Iraqi army command was not alerted that a few hundred guards were moving into the IIP.

There was one bright spot in the fraught relationships of Iraq's top leaders. Talabani, his fellow Kurdish deputy prime minister, Barham Salih, and foreign minister Hoshyar Zebari were the closest thing to true statesmen Iraq possessed. It was supremely ironic that these Kurdish politicians, formally pledged to a separate state, worked the hardest to pull together the fractious government. Although they certainly looked out for Kurdish interests, these men were also willing and able to horse-trade and make compromises for the greater common good. No Kurd in his heart wanted to be part of Arab Iraq; Kurds had long sought their own state. But these three leaders recognized that to pursue statehood invited certain war with Turkey, because an independent Kurdistan would ignite the irredentist movement in Turkey's own substantial Kurdish population. That left Kurdish leaders with the violent, fractious mess of Iraq as their people's life raft for the present and foreseeable future. The only way they could secure their own interests was to induce the Arab Sunni and Arab Shia to stop fighting. The Kurds had been subjected to genocidal repression under Saddam Hussein's regime, but most Kurds were Sunni Muslims, which provided a common cultural link to Arab Sunnis. The Kurds also had strong interests in common with the Shia: they both wanted to maximize control over oil in their regions and maximize their autonomy through a strong federal system with a weak central government.

Talabani's lifelong rival and the head of the Kurdish Democratic Party, Masoud Barzani, was president of the Kurdistan Regional Government, which had been formed from the three Kurdish provinces. Barzani pushed Kurdish parochial interests like the old-time warlord he was, but when Talabani had his statesman hat on, the ailing seventy-three-year-old president strove to stitch the fraying seams of Iraq back together. The portly, mustachioed Talabani was a wily old pol. One favorite tactic was what his chief of staff, Kamran Karadaghi, called Talabani's "lunch policy": he would invite the various feuding officials for lunch or dinner, without telling either that the other was invited, and then maneuver them into the same room to talk. On occasion Talabani would actually use his enormous bulk to wedge the men into a corner. This was particularly necessary in the case of Prime Minister Maliki and Vice President Hashimi, who could not stand each other. Their mutual antipathy was so deep that a simple conversation was difficult. Hashimi and Mahdi, on the other hand, got along well personally, but their two parties' positions were deeply divided. The perennial problem, in Hashimi's view, was that the Shia-led government had made no concessions to the Sunni but used his participation to claim it was a national unity government. It became increasingly difficult for him to justify his continued presence to his constituency.

SHIA POLITICS WERE THE MOST complicated of any Iraqi group's. The basic dynamic was a three-way power struggle between the best-organized Islamic Supreme Council of Iraq (ISCI), Muqtada al-Sadr's movement, and the Islamic Dawa Party. ISCI had won the most seats in parliament—thirty-six, compared with Sadr's twenty-nine and Dawa's twenty-five—and eleven governorships. Vice President Adil Abd al-Mahdi represented ISCI. But he was only one of several significant players in the party, which was founded in Iran in 1982 by Muhammed Bakr al-Hakim, with support from Iran. Bakr was killed in 2003 shortly after returning to Iraq from Iran, in one of the war's fateful early assassinations. Abdul Aziz, the lesser known brother, took his place but was suffering from lung cancer. Abdul Aziz's son Ammar, age thirty-six, was the heir apparent, but Hadi al-Ameri, the head of the Badr Corps, the party's militia that the Iranian Revolutionary Guard had formed, trained, and armed, was also a competitor who had recast the militia as a political force. Mahdi, who had been educated at the Jesuit Baghdad College, left Iraq in 1969 for France, where he edited magazines.

Upon his return to Iraq, Mahdi had become close friends with Meghan O'Sullivan, the deputy national security adviser for Iraq and Afghanistan, when she came to Iraq in May 2003 as a member of the Coalition Provisional Authority's governance team. Ryan Crocker assigned her as the liaison to Hakim's party, since the Americans had no standing contacts with the group, unlike with the other London-based exiles. O'Sullivan came to know Mahdi's family and developed a close relationship with him. O'Sullivan had not started out as an Iraq expert, but she was one of several smart, aggressive women who rose through the White House bureaucracy to wield a great deal of clout. In Iraq she worked on the elections and the constitution and then from her National Security Council perch had coordinated—and, some of her critics alleged, micromanaged—policy execution in Iraq. After four years of working long hours, she announced her intention to leave the administration in early 2007 but was then persuaded to stay on.

In O'Sullivan's view Mahdi was the Shia intellectual who was most willing to bargain with the other parties, but ISCI was the closest to Iran of all the Shia parties. It also proposed a super region created from the nine Shia-dominated provinces in the south, which, if implemented, would very likely tear Iraq apart. The 2005 constitution permitted the formation of powerful regions, but any implementation was postponed until 2008 through Khalilzad's intervention to head off another conflict with the Sunni, who adamantly opposed a regionalism that left them a few provinces that lacked oil resources.

The intense intra-Shia competition within the Islamist parties of the ruling coalition, the United Iraqi Alliance (UIA), centered on a very personal rivalry between ISCI's Hakim family and Muqtada al-Sadr. Hakim represented the upper-class Shia and had largely lived in Iran after most of his relatives were killed. Sadr was an upstart cleric who had stayed in Iraq and rallied support among lower-class Shia. From the spring of 2003 it was clear that Sadr intended to challenge the more established Shia clerics and parties by trading on his own clerical lineage. His father, the Ayatollah Mohammed Sadiq al-Sadr, had rallied poor Shiites to oppose Saddam's rule and was executed in 1999 along with Muqtada's two brothers. This legacy gave Muqtada a base among the Shiite poor, although his movement was less organized than Hakim's party and militia, which had been around for a quarter century. In the parliamentary maneuvering after the 2005 elections, Sadr threw his support to Islamic Dawa to deny ISCI the prime ministership in the 2005 transitional government and again in 2006.

When Maliki became prime minister, he was a virtually unknown commodity. He had served as deputy of the de-Baathification commission with Ahmed Chalabi, the secular Shia exile politician who was the darling of the American neoconservatives. Maliki had lived most of his years in exile in Syria. There he had helped run the Dawa underground guerrilla movement, which, among other things, plotted many assassination attempts of Saddam and his senior officials. Along with other Dawa members Maliki had been sentenced to death in absentia by Saddam's regime in 1980. Americans hoped he would prove to be a more efficient leader than Jaafari, and indeed he was blunter and more decisive, but also secretive and easily swayed by the conspiratorial whisperings of his closest advisers.

Shia leaders were resolved not to repeat the mistakes of the 1920s, when the Shia's rejectionist stance led the British to empower the Sunni minority and set the stage for seventy years of marginalization and oppression. As soon as the bombs stopped falling in April 2003, Dawa and especially ISCI (then known as SCIRI) had aggressively moved into southern Iraq to begin organizing, recruiting members, and demonstrating. ISCI and Badr Corps streamed across every border crossing from their home in exile in Iran. In the city of Kut, they took over the city hall in April 2003 and barricaded themselves inside. They staged street demonstrations calling for a religious government and denouncing Ahmed Chalabi, then rumored to be the Americans' choice to lead Iraq. The Shia Islamist parties supported Islamic rule to varying degrees, but the parties had different and evolving positions. Dawa had traditionally favored Islamic-influenced civilian (*umma*) rule, while ISCI had favored rule by clerics (*ulema*) along the lines of the Iranian model. This intra-Shia power struggle had no certain winner.

IF THERE WAS ONE DIPLOMAT capable of navigating Iraq's complexities, it was Ryan Crocker, sworn in as Khalilzad's replacement on March 29, 2007. A shrewd, slightly built veteran of the State Department's Near East bureau, he was fluent in Arabic and was the type of muddy-boots diplomat who preferred to be abroad rather than at the State Department headquarters in Washington's Foggy Bottom neighborhood. He had spent his entire career in the region and had been named ambassador five times—to Lebanon, Kuwait, Syria, Pakistan, and now Iraq. He was in the region continuously from 1990 to 2001, when he was dragged back to Washington for a tour as the deputy assistant secretary of state. He opened the embassy in Afghanistan after the 2001 invasion that toppled the Taliban and was posted to Pakistan from 2004 to 2007. After being named ambassador to Iraq, Crocker recognized the urgency of the situation and flew directly to Baghdad. Instead of being sworn in by Secretary of State Rice in the ornate Benjamin Franklin room at main State, Crocker asked a young foreign-service officer, Tina Tran, to administer the oath, to salute the new crop of diplomats who had joined the service after 9/11. Tran had followed him from Pakistan and to Iraq.

Crocker had met his wife, Christine, on his first tour in Baghdad in 1979, and they had both lived through the dark days of the 1983 Beirut embassy bombing and had watched as Lebanon was torn apart in a brutal civil war. That searing experience, which included the Israeli invasion of Lebanon in 1982, informed the silver-haired diplomat's perspective as he arrived to take up his post alongside Petraeus. Far less fanfare had greeted his nomination, confirmation, and arrival than had accompanied the general's, but Crocker was formally in charge of the most important and difficult part of the assignment—the search for political reconciliation—even if, as military commander, Petraeus wielded the most potent sticks and carrots. Petraeus was determined that they would operate on the principle of "one team, one mission," as he put it. Echoing his sentiment, Crocker pledged in his remarks at the swearing-in ceremony to aim for "unity of effort" with the military.

U.S. civilian-military relations had been fractious since the war began in 2003. It was worst under Paul Bremer and Lt. Gen. Ricardo Sanchez, but there were institutional and political reasons for the hostility. It was hard for the State Department not to feel like the tail of the Pentagon dog in a country dominated by some 170,000 U.S. troops and a massive military infrastructure. The U.S. military had a budget and manpower that dwarfed any other U.S. agency by several orders of magnitude. Many foreign-service officers felt that their diplomatic expertise had been shunned by the administration and by Rumsfeld's Pentagon in particular, and that they were now being tasked to pick up the pieces of a war that had gone awry. For their part, uniformed officials frequently commented that they were carrying the full load of the country's decision to go to war.

Crocker, the son of an air force officer, had no antimilitary prejudices, and he kept his feelings about the wisdom of the war from interfering with the mission at hand. He was as confident and decisive as Petraeus, although his style was low-key. There was no way to get around the fact that the military was an eight hundred–pound gorilla, compounded by the fact that Petraeus was a high-profile and outspoken general. But Petraeus had said in his confirmation hearings that Iraq needed a political solution, which in turn called for diplomatic expertise. His tenure would be judged on whether the military and political efforts could at last be united. As it happened, the two men hit it off. Both were avid runners and would go for five-mile runs together whenever their schedules meshed. Soon after his arrival, Crocker called for the entire embassy staff to join the troops on a ten-kilometer run. The two men made a point of coordinating their work schedules, even if it required extra helicopter trips. They also established a habit of meeting jointly with the prime minister so they would be fully aware of his responses and could broadcast their unity to the Iraqi government.

In their meetings with Maliki, the two men would take turns sitting next to him. When Crocker finished presenting his agenda to the prime minister, he would switch places with Petraeus. They developed something of a "good cop, bad cop" routine. Crocker admitted that he played this card, telling Maliki or other Iraqi leaders that "if you don't agree to do this, you're going to have to deal with him," jerking his thumb in Petraeus's direction. Whereas Crocker was the model diplomat with a perpetually modulated voice, Petraeus had a sharper temperament that could turn fiery. Petraeus also confessed that he simulated anger on occasion, when he felt it would make his point more persuasively.

Crocker knew the key Iraqi politicians, but even more important, he had a deep grasp of the country's history and the psychological scars that had made it so hard to bring peace to Iraq. The western notion of compromise was simply not palatable, or even rational, to a group of men who had spent thirty-five years—their entire adult lives—as conspirators, guerrillas, and insurgents, trying to topple a dictator while staying alive. "The prime minister's party suffered enormously at the hands of the regime. Dawa went underground and survived by trusting no one," Crocker said. "Look at the prominent Sunni party, the IIP, exactly the same thing. It suffered horribly at the hands of Saddam. They all lived secretly and stayed alive by trusting no one. What might seem to us a no-brain kind of compromise does not look that way to them. There is this pervasive fear that the Baath will be back. There is a Baathi behind every lamppost."

The paranoia was so strong that Talabani's "lunch policy" aroused Dawa officials' suspicions whenever a meeting did *not* include them. They believed the other parties were plotting a parliamentary coup to depose them. Trusting the United States did not come naturally either. The U.S. government had called on Iraqis to overthrow Saddam in 1991 after the Gulf war and then stood by as he crushed a massive uprising that had taken over most provincial cities—and killed more than ten thousand Iraqis. The Kurds went through the same experience again a few years later when the CIA encouraged a coup attempt, then turned its back. And during the 1980s, when the United States had supported Saddam's regime against Iran, it designated Dawa a terrorist group.

The mounting violence stoked these lifelong conspirators' fears and suspicions like gasoline on a fire. Crocker was with Maliki in his office on April 28, 2007, when they received word that a car bomb had exploded near the sacred Imam Hussein shrine in Karbala. The prime minister was beside himself as he watched Iraqi television broadcast scenes of hundreds of people screaming and crying, searching for their dead or wounded relatives. A child, one of six killed, lay on a stretcher. People beat their chests in grief and set two ambulances on fire. Fifty-six Iraqis were killed and seventy wounded. The next day, angry mobs stoned the office of the Karbala governor, demanding his resignation, and then set the building on fire. The furious Shia rampage could easily spread all over the country. Reconciling with Sunnis was the furthest thing from Maliki's mind that day.

The country teetered on the brink of all-out, irreversible war. Crocker had seen countries at the breaking point before. Sunni insurgents had unleashed their deadliest string of car bombings of the entire war. Sixteen car bombs were detonated in April, killing many hundreds of Iraqis in crowded markets. Karbala had been bombed two weeks earlier in almost the same spot; 47 were killed and 224 wounded. The insurgents were obviously determined to destroy one of the Karbala shrines or the one in Najaf, which would have an impact far beyond the bombing of the Shia mosque in Samarra because these latter sites represented the very heart of Shiism. If they were hit, the country would literally come apart. "In a sense we are one car bomb away from utter devastation," Crocker said. "There's a limit beyond which society just begins to come unglued. There is no way that all car bombs can be stopped, but we've got to do everything we can to keep them from hitting a target of cataclysmic proportions."

The ambassador realized that his effectiveness in such a febrile situation depended first of all on Iraqis' willingness to listen to him. He had to be seen as open to their views. "I don't think it works for me to say, 'This is what we need, do it, dammit,'" he said during this time. Since arriving, he had tried to gain the confidence of the various factions and convince them that "wherever the knives are coming from, I don't have any in my hand." He tried to establish himself as a neutral party, but he honestly did not know if he could make a difference.

Crocker's only certainty was the solid partnership he had formed with Petraeus. "Lord knows where this is going, but Petraeus and I are committed to getting there together, wherever it is," he said. A new embassy was being built a short distance away on the Tigris River. Crocker had already given orders, much to the builder's chagrin, to change the construction plans to replicate the joined suites of offices he and Petraeus had in the Republican Guard palace so they could maintain their close coordination and frequent face-to-face conversations. That way it was much easier for them to go visit the prime minister together at a moment's notice. Like Petraeus, the ambassador made a point of visiting Baghdad neighborhoods and other parts of the country. "Palacitis is not a disease I wish to contract," he said drolly, as if his career gave any indication that he was prone to staying indoors where it was safe. He found ordinary Iraqis surprisingly outspoken, and he listened. He heard how bad their lives were, how the only medical care some of them received was from U.S. medics, since all the Iraqi doctors had fled the country. It was Lebanon all over again.

Petraeus and Crocker would tag-team issues that required their joint involvement, but the formal division of labor was that Petraeus took the lead on security issues and Crocker pushed forward on the political and economic portfolio. In fact, however, Petraeus liked to get involved in everything, and the reality was that the toughest security issues were intrinsically political. Furthermore, Iraqis were constantly seeking meetings with Petraeus, as the man with the guns under his command. "I try to get everyone to meet in a group as much as possible, but everyone wants a secret, private meeting," he observed.

Petraeus assured Maliki that U.S. forces were aggressively going after Al-Qaeda, which aimed to fracture Iraq with its car-bomb campaign and set up an Islamic state in its remains. But he made an early pitch for Maliki to reach out to Sunnis. In one of his first meetings with Prime Minister Maliki, Petraeus suggested that Maliki pay a visit to Ramadi, the capital of Anbar province, where Sunni tribal sheikhs had joined with American troops to fight Al-Qaeda in Iraq (AQI), which had declared Ramadi its de facto capital.

Maliki had never been to Anbar and was not eager to go. Petraeus pointedly noted that he had visited Iran but not several provinces of the country he governed. "This will show them that you are the leader of all Iraqis," Petraeus said.

On March 13 Maliki flew with Petraeus in his Black Hawk helicopter to Ramadi. When they landed at Camp Blue Diamond, Petraeus exited on one side of the helicopter while Maliki and his entourage climbed out the other side to be photographed and filmed by the press. Petraeus toured the city, visited troops, and inspected infrastructure. Maliki opted to stay at the base, where he met with dozens of sheikhs who had traveled from every corner of Anbar. Sheikh Abdul Sattar Bezia al-Rishawi, the Ramadi chieftain who was the founder of the Anbar Awakening, as his movement had come to be called, urged the prime minister to permit provincial elections in Anbar at the earliest possible date. Most Sunnis had boycotted the January 2005 provincial election either as a protest or because they were intimidated by the violence. Maliki agreed elections were needed.

Maliki chafed at criticism that he was not doing enough. The constitution had established a weak central government and Iraq's armed forces were still weak. He and other top officials rightly complained about the inadequate equipping of the Iraqi forces. Four years into the war they had only three C-130s and no attack helicopters. The United States had supplied 2,700 armored Humvees of the planned 3,300, only half of the promised 1,200 personnel carriers, and 440 vehicles with V-shaped hulls for clearing mines and transporting troops. The Iraqis had decided to use the U.S. foreign military sales program to acquire materiel, but the American bureaucracy was proving to be excruciatingly slow. In frustration, President Talabani went to China and signed a deal to buy 150,000 AK-47 automatic rifles.

The Iraqis also complained that the Americans were holding out on their best technology: they frequently asked for the "special technical devices" the Americans had for defending against bombs. The Pentagon's counterbomb task force had not yet developed any silver bullets, even though it had equipped most of the American Humvees with Warlock jamming devices that were effective against some radio-controlled bombs. There were concerns that such technology, if shared, might well end up in the adversaries' hands. Iraq also finally started to spend more of its own substantial resources: in 2007, for the first time since the invasion, the country spent more on its own armed forces than the United States did. The budget included $4.1 billion for the defense ministry and $3.2 billion for the interior ministry.

DEVELOPING CAPABLE SECURITY FORCES was a long-term project, and the United States would need to keep at it to succeed. But the more urgent question was whether Maliki was determined to use the army and police to consolidate the Shia's hold on power and retaliate against Sunnis. Many U.S. officials in Iraq believed the answer was clearly yes. Petraeus had seen the classified reports on secret ministry of interior prisons that had been found in late 2005 with detained Iraqis—former regime members and Sunnis—bearing signs of torture. He was resolved to confront the issue of sectarianism head-on with Maliki.

Some of the most egregious abuses were occurring in Baghdad's hospitals. The Sadrist health minister had packed the ministry and hospitals with militia members. Sunnis were going in and not coming out. They were being either killed or kidnapped and held for ransom. Petraeus decided it was a good place to start and threw down the gauntlet to Maliki. U.S. and Iraqi troops arrested the deputy health minister and the head of his facilities protection service, who had been implicated in the abuses. Petraeus urged that they be charged and brought to trial. The health ministry was not the only ministry whose security force, dressed in uniforms similar to the police, staged brazen kidnappings. In May, such men kidnapped five British contractors working at the finance ministry.

Over the past year Lt. Gen. Marty Dempsey had worked to purge the sectarian National Police force. Eventually all of its brigade commanders were replaced. Dempsey had hoped that five of them would be prosecuted for their sectarian and criminal behavior, but he settled for what he could get. The entire rank and file of the National Police was purged and put through a new training program. Dempsey also instituted what he called a "quick look" assessment for the local police, conducted by

U.S. advisory teams, who were to recommend changes to the ministry. There were insufficient U.S. police advisers to embed with every police station, so the teams that did exist adopted a circuit rider approach to visit their assigned precincts.

Maliki had promised to allow targeting of Shia JAM forces who were violating the law. But any operations against Shia targets still usually provoked some degree of crisis, and that usually meant hours of phone calls to Maj. Gen. Dave Fastabend, the MNF-I deputy for strategic operations, and to Sadi Othman.

Fastabend had just returned from the dining hall one evening when his cell phone rang. His executive officer had sent him off to the mess hall for dinner, one of the few breaks in his hectic eighteen-hour days. Fastabend sat in his chair and listened to the frantic voice on the other end of the line with his usual bemused smile. "I will check it out and let you know," he said and then hung up. He called to his aide in the outer office. "The PM's office says that the Office of the Martyr Sadr in Karbala is under attack from coalition troops. Will you check with the CHOPS [chief of operations]?" In a few minutes the officer appeared in the doorway. No military operations were under way in Karbala. Fastabend called the prime minister's office and said there was no activity.

The next call was from Gen. Graeme Lamb. According to a new report, the attack was apparently occurring in Kadhimiya, the JAM-dominated Shia neighborhood in west Baghdad, not Karbala. The prime minister was highly agitated, the British general reported. Fastabend rang off and tracked down the details before calling back. "The troops took fire from the building and responded in kind," he reported. "But only the Iraqi army went into the building." The calls continued to come in. Iraqi civilian officials wanted a cordon around the building, the U.S. liaison officer reported. Fastabend told him to tell the Iraqi civilians that their advice was noted but that the commanders on the ground would make the tactical decisions.

After the standoff with JAM in Kadhimiya was resolved, Fastabend placed a video call with his computer to the MNF-I chief of staff at the Al Faw palace. The chief of staff's face did not appear on the screen. Instead, Mr. Potato Head appeared and asked Fastabend for the latest news. After a good laugh, the two men discussed the events of the day and then signed off for the night. It had been a typical day of crisis management, leavened by humor and camaraderie. As the man who signed the orders that lengthened troops' tours, Fastabend was keenly aware of the rising casualties and the increased burden soldiers were bearing.

Maliki's desire to command his military directly rather than through the military chain of command fueled many officers' concerns about his sectarian intentions. The Americans were trying to set up a depoliticized professional army on their own model, but personalistic control was the model that had been common in Iraq under Saddam and elsewhere in the Arab world. Maliki insisted that a military unit be placed under his direct command. The Americans agreed to a compromise: one brigade would be designated as an emergency reserve force. But this did not satisfy the prime minister. The Counter-Terrorism Bureau was set up to serve as his link to the Iraqi special operations forces, the most competent unit in the military. Special Forces advisers in the office worked to keep it from being turned to sectarian purposes.

Maliki also set up the Office of the Commander in Chief (OCINC), which would become the source of many headaches and great suspicion over the course of the year. Orders emanated from it that no one else knew about, and when the orders were discovered, the intent often appeared to be sectarian. The woman in charge of it, Bassima al-Jaidri, was not a military officer but people took to calling her General Bassima.

In the spring of 2007, a new National Police brigade was created to safeguard the Shia Al-Askari mosque in Samarra. The original roster of recruits submitted for the unit was roughly half Shia and half Sunni. OCINC then dismissed the brigade's Sunni commander, Lt. Gen. Adnan Thabit, and replaced the recruits with almost all Shia, including officers linked to Shia militiamen, even though Samarra's population is largely Sunni. Then, unbeknownst to the Americans or the Iraqi high command, the prime minister's OCINC issued a directive giving the brigade responsibility for guarding the main highway from Samarra to Baghdad. The U.S. military advisers working with the unit reported what had happened. Fastabend drafted some talking points for Petraeus, who, with Dempsey, went to the mat with Maliki, threatening to withhold aid and training for the unit. Maliki grudgingly reinstated the original commander and revamped the unit's composition and assignment.

OCINC also gave orders to Iraqi brigade or battalion commanders, bypassing their chain of command, to hit specific targets. Virtually all the target lists that emanated from the Iraqi government were Sunni; the Shiite militias were almost never included. Commanders were also changed on OCINC orders. Iraqis whom the Americans considered solid, impartial officers were sacked, including the one who had detained the health ministry security chief. Other commanders were removed and placed under investigation. One tactic to remove commanders was the use of "judicial warrants" produced by the OCINC, which had no basis in the Iraqi court system. Other military commanders who seemed inclined to take a sectarian approach to Iraq's security were appointed, promoted, or protected.

After a half-dozen Iraqi army battalion commanders were forced out in spring 2007, U.S. military officials decided to publicize the details in an attempt to push back against OCINC interference. The Americans raised the matter with Maliki on a case-by-case basis. For example, when seventy members of the Iraqi army were ordered purged in Tal Afar, based on a de-Baathification order from a defunct commission, Maliki reversed it after the Americans brought it to his attention. But the incidents continued. A commander from Karbala was arrested and was being investigated, and Sunni intelligence officers were fired. "If we have to go to the prime minister every time, obviously that's a problem," commented Petraeus aide Pete Mansoor.

One general believed that much of the sectarian intent of the Maliki government came from National Security Adviser Mowaffak al-Rubaie, whom he held responsible for the lynching atmosphere of Saddam's execution. He watched on many occasions while Rubaie told the Americans what they wanted to hear and then told Iraqis the exact opposite. The officer grew more troubled when U.S. armored cars provided for Rubaie's protection were reported as stolen and then turned up in the possession of Sadr's JAM militia. Rubaie had asked for additional vehicles, prompting an investigation into what had happened to the original ones. When confronted, he smugly said that Washington would never abandon the Shia government. The general was appalled at Rubaie's brazen attitude, but the Iraqi had correctly deduced that Washington would not hold him accountable.

Maliki's governing style was secretive and insular. He relied on Rubaie, Jaidri, and a handful of Dawa advisers and cut out other officials, even those responsible for the issue. When Maliki toured the Middle East in the spring, he did not bring his foreign minister. The pattern repeated itself on most political, economic, and security matters. The other Iraqi parties who were part of the cabinet were increasingly angered by this behavior. The national unity government was a sham.

At a cabinet meeting in late April, the tensions within the Iraqi government boiled over. "We are at a very grave, critical juncture and we need to do better," Barham Salih, deputy prime minister, told his colleagues. "We cannot pretend that we can continue as we are."

More than any other politician, Salih saw the urgency of the need to rise above the factional fighting that was pushing Iraq into ruin. The eloquent, clear-eyed technocrat was probably the closest to a Nelson Mandela figure, in terms of his vision and talent. He used the fact that he was Kurdish to reach out to Arab Sunnis and Shias. But, at forty-eight, he was junior to Talabani, his party's founder, and one rung below the other parties' senior leaders. Nonetheless, he had played a crucial role in brokering the one substantive agreement the cabinet had managed to reach, in February, on a draft framework law regulating the oil and gas industry. The key compromise gave a nationally appointed body the right to approve oil contracts signed by the regional governments, thus striking a balance between national and local power. But the bill had languished and not been voted on in parliament.

Salih was on the verge of despair by late spring. In a room upstairs in the large house he lived in on a tree-shaded road in the Green Zone, the father of two huffed and puffed on a treadmill while he watched the television news. A bomb had just gone off in Bayaa, a couple of miles away across the airport road. He had heard the boom. In a few minutes the Al-Iraqiya television network was broadcasting a view of the skyline filled with a black plume of smoke. The Green Zone had lately come under increasingly accurate mortar attacks, launched from Sadr City across the river. Although much of Sadr's militia had disappeared from the streets, rogue elements had continued to fight. They either had a spotter inside the Green Zone to direct the fire, or they had new and more accurate rockets, or both. That week the latrine trailer was blown up at LZ Washington, the landing zone helicopter pad next to the Republican Palace that Petraeus, and every other important visitor to the Green Zone, used every day.

Salih's fellow Kurd and longtime friend, environment minister Narmin Othman, sat on one of the couches by the treadmill. The room served as Salih's office and general headquarters. Papers were stacked on chairs and coffee tables. Between calls on Salih's constantly ringing phones, they discussed the deadlock in the cabinet. Othman had been a *pesh merga* fighter in her youth and was a veteran politician. The violence prevented her from going to her downtown office many days. She had just launched a citizens' movement to protest the endless cycle of violence. It was called Bas, which was Kurdish for "enough." The only place they had outdoor rallies was in the Kurdish north, where it was much safer. They planned to conduct their campaign through the media, since suicide and car bombers were likely to attack any public gatherings.

Salih had left Iraq in 1979 and received a degree in statistics and a doctorate in engineering in England. He had been the spokesman for his party, the Patriotic Union of Kurdistan, in London and later Washington, before returning to northern Iraq in 2001 to serve as prime minister of the autonomous Kurdish region. Salih had won a seat in parliament in 2005 and had served in the interim and transitional governments that had preceded Maliki. With wire-rimmed glasses and a balding head, Salih looked like an accountant but spoke with the passion of a preacher. He did not know if he could persuade Iraq's feuding warlords, suspicious conspirators, and old guard to rise above their factional interests, but he was determined to try.

In a country where delay was a time-honored tactic, the Kurd was a whirl of activity. He made it his mission to disburse more government funds to the provinces, in particular the Sunni ones that had received little help from the central government. He traveled nonstop to sign up sixty countries to pledge debt relief and $30 billion in aid for the International

Compact for Iraq, which would be launched in May with its cosponsor, the United Nations.

Salih believed the only road to peace required a power-sharing agreement among Iraq's three groups. "It is not impossible, but it requires leaders, it requires vision, commitment and I daresay it requires American leadership," he said. His formula for achieving it was to form a government of the moderate elements of the Shia, Sunni, and Kurdish communities. He believed that only such a multisectarian coalition could end the struggle between the Arab Shias and Sunnis. He realized Americans' patience was waning, but he said, "This is not a battle that could be won in any cycle of any administration, and it will not be subject to American political timetables."

Salih was counting on Petraeus and Crocker's help to achieve his "grand bargain." He knew they embraced a "tough love" approach to Iraq and would not allow themselves to be played by the Iraqi factions. Salih had met Petraeus during his 2003 tour in Mosul, when the general had helped Salih transport computers he had ordered from Dublin to Sulaimaniya and helped build the city's airport. Salih had known Crocker for years, and one of their encounters was engraved on his memory. The ambassador had come to Kurdistan on April 2, 2002, to visit Talabani as the war planning began. As Salih left his home to pick up Crocker at his hotel, a group of Kurdish extremists belonging to Ansar al-Islam tried to assassinate Salih. He escaped injury but five of his bodyguards were killed.

Salih had sacrificed his personal life to the cause of Iraq. His wife, who did not expect to see him more than a few days a year, would admonish their son and daughter: "Do not feel sorry for yourselves for not having Baba ["Dad" in Kurdish] here with us. At least we have each other. He is alone in Iraq working for the greater good. We cannot be selfish and expect him to stay with us. We must be supportive of him." Somehow, through the years, Salih had managed to be there for his family. His daughter, Cale, called him frequently to pour out her teenage problems, such as her mother's prohibition on her wearing fashionably tight jeans or her insistence on chaperoning a seventh-grade dance. Now a student at Princeton, Cale rarely saw her father but often sought his advice and support. From afar, he coached his children on their schoolwork and enforced his own high standards. As Cale wryly noted, "An A- in my father's household was just barely tolerable."

MALIKI'S GOVERNMENT BEGAN to fragment in the spring of 2007. The cabinet ministers loyal to Muqtada al-Sadr split first. Sadr had successfully played the nationalist card since the spring of 2003, when he had denounced the American occupation in fire-breathing sermons he delivered in the holy city of Kufa outside Najaf. The young cleric had built a huge grassroots movement of loosely organized militias to defend Shia areas and welfare centers to help the Shia poor. They also set up "Sharia courts" to enforce Sadr's version of Islamic law. Young men were beaten for cutting their hair or not growing beards, and women were admonished for not wearing the *hijab*, or headscarf.

In exchange for supporting Maliki's election as prime minister, Sadr received five cabinet ministries. The Sadrists were shrewd enough to hold out for ministries where they could hand out jobs as patronage and provide services to constituents: transportation, health, agriculture, and tourism. Once the Sadrists entered government, two things happened. They had access to power and resources, and a portion of the JAM and other Sadrists turned to crime and graft. Others flowed into the facilities protection service of the ministries and used that as a base to extend their reach through force. The black-shirted JAM youths with guns gained increasing sway over Sadr City, Shula, and Kadhimiya first as neighborhood guards who were protecting Shia from Sunni insurgent attacks because the Americans and the fledgling Iraqi security forces were not, and later as the neighborhood bosses. They then took the offensive, pushed Sunnis out of mixed neighborhoods, and attacked Sunni neighborhoods.

Sadrists also exercised their influence in parliament. Many legislators and other officials spent a great deal of time out of the country, and others remained in their home districts when they felt it was not safe enough to travel. Even Ali Dabbagh, the prime minister's spokesman, lived in Dubai. But not Nassar al-Rubaie, the head of the Sadr bloc in parliament, a large man with a black beard who wore thick glasses and a dark suit that strained to cover his bulk. He lived in Sadr City and rarely missed a session. Like all the Islamist politicians in Iraq, Rubaie declined to shake women's hands and instead used the classic greeting of placing his hand on his chest. After a March bombing in the cafeteria of the convention center where the parliament met, Rubaie was at work in the parliament even though many legislators had fled. Generator cables snaked up the darkened stairway of the nearly vacant building, and the fountain and reflecting pool outside were cracked and dry. Rubaie had just read a letter from Sadr to the parliamentarians who had gathered for a session, even though, like most days, members of parliament had failed to achieve a quorum.

The letter announced that Sadr was leaving the Maliki government. "From the beginning, we have asked the Americans to leave," said Rubaie. "They said they cannot because the Iraqi security forces are not ready. Why are they not ready?" The five Sadr ministers were withdrawing from the cabinet because Maliki had refused to set a deadline for the Americans' departure. "We will not accept them forever," Rubaie said. The majority of Sadr's militia, in response to pressure from Maliki, had been relatively quiet for the first three months of the Baghdad security plan. U.S. and Iraqi troops had run sporadic patrols into Sadr City without encountering resistance from JAM. Many senior Sadr figures were gone or in hiding, and about seven hundred fighters had been detained since the previous fall. Since January, most Sadrists had adopted a tacit wait-and-see posture. Now it seemed they were ready to up the ante.

Rubaie blamed the Americans for Iraq's violence. He recalled that he had been able to drive freely around Iraq, from Najaf in the Shia south to Tikrit in the Sunni north, for the first eight months after the invasion. He broke out of Arabic and said in English for emphasis: "No violence, no nothing, *baby*." He warmed to his topic as he sat in the convention hall auditorium. "Foreign hands and foreign politicians are pushing the Iraqis to fight each other," he said, resuming in Arabic. "The cause for the violence is that the Americans are staying. Americans' presence here is attracting the terrorists. American military operations show that they are just protecting themselves and not the Iraqi people."

He said the U.S. military had done nothing to help the residents of Sadr City. "After four years we don't see them building security in Iraq," Rubaie said, "so we ask them to leave." He added, "While we remain under the hand of any occupier, don't expect that we will deal with them nicely."

Petraeus did not want an all-out confrontation with Sadr. He hoped to separate the hard-core militants from the Sadr nationalists such as Rubaie and to seek a political solution with the latter. Intelligence officials estimated that 90 percent to 95 percent of JAM members were motivated by the desire to protect their neighborhoods or improve their personal fortunes. Many may have become hoodlums but were not irredeemable. Yet neither the U.S. military nor anyone else had a clear picture of who the reconcilable "good JAM" were. "We're still looking for the right people to talk to," one American general admitted. "We don't really know who is doing what to whom. We'll have to wait until JAM sorts itself out." Muqtada al-Sadr had gone to Iran early in 2007 and communicated mostly by letters, which were read by his followers at Friday prayers at his mosque in Kufa.

THE U.S. MILITARY WAS RESOLVED to counter the violent JAM militants who appeared to be acting on their own and with increasing barbarity. Iraqis were dragged into makeshift Sharia courts in homes or prayer halls, and harsh punishments were exacted. Acid was poured on women who were not veiled. Torture with electric prods, hot irons, and other implements was common. Special operations forces rescued some Iraqis being held in these mock courts. Other victims, both Shia and Sunni, were dumped in the street, having been blindfolded and shot. A signature tactic of these extremist cells, which the U.S. military began calling "special groups," was to drill holes in their victims' bodies, heads, and hands with power drills and nail drivers before killing them. With astonishing rapidity, the people who had once been brutalized adopted their oppressors' practices and added their own grisly refinements.

The special groups were also attacking U.S. troops with a bomb the military dubbed explosively formed penetrator (EFP) because the molten metal projectile could pierce the heaviest armor in the U.S. military's inventory—even a main battle tank. The EFPs had appeared first in the south, then in eastern Baghdad around Sadr City, and then all over Baghdad and Diyala province. Although they accounted for less than one-fifth of all the bombs found or detonated in Iraq, the EFPs were much more lethal than the average bomb. Loss of limb, if not life, was a high probability if one hit a Humvee. The Iraqis became more adept at using EFPs and frequently set up arrays of charges aimed to hit seats in a given type of armored vehicle. They were molded in foam blocks that were painted to look like curbs. The special groups did not heed Sadr's decision to lay low in early 2007; in fact, the use of EFPs escalated steadily, as did mortaring of the Green Zone.

U.S. officials believed that Iran was supplying the JAM special groups with EFPs, other materiel, training, and guidance that made them a more lethal threat to U.S. forces. They did not have definitive proof, but they had not found any signs that the key EFP components were being made in Iraq. The torture tactics, the new weapons' lethality, and the suspected Iranian connection were all matters of great concern to Petraeus. It seemed that at least part of Sadr's movement was becoming increasingly tied to Iran.

While the classified, or "black," special operations forces under Lt. Gen. Stan McChrystal's command were largely focused on the hunt for high-value targets affiliated with Al-Qaeda in Iraq, the "white" special operations forces, along with the Iraqi special operations forces, took on the job of going after JAM special groups as well as midvalue Al-Qaeda targets. A winding road led to their hilltop headquarters outside Baghdad in a palace complex with guest villas and orchards where Saddam's private zoo and hunting preserve of exotic animals once roamed. Two battalions from either the army's 5th or 10th Special Forces Group traded places every six months at the base, augmented by one company from either the 1st or 3rd Group that specialized in direct-action missions. These units had trained, advised, and fought alongside the Iraqi special operations forces since their formation in 2003 as the 36th Iraq Civil Defense Corps, made up of Shia and Kurdish militia members. Since then it had grown to two battalions, a support battalion, and a brigade headquarters led by Gen. Fadl Barwari, the original Kurdish pesh merga leader of the Iraqi Special Operations Forces, or ISOF. The ISOF had received the same equipment U.S. commands used. A school, training ranges, shooting houses, and living quarters were built near the palace. The school was modeled on the Special Forces' selection course, and the intensive training and mentoring by the same U.S. units for four years had produced what was widely considered the single best organization in the Iraqi security forces. The key to their success rate was that the U.S. and Iraqi units operated together every day, with the Americans serving as combat advisers in the field.

In 2006, the ISOF and their American partners had concentrated on Baghdad, but during 2007 they became much more expeditionary, expanding their operations in the south and along the Iranian border. The task force also commanded twelve-man Operational Detachments Alpha in southern Iraq, who served as combat advisers to SWAT-type units they had trained and mentored. The first of these units was the Hilla SWAT, followed by the Karbala Emergency Response Unit. Unlike the ISOF, the Hilla SWAT team used pickup trucks with machine guns mounted on the truck beds. "Those guys do a lot with a little," said Lt. Col. Sean Swindell, the commander who was on his second tour leading the U.S.-Iraqi special operation task force based at the Baghdad Radwaniya complex.

Swindell answered to his boss, Col. Ken Tovo, in Balad, where the Combined Joint Special Operations Task Force-Arabian Peninsula had been based since it moved out of Radwaniya in 2004. After the ISOF was transferred to Maliki's control, Swindell was also directed to brief Maliki numerous times on their missions. In 2006 the Iraqi government frequently objected when they hit Shia JAM targets, in one case suspending ISOF raids for four months. ISOF procedure required detailed target packages that included evidence and sworn statements that provided the basis for going after an individual, but to preserve operational security, the precise time and location of raids were never divulged to Maliki. Most often the raids were launched on short notice, once the target had appeared or was supposed to appear at a given location. Very often one raid would lead to others in the same night, while the intelligence was still fresh. This method, known as time-sensitive targeting, had become standard operating procedure for all units, conventional and special, in this war.

As the United States began to pick apart the JAM special groups' structure in nightly raids into Sadr City and other JAM strongholds through early summer 2007, more intelligence was produced. The original leader of these special groups, according to a special operations officer charged with capturing them, was Abu Mustafa al-Sheibani. His brother allegedly was the primary source of weapons from Iran. A pair of brothers named Laith and Qais Khazali had formed their own special group alongside Sheibani's. Some three hundred fighters were organized into separate cells. Qais Khazali had acted as a Sadr spokesman, but U.S. officials believed the special groups were breaking away from Sadr's control.

In March 2007, Iraqi and U.S. Special Forces captured their long-sought targets, the Khazali brothers and Sheibani in Hilla, Basra, and Baghdad. Working with the British, the Special Forces team based in Basra, Operational Detachment Alpha 044, captured Qais Khazali. The Khazalis' computer hard drives yielded a wealth of information, linking the brothers definitively to one of the most sophisticated enemy operations of the entire war, the January kidnapping and killing of five U.S. soldiers in Karbala. The Iraqis had passed easily through the checkpoints at the Karbala provincial government coordination center wearing U.S.-type uniforms and driving SUVs similar to the Americans'. They knew exactly where the Americans would be and moved in quickly to capture them. One was killed on the spot, and the other four were taken away. One of them was found barely alive but died en route to the hospital. The dead soldiers' identification cards and driver's licenses had been scanned into the Khazalis' computers, which also contained a twenty-two-page account of the operation written by Qais and accounts of other attacks on American and British forces. Following the March captures, in a subsequent raid in Sadr City on May 19, the Khazali cohort who led the attack on the American soldiers in Karbala was killed.

Two officials who saw the tape of Qais Khazali's interrogation say he also supplied detailed information on arms, training, and support they received from the Iranian Revolutionary Guard's al-Quds Force, which was the entity devoted to supporting foreign military forces including the Islamic fundamentalist group Hezbollah. This treasure trove of intelligence that finally confirmed the Iranian link Petraeus had suspected for some time. The detainees said they would not have been able to mount their operations without Iranian help, although the Iranians had not been directly involved in the January kidnap-murders. The Khazalis' statements also helped establish Iran as the source of the deadly EFPs, 240 mm and 107 mm rockets, advanced surface-to-air missiles, and rocket-propelled grenades.

Although it was not announced at the time, special operations forces had also captured two other extremely important people in March. They had captured the brother of Abu Mustafa al-Sheibani, the original special groups' leader, who was a principal transporter of weapons from Iran. And they caught a man in Basra who turned out to be a Lebanese Hezbollah leader. During his interrogation, Ali Musa Daqduq at first pretended to be a deaf mute, but when he finally spoke the translators quickly realized by his accent that he was Lebanese. His interrogation, which was also taped, yielded explosive information. Daqduq was the deputy commander of Hezbollah's Department 2800, a unit set up to help JAM special groups become a Hezbollah-like organization, and Yussef Hashimi was its leader. Hezbollah, long supported by Iran, was serving as Iran's proxy in Iraq to aid the special groups. JAM members were also receiving training at three camps outside Tehran, in groups of up to sixty. In addition to weapons, Iran was supplying $750,000 to $3 million a month to the special groups.

Petraeus and Crocker shared the information with Maliki. "We showed the prime minister the information on the people he was dealing with. He did not know what they were doing," said one general. A senior Iraqi official confirmed that Maliki was alarmed. MNF-I chief spokesman Brig. Gen. Kevin Bergner released a number of details about the captures of Khazali and Daqduq in a July 2 press briefing. According to Bergner's briefing, Hezbollah's senior leadership had sent Daqduq to Iran in 2006 to help the Quds Force train the Iraqi special groups. The Quds leadership then sent Daqduq to Iraq. Bergner also said al-Quds had provided intelligence for the attack on the U.S. soldiers in Karbala.

The information on Iran's activities drove a wedge between Maliki and Iran, and between Maliki and Sadr. Maliki became far more willing to allow the targeting of JAM special groups, and twenty-one senior figures of JAM special groups were captured. It would take time to determine the effect on JAM and Sadr—whether the groups would regenerate or whether the pressure would catalyze a definitive split between the Shia "irreconcilables" and "reconcilables" and induce the bulk of JAM to turn away from radicalism. The aggressive campaign was coupled with an effort to open a dialogue with Sadr moderates—and in a major departure from its previous policy, the Bush administration decided to begin a dialogue with Iran about Iraq.

7

Downsizing Expectations

Spirits were low in Iraq as summer arrived. There was no sign the violence was abating or that Iraq's politicians were coming together on the issues that divided them. In May Congress passed a war funding bill that required the administration to report by September 15 on whether eighteen benchmarks were being met in Iraq. The measure set a clock ticking to produce results or otherwise declare the surge a failure. Petraeus and Crocker were still finalizing their formal campaign strategy, but they both agreed that expectations in Washington would have to be downsized. They were not going to get reconciliation in the next three months. Indeed, the past four months had demonstrated just how difficult it was to make any meaningful progress. Nonetheless, they would have to produce some progress or face irresistible pressure to concede defeat and prepare for withdrawal. Crocker would tackle the political reconciliation from the top down while also trying to make headway on the economy and local governance with the provincial reconstruction teams. Petraeus would work on security and reconciliation from the bottom up.

Six of the eighteen benchmarks were the core political reconciliation issues that the Iraqi government had embraced—at least rhetorically—at former ambassador Zalmay Khalilzad's prodding in 2006. They were to (1) revise the de-Baathification law to allow more former regime members to take part in government, (2) pass legislation governing the country's oil resources, (3) pass a law that stipulated the powers of the provincial governments, (4) set a date and hold provincial elections, (5) promulgate constitutional revisions that had been promised to the Sunni minority under a bargain extracted by Khalilzad, and (6) agree on terms for amnesty and demobilization of militias. Reaching agreement on these issues would go a long way toward achieving the "political solution" among Sunnis, Shias, and Kurds, which had eluded Iraq since the war ended in 2003. The other nine benchmarks pertained to supplying the promised number of Iraqi troops for the surge, increasing the overall size and capability of the Iraqi security forces, and judging whether the Iraqi government was using the armed forces in a sectarian manner, equitably targeting all groups that violated the law, and treating military officers evenhandedly.

With the Iraqi government paralyzed by infighting, progress on the core benchmarks was a very tall order. But Crocker was determined to try. He had also been given the green light to talk to Iran. It was a testament to the diminutive ambassador's reputation that he was able to recruit a first-class team of diplomats to join him in Baghdad—by far the least popular assignment. He sent the State Department a blunt request to staff the embassy fully with qualified personnel, while he reached out personally to high-ranking colleagues and trusted friends.

Within two months, he had assembled an impressive roster that included three ambassadors and three deputy chiefs of mission. He needed a number-two with the managerial skills to oversee a thousand embassy personnel and their relocation to the new embassy compound, which was finally nearing completion. Pat Butenis gave up her ambassadorship to Bangladesh to join him. A no-nonsense woman with close-cropped brown hair, Butenis had been his deputy chief of mission in

Pakistan. She had overseen the largest and longest humanitarian airlift operation in U.S. history after a devastating earthquake in Kashmir in 2005.

Two other ambassadors understood the urgency and answered Crocker's call: Marcie and Charles Ries, ambassadors to Albania and Greece. Marcie was ending her tour and looking forward to joining Charlie in Athens, but the couple agreed to live in a trailer behind the Republican Guard palace instead. Charlie took on the portfolio of all things economic, including oil and other economic legislation as well as the myriad problems slowing the disbursement of budget funds and the functioning of ministries. Marcie was in charge of political-military affairs, which included liaison with the U.S.-led coalition forces and soon expanded to include security matters involving Iran and Syria. Crocker also persuaded his friend former State spokesman Phil Reeker and Arabist Matt Tueller to join him. Phyllis Powers left her deputy job in Peru to oversee all provincial reconstruction teams. No one could now say that the foreign service had not sent its best and brightest.

The chances of legislation being enacted appeared remote. In the Council of Representatives, the brand-new exercise of parliamentary democracy was chaotic in the extreme. By midsummer both the Tawafuq and the secular Iraqiya Iraqi National Alliance were boycotting the Council of Representatives, and the parliament was due to recess at the end of June for the last two blistering months of summer in Iraq.

Another party, Fadhila, had split from the governing coalition in 2006 in protest over its sectarianism. It held fifteen seats and the Basra governorship. Bassim Sharif, a tall, bespectacled doctor from Kut who was one of the Fadhila legislators, said his party had drafted a reasonable de-Baathification law that barred only those convicted of crimes and limited top Baathists from the highest offices. Sharif had gone to school in Mosul and lived in Sunni-dominated Adhamiya. "We in Fadhila have no problem with Sunnis. We are all Iraqis. I like them more than Muslims from outside Iraq," he said in a pointed jab at the Iranians next door. His party was a nationalist, moderate one. "We need a national project to save Iraq," he said, but achieving it would require a different, less sectarian government.

In Washington, Iraq's ambassador, Samir Sumaidaie, tried to dampen expectations that any of the reconciliation legislation could be enacted by September. "There is far too much emphasis on this legislation. I'd rather have a benchmark that says how many families can go back to their homes," he said. He tried to fend off alternative proposals floating around Washington, particularly ones that would further weaken Iraq's central government through increased federalism. In his view, the original problems had to be corrected to resolve the conflict. "Elections were held too early, before the country was ready," he said. "In my personal view, the constitution was written too early by the wrong people." To undo the damage done and amend the constitution "requires the statesmanship of those who gained by it," he said. Sumaidaie also dismissed the notion that violence could be controlled by repositioning troops in bases on the border or over the horizon. "Either you have control of the territory or you don't," he said. "You might as well go back home as sit in bases defending yourself." As the drumbeat for U.S. withdrawal grew, Prime Minister Maliki defiantly claimed that Iraqi forces were capable of defending the country. "There is a lot of talk inside the government about how to adjust ourselves to that eventuality," Sumaidaie conceded. "But he knows and we know that our security forces are not strong enough, and there would be a lot of bloodletting."

Because the relationships among the top Iraqi officials were so toxic, Crocker and Tueller tried a different gambit. They convened the second-tier leaders from the major parties and proposed a series of working groups to discuss each of the core reconciliation issues in depth. The embassy would contribute papers outlining possible solutions or compromises that might break the various logjams. The key Iraqis were Iyad Samarrai for the Sunni Iraqi Islamic Party, Ali Adeed for Dawa, Humam Hamoudi for ISCI, Hadi al-Ameri for Badr, and Rowsch Shaways and Barham Salih for the two Kurdish parties. Tueller found that these Iraqis realized the seriousness of the impasse. "They are not blind," he said. "They could see that this paralysis is leading toward a failed state."

Meanwhile, the embassy's economic czar, Charlie Ries, took another avenue of attack to send money to the provinces and improve services and infrastructure. He delved into the minutiae of Iraq's economic situation and quickly absorbed the details. He was perfectly suited to the task, since he had spent the past decade in senior economic positions negotiating trade accords. His top priority was to ensure that economic activity, using both U.S. and Iraqi funds, immediately followed the surge to bolster any security gains. He prodded Iraq's government to spend its $33 billion budget—which it had largely failed to do the previous year due to paralysis, incompetence, and infighting—and boost the banking, finance, transportation, and agriculture sectors. Ries was particularly concerned that growth in agriculture, which employed a quarter of the population, had been flat or negative. Iraq had greater potential in this sector than most of the Middle East because it was watered by the Tigris and Euphrates rivers. Electricity and water were two enormous infrastructure challenges. Ries saw the problem through an economist's lens: because electricity was essentially free, demand had shot through the roof. Price controls also fed corruption and a black market in oil. If Iraq could agree on the legal framework, the potential existed to nearly double oil production in short order. The Rumaila oil fields in the south were full of easy-to-extract oil; extraction in the Kurdish north was more difficult, so the Kurds wanted the right to offer production-sharing agreements to foreign companies.

Crocker's veteran professionals were matched to the right tasks. To ensure they were not working at cross-purposes with the behemoth Multi-National Force-Iraq (MNF-I) command, as had been the case for much of the previous four years, the senior members of Crocker's team began each day by attending the MNF-I battlefield update briefings, where they received a torrent of information. Given Petraeus's keen interest in the all-important economic portfolio and dysfunction in the ministries, Ries frequently spoke up in the briefings. Interagency "fusion cells" were created to address big problems such as oil and power generation. These mechanisms provided the missing integration of the "lines of operation" at the strategic level that had previously been attempted at the tactical level alone.

Petraeus and Crocker's efforts were handicapped by the White House in two critical respects. President Bush was not disposed to issue Maliki anything approaching an ultimatum. Moreover, that the president continued to hold biweekly video teleconferences with Maliki reduced the impact of any other U.S. officials' urgings—and indeed his own. By establishing such routine contact, the administration had devalued a major diplomatic tool. Normally, foreign leaders meet with a U.S. president to reach substantive agreements after months of staff work, or to seal a deal their cabinet officials have struck. Bush's routine presidential contact produced no significant breakthrough. Furthermore, the regular videoconferences had become a trap: White House officials were reluctant to stop them because they feared losing influence over Maliki. One aide said ceasing presidential videoconferences would be interpreted as a break in relations. The administration had gambled the president's prestige on the hope that giving a bear hug to Maliki would empower and embolden him to take the steps the United States wanted. But no one reckoned with the downside if he did not, or could not, respond accordingly.

Nonetheless, Petraeus was determined to use all the levers at his disposal. He had grown increasingly frustrated with the Maliki government. When the time came to write the report Congress had requested by July 15, Petraeus told his aide Col. Bill Rapp, chief of the Commander's Initiatives Group, "Tell it like it is." Rapp and his deputy, Lt. Col. Charlie Miller, sat down with the legislation outlining the eighteen benchmarks and wrote a scathing draft report. Petraeus edited the draft in his typically detailed fashion, but the aides had reflected his assessment accurately. The White House put out the report without changing any of Petraeus's substantive judgments.

The "Initial Benchmark Assessment Report," made public on July 12, 2007, found that "unsatisfactory" progress had been made on ten of the eighteen benchmarks, including the most important items on the political-reconciliation agenda. The report bluntly stated that sectarian behavior was rife within high levels of government. It found ongoing "sectarian bias in the appointment of senior military and police commanders" and "sectarian-based decisions . . . evident through intelligence channels." It bluntly stated that in the ministry of interior, "some senior officials responsible for abuse continue to hold positions of responsibility" and that efforts to detain them had been "inadequate."

Petraeus did not always play hardball with the Iraqi leaders. The most valuable instrument in his effort to influence them was his adviser Sadi Othman, who was on the phone with them day and night. Othman had started out as Petraeus's translator, but he was much more than that. His importance was reflected in his title, which was equal to that of the other inner-circle members: senior adviser to the commanding general. Othman had first worked for Petraeus and the 101st Airborne Division in Mosul in 2003–2004. Born in Brazil to Palestinian parents, the towering six-foot-seven-inch Othman was raised in Jordan and emigrated to the United States, where he became a citizen in 1977. He attended a Mennonite school, Hesston College, in Kansas, where the teachings of peace and brotherhood deeply impressed him. He moved east to New York and worked at a variety of jobs: running a deli, then a grocery store, as a salesman, and as a taxi driver. When the 9/11 attacks occurred, "as an Arab-American from the Muslim tradition, I felt humiliated that those who carried out the attack were Muslim," Othman said. "I wanted to do something . . . and a friend told me that the American military was looking for linguists and cultural advisers."

After a background check, Othman left his wife and daughter in Queens and went to Iraq. Petraeus saw that Othman had a gift for connecting with Mosul's kaleidoscope of religious and ethnic communities. A news junkie, he had followed the developments in the Middle East, so he grasped the bigger picture. Othman stayed on in Mosul to work for Petraeus's successor. When Petraeus returned as Multi-National Security Transition Command-Iraq commander, Petraeus flew to Mosul to pick Othman up.

When Maliki became prime minister, he told Othman he'd heard good things about him from his predecessor. The gaunt, white-haired man gained a reputation among Iraqi officials as a reliable channel who would transmit their message without prejudice—and deliver an answer. "They know I don't side with one over the other," he said. Othman frequently talked with senior officials until 1, 2, or 3 a.m. "The top leaders trust him, and a lot of military guys get their credibility with the Iraqis from Sadi," said Maj. Gen. Frank Helmick, who had been Petraeus's deputy in Mosul.

The Iraqis knew that when Othman called, Petraeus was calling, but they were also more willing to respond because "the big Sad" was their friend, and a friend of Iraq. Some $37 million in reconstruction money for Tal Afar, in the Sunni northwest, had been stalled for a year. Petraeus told Othman to call the finance minister to shake it loose. After doing so, Othman called the ministry responsible for carrying out the work. He also helped unlock funding for the rule of law complex.

Petraeus often used Othman to deliver a message that might ruffle feathers if he conveyed it directly. After a chorus of calls for Maliki's ouster, including from France's foreign minister and Sen. Carl Levin, Maliki lashed out, saying that Iraq would find better friends elsewhere. He made this remark while visiting Syria, so it was assumed that he was referring to Syria, his former home in exile. Petraeus asked Othman to call Maliki and offer him some friendly advice. "Tell him to rise above this and be statesmanlike. He doesn't have to name names and poke people in the eye," Petraeus said. "He's playing to the bloggers."

Othman delivered the message as friendly advice rather than admonishment, and Petraeus knew face-saving was an important part of the culture. He was not afraid to confront Maliki but saved those confrontations for important matters. Petraeus trusted Othman implicitly and appreciated his dedication to the Iraq cause. The two had an open and easy relationship, eating many meals together and joking a lot. After a particularly late-night marathon of phone calls, Othman might sleep in and miss the morning briefing, but he was rarely far from the general's side.

TRY AS THEY MIGHT, THERE WAS no progress on reconciliation among the national political leaders. Petraeus adopted a phrase to characterize the situation: the Washington clock was moving much faster than the Baghdad clock. It was time to officially adjust the expectation of what was achievable. The Joint Campaign Plan, which was formally adopted at the end of July, defined national reconciliation as a distant goal. The near-term goal was to reach local political accommodations that would help bring down the violence. Reconciliation would not come in a big bang. There was no alternative, in Petraeus's view, to a localized approach that would nudge the ball forward one area at a time.

The JSAT's recommendation of dramatic steps to tackle the national political impasse was not adopted, but the Joint Campaign Plan did adopt the team's vision of seeking a series of accommodations among the parties that would produce pockets of "local security." The essential concept was represented by a puzzle diagram in the campaign plan that showed three circles. The first circle represented the near-term goal of localized security via accommodations that would be sought through whatever combination of security, political, economic, and diplomatic operations made sense in a given area. Demobilization, jobs programs, infrastructure repairs, representation on governing councils, and other measures could be brought together in a deal that suited the needs of a province, city, or even neighborhood. The JSAT believed that localized security could be achieved by the end of 2007, but the campaign plan set a more modest goal of mid-2008.

The plan envisioned that enough of these local deals could be reached all over the country by June 2009 to achieve a nationwide state the plan called "sustainable security." That was represented in the diagram by the second circle, showing Iraq covered with little puzzle pieces representing local deals. The final phase was labeled "national reconciliation," signified by an Iraqi flag covering the whole country, but instead of affixing a target date, the planners deemed this long-term goal a "generational" one. It was without a doubt the most realistic campaign plan that had been developed over the past four years. It did not abandon the goal of national reconciliation, but it recognized that it would likely take years to reach the necessary agreements and laws, build capable security forces, and establish the rule of law and a functioning state. Knitting the country together again would take a generation.

By making the quest for political accommodation the goal of all the lines of operations, Petraeus elevated Lt. Gen. Graeme Lamb's strategic engagement initiative to a central role in the campaign. The official goal was not a classic military defeat of the enemy but rather a negotiated settlement—in fact, a series of them.

Not everyone embraced this idea of cutting local deals, including Rick Olson, a retired two-star general at the embassy. "If tribes and sheikhs start taking a role, what will this do to governors' roles and their legitimacy?" he asked. Olson also noted that the wrong tribes or individuals could be empowered if the interlocutors did not know what they were doing or who was who. "The danger of dealing with the wrong person can be enormous," he said.

Petraeus and his subordinates knew they were taking a gamble, but they felt it was warranted. One adviser said they calculated that they could recover if the gambit didn't work. But they had to try something to change the war's dynamic. They were in the last inning of the military game. Kilcullen and others openly discussed scenarios of drawing down by as much as three-quarters in the next couple of years. Petraeus's intelligence adviser, Derek Harvey, still believed they had less than even odds of turning around the war in Iraq. But he was heartened by several new developments, including the strength of the Petraeus-Crocker partnership and what he believed to be a new moderation on the part of the Shia Islamic party ISCI and particularly Vice President Adil Abd al-Mahdi. It was not enough by itself to shift the Shia equation, but it was something.

Harvey was also encouraged that the Defense Intelligence Agency had finally gotten its act together and fully staffed Iraq with the intelligence analysts it needed. There were now four hundred analysts in Iraq, and they were all Middle East specialists. For the first time the commanding general and the ambassador could ask who were the top ten sectarian actors in the interior ministry and get a documented answer that they could take to the prime minister. Even so, Harvey's revised odds of success were still only one in three.

Petraeus also sought to shape public expectations by giving frequent interviews to the media. He knew Americans' deep disenchantment could force an end to the troop surge, so he tried to temper the expectations while also showing reason for hope. Several of his attempts to highlight improvements were criticized as exaggerations, but he continued to speak out. In sharp contrast to Gen. George Casey's, his philosophy was the more information the better. In the daily briefing, a long list was displayed of the journalists who were conducting interviews with officials or embedded with troops. Petraeus was adamant about pushing dozens of reporters down to the brigade and battalion level. Steve Boylan,

Petraeus's spokesman, kept a list on his whiteboard of all the major media organizations and how many times they had been out on a "battlefield circulation" with the general. Petraeus preferred individual interviews, but his Strategic Effects general, Bill Caldwell and then Kevin Bergner, along with Iraqi officials, gave press conferences every week or two.

The frequency and visibility of Petraeus's outings made friends and family back home nervous, even though he traveled in a robust security bubble that included overhead drones and attack helicopters. Army officers in Washington grumbled when they saw photos of him walking around in a soft cap instead of a helmet. It was a commander's prerogative to set his own dress code, but army generals worried that he was sending the wrong message to the troops that would result in fatalities. On the other hand, talking to a vulnerable Iraqi citizen when dressed in full military kit did not exactly send a message of solidarity and confidence.

Petraeus avidly read the press coverage. Rapp and Miller, of his Commander's Initiatives Group, prepared daily press digests for him. Petraeus's views on the power of the news media went beyond a keen sense of its ability to make or break someone's career and personal reputation. He certainly tended his image, but he also believed that wars could be won or lost through information and perception, a realm the military had taken to calling information operations. He held fast to his philosophy that "you can't win if you don't play." That included taking media to task for stories he and Boylan felt did not meet basic standards of accuracy, proper context, and correct characterization.

Finally, in June, Petraeus was ready to launch his first major offensive. He felt like he had been marking time as he waited for all of the surge troops to arrive. All five brigades were now place and ready to launch a broad military campaign to attack Al-Qaeda's sanctuaries in a rolling series of operations around the country. He sought to regain the psychological momentum with a command climate he described tersely in one word: "determination." On June 15, Operation Phantom Thunder was launched in the belts around Baghdad and Diyala province to the north. It was the beginning of a series of operations that would keep the insurgents on the run for the rest of the summer.

As soon as Operation Phantom Thunder concluded, Operation Phantom Strike was launched to chase the fleeing insurgents farther north in the Diyala River Valley. Much of this campaign took place at night, in secret, as the Joint Special Operations units (Task Force 27) stepped up their already intense pace to target the top insurgent leadership with high-tech tools and a large intelligence unit that helped them discover the identities, relationships, and cell phone numbers of Al-Qaeda's top three tiers of leaders, financiers, bomb-makers, and facilitators. The Al-Qaeda in Iraq (AQI) organization had proven its ability to regenerate almost as fast as the commandos captured or killed its leaders. The hope now was that if they could take down most of these targets nearly simultaneously, they would be able to deal Al-Qaeda a crippling and possibly fatal blow. Doing so required a tip on one suspect's current location, to permit "time-sensitive targeting," and his capture would lead to the next, and the next. On one single night, for example, twenty-seven Al-Qaeda targets were successively captured. "The Iraqi government does not know how much we are doing to knock AQI off balance," commented a U.S. general.

The United States also sought to attack Al-Qaeda's appeal with the "anaconda strategy," which aimed to go after the terrorists from every angle. "You can't do in Al-Qaeda with just counterterrorist forces," Petraeus said. "You've got to reduce any threat that gives a reason for Sunni Arab communities to want to support Al-Qaeda as a bulwark against them. You've got to get services, education, jobs. The religious side is important. . . . You've got to get out there in cyberspace . . . and you have to get with all the source countries."

Meanwhile in Baghdad the troops were engaged in an uphill battle. In April and May U.S. forces had suffered their highest casualties since the war began, as the city remained the epicenter of sectarian cleansing and the Sunni insurgents' bombing campaign. The fighting was especially intense in Sunni neighborhoods like Adhamiya and Ameriya, where the soldiers had struggled for more than a year to quell Iraq's murderous violence and turn around a situation that had been careening out of control since the summer of 2006.

8

The Blue Spaders
in the Inferno

Amid the maelstrom of violence, troops on the ground endeavored to walk the country back from the brink of all-out civil war. At the center of this effort in eastern Baghdad was 1st Battalion, 26th Infantry Regiment, which had arrived in Iraq in August 2006 when Operation Forward Together was foundering and Generals George Casey and Peter Chiarelli desperately needed more troops to try to tamp down the spiraling violence. That 1-26 had been thrown into the breach was rather fitting, given the unit's history; it had been formed quickly in 1901 when the United States needed more forces for the Philippine War, and thereafter it deployed for repeated stints in the Indian Wars, World War I and II, Vietnam, and the Balkans.

Known as the Blue Spaders for the unit's regimental emblem, 1-26 landed in Kuwait on August 5 and was in combat eleven days later in Baghdad. The Blue Spaders were to fight the entire tour as a battalion under other brigade commands. They were sent ahead of their own brigade command, 2nd Brigade, 1st Infantry Division, which followed later in the fall from its home base in Schweinfurt, Germany. The brigade commander, Col. J. B. Burton, a hearty Tennessean, did his best to watch over them from western Baghdad when he arrived, but the Spaders were pretty much left to figure things out for themselves on the other bank of the Tigris. They were in for a tumultuous tour in every imaginable respect.

For all the disadvantages of their situation, 1-26 possessed some distinct advantages as well: leadership, unit cohesion, and experience. The battalion commander, Lt. Col. Eric Schacht, was a taciturn, unflappable man who was well liked by his staff because he gave them latitude to do their jobs and make decisions. The forty-three-year-old shunned theatrics but could be counted on to back up his men and stand firm on what he believed was the right decision. Schacht had commanded 1st Infantry, 26th Regiment since July 2004, an unusually long stint, so he knew every soldier down to the lowest private. He was leading the battalion into combat in Iraq for a second time; the first had been in 2004–2005 to Samarra, which was then falling under the grip of insurgents, where they saw serious combat including a car bombing of their base.

The battalion was also fortunate to have a first-rate staff, which would be asked to handle demands far beyond those normally asked of junior officers. The two field-grade officers were operations officer Maj. John Meyer, thirty-five, a cerebral recent graduate of the School for Advanced Military Studies, and the executive officer, Maj. Clay Padgett, thirty-eight, Schacht's quick, wisecracking number-two. Both would be promoted below the zone (ahead of their year group) to lieutenant colonel before the end of the tour. When word came that their brigade would be sent back to Iraq, the brigade commander imposed a stop-loss order, which prevented many who were scheduled to rotate to other units or leave the military from doing so. The unit strength would have been depleted without the order, but it made some soldiers exceedingly bitter. But whether they remained in 1-26 by choice or by force, the unit camaraderie grew as they returned to a much more dangerous Iraq.

When the battalion reached Baghdad on August 11, it was divided between two forward operating bases (FOB) on the southeast edge of the city, FOB Rustamiyah and FOB Loyalty. The battalion's Charlie Company was sent ahead to Adhamiya, in the northeast corner of Baghdad. The old-line Sunni neighborhood had been the symbolic home of the insurgency since 2003. It was where Saddam Hussein had made his last, defiant public appearance in April 2003 before going underground until his capture in December. The spot he chose was outside the Abu Hanifa mosque, one of the most revered sites for Sunnis in Iraq. The mosque became identified with the Al-Qaeda insurgency and was raided four times in 2003–2004. Adhamiya's Sunni middle-class residents had been part of the ruling class; former regime members, intellectuals, and professionals lived there. It was a receptive environment and recruiting ground for the most extreme opponents of the U.S. occupation and the Shia-led government that came into power in 2005.

In April 2006 Shia militia attacked Adhamiya. The two sides waged a pitched seven-hour battle in the streets. From then on, the Sunnis were under siege, their backs against the Tigris. The once-proud neighborhood was a portrait of dilapidation and destruction. Gracious buildings were pockmarked with bullet holes, especially around the mosque where the fiercest fighting occurred. Trash filled the streets and tangled wires ran from homes to jury-rigged connections and generators. Adhamiyans received just an hour or two of city-supplied electricity a day, and it galled them to look across the Tigris to see the Shia shrine in Kadhimiya brilliantly lit every night. An average of ten dead bodies turned up on the streets each day.

The 1-26 moved into a tiny compound appropriately named Combat Outpost Apache, where a Special Forces team had been the lone U.S. unit since 2003. The compound sat on the banks of the Tigris, ringed by twelve-foot concrete barriers, next to a military museum that had been turned into barracks for the Iraq army's 2nd Brigade, 6th Division. A high metal gate divided them. Life at Apache was as austere as it was dangerous. There was none of the support structure the larger forward operating bases typically provided. Charlie Company took care of its cooking, laundry, and upkeep with a cook from the support company, while their comrades could get made-to-order omelets and stir-fry in their dining halls, steak and lobster on Friday, and myriad other services including Internet, satellite TV, phone centers, gyms, PX stores, and laundry service. Charlie's 1st sergeant did what he could to make life at Apache better: he ordered weight machines and cardio equipment for the patio.

Charlie Company patrolled Adhamiya daily. Each platoon normally spent about twelve hours a day on patrol, in three and a half hour stints. The specific missions varied, including cordon and raid on a developed target, overwatch of an area where insurgent activity was thought to be occurring, or cordon and knock to gain information from residents and find out if they were having problems the soldiers could address. Nighttime was raid time since the Americans' night-vision technology gave them an edge and most noncombatants were in bed. U.S. military and intelligence officials believed that senior members of the Sunni insurgency used Adhamiya as a safe haven and that one of the principal car bomb networks was based there.

The leader of Charlie Company's 3rd platoon was 1st Lt. Matthew Martinez, twenty-three, a recent graduate of Cal Tech who had decided to join the army. He was the youngest in his officer basic course and sapper, or combat engineer, school, but his serious manner and deep baritone made him seem years older. Martinez could have easily landed a good engineering job, but he was drawn to the idea of serving his country. His father, a patriotic first-generation Mexican American, had served in the air force and every weekend put the flag outside their house.

Martinez's platoon sergeant, Sgt. First Class Widmark Quashie, a warm Haitian American, expected to help the new officer learn the ropes, but he was amazed by the young man's maturity. "I thought I'd be teaching him, but instead I learned from him. He's the most intelligent officer I've ever had," the forty-three-year-old noncom said.

Martinez and Quashie initially hoped that acts of kindness would win over the Adhamiyans. The platoon made food deliveries that the Shia-led government bureaucracy had stopped sending to the Adhamiya state ration stores. On another occasion, when a grenade landed outside the Abu Hanifa mosque and wounded several Iraqis, including an old man, the soldiers administered first aid in a nearby home and took the seriously wounded to Apache's medic. They hoped that word of their good deeds would spread and people would come forward to help them.

It didn't happen. Adhamiya was ensnared in a deep psychosis of violence. Each day the streets were littered with bodies, and violence was apt to break out at any moment. One day in October a group of agitated Iraqis at the scene of a bloody gunfight waved down a patrol. Staff Sgt. Jose Narvaez got out of his Humvee to check whether two people lying in the street were still alive. He was shot and killed, and the rest of the patrol came under fire from men on a hospital roof. Another day one of their interpreters was shot as they uncovered a bomb in the park. A resident described a scene that perfectly captured the horrors of Adhamiya. As children played soccer one day beside the Abu Hanifa mosque and cemetery, a man and his wife were killed. The woman was raped, and the man's head was put in a bag and hung from a lamppost. "The guys we are fighting are just insanely brutal," Martinez said.

For three months the rest of the battalion suffered casualties on the dangerous daily commute from bases in the southeast to northeast Baghdad patrol areas. On this deadly journey, Task Force 1-26 lost eleven soldiers in all, most of them felled by EFPs (explosively formed penetrators). Brig. Gen. John Campbell, the Baghdad deputy commanding general, advised the battalion to move to Taji, just north of Baghdad. Burton agreed. The route from Taji south to the battalion's area of operations was much safer. The move also made sense because the division was about to redraw the lines for the Baghdad security plan. An additional brigade command was arriving to oversee northeast Baghdad, and it would also be based at Taji. TF 1-26 would fall under that new brigade commander, but Campbell kept a close watch on Schacht and his men and visited them regularly. He knew they were in the belly of the beast. The drive from Taji was safer, but not safe. One of operations officer Meyer's Humvees was hit by an EFP that decapitated the driver and severed the legs of the truck commander. Eventually the battalion moved into the old defense ministry complex next to Adhamiya.

The first task the battalion was assigned when the Baghdad security plan began in February was to set up a joint security station (JSS) in the Suleikh neighborhood. Capt. Scott Gilman, a fresh-faced blond from Decatur, Illinois, fortified the blue-and-white police station with sandbags and posted a soldier with an MK-19 grenade launcher on the roof around the clock. The policemen were used to slipping into the station in civilian clothes and changing into their uniforms there, to avoid being targeted on the way to or from work. After a few weeks of joint patrols with the American platoons that rotated in and out of the JSS Suleikh, residents of the neighborhood began coming to the station's guardhouse at the entrance barriers to report tips on crimes.

Opening Joint Security Station Adhamiya, a few miles south, was a very different story. A firefight broke out within hours of Gilman and his company moving into the Adhamiya police station. Insurgents shot at them from two schools next door. The American snipers on the rooftop spotted an Iraqi burying a bomb and shot him. Rarely a day went by without mortars raining down on the pockmarked concrete at the station's front door. Gilman erected a high chain-link fence to keep out grenades, and concertina wire was strung in coils around the station. Soldiers took turns on twenty-four-hour shifts to give each other a break from the attacks. No U.S. troops had been regularly patrolling Adhamiya for a year, and now that they were in, they were not leaving.

By now, seven months into its tour in Iraq, 1-26 was a combat-hardened battalion. In the fall the soldiers had fought the only serious battles waged in Sadr City, after a U.S. soldier was kidnapped and taken there. They had been in a nasty firefight after being called to recover the remains of Blackwater security contractors whose helicopter had been shot down in their sector. And they had repelled a concerted attack on Combat Outpost Apache the night Saddam was pronounced guilty in the Dujail massacre trial and launched an hours-long counterattack through the streets of Adhamiya.

Most of their work was the painstaking, intelligence-driven hunt of counter-guerrilla warfare. Much of it was frustrating, for residents were loath to give up any information. One family brazenly hid a suspect while the soldiers questioned them and then helped him scramble over the back wall. But a key break came when the battalion raided a guarded house full of weaponry and bomb-making materials. Elite units and their own intelligence officer, Capt. John "Yoda" Nakata, helped lead them to related targets. In the middle of a sandstorm one day, a gunner's practiced eye spotted a car that was a nearly finished bomb.

The rash of truck bombs had collapsed bridges around the city, including the nearby Sarafiya bridge's center span, which lay in the river. Matt Martinez and his platoon picked up four men who said they were shopping for a van. Adhamiya did not have used car lots, but it was a thriving bomb factory. Using their Humvees to close off the narrow street, the soldiers carefully searched the Iraqis' pocket litter and cell phone registers but in the end found no grounds for detaining them. Martinez was still suspicious. In his first weeks in Adhamiya, he had let go men whom he later caught operating as a hit squad, with guns, hit lists, and a blood-covered car. After months of work, the battalion finally dismantled the Rusafa network, which had been responsible for most eastside bombs. Over the spring they also caught seventeen senior Al-Qaeda insurgents, including the "emir" of Adhamiya.

In addition to targeting the Sunni insurgents holed up in Adhamiya, 1-26 was tasked with stopping the sectarian cleansing campaign being mounted by the Shia militia JAM, which was now on Adhamiya's doorstep. Militiamen fired EFPs at the soldiers and mortars into Adhamiya. In the mixed neighborhoods next to Adhamiya, JAM chased out Sunni families by breaking into their homes and leaving a threatening note or one bullet per family member. JAM had consolidated its hold on Shaab and Ur and was now seeking to do the same in Adhamiya. The Americans used two approaches: targeting EFP cells and enlisting the civilian population to resist JAM's encroachment. They used night raids for the former and daytime house calls for the former.

These were also difficult tasks. Many residents were irate at the lack of security and government services, and the local army commander was either turning a blind eye to or collaborating with JAM. But some Iraqis responded to the Americans' overtures, despite the risks. Omar Rachmani continued to serve on Adhamiya's advisory council after two chairmen and six members were killed. "I was angry for the first days of the invasion," he said. "Then I decided I'd better get involved." The soldiers met regularly with the council to fund reconstruction projects of its choosing and answer complaints, usually about relatives who had been detained. Schacht even had backdoor meetings with the older, less radical of the two imams at Abu Hanifa.

As TF 1-26 attacked the Al-Qaeda network in Adhamiya in March, the battalion was also overseeing the construction of a wall of twelve-foot concrete barriers around the entire neighborhood. Each night the engineer teams came in to lay more walls, an operation that Petraeus took to calling the "concrete caterpillar." The teams could put down five hundred meters of T-walls—or Texas barriers, as they were called—a night, carefully lining up the edges.

The concrete caterpillar crept down the Khalid bin al-Walid Expressway, or Route Brewers, as the military called it. When the wall was complete, six kilometers of concrete barriers ran along the eastern and southern borders of Adhamiya. Two openings were left for cars to enter or leave, after being searched by police or soldiers at checkpoints, to prevent weapons and bomb-making materials from being brought in or ready-to-detonate car bombs from being driven out. The walls were also intended to protect the Adhamiyans from the Shia militia attacks.

The wall of Adhamiya caused a huge controversy and became a magnet for criticism of the entire program of concrete walls around Baghdad's most violent neighborhoods and markets. Over loudspeakers imams of the Abu Hanifa mosque denounced the wall and called on Adhamiyans to protest. Over a thousand people gathered at the mosque and marched to the checkpoint at Antar Square. The national and international media covered the story extensively. When asked about the wall, Iraqi Prime Minister Nouri al-Maliki, traveling in Egypt at the time, criticized it, comparing it to the walls in the West Bank and in Berlin during the Cold War. But privately Maliki told Petraeus to continue. He, the Iraqi military command, and the neighborhood council had all known and approved of the plan.

Perceptions aside, the facts were that controlling the flow of traffic and people was the one tactic that had not been tried to stem the bombing campaign. The intent was not to make life more difficult for Adhamiyan

Change of Command: CENTCOM chief Gen. John Abizaid passes the unit colors to Gen. David Petraeus in the ceremony marking the change of command of Multi-National Force-Iraq from Gen. George Casey to Gen. Petraeus on February 10, 2007, in the atrium of the Al Faw palace at Camp Victory, Iraq.

Petraeus with Sheikh Sattar (Sheikh Abdul Sattar Bezia al-Rishawi), one of the most important tribal leaders who contributed to the pacification of Anbar province, known as the Anbar awakening. He was killed by a bomb outside his house in Ramadi in September 2007.

Center and bottom: After ten months in office, Prime Minister Maliki pays his first visit to Ramadi on March 13, 2007, under Petraeus's personal escort, as part of the process of encouraging the government of Iraq to govern for the entire country.

Petraeus typically tried to avoid wearing a helmet or flak jacket when mingling on the streets of Baghdad to normalize ordinary human contact as much as possible.

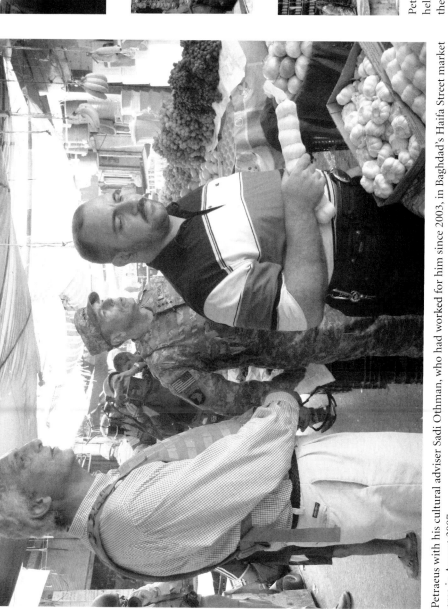

Petraeus with his cultural adviser Sadi Othman, who had worked for him since 2003, in Baghdad's Haifa Street market area in August 2007.

Petraeus and President Jalal Talabani, who could — and did — use his bulk to prevent feuding Iraqi ministers from leaving the room until some agreement was reached.

push-up contest. The soldier in the right foreground bested Petraeus in this particular contest.

Camp Victory staff run.

Brigadier General Campbell, deputy commanding general of Multi-National Division-Baghdad, talks to a sheikh in Taji with the help of his interpreter.

Campbell and Lt. Gen. Abboud Qanbar, head of the Baghdad Operations Command, visit the Shorja market in Rusafa, the site of numerous car bombings. (Photo courtesy of Lt. Col. Scott Bleichwehl)

Campbell and Lt. Col. Van Smiley, commander of 1st Battalion, 23rd Infantry Regiment (Stryker).

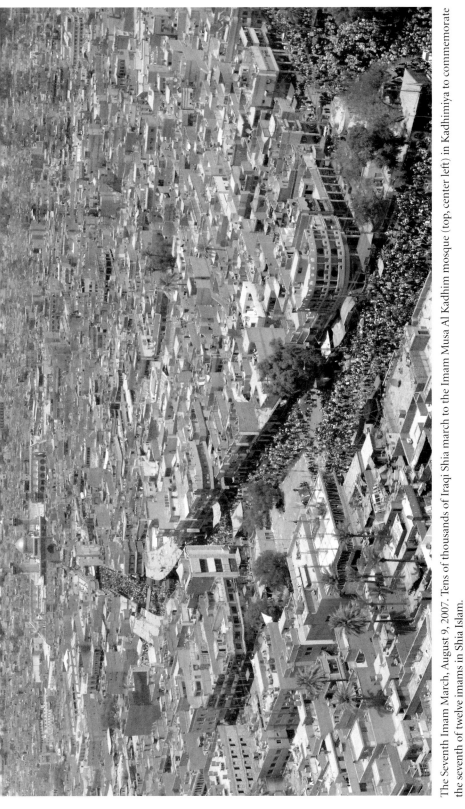

The Seventh Imam March, August 9, 2007. Tens of thousands of Iraqi Shia march to the Imam Musa Al Kadhim mosque (top, center left) in Kadhimiya to commemorate the seventh of twelve imams in Shia Islam.

The soldiers of Charlie Company, 1st Battalion, 26th Infantry Regiment "Blue Spaders" at Combat Outp[ost] Apache in Adhamiya listen to Cpt. Ed Choi on Thanksgiving Day. (Photo courtesy of TF 1-26)

Outside COP Apache, Charlie Company commander Cpt. Mike Baka and 1-26 operations officer M[aj.] John Meyer stand in front of up-armored Humvees. (Photo courtesy of TF 1-26)

The Blue Spaders at FOB Shield, East Baghdad. Battalion commander Lt. Col. Eric Schacht (center) with Maj. John Meyer (left) and Command Sergeant Maj. Steven McClaflin (right). (Photo courtesy of TF 1-26)

rd Platoon, Charlie Company, 1st Battalion, 26th Infantry Regiment "Blue Spaders" in Adhamiya. Photo courtesy of Lt. Matt Martinez)

On patrol with 3rd Platoon, C/1-26, in Adhamiya. Squad leader Staff Sgt. Juan Campos (right) and h[...] squad members (left to right) Sgt. Oscar Gonzalez, Sgt. Eduardo Rodriguez, and Pfc. Omar Avila sear[...] a possible car bomb they have discovered. At left, masked, is their Iraqi interpreter. (Photo courtesy [...] Lt. Matt Martinez)

Platoon leader Lt. Matthew Martinez (left) discusses patrol details with platoon members Staff Sg[...] Nicholas Simon (center) and Sgt. Jeremy Rausch (right). (Photo courtesy of Lt. Matt Martinez)

Abu Abid's volunteers riding to a target on the back of a Bradley Fighting Vehicle. (Photo courtesy of Lt. Gregg Caravella)

Platoon Sgt. Joseph Frye (second from left), platoon leader Lt. Gregg Caravella, and platoon members at Abu Abid's house in Ameriya. (Photo courtesy of Lt. Gregg Caravella)

Lt. Col. Dale Kuehl (back row, center) and staff officers Maj. Chris Rogers (lower right) and Maj. Chip Daniels (lower left) with Sheikh Khaled and other community leaders in Ameriya. (Photo courtesy of Maj. Chip Daniels)

Petraeus meets Abu Abid, leader of the volunteer group "Knights Between the Rivers" in Ameriya on August 15, 2007. Abu Abid, with dark hair, sits next to Lt. Col. Dale Kuehl, commander of 1st Battalion, 5th Cavalry Regiment, assigned to Ameriya. To the right of Petraeus is Deputy Prime Minister Barham Salih.

Petraeus and Iraqi Defense Minister Abdul Qadir Jassim look on as Deputy Prime Minister Barham Salih talks to one of Kuehl's company commanders, Cpt. Brendan Gallagher, at Combat Outpost Bushmaster in Ameriya.

The crucial partnership—force and diplomacy—Petraeus and Ambassador Ryan Crocker.

Key Petraeus aides: press aide Col. Steve Boylan, adviser Col. Mike Meese, and Col. Pete Mansoor, ch[ief] of staff.

Prime Minister Maliki flanked by his national security adviser, Mowaffak al-Rubaie (left), and adv[iser] Amb. Sadiq al-Rikabi (right).

Petraeus meets with Iraqi sheikhs, the "Sons of Iraq" volunteers who allied with U.S. and Iraqi soldiers, and Iraqi police in October 2007 in Yusufiyah, in an area south of Baghdad once called the "Triangle of Death" for its violence.

Playground built in Ameriya on what was once called Body Dump Field. (Photo courtesy of Maj. C Daniels)

1st Battalion, 5th Cavalry hosts a soccer game with its Iraqi army, police, and Sons of Iraq partners. Lt. C Muqadam Wa'il was the 2nd Battalion, 1st Brigade, 6th Iraqi Army Division (2/1/6 IA) commander at time. He is in the foreground with sunglasses on. Lt. Col. Dale Kuehl, 1-5 Cavalry commander, is sea to his left. Sons of Iraq leader Abu Abid is standing, dressed in a track suit. (Photo courtesy of Sgt. J Androski)

noncombatants, but it was an unfortunate side effect. The irony was that Iraqis had been setting up protective barriers around their homes and neighborhoods for a long time. Anyone who drove around Adhamiya or other Baghdad neighborhoods could readily find makeshift barriers residents had erected to keep people out.

Construction of Adhamiya's wall paused briefly while the concrete caterpillar went to replace the barriers in Sadriya, but it was completed in May. The wall did have an immediate and dramatic effect of reducing Iraqi deaths: the number of dead bodies in Adhamiya attributed to sectarian killings declined to two a week from an average of ten a week. The violence in the surrounding area also fell because Sunnis who had previously left Adhamiya to battle the encroaching JAM militias were now unable to move freely. The car bombs in the east side abated dramatically, likely due as well to the targeting campaign TF 1-26 had just carried out. But there was also another dreadful consequence of the wall, which no one foresaw and certainly no one intended, that would play out in the coming weeks.

Schacht saw that Adhamiya was a microcosm of the larger battle, in which the Shia government was trying to eliminate the Sunni enclaves. Three months into the Baghdad security plan, he saw what was required. His men were targeting insurgents, funding small projects, and reaching out to local politicians and even the Abu Hanifa imams. That was not enough, he said, "if reconciliation doesn't occur at the government of Iraq level, and its resources aren't cut loose to help this part of the city, we will end up with the status quo." Adhamiya was the home of the hard-core Sunni insurgency, and it would not give up so long as it believed the Maliki government was bent on the Sunni's destruction. Resolution of the conflict there required a national settlement.

After constant patrols and ferocious battles over six months, Schacht's battalion knew Adhamiya. So when their brigade command in Taji demanded that they conduct all their patrols on foot, Schacht resisted. That might work elsewhere, but the level of hostile contact in Adhamiya was just too high. Schacht had been on the ground for six months, on his second combat tour, and the brigade commander, Col. Billy Don Farris, had just arrived in February. As of April, the battalion had suffered nineteen killed and many more wounded—the highest casualty rate of any unit deployed in Iraq.

Farris came to visit 1-26 on May 3. He wanted to inspect the wall of Adhamiya, so operations officer Meyer and his security detail accompanied him. Farris insisted on dismounting to take a closer look at the wall. Meyer suggested that would not be a good idea since it was broad daylight and they had not done any clearance, set up a perimeter, or made any other preparations. Route Brewers, the highway that bordered the wall, was a virtual shooting gallery. A sniper lined up Col. Farris in his sights and shot him in the groin.

Meyer quickly loaded the colonel into the Humvee and sped the convoy to Apache, where the battalion physician's assistant, Capt. Joe Welchel, otherwise known as Doc Welchel, stopped the colonel's bleeding, stabilized him, and put him on the medevac. Luckily Farris's femoral artery had not been hit, but it was a complicated wound. Farris was evacuated to the United States via Germany. Meyer felt terrible about the injury to the brigade commander, but they had tried to tell him how dangerous their neighborhood was. They had paid for that knowledge with their own blood.

As the physician's assistant providing immediate care to battlefield injuries in Adhamiya, Welchel had a graphic appreciation of how the enemy's methods had evolved over the unit's tour. At first grenade and sniper attacks were the norm, and 1-26 successfully adapted its tactics to counter them. Then EFP attacks began to rise. An EFP could kill one, two, or three in a Humvee, depending on its size and where it hit the vehicle, and would often rip off limbs. Compared to their first tour in Samarra, according to Welchel, this tour was incomparably more lethal. "There have been many more amputations, a lot more lethality, shattered bones," he said. "Other soldiers see other parts of Iraq. They see kids in the streets and stuff like that. All I see is the destruction."

A UNIT'S STRENGTH USUALLY RESTS on a few individuals who provide its esprit de corps and make the sum greater than its parts. 1-26's Charlie Company had a reputation as a strong unit, and its three platoons carried on a friendly rivalry. Platoon sergeants Widmark Quashie and Tim Ybay traded boasts one night at Old MOD. "Everyone says their platoon is the best, but ours *is* a very tight unit," Quashie jousted. One of the main reasons was Staff Sgt. Juan Campos, from McAllen, Texas. At twenty-seven, a veteran of Iraq and Kosovo, Campos was a charismatic leader of the best and most motivated squad. "He's the heart of the platoon," said Quashie, who marveled at Campos's gift for navigation. "He could visualize a grid in his head. He'd wait until I was done explaining how we were going to get somewhere, and then show me a better way."

Campos's company commander, Capt. Mike Baka, had the same high opinion of him. The sergeant was one of the few who would challenge Baka when he did not agree with a mission. Campos had reenlisted for another five years, despite the toll army life had taken on his wife, Jamie, and son, Andres, who was eight. He would get a break from deployment after this tour with a two-year assignment to the school at Fort Benning, Georgia. Campos was young, but he was responsible for the life and death of younger men in their late teens and early twenties. He knew the better the squad functioned, the better chance everyone had of coming out of a battle alive. In the quasi-familial relations of the ground units, the squad leader functioned as the big brother, the platoon sergeant as the father. The closeness of Campos's squad was mirrored in its physicality. The soldiers would wrestle with each other and sprawl together in a heap to watch movies. Their bonds, their youth, and their confidence made them feel invincible.

In early May, their platoon leader, Matt Martinez, was brooding. Over the past two weeks his soldiers had found more and more homemade explosive powder, which the soldiers called HME. A sergeant stepped on some and the blast cut a hole right out of his foot. A few days later, one of their gunners was wounded by a bomb made with HME. Shrapnel blew up through the bottom of his Humvee. It was clear to Martinez that they needed new countermeasures.

Martinez was the kind of person who thrived on finding solutions to problems. His natural bent, as an engineer, was to keep close tabs on all the infrastructure projects that had been started, and mostly left unfinished, in their area. The army had drilled into the head of every soldier going to Iraq the importance of rebuilding the infrastructure and the economy, but few young infantrymen were intrinsically interested in sewage systems or power lines. Martinez was the exception, and his soldiers kidded him about it. He was frustrated by the unfinished projects, such as the new transformers sitting next to the gas station, a project funded by the French embassy. The transformers sat there, useless, because no one had connected power lines to them. He passed information on what he saw during his daily patrols to the company's designated civil affairs officer, who was quadruple-hatted as fire support, public affairs, and psychological operations officer. When a trained major from the 96th Civil Affairs Brigade arrived in Adhamiya to take charge of this critical aspect of counterinsurgency, Martinez fed him constant updates.

Martinez kept a close eye on the infrastructure projects for another reason. Any project to repair or replace water, sewage, and power lines required digging holes in the streets, sidewalks, or nearby soil. The insurgents frequently used these excavations to plant bombs. The attackers did not care whether people had electricity, drinking water, or sewage lines. Many of the soldiers begrudged residents' failure to band together to stop this destruction. Martinez fought bitterness, noting that all of the bombs they had found were discovered with the help of the locals.

On May 14, Martinez and 3rd platoon were on patrol in Adhamiya near the mosque. Sgt. Oscar Gonzalez was in the lead Humvee, followed by Martinez's and two other Humvees. As they drove by the cemetery, a rocket-propelled grenade flew between the first two Humvees and exploded into the cemetery wall. There was no one on the street. "What was that?" one of them yelled over the radio. Martinez believed the grenade had been mounted on the wall of a house opposite the cemetery and fired remotely as they went by. They turned onto the street leading to the mosque. As the lead vehicle approached the next intersection, Chirdag Street, the driver saw people scatter. He radioed back to Martinez: "Hey, there's something wrong with this street. Everybody ran away."

Martinez told the driver of his own Humvee to take the lead, as he usually did when they came under attack or saw something suspicious. It was the most dangerous position, but it enabled him to assess the situation.

He looked at the covered manhole in the middle of the street and directed his driver to swing wide around and turn onto Chirdag. The others followed. The street was dirt: the pavement had been dug up by contractors Americans had hired to lay new sewer lines. The contractors had not come back to lay concrete over the dirt. Sgt. Campos's Humvee followed Martinez's.

Suddenly there was a deafening explosion. Thirty meters ahead Martinez saw dirt shoot out of a building—probably propelled up out of the sewer system. He radioed for all the Humvees to report their status. His gunner swung his turret around to look at the Humvee behind them and said, "They're on fire."

Campos's Humvee was thrown into the air as the explosion hit the vehicle's fuel line, driving fuel into the cab of the vehicle and setting the five men inside on fire. His gunner, Pfc. Omar Avila, was slammed against the edge of the turret. The force broke both of his femurs in open fractures just above the knees. Pfc. Nicholas Hartge, twenty, who was sitting in the right rear seat behind Campos, was swallowed up in flames and incinerated.

The platoon had rehearsed what they would do in case of fire. The drivers jumped out and grabbed their extinguishers, which were mounted behind their seats. Martinez and Staff Sgt. Octavio Nunez ran back toward the burning Humvee. Iraqis with AK-47s were shooting at them. Sgt. Terry Fleming had climbed out of the Humvee and was running toward them. He was on fire. Nunez forced him to the ground and yelled at Spc. Michael Alexander, the driver of the vehicle behind the burning truck, to come quickly with the extinguisher. Alexander sprayed foam all over Fleming, putting out the fire. Martinez carried Fleming to his Humvee and gently placed him in his seat.

Private Avila was huge. He weighed 250 pounds and, with his vest and gear, close to 300. He was also extraordinarily strong. He was on fire and both legs were broken, yet he somehow managed to pull himself out of the turret. Sgt. Nunez dragged him away from the burning truck as rounds began cooking off. It took three men to pull him to safety. Avila lay on his side, still burning, and Pfc. Sean Cousino extinguished the flames. Martinez and Alexander went to their Humvee for a backboard.

With Cousino's help the three loaded Avila, with his torn legs, onto it and carried him to a doorway alcove on the sidewalk. Cousino stood guard while Sgt. Robbie Flowers, the medic, began to work on him. Avila had second- and third-degree burns over 60 percent of his body. "You're gonna be okay," Martinez reassured Avila, bending over him to comfort him.

Martinez sent Nunez back to his truck to radio for help. The Humvee was still burning, and two buildings next to it had caught fire. The men were cut off from the two trailing Humvees. The roar of the fire was deafening. Martinez realized they were still being shot at from the alley to the north. AK-47 shots pinged off the walls and the Humvees. All kinds of ammunition inside the burning Humvee began to explode. The truck was full of ordnance: it was rigged for both a 50 cal machine gun and an M240B machine gun, and one of the men carried an M203 grenade launcher. There were thermite and flash-bang grenades. Rounds were going off in all directions.

As soon as he saw the fireball, Pfc. Chad Chalfant, the gunner in the truck behind Campos's, had leapt out of his turret, jumped to the ground, and run to the burning Humvee. Private Jarrod Taylor was steps behind with the extinguisher, which he threw to Chalfant, who reached Campos first. Their squad leader was engulfed in flames and had collapsed onto the ground. Chalfant extinguished the flames, and Taylor dragged Campos to one of the Humvees, burning his own hands. Campos was severely burned over 85 percent of his body. Taylor was knocked over by shrapnel from an exploding grenade, but it caught the edge of his flak jacket and bounced off. He ran back to the truck to Pfc. Andrew Catterton, whose face and fingers were badly burned. His fingers were "gloving": the skin was peeling back to expose bone. His shirt and armored vest were gone and he was wandering in shock. Taylor grabbed Catterton and put him in the truck and then helped others who were loading Campos.

A pair of UH-60 Black Hawks happened to fly over Adhamiya just then. Helicopters routinely flew a ring route around Baghdad's various military bases. These were probably on their way from the Green Zone to Combat Outpost War Eagle or Taji. Choppers usually flew up the Tigris, and Adhamiya sat on its eastern bank. The pilots saw the burning Humvee and the billowing smoke. They immediately flared and hovered over the attack site. The door gunner swiveled his .50 caliber machine gun in an arc, looking for the attackers. Martinez looked up gratefully as the helicopters came lower, no more than twenty meters off the ground, to stand guard as the soldiers struggled with the wounded.

While the choppers hovered above, Private Naryan Curtis, on the ground, fired his M249 Squad Automatic Weapon at the attackers. When he ran out of ammo, he moved to the turret of his Humvee and began shooting the M240 machine gun. Meanwhile, Flowers, the medic, who was feverishly treating Avila and Fleming, told Martinez that their airways were going to start collapsing soon if they did not get to the doctor. Flowers did not want to perform emergency tracheotomies there on the road under fire. "We've got to get them to medevac right now," he said.

Martinez went to his Humvee and radioed Staff Sgt. Christopher Cunningham, who was on the other side of the conflagration. "Account for all personnel," he said. As he stood with the radio in his hand next to Fleming, who was in his seat, Martinez saw the soldier begin to shake. He was going into shock. Martinez saw that Fleming's bulletproof vest and web gear were still smoking. The plastic zippers had melted. Martinez unsheathed his knife and cut the vest off him.

The other vehicles were not yet loaded with the wounded, so Martinez decided to send the Humvee with Fleming and Avila back to Apache by itself. Cousino volunteered to stay with Martinez. They, Nunez, and their interpreter ran several blocks through the alley; it was the only way to the other vehicles. When they reached the other side, the soldiers were trying to stabilize Campos and Catterton. Martinez looked at Nunez and saw tracer bullets flying by him and realized they were under fire again. He ducked and ran between the vehicles, directing Catterton to be shifted to the other truck so shooters were distributed evenly to protect them on their dash back to Apache. Cunningham radioed Apache to let them know they were on their way with more wounded.

In the chaos, Martinez made one more check to see where the empty seats were. He put Nunez into the last one. Then he grabbed the interpreter and ran to the back of the last Humvee. He opened the trunk hatch and threw him in. Since there was no more room, Martinez piled in on top of him, leaving the hatch open since his six-foot-plus, 200-pound bulk would not fit. "Move out, move out," he yelled.

As they careened into the winding entrance to Apache about five minutes later, the truck ahead of them got stuck rounding one of the turns. There was not a moment to spare. Martinez jumped out and helped carry Campos the last two hundred yards down the road and past the twenty-foot metal door into their compound, which was standing open to receive them. They took Campos straight to the open garage shed where Doc Welchel and four or five medics were already at work on Fleming and Avila. Their throats had started to close, as Flowers had warned. They had arrived just in time.

Martinez had been forced to leave Private Hartge's body on the sidewalk. The helicopters hovered over his corpse. In a few minutes the quick-reaction force—2nd platoon, the fire truck, and a recovery vehicle with a winch—arrived on the scene to get him. The company commander told Martinez his platoon did not have to go back out. They gathered around as Welchel's medics made the final preparations to put the four wounded soldiers on the helicopters. It was a horrific sight. The men were all severely burned: Avila, Fleming, and Catterton had third-degree burns over much of their bodies. Campos, their squad leader, was in the worst shape. No one knew whether they would make it.

The medevac helicopters arrived and whisked the four away on the five-minute flight across the river to Ibn Sina, the combat support hospital in the Green Zone. After surgery to stabilize them, they would be evacuated to the United States, via Germany, to Brooke Army Medical Center in San Antonio, Texas, which was the army's main facility for burn treatment. They were on their way to Landstuhl, Germany, in a few hours. In a stroke of luck, a team of burn experts from Brooke just happened to be at the base in Germany that day, flying home from a trip to Norway. They attended the soldiers en route.

A day or two later the rest of the platoon went to the mental health clinic at Taji. The men were shaken. After an hour and a half of listening to them pour out their emotions, the counselor said, "Time's up." But the floodgates had been opened, and the young men had no idea what to do next. There was no miracle cure, no drug they could take to hold back or dissipate their feelings of horror, grief, fear. "There is no preparation in our training for the mental health struggles that come later," Martinez said of their attempt to grapple with the traumatic event.

On June 1, Staff Sgt. Campos died at Brooke. His wife made the excruciating decision to take him off life support after the doctors told her there was no hope of his recovering consciousness. The other three remained in critical condition. Catterton and Avila would eventually start breathing on their own, but Fleming remained on a breathing machine, his fate uncertain. He nearly died several times but kept fighting, though he had third-degree burns over 70 percent of his body. In October he walked and talked for the first time, and his father was overjoyed to hear his son's voice. The road to recovery for all three men would take years of multiple surgeries, grafts, and painful therapy.

Everyone in the company was affected by the deaths of Hartge and Campos. Their former company commander, Mike Baka, was devastated. He had helped Hartge apply to West Point, but Hartge had then decided to postpone his matriculation so he could return with the platoon to Iraq. He had not wanted to leave them shorthanded. So far, Charlie company had lost seven men in the war. Those who had labored to rescue the soldiers were nominated for Bronze Stars with Valor and Silver Stars for their heroism, but medals would not bring back the dead or restore those who lay in agony.

Campos's death sent ripples throughout the company. "We felt that if God could take him, he could take me in a second," Quashie said. The remaining squad members had trouble sleeping. Martinez had to keep pushing them. After patrols they would hook up the video game *Guitar Hero* and play it for hours. They put on wigs and pretended they were dueling guitarists in a rock band, not young soldiers losing their buddies in a war. When it was time to go on patrol again, they loaded their weapons and put on their vests, pushing away the thought that this might be their day to die. As they left the base, adrenaline fired them into a state of hyperalertness. In automatic, orchestrated movements they scanned the street for signs of bombs. Inside the Humvees for hours on end, men bonded by danger and death poured out their thoughts to each other. "The Humvee was our foxhole," Quashie said. "We would talk about everything—God, man, obscene and crazy stuff."

Martinez was deeply concerned. Since the May 14 attack, they were getting hit almost every time they went out, and the bombs were getting bigger. One bomb crater he measured was five by four feet. The trend was clear: the concrete wall had sealed off the insurgents from their Iraqi targets in the city, so they were turning their full fury on the Americans. "The focus of the enemy changed from Iraqi civilians to coalition forces. I noticed the increase in IEDs [improvised explosive devices] as soon as the wall went up," Martinez said.

He went to see the company commander. "Sir, something is going on in the city. The enemy is escalating very quickly. If we don't respond to it, we are going to lose a lot more guys," Martinez said. "We need to lock the city down." A few days later, he took his case to Meyer. The wall gave them the means to close Adhamiya, he argued. After the next bomb they could close the checkpoints for a day. If there was another bomb, they could shut down for two days. They could deny the insurgents freedom of movement. Meyer saw the logic of the proposal, but there could be other consequences. U.S. forces had launched a citywide effort to woo Sunnis and get them to volunteer as neighborhood watchmen. Punitive action against Adhamiya would fly in the face of that initiative. It would also cause a furor, as putting up the wall had. The Sunnis of Adhamiya were already paranoid, and trapping them inside the neighborhood would certainly fan those flames.

The platoons started patrolling in Bradley fighting vehicles, the army's heavily armored, tanklike personnel carrier. Sometimes they would take two Bradleys and two Humvees; others would take four Bradleys. Martinez switched to a Bradley so his crew would feel safer.

On June 21, Charlie Company's 2nd platoon was on patrol in the heart of Adhamiya. The lead Bradley in the patrol turned left off Route Remy, one of the main east-west arteries, onto a residential street. It was a wrong turn. The Bradley stopped and began to back up. Sgt. Ybay, the acting platoon leader, was in the second Bradley. He was in the commander's seat in the turret on the Bradley's right side, with the hatch closed. As the first Bradley turned around, Ybay scanned the street through his sights. He saw a young boy about seven playing on the sidewalk near a teenager. Outside the house on the corner an adult looked after two toddlers in the yard.

Then Ybay heard a deafening roar. It was a bomb like he had never heard or seen before. The entire street blew up, lifting the massive Bradley in front of him into the air and flipping it upside down. The force of the explosion ripped through the Bradley into the turret and blasted the hatch off. It was a shocking, almost incomprehensible thing to see such a vast hunk of metal so quickly and totally destroyed. The insurgents had stuffed so much explosive into the sewer system that they now had enough power to destroy a Bradley. The Bradley weighed thirty-five tons, combat loaded, with its stock of munitions and special reactive armor tiles. The add-on tiles were steel boxes filled with explosives designed to blow outward and detonate incoming rounds away from the vehicle. But the tiles were of no use against these bombs, which blew through the flat underbelly.

In fact, nothing in the U.S. inventory could withstand the explosive force of these new deep-buried explosives. The bomb detonated under Ybay's platoon was estimated at over two hundred pounds of explosives, packed into the drainage pipe under the road. By comparison, a tank-killing 155 mm artillery shell contained eighteen pounds of explosives. In recent months the soldiers regularly had been finding the homemade explosive powder, made from urea nitrate or ammonium nitrate and other common fertilizer, in houses they searched. It was cooked and then spread out to dry, an inch or two thick, on roofs or floors of vacant homes in the area. There was usually no way to safely remove the highly unstable substance. Explosive ordnance disposal teams were called in and the houses were blown up, after the neighbors were warned. One of Schacht's soldiers had lost his foot in April in one such house in Qahira.

Sgt. Ybay and his soldiers dismounted. Flames and black smoke billowed out of the Bradley. Someone started shooting an AK-47, and the ammunition inside the burning Bradley began cooking off, both of which forced the soldiers to take cover and return fire. Ybay had been the acting platoon leader since March. Called Platoon Daddy by his soldiers, he often pulled pranks on his charges when they were asleep or not paying attention. He was born on Clark Air Base in the Philippines into a military family, and his siblings were scattered around the world in various branches of the armed services. Now he was forced to watch his young charges die. He could do nothing for the five Americans and their interpreter inside the Bradley.

Two were sergeants, Alphonso Montenegro and Ryan Wood, who had served with 1-26 in Samarra in 2004–2005. Both were college-bound, and Montenegro's twenty-second birthday had been just two weeks earlier. The other three were newly engaged Daniel Agami and best friends Anthony Hebert, nineteen, and Thomas Leemhuis, twenty-three. In the days and weeks ahead, Ybay was haunted by the fact that 1-26 originally had been scheduled to go home on June 20, before their tour was extended to fifteen months. It seemed to him a judgment.

Maj. John Meyer was on patrol in the neighborhood and heard the explosion. The reverberating boom told him it was bad. He had already turned his protective security detail toward the sound when the call came over the radio. They were the first to reach the site and saw the Bradley, upside down and on fire. Meyer radioed for all available units to come immediately.

For the next three and a half hours, Ybay and Meyer struggled to get the chaos under control. They first set up a security perimeter to prepare for the recovery. A platoon of military police attached to 1-26 responded to Meyer's call. He sent them to Route Absolut, the major street intersecting Remy. Martinez's platoon arrived next, and Meyer went to the MP position just as it came under attack. A rocket-propelled grenade slammed into one of the MP Humvees and decapitated a female MP inside. Meyer rushed to aid four other MPs who were wounded, stifling his agony over one more death as he threw himself into action. The M88 armored recovery vehicle, a seventy-ton crane, arrived and its crew repeatedly risked their lives as they aided Meyer under intense gunfire and rocket-propelled grenades.

Back at the Bradley site, Maj. Pete Zike, the embedded U.S. military adviser to the Iraqi battalion, had arrived. He left Apache as soon as the radio call went out. A little while later, the fire truck arrived and tried to douse the flaming Bradley. Apache helicopters flew over the area to provide cover and look for attackers. Zike began picking up body parts. No man could discuss this gruesome day afterward without tears in his eyes. The blast was so powerful that the soldiers had been dismembered. The children and other Iraqis who had been at the street corner were also blown apart. It was impossible to determine to whom many of the remains belonged.

Capt. Ed Choi, the battalion chaplain, also responded to the radio call, but en route to Adhamiya, his Humvee was hit by an IED. The bomb went off underneath the right front seat, breaking both of the truck commander's legs. Choi, seated behind him, was wounded in the left knee and right foot. They continued on to Apache, where Doc Welchel treated them, and Choi comforted the distraught 2nd platoon soldiers as they came in from Route Remy.

As the men labored in Apache's open garage shed, the body bags slowly filled up. Five Iraqis, whose remains would be given to the families as soon as they were identified. Five soldiers. One female MP. One interpreter. And a final bag for the strewn parts whose owners could not be identified. Doc Welchel worked stoically, his medics at his side, while others struggled at the grisly sight of their dismembered comrades and the smell of death as the scorching sun beat down on the shed.

Two Black Hawk helicopters flew across the brown Tigris, which glinted in the late afternoon sun. They settled down on the gravel outside the walls of the little compound for the "hero flights" that would take away the dead. The soldiers gathered there for a ceremony to pay their last respects as the body bags were loaded aboard. There were so many body bags that the helicopters had to make three trips.

For the previous two hours Clay Padgett, Meyer, and the chaplain had been keeping an awful secret, a final blow dealt to 1-26 on that terrible day. Padgett had received a call from their brigade commander across the river, Col. J. B. Burton. Padgett took the message and told Schacht, "Col. Burton needs to see you at Camp Liberty." Schacht could not fathom why Burton would call him away from his men at such a time. He said he would go on the last flight carrying the body bags.

As Schacht stood at the landing zone with Meyer and Padgett, it dawned on him why Burton was calling him over. He was going to relieve him of duty because so many soldiers had been killed. "No, he just needs to know you're okay," Meyer reassured him. They knew the real reason but it was not their place to tell him.

Burton had told them to send Sgt. Maj. Steve McClaflin, Schacht's battle buddy and close friend, along with him. The two men boarded the chopper and landed in a swirl of dirt about fifteen minutes later at Liberty Pad, on the sprawling main base complex that surrounds the Baghdad airport. Burton was waiting on the tarmac. The last body bags were loaded into the waiting graves registration van. Burton then gave his favorite battalion commander the hardest news he'd ever had to deliver. "Your son Justin died today," he told him.

Shacht's sixteen-year-old son had returned home to Schweinfurt that day after a summer youth group trip to Rome. His mother and siblings were in the United States visiting relatives. After walking the dog and taking a shower, he was supposed to go to a neighbor's house. When Justin did not appear, the neighbors went to his house on Jackson Street. Looking in the window, they saw him slumped over on the couch, a plate of food on his lap. The autopsy was inconclusive, but it appeared that Justin, a healthy young man, had choked to death in a freak accident.

The men sat on the tarmac and stared at the sky as Schacht struggled to absorb the tragic news. Burton took them back to his office. McClaflin comforted his friend as he cried. The stalwart lieutenant colonel had borne the heavy responsibility a commander carries when his soldiers die doing things he has ordered them to do. After almost three years commanding the battalion, he knew every member down to the lowliest private and felt each loss keenly. As Schacht grappled with this devastating blow and prepared to leave on the flight to Balad, the first leg of his journey home, Burton brought up the decision that lay before him. "You are going to have to decide whether to give up your command," the colonel said. "Don't make the army make this decision for you." He knew Schacht would feel he was abandoning his soldiers. Schacht agreed to think about it. The next day he flew home to Germany to claim his son's body. "Where shall I bury my son?" Schacht asked Burton and Chaplain Choi. "I don't have a home." At the division's request, he had moved his family to Germany from Hawaii in the year between the Samarra and East Baghdad deployments. Burton and Choi helped Schacht arrange for Justin's burial in Arlington National Cemetery. Choi attended the funeral and prayed afterward with Schacht and his family. Schacht hated to leave his troops when they most needed him, but he could not compound his wife Amy's grief by leaving her alone. "Your family needs you now," Choi told him.

True to their fighting form, Meyer and Padgett had not let grief stop them for a minute. The night of June 21, they launched the first of several raids to seek justice. Neighborhood informants and intelligence gathered by technical means helped them find some of those responsible for that day's attacks, the carnage of which had stunned even the war-hardened Adhamiyans. Over the coming week, the battalion rounded up fifteen suspects who were part of the homemade-explosives business.

Petraeus attended the memorial service for those who died on June 21. He had been informed of the attack immediately, as he had been on May 14, the day Martinez's platoon was hit. He knew 1-26 was in an inferno, and he hoped that his attendance at their ceremony at the former defense ministry (Old MOD) would lend some moral support. He sat in the front row of folding chairs. While conducting the service, Chaplain Choi broke down and had to pause to regain his composure. Afterward, Petraeus talked to the battalion staff. The services were intended to help the unit begin to reach closure, but it was only a first step. "Adhamiya was exceedingly hard," Petraeus said. "This unit was really having a tough time."

After a platoon lost soldiers, the battalion policy was to give the unit forty-eight hours off the line, to reduce the chance of revenge killings and to reinforce military discipline. It was a natural human desire to want payback, especially after such horrific deaths. Anger, grief, and fear were churning inside the men, and Sgt. Ybay tried to address each man's needs. "A lot of guys were angry," he said. "Some wanted to talk; others just needed time to themselves." There wasn't much Ybay could offer his men in their highly demanding circumstances and austere environment.

Their only respite was satellite TV, which the 1st sergeant had installed at their combat outpost at Old MOD. Beyond their two weeks of home leave, Ybay gave each soldier four days of extra leave at Taji, a large base away from the front lines.

Ideally Ybay wanted to allow each man one day for himself each week, to relax at the outpost. But he just couldn't manage it, since the platoon had to run multiple patrols around the clock. They had lost too many men. His platoon, originally thirty-eight soldiers, was now down to twenty-five. Eleven men had been killed or so severely wounded that they could not return to duty. The other two had been transferred. Ybay himself did the jobs of two men—platoon sergeant and platoon leader—from March through July, as the casualties escalated. Desperately needed reinforcements were slow to come, and the soldiers who did arrive came straight from basic training. Ybay and his squad leaders tried to prepare these new GIs for what they would encounter outside the gate. Charlie Company had a reputation as an extremely professional outfit that soldiers were pleased to join, but Ybay recognized that the losses of the past eleven months had bound his original platoon members into a fraternity that was impossible to enter.

The carnage of June 21 affected the entire unit. The soldiers had regarded the Bradleys as invincible; the vehicles had seen them through the 2006 battles in Sadr City, through the Blackwater recovery battle, and in countless other missions to capture militia leaders and car-bomb makers. Now the enemy had ripped away their security blanket. They felt naked.

"I knew the Bradleys were my guys' last bastion of hope. That's what they were holding on to," said Matt Martinez. Now they wondered, "What do we do now? If I'm not safe in a Bradley, where am I safe?" The day after the June 21 attack, his entire platoon went to Taji for counseling, and when they returned Martinez sat down with them to sort out how each one felt. Both his platoon and Ybay's platoon were struggling. They decided that 1st platoon would take the lead on the night shift, when most time-sensitive targeting and raids occurred, and Martinez's 3rd platoon would take most of the day patrols to give Ybay's a break.

Martinez had tried to balance the individual soldiers' needs with the entire unit's morale. After the first Charlie Company deaths in 2006, a few soldiers had gone to Taji for mental health counseling but after a week there they did not want to come back to the front line. That led to resentment among those who continued the dangerous daily patrols. "Every soldier has seen terrible things," he said.

The soldiers continued to go out on patrol, but ten to twenty Charlie Company soldiers were flooding the mental health clinic at Taji every day. The administrators of the clinic began calling the command to ask what was going on. Gen. John Campbell at the Baghdad division headquarters felt it was time to pull 1-26 out of Adhamiya. Burton also wanted to get his men out of the inferno, but he was in a particularly difficult position. 1-26 was his battalion, trained, raised, and mentored by him, but he was not their commander in the field. He was, however, still responsible for the brigade's eleven thousand family members back in Schweinfurt.

Burton called the brigade commander based in Taji. Acknowledging that it was the commander's call to make, Burton said, "I'm worried about my boys. I want you to find a way to get my soldiers out of there." He did not want to see Charlie Company and Alpha Company leave this war with nothing left. The decision was made to move Charlie Company from Apache to join the rest of the battalion at Old MOD.

Martinez was grateful. "Someone recognized that they could not continue to work us the way we were being worked," he said. There was no doubt in his mind: the soldiers of Charlie Company had done their time. No unit had endured more during the entire Iraq war. Whereas in World War II, troops would be pulled off the front lines for a reprieve every few weeks or, at most, months, these men had been on the front lines in Baghdad's most violent neighborhood every day, rarely getting a break. The company had lost two dozen men, and they had worked around the clock, detaining hundreds of high-value targets, hundreds of low-value targets, and discovering more weapons caches than they could recall.

The Baghdad division had just received two battalions of the final surge brigade and sent one to Adhamiya. The new battalion-sized unit—3rd Squadron, 7th Cavalry Regiment—was scheduled to take over Apache on July 20. Charlie Company patrolled with them for several days beforehand to orient them to the neighborhood, and 1-26's

Alpha Company would continue to patrol Adhamiya along with the new unit. This new arrangement meant that four companies plus a battalion headquarters would replace the lone Charlie Company's daily patrols in Adhamiya proper. Quadrupling the number of troops was tacit recognition of the heavy load Charlie had carried. They just did not have enough troops.

Ttragedy continued to stalk the battalion. On July 11 Alpha company 1st Sgt. Jeffrey McKinney, forty, took his own life in front of his vehicle crew. He stepped out of his Humvee and put his gun to his head. A week later, on July 18, an Alpha Company patrol was returning to Apache after making a bereavement payment to the family of a woman who had been killed in a firefight with insurgents a few days before. Such payments were standard practice when civilians were killed, even when enemy fire was responsible. The death of noncombatants could turn an entire family against the Americans and the Iraqi government, and the payments were an effort to prevent that. Soldiers were fighting a war among civilians, and even the strictest rules of engagement could not prevent innocent deaths.

The soldiers were a few blocks from the dreaded mosque when the street heaved up under the lead Bradley. It was as if the same horror film were playing again: over one hundred pounds of homemade explosives planted deep under the street was detonated as the soldiers rolled over it. The Bradley was launched into the air and tossed upside down as if it were a toy truck, and a massive fireball consumed it. The fire was raging and the motorized hatch, which weighed several tons, was not able to open against gravity, assuming anyone was still alive to open it. The fire suppression system may well have asphyxiated everyone inside. When the four soldiers inside were finally retrieved, they had been burned beyond recognition.

The dead included Sgt. First Class Luis Gutierrez Rosales, one of the most popular men in Alpha Company and one of its four senior noncommissioned officers. The gregarious platoon sergeant, thirty-eight, had been a big brother to all the company's younger soldiers. Three specialists also perished: Zachary Clouser, nineteen; Richard Gilmore III, twenty-two; and Daniel Gomez, twenty-one. Like so many squads, these soldiers hailed from all over America: California, Pennsylvania, Alabama, and Georgia.

The July 20 attack, coming within a month of the previous multiple-casualty attack, struck at the foundation of the unit's morale. Throughout the year they had grown accustomed to losses by ones or twos, but it was crushing to keep losing so many men in catastrophic attacks they stood no chance of surviving. Ybay had been trying to nurse 2nd platoon back to functionality. "The scab had barely formed," he said, "and this ripped it off." Several of his soldiers had flashbacks.

Operations officer Meyer described the cumulative effect on a soldier's psyche of the months of losses and daily patrols that were a deadly roulette. "You've been in fights that last for hours. Almost every day you go out the gate. You are a second away from another IED strike every time you go out the gate. It is over 100 degrees. You've been here for thirteen months. The only break the soldiers have had for a year is two weeks of R&R. Almost every day you go out on patrol, and whether or not you make contact, you've just seen the day before a Bradley flipped over on its top with five soldiers whom you've known and you can't recognize those five because that blast didn't burn, that blast blew everybody apart. Or the one with Alpha Company; it doesn't blow anybody apart, they're burned and you don't recognize them. The soldiers see that, and it adds up over time. So every time they go out the gate, they think, 'Am I going to get blown up? Am I going to get shot?'"

It was the junior and noncommissioned officers, Meyer said, who kept their soldiers putting one foot in front of the other. "Sgt. Ybay, Sgt. Quashie, Lt. Martinez, Capt. Baka—I could go down the list," he said. "The lesson learned for a small unit is that it all comes down to leadership, discipline, doing the basics well. To get your soldiers to go out the gate is nothing but pure leadership. To get them to do the right thing is pure discipline. . . . The discipline to come back, clean your weapon, make sure your vehicle is fueled, make sure the ammo is clean, make sure your radio and kit are taken care of, to scan your sectors, to go out there day in and day out."

The more resilient soldiers helped carry the others. Padgett's driver, Spc. Chris Matthews, created a memorial for Zach Clouser, his best

friend since basic training, on his MySpace site. Losing Clouser reinforced Matthews's wish to become a noncommissioned officer and lead
men in such times. He kept the wedding photo of his wife taped to the
radio in his Humvee and reminded her that she had encouraged him to
join the army. Despite Padgett's half-serious complaints, Matthews had
mastered the art of driving like a bat out of hell to avoid the ubiquitous
bombs—and so far had succeeded. A genial fellow, he bucked up the
spirits of his gunner, who had been stop-lossed before deployment and
yearned only to be free of the army and the war.

A turning point for Adhamiya, or the possibility of one, came two
weeks later. Two relatives of a prominent sheikh, Wathiq al-Ubaidi, were
killed. The sheikh had been on the Americans' list of bad guys since Pete
Mansoor's brigade of the 1st Armored Division had patrolled Adhamiya
in 2003–2004. The sheikh had been an imam at the Abu Hanifa mosque,
preaching resistance to the Americans, but left after a falling-out with
the other preachers. When insurgents would not allow him to bury his
relatives at the Abu Hanifa cemetery, the outraged sheikh denounced
the "terrorists" being harbored at the mosque. He gathered about eighty
members of his clan, and they forced their way into the grounds of Abu
Hanifa on the afternoon of August 5.

Soon after the melee broke out, the local Iraqi army unit showed up
and detained thirteen suspects in and around the mosque. Later that
evening the Iraqi troops returned to an outer courtyard of the mosque
and unearthed a massive weapons cache containing IEDs ready for use,
dynamite, mortars, rockets, land mines, and a variety of weapons.
Around midnight another raid was carried out at the nearby Al Assaf
mosque, a few blocks east. They then returned to Abu Hanifa, where
more weapons including a sniper rifle, IEDs, grenades, detonation devices, and mortars were found in the cemetery. The soldiers knocked
on the tomb lids to determine which were full of materiel. In all, forty-
four suspects were detained that day.

Several times over the past year 1-26 had sought permission to go into
the mosque, which they knew was the insurgents' sanctuary and an arms
depot. Because raids on the religious site had caused an outcry in previous years, they were banned from entering the mosque grounds without

the permission of either the prime minister or Multi-National Force-Iraq (MNF-I). What apparently catalyzed the August 5 raids was that Sheikh Wathiq happened to be the uncle of Gen. Riyadh Jalal Tawfiq, the commander of the Rusafa Area Command, which directed the Baghdad security plan in the eastern half of the city. When Riyadh learned what had happened, he swung into action and went to Adhamiya himself. The necessary permissions were forthcoming. "Was it the death of Riyadh's family members that made the difference?" Meyer wondered. Another soldier remarked sardonically that it was not surprising that Wathiq would know where the weapons were hidden at the mosque since he used to be an imam there.

"Everything bad that ever happened to us happened within earshot of that mosque," Widmark Quashie said. The battalion certainly hoped the events of August 5 signified that the residents of Adhamiya had finally decided to turn on the killers in their midst. It would mean that the soldiers' toil and bloodshed were leading to something. The battalion was too experienced to leap to facile conclusions, however. Capt. Nakata, the battalion intelligence officer, knew insurgent leaders readily moved among their various safe havens in Fadl, Adhamiya, and west Baghdad. They would not give up Adhamiya without a fight. A few days after the roundups in the mosques, Sheikh Wathiq's home was bombed. He was seriously wounded and three more of his relatives were killed.

The Abu Hanifa's chief imam, Sheikh Amer, fled to Syria. A guest imam, Sheikh Yasser, arrived at the Abu Hanifa mosque and adopted a far less belligerent tone. He attended all the District Advisory Council meetings and urged the councilmen to work together. At one meeting the middle-aged, bearded imam listened attentively for much of the meeting before speaking. He asked the American officers sitting at the table to provide a list of detainees held by the Americans and the Iraqis. Adhamiyans did not know whether their sons had been detained, killed, or were with the insurgents.

In late August a trickle of Sunni volunteers came forward to work as security guards on contracts paid by CERP (Commander's Emergency Response Program) funds. They had shunned Schacht's earlier attempt to recruit them into the Iraqi army, but this new effort at engagement did not require them to leave the neighborhood. After verifying that they were not wanted for any crimes, the Americans put the first thirty volunteers through a quick training course at Apache. They started work as guards outside Adhamiya's Al Numan hospital, the only one in eastern Baghdad where Sunnis could safely go for treatment. Another thirty guards were put to work at the newly reopened gas station in Adhamiya in an effort to prevent it from falling under criminal control once again.

Martinez's platoon was now patrolling Waziriya, which abutted the southeastern corner of Adhamiya. Bomb factories, militia members, and insurgents had been found there too, but it was worlds away in lethality. "My guys appreciate being able to go on a cordon and knock and not have someone throw a hand grenade at them," he said. Residents in Waziriya often extended traditional Iraqi hospitality to the soldiers who came to ask questions and search their homes. They would serve soft drinks, chai, or, as on one hot August day, ice cream to the men sweating in their bulletproof vests.

THE END OF THEIR FIFTEEN-MONTH TOUR was finally in sight for the Blue Spaders. They were the first active-duty unit to serve the extended tour, and the extra three months in Baghdad's most violent neighborhood had taken its toll. Nearly every day of their 443-day tour was a combat patrol. Of the battalion's 800 soldiers, 35 had been killed in action and 122 wounded, three times the casualty rate of 1-26's previous deployment to Iraq in 2004–2005. It was the highest casualty rate any battalion had suffered since the Vietnam War. Six soldiers had lost one or both legs, and many more suffered lifelong injuries. Thanks to Doc Welchel and the medics, many wounded men had survived, but there were grievous injuries, including ones that would not surface for months. Many traumatic brain injuries caused by bomb blasts were not diagnosed until later.

Chaplain Choi believed the extra three months had caused an exponential increase in stress and fatigue. "I've only got twelve months of Iraqi patience," Padgett joked. The battalion had lived in dangerous, spartan outposts with none of the amenities most U.S. soldiers in Iraq took for granted. To help the men cope with their grief and prepare for the transition from war to home, Choi and the new battalion commander launched Operation Healing Heart, a program to treat the whole person with physical, spiritual, and mental activities. He organized weight-lifting and other contests and card- and video-game tournaments. In between patrols the soldiers played soccer and basketball in the walled streets outside their ministry buildings-cum-barracks. Choi conducted Protestant services and found a Catholic priest to celebrate mass.

His most popular innovation was "combat stress groups." Each month he met with a different platoon and asked the soldiers questions designed to get them to start processing their experiences. What has been your biggest struggle here and why? What is something positive about the deployment? How has your outlook on life changed? If invited to speak to third- and fourth-graders about your experience, what would you tell them? The soldiers discussed their responses first in small groups and then shared them with the platoon. Choi held more than 120 individual counseling sessions, but he knew the men's needs were far greater than one chaplain could meet. He believed each company needed a combat stress team, soldiers who were specially trained to help other soldiers deal with death and other traumas. The sooner they received treatment, he said, the better their chances of recovery.

Most of the men were emotionally numb as the deployment ended. The atmosphere at Old MOD was subdued. Jared Purcell, the spunky effects captain, tried to get guys to grow mustaches, and Clay Padgett was still quick with a smile or a joke. Meyer maintained his iron composure, but he was drawn and pale, and the strain of sleeping only a few hours a night showed in his solemn brown eyes. Choi fretted over soldiers who had been unable to grieve, as they would be most at risk of post-traumatic stress disorder (PTSD), drinking, drug abuse, or other infractions or illegal behavior once they returned home.

Choi knew from previous deployments that most of the PTSD cases would develop after the soldiers had been home for about three months. On the last deployment the troops seeking help had had to wait four months for counseling. The staff of mental health workers at

Schweinfurt had shrunk from four to one since then as the base had been downsized. Choi made an appeal to the division headquarters at Wiesbaden that all available mental health professionals stationed at bases in Europe be sent to Schweinfurt for six months of temporary duty. He reiterated the request to the commander of all U.S. Army forces in Europe, Gen. David McKiernan.

Meyer was fiercely proud that the soldiers had maintained their discipline in the face of the daily brutality inflicted on them. "These soldiers are disciplined. Even though all this has happened, not one civilian has been abused. They still treat people with dignity and respect, and it is unbelievable," he said. A few days earlier, his own self-control had been tested. A JAM cell leader in Qahira wanted for killing four soldiers with EFP projectiles on Route Brewers had finally been captured. Meyer had been there when the Iraqi was brought in. "I looked at him—and I'm a field-grade officer—and the anger boiled up in me," he confessed. After a white-hot moment, Meyer turned and walked away. "All the soldiers have done is just walk away, because they are disciplined soldiers. And that's what makes this a great unit," he said. "This is a disciplined military organization of the U.S. Army. Our soldiers do not go out and do things you hear about on TV."

There was certainly ample hatred of Adhamiya voiced by many soldiers. Some felt that way about all of Iraq. "This is a trash pile that needs to be blown up," said Charlie Company's Sgt. John Gregory. One night in the company break room, he vented about the ignorance, indifference, and violence he had witnessed among Iraqis. "All the surge means is more of us for them to kill," he said bitterly. He was also scathing in his criticism of the war. "This is a stupid war," he said, excoriating President Bush. "We've tried every different angle; all of them have failed. We're too afraid of offending Iraqis." Gregory said 80 percent of those the soldiers detained were released within days. "The Iraqis know we won't kill them," he added, fuming that many restraints had been placed on firing the Bradleys' cannons in the city.

"My only goal is to make sure my guys get back home alive," Gregory said. He leaned forward and his intensity increased as he recounted pulling his best friend and fellow soldier out of a Humvee after it was hit by an EFP. "He had no legs. He bled to death," the sergeant spat out. "I've watched the road blow up in front of me I don't know how many times and rain asphalt all over my hood." With eight years of military service to go, Gregory saw no end in sight to his Iraq deployments. "I'll be coming over to Iraq until I get killed," he said.

Martinez had come into the company's break room and taken a seat nearby. He listened quietly. As Sgt. Gregory got up to leave, he said angrily to Martinez, "Tell the truth, Lieutenant." Next to a computer on a table in the room, where a television blared at high volume and soldiers sat mesmerized, eating popcorn, lay pencil sketches some soldier had drawn. They were strange and violent drawings, with captions like "You're next, bitch."

Martinez did not try to soften Gregory's comments or excuse his bitterness. Blowing off steam verbally helped the men conquer their feelings to do their jobs the next day. Martinez was also frustrated by the losses, the unfinished reconstruction projects, the Iraqi army's inability to supply its soldiers with flak jackets and other essential gear, the political system's inability to produce solutions, the Iraqis' timidity in the face of violence. His wife Lauren's love had helped him maintain his sanity, he said, but he did not know if there was hope for Adhamiya. It was easy to remember the bad people, he said, but some Adhamiyans had stepped up to help. Sunni nationalist insurgents had caught one of the worst killers the battalion had sought, and a shopkeeper had saved Martinez's life in January by warning him about a bomb in a box.

Martinez planned to return to Iraq, he hoped with the Blue Spaders. He had twice requested a permanent transfer from his engineer battalion to 1-26. Army rules required him to serve thirty-six months in his first unit, but 1-26 wanted to keep this extraordinary young man, already wise and steady beyond his years, who had proven his mettle in the deadliest part of Baghdad. Either way, he was destined to return to Iraq after a year at home. After being bloodied and battered with 1-26, he wanted to serve with them on the front lines again. Living, sleeping, and dying together had forged the deepest of bonds. Trying to explain it, he said, "You've worked through some of the hardest experiences of your life that you'll ever have with these men."

Some of the Blue Spaders' most experienced soldiers would leave the unit after the tour in Adhamiya. At age forty-three, Quashie was retiring after twenty-three years in the army. His wife and two girls eagerly awaited his return. He thought he might become a teacher. Sgt. Ybay was leaving too. "I promised my mother, no more war," he said. After fourteen years of army life he wanted to spend more time with his three children before they were grown and gone. The men's personal reasons for leaving the army were understandable, but the loss of platoon sergeants such as Ybay and Quashie would be keenly felt. They were the unit's father figures, and "Platoon Daddy" Ybay knew it. The army leaders were keenly aware that the growing attrition of such noncommissioned officers and captains posed a huge problem for an army still in the middle of a war and for the institution's long-term health.

John Meyer would be coming back. He was promoted to lieutenant colonel and given command of the battalion, which he would no doubt lead from the front as he had every day of the past year. His first charge was to mend his men and get them ready. Their bravery under almost constant fire was recognized as the army began to bestow combat medals. Thus far, 76 medals for valor had been awarded or were pending, including a presidential citation for the battalion, 5 Silver Stars, 15 Bronze Star Medals with Valor, and 55 Army Commendations with Valor. In addition, 122 Purple Hearts were awarded to the wounded. The country's highest award, the Medal of Honor, was bestowed posthumously on Spc. Ross McGinnis, nineteen, of 1st Platoon, Charlie Company. He was only the third service member of the Iraq war to receive the honor. McGinnis died in Adhamiya on December 4, 2006, when a grenade was thrown into his Humvee. Rather than jump out, he smothered it with his body and saved the lives of the other four men inside.

NO ONE COULD BE SURE what the endgame for Adhamiya would be. Even though the new unit, 3-7, came in with a large infusion of money to pump the neighborhood full of reconstruction projects and engagement initiatives, Meyer believed a purely nonlethal, or nonkinetic, approach would not work there. "You have to be able to secure the population to have a solution in Adhamiya," he said. "And you have to defeat AQI [Al-Qaeda in Iraq] so you can secure the population. You have to have enough combat power inside the wall to be able to do that. Where we had one company, there are now four." But in his view, even that probably was not enough. A full-scale clearing operation according to army doctrine would require an entire brigade—more than twice what was there.

It was late at night and Meyer had missions to run till 4 a.m. But he got out his marker and started to draw on a whiteboard, littering his arguments with references to military history and contemporary strategic literature. In another life he might be a professor. These were the war's burning questions, and he thought about them constantly. The most critical element for succeeding there, he said, was time. Despite the pressure from the American public, he said, doing the job in Adhamiya simply required more time. Rocking back on his heels, he asked the question that haunted most officers in Iraq: "How much time do we have to make a difference?" Meyer also knew there was a limit on how much a volunteer army this size could take.

A solution in Adhamiya required two other elements, in addition to more time and more troops. As Schacht had realized early on, a permanent peace in Adhamiya would require action by the national government. This neighborhood represented Iraq's Sunni leaders, and if they did not believe they had a place in the new order and assurances that they would not be liquidated or forced out of their homes into a refugee existence, they would continue to support or at least tolerate those who were fighting the government.

Meyer also believed that enemy forces had to be killed or captured; securing the population was not enough by itself. It had proven impossible to play defense against this enemy's tactics, and the population could not be protected by defensive measures alone. But the offense had to be very precise so as not to kill innocents and create more recruits to the cause. "I think for Al-Qaeda in Iraq it *is* a kinetic solution," Meyer said. "I mean the actual AQ, not the guy who they pay fifty or a hundred dollars to plant something." Although Al-Qaeda in Iraq attracted foreign leaders and foreign suicide bombers, it had planted roots in Iraq. Meyer said they had not caught one foreigner in Adhamiya. The radical clerics at the Abu Hanifa mosque had recruited many Iraqis and spread the group's extremist agenda and beliefs.

The embedded military adviser to the Iraqi battalion, Maj. Pete Zike, shared Meyer's view that the lethal, die-hard killers had to be taken out of action. "We were not kinetic enough initially in this war," he said. "This is a culture that respects absolute power and death. We had to knock heads in Adhamiya to get to reconciliation." Zike had been an indispensable link between the Iraqi battalion and the Spaders, since the Iraqi commander was inclined to go off on his own operations. Zike suited up and went out with Iraqi patriots day and night, and kept the Spaders in the loop. The artillery officer loved the job so much he signed up for a second tour.

Another who agreed was Lt. Col. Sean Swindell, who over the course of two tours in Iraq had led the special operations battalion based in Baghdad that targeted many high-value targets, car bomb networks, and the JAM special groups. One of his teams lived at Apache and worked with 1-26, but Swindell regretted that he had not been able to send more help to Adhamiya to keep the cells from regenerating. He believed they had yet to track down a few key individuals based in Taji or Tarmiya who used Adhamiya as a staging ground.

Petraeus agreed that Adhamiya was probably the toughest nut to crack in all of Baghdad. He shared the officers' skepticism about whether a local peace was possible there. "It seemed to have an extremist fervor to it that other areas didn't have," he said. "It was such a tough place to get established in. We had to fight to get the JSS in, and fight AQ continually. They were very hard-core, very resilient. It really appeared to be one of those areas, candidly, where you wonder if you can solve it with the resources you have."

9

The Knights of Ameriya

In many respects Ameriya was western Baghdad's equivalent of Ad-hamiya. It too had become a haven for the Sunni insurgency, though the battle there took a different turn. Its spacious two- and three-story mansions were home to the ruling elite of Saddam Hussein's regime. Army officers, former officials, and many doctors and other professionals lived in the tan stone and stucco buildings of modern design, with high ceilings, tall windows, and arched atriums over the front doors. Many homes bore evidence of the ferocious battles that had been fought. They were pockmarked with holes from automatic rifles and machine guns, including most of the houses lining the infamously violent airport road that marked Ameriya's southern boundary. The homes' flat roofs were perfect for snipers and spotters who remotely detonated bombs against the passing U.S. convoys. Some homes' walls or roofs had caved in, and a few had been reduced to rubble. At least half the houses were vacant, abandoned by families who had fled to Jordan, Syria, or Anbar province as the violence escalated in 2005 and especially 2006. As in Adhamiya, city services were virtually nonexistent. Corpses were dumped on the streets or in a large field, nicknamed Body Dump Field, in the middle of the neighborhood. Ameriya had become a safe haven for the most extreme insurgents not only because the disgruntled former Sunni elite welcomed them, but also because it was located along the main highway from insurgent-ridden Anbar and the Abu Ghraib neighborhood to the west. Nationalist insurgent groups like the 1920s Revolution Brigade and the Islamic Army of Iraq made common cause with the radical Al-Qaeda-affiliated fighters.

The 1st Battalion, 5th Cavalry Regiment of the 1st Cavalry Division arrived in Iraq at the end of November 2006 and was assigned to Ameriya and the western part of Mansour. When the Baghdad security plan was launched, 1-5 CAV set up joint security stations (JSS) in Bonsai in an old wedding hall in Jamia in January and in a mall in Adl in February. In March the battalion commander, Lt. Col. Dale Kuehl, moved his headquarters from the battalion's base at nearby Camp Liberty to the JSS Khadra in a police station so he could lead from the front and have ready access to the battle space. Ameriya was too violent, and there was no Iraqi security presence whatsoever, so the construction of outposts there would await the spring clearing operations.

When 1-5 CAV arrived, the U.S. strategy had been to transition areas to Iraqi control and withdraw, but by mid-December 2006 they received word that the strategy was changing. The battalion was quick to reorient to the population-security approach. The staff officers had already read their former colleague Doug Ollivant's *Military Review* article about battalion-led counterinsurgency operations and had discussed ways of putting the ideas into practice. Ollivant had been 1-5 CAV's plans officer on its previous tour. The current executive officer, Maj. Chris Rogers, was a close friend of Ollivant's, with whom he had attended the School for Advanced Military Studies after their return from Iraq. The battalion was eager to see if it could implement enough of the counterinsurgency initiatives to make the area a model and advance the oil-spot approach of making progress one neighborhood at a time. They drew up contracts for road repairs and trash pickup to stimulate economic activity, and undertook a frustrating, months-long effort to reopen a bank branch in the area.

Even before clearing operations were conducted, Lt. Col. Kuehl began the slow work of sending out feelers, making contacts, identifying influential locals, and trying to build a network of relationships that would enable him to understand what was happening in Ameriya, and then, he hoped, to influence it. It would take him four months to lay the foundations. As a foreign area officer, he had appreciated the cultural demands of such work. Although his area of expertise was Korea, his years abroad had taught him the importance of keeping an open mind and learning to adapt to other cultures. He had been the only foreigner in a class of fifty students, and he had traveled extensively in Asia and Russia before serving a second tour in the U.S.-Korea combined forces command. Kuehl had never attempted to penetrate a foreign culture in such hostile conditions—few U.S. soldiers had—but he understood that this was his primary mission. He had to be a soldier, spy, and diplomat in a neighborhood that was under fire every single day. Kuehl was well suited to the task: he had a sharp, skeptical mind and read people well. He did not hesitate to take risks when he believed the opportunity warranted it. Ameriya was a situation replete with risk.

His predecessor, Lt. Col. Gian Gentile, of 8-10 CAV, had introduced him to the five most influential imams of Ameriya, who became the main focus of his outreach. Whereas tribal leaders dominated in much of rural Iraq, in the city the mosques were centers of influence. In February some of the imams agreed to meet with Kuehl. Sheikh Khaled Muhamed Ahmad Mizwid al-Ubaydi, of the Abbas mosque, was the most important imam of the five, with political connections throughout Iraq. Kuehl found him to be articulate and very intelligent. He held a master's degree and was pursuing a doctorate in religious studies in Jordan. They discussed local matters such as the need to bring services into Ameriya and to form representative local councils, but they also discussed politics, Al-Qaeda, sectarian influences in the Iraqi government, Iran's influence, and Iraq's importance in Middle East geopolitics.

Sheik Walid, of the Firdas mosque, had an engaging personality and was the imam most open to meeting with the Americans. As were other imams, he was involved with some of the insurgent groups. Walid even fancied himself a *mujahedeen,* an Islamist fighter, but Kuehl rather doubted it. Regardless, the battalion commander wanted to talk with them all to help him understand who was who. Not all of the imams were receptive. One older imam was hostile and did nothing but complain. He was hostile because he had had a very rough relationship with the previous Iraqi army unit, which had stationed soldiers around each mosque. When a soldier was killed, his mosque was raided and nearly destroyed.

Clearing operations in Mansour and Ameriya began in March and continued into April. They were carried out by elements of Col. Steve Townsend's 3-2 Stryker Brigade and the Iraqi army's 5th Brigade in conjunction with Kuehl's battalion. From the outset Kuehl had operated with less than a full battalion. Two of his companies had been sent to other areas: one to Dora in southwest Baghdad and one to neighboring Mansour. Kuehl assigned his remaining two companies, Alpha and Bravo, to west and east Ameriya, respectively. Because he was shorthanded, Kuehl was also given temporary command of one of Van Smiley's Stryker companies, Alpha Company of 1st Battalion, 23rd Regiment, to help control the battle space once the clearing operations had finished. After the clearing operations, Kuehl's two companies set up two combat outposts, Annihilator in west Ameriya and Bushmaster in east Ameriya, with Iraqi liaisons posted there. In late May Kuehl's Delta Company returned from Dora and became the battalion's nighttime force to conduct targeted raids against insurgents and go after the bomb-layers.

During the March and April clearing operations, Kuehl met daily with Townsend and the Iraqi army commanders, including Brig. Gen. Abdul Ameer, who led the 6th Division and commanded operations for the Baghdad security plan in all western Baghdad. In the course of these meetings, the American and Iraqi commanders had ample opportunity to take measure of each other.

Kuehl was inclined to call things as he saw them. Early on he spotted his Iraqi army counterpart, Lt. Col. Sabah Kadam Fadily, extorting local businesses and did not hesitate to raise the matter with the 5th Brigade commander, Col. Ghassan, and Brig. Gen. Ameer. In response Abdul Ameer asked that Kuehl be fired. Kuehl's boss, Col. J. B. Burton, not only defended him but also began a detailed collection effort to track Iraqi army commanders' connections to political figures, militias, and criminal enterprises. Often just sharing that information with the officers themselves or their superiors had a salutary effect. When necessary, efforts were made to have the commander removed. But Ghassan, whom Kuehl and others regarded as an excellent officer, was always a little cool toward Kuehl thereafter. Kuehl had a ready smile that crinkled the corners of his eyes, but also a steely side that everyone who came into contact with him experienced.

Almost immediately after the clearing operations finished in Ameriya, all hell broke loose. It made Kuehl question the value of the clearing operations and the quality of the intelligence that drove them. It was obvious that plenty of insurgents remained in Ameriya. As he looked back on the operation, he mused that the control phase might need to come *before* the clearing phase so that units would gain the needed understanding of the neighborhood and the intelligence to carry out targeted clearance.

In May, thirty-five bombs went off, and fourteen soldiers were killed. Until then the battalion had lost only three soldiers in the previous six months. On May 2 a female MP attached to the battalion was killed. On May 3 a bomb exploded at the intersection of two main streets, Market and Honey, which the soldiers had dubbed Screaming Lady for a statue at the crossroads of a woman that appeared to them to be screaming. The battalion was being targeted with the same deep-buried bombs that were decimating 1st Battalion, 26th Infantry Regiment in Adhamiya. The daily drumbeat continued, with bombs going off on the main north-south thoroughfares, Market and Jordan streets, Screaming Lady, and one the troops had nicknamed Ferris Wheel.

ON MAY 19 1-5 CAV SUFFERED its worst loss in a single day. That afternoon the battalion's Alpha Company had moved out to seize and secure the buildings that would become its first combat outpost in Ameriya, Annihilator, in an unused trade school. They would live in the outpost and provide security for the surrounding population. While they secured that site, 1st platoon, Alpha Company patrolled the neighborhood to the south and east in their M2A3 Bradley Fighting Vehicles.

Back at the motor pool at Camp Liberty, Sgt. First Class Joe Frye was suiting up for his patrol. The platoon sergeant could see that his soldiers were absentminded. In the past weeks they had seen the hardest fight of their tour. There had been eighteen bomb attacks that week, and twenty-two the week before. This was just a fraction of the hostile actions recorded as "significant activities," or SIGACTS, including gunfire and mortars, which were running at an average of thirty-one a day. In their own 2nd platoon, one soldier had been killed and two others wounded during this spate of violence. Many of the men had seen soldiers die in front of them.

To Frye, it seemed as though the unit was on the verge of a collective breakdown. He spent more time talking to the men about their emotions than about the mission ahead of them. He too found it hard to put the past weeks out of his mind, but he tried to change the subject. He started off his mission brief with a few jokes and instigated some friendly wrestling with some of the guys. It succeeded in lifting the gloom a bit, and Frye launched into the day's action plan. He had barely begun when he was interrupted by a dull roar in the distance.

"We all knew the battle drill for the sound of a blast," Frye recounted later. "One, hope it's not one of your own. Two, turn the speaker up in the back of the Bradley as high as it could go [to hear the radio transmission]. Three, look toward the city of Ameriya for a cloud of smoke." That day they saw the smoke first. It rose high above the city and continued to billow upward instead of dissipating, as it usually did. The soldiers' faces darkened with concern, then determination. They rushed to their gear, threw it on, and dove into their Bradleys. Gunners, drivers, and riflemen raced through the preparations for departure.

Inside the tank commander's turret, Frye put on his headset as the first report came over the radio. At 4:59 p.m. 3rd platoon had been hit by an IED. One of the Bradleys was on fire. There were six casualties. Frye felt relieved: casualties, not KIAs. His relief would come back to haunt him. On the internal radio, Staff Sgt. Damion Andrews told Frye that the men and Bradleys in his section were loaded and ready. He had heard part of the report that Frye missed: no one had gotten out of the Bradley. Andrews hoped no one else had heard it. Like Frye, after each day's casualties over the past month, Andrews had spent a lot of time comforting soldiers and reassuring them that they would be okay.

Frye radioed the battalion's executive officer, Maj. Rogers. He was in command that day since Kuehl had flown to the Counterinsurgency Academy to speak to incoming soldiers assigned to Mansour. "We're REDCON1," Frye radioed as soon as they were ready. They were told to go to checkpoint 3. A fire truck was being readied and would link up with them at that checkpoint exit from Camp Liberty. "Roger," Frye replied.

The Bradleys rumbled out toward checkpoint 3. Rogers radioed them en route to go instead to checkpoint 4. Frye ordered the other Bradleys to follow him as they U-turned to head to the other exit. Halfway there, another call came redirecting them to checkpoint 3. When they arrived, the soldiers watched the cloud still billowing over Ameriya. They were anxious to be on their way to the rescue. They were expecting a fire truck to show up, but the only thing the 299th Forward Support Battalion had available was a flatbed truck with a five hundred–gallon drum of water mounted on its back. About fifteen minutes after the bomb had gone off, the rescue team was finally on its way. The drivers gunned the massive Bradleys through the winding access road onto the airport highway. At the first exit they turned left into Ameriya. As they approached the site, Frye radioed 3rd platoon, which was already on the scene. It was 5:36 p.m. He turned the fire truck and the M88 recovery vehicle over to 3rd platoon and set up a security perimeter with his Bradleys facing south on Market Street.

It was the same bad intersection—Market and Honey ("Screaming Lady")—where they had suffered their first catastrophic IED hit on May 2. Just in the past week five dead Iraqis had been found within two hundred meters of the intersection. Kuehl believed Al-Qaeda was killing residents to intimidate the neighborhood and increase its freedom of maneuver.

It wasn't long before the fire truck drained the five hundred-gallon drum. The Bradley was still burning, and the truck departed for Camp Liberty to refill. Frye then radioed the commander. "Do you need us for cas-evac?" Frye asked, eager to help with casualty evacuation. "No one has gotten out of the vehicle," Rogers told him.

The mood inside Frye's track shifted from determination to anger, rage, pure hatred toward everything and everyone who was not American and not a soldier. "I, along with everyone in my vehicle, wanted to inflict as much pain and suffering as possible," Frye later recalled with brutal honesty. "It was directed at every single individual around us. It did not matter whether they were innocent or not."

One of the soldiers in the back of Frye's track asked if they could go to the vehicle to help. The Bradley was still engulfed in flames. Frye and his men knew that if nothing was done there would be neither survivors nor their remains. He took three men and moved to the scene with their fire extinguishers. They emptied their fire extinguishers onto the blazing Bradley. It was as if they had done nothing. The fire raged on. Fighting hopelessness and covered in soot and sweat, Frye and the soldiers ran to a house in front of the burning vehicle. They found a garden hose and some old buckets, filled them with water, and began trying to douse the fire with buckets. After a few trips, two Iraqi men came out of the house and began to help ferry buckets to the Bradley. Despite his surging emotions, Frye was touched by their gesture. "It was something we did not expect. It was much-needed help."

Sgt. Andrews wanted to take a Bradley to the fire station in Ameriya to get a fire truck, but if he was hit en route they would not have the combat power to respond to two emergencies at once. Instead he continued to provide security and then took over for 3rd platoon when Rogers ordered the latter platoon to Bushmaster to proceed with the scheduled opening of the combat outpost that day. Andrews did not understand why the opening could not be postponed so the unit could put all hands on deck for the recovery. Rogers's answer: "Negative, we are not going to give them the satisfaction."

The answer came over the company net. Everyone heard it. Andrews couldn't understand Rogers's logic and he knew how it would sound to the soldiers. All they wanted to do was get to their buddies, rescue them, and find those responsible. Andrews himself was churning pain, anger, and rage. "It was the hardest thing I ever had to do . . . not to inflict as much pain and suffering as was humanly possible. Someone had just killed members of your family, and you have to swallow hard and just pray that someone shoots at you or tries you," he wrote later. "But no, the locals just kept going about their day."

As Frye and his crew tried in vain to douse the fire, Andrews received a radio call from overhead reconnaissance that a group of men was moving white powder off a nearby rooftop. Homemade explosives. He wished he had more men so he could send them over to the site. Andrews was furious at Rogers's decision.

At 6:00 the Stryker platoon, which had been investigating the area, found a command wire leading from the blast site to another house nearby. The hands of three men inside tested positive for explosive residue, and they were detained.

A request came over the radio to confirm the battle roster of those in the burning Bradley. As the names were radioed back, Andrews's anger was further stoked. A little while later, someone at the battalion asked if the vehicle would have to be towed or skull-dragged back. Andrews raged at the thoughtless remark. The water truck returned. By 7:20 the fire was sufficiently under control for the recovery work to start. So the soldiers of 1-5 CAV would not have to do it, the Stryker platoon moved in to pull open the rear ramp door of the charred hull. It was a ghastly scene. They found the remains of five soldiers and the interpreter, but they could not find the driver or the gunner.

In the meantime Lt. Col. Kuehl and the battalion's sergeant major arrived at Liberty. Rogers gave them a quick situation report and they headed to the site. Even though he had ordered his men to use Bradleys instead of Humvees, Kuehl and his detail were using theirs. He was nervous, especially as they drove past known IED sites. They arrived at about 8 p.m. as the Bradley's turret was being lifted by a crane. The hull had already been righted. Pieces of the Bradley were scattered everywhere. The familiar smell of burned asphalt filled the colonel's nostrils. He talked to Frye and the Stryker platoon sergeant. Then he noticed that two bodies were still in the turret that was hanging from the crane.

Kuehl held a flashlight while his sergeant major, Fidel Gomez, and another soldier grimly struggled to pull the tank commander's body away from the melted metal, wires, and charred equipment. The body was stiff and curled into a ball, the uniform and skin completely gone. The body was still hot, so they had to handle it in gloves. Then they freed the gunner, who was also inside the turret. It took them about twenty minutes, but it seemed like hours. Despite two decades in the military, Gomez was not prepared for the feelings that came over him when he saw his fellow men violently blown to pieces and burned beyond recognition.

The Stryker platoon had removed the rest of the remains from the Bradley. They had been there for hours. Kuehl told their platoon sergeant that they could leave and directed Frye to take over security of the area. A week later that sergeant would lose a leg when a house filled with homemade explosives blew up. Kuehl rested on one knee and gazed at the horrible scene as the Bradley was hoisted onto a flatbed truck.

The forensic analysis conducted after the blast calculated the bomb buried under the street had been concocted from at least one hundred pounds of homemade explosive. Like other such megabombs, it had been powerful enough to rip through the Bradley's underside, flip it upside down, blow off its turret, and carve a twelve-foot-wide and four-foot-deep hole in the street. The soldiers killed were Staff Sgt. Christopher Moore, twenty-eight, of Alpaugh, California; Sgt. Jean P. Medlin, twenty-seven, of Pelham, Alabama; Spc. David W. Behrle, twenty, of Tipton, Iowa; Spc. Joseph A. Gilmore, twenty-six, of Webster, Florida; Pfc. Travis F. Haslip, twenty, of Ooltewah, Tennessee; and Pfc. Alexander R. Varela, nineteen, of Fernley, Nevada. Their Iraqi interpreter, Aziz Abdal Saahib Aziz, was also killed.

Frye's platoon remained to finish the job. He circled the Bradleys for protection and made a plan to exfiltrate with the destroyed Bradley back to Liberty. Andrews's Bradley followed behind it, with him standing in the turret. The smell of fire and death and the sound of the scraping metal tore at his heart.

It was after midnight when they reached the motor pool. Andrews and Frye immediately went to comfort the surviving men of 1st platoon. The battalion chaplain was there, as was Rogers. Andrews and Frye did not say much. They were there to listen, to provide the shoulder to lean on, a hug. They told their platoon to provide moral support for 1st platoon. Meanwhile, Delta Company had also suffered two IED attacks. Two of their tanks had to be towed in, and one of the wounded soldiers was flown to the 28th Combat Support Hospital in the Green Zone with a spinal injury.

Everyone gathered by the Bradley. The maintenance team had set up generators and lights so the final recovery work could be completed that night. The mechanics had to cut the driver's compartment from the vehicle. The physician's assistant, the battalion's senior medical officer, climbed inside the hatch to look for the last soldier's remains. He found them on the roof of the compartment. Andrews thought, *How do I tell my soldiers that they are going to be okay now? What will we do to react to what just happened? Why are we not locking down Ameriya right now?*

Frye and Andrews hoped that the soldiers had been killed by the concussion of the blast so they did not suffer the agony of being burned to death. Frye tried to console himself and his men with the knowledge that they had done everything in their power to rescue their comrades. It was by far their darkest day. Yet Frye also took great pride in the unit's professionalism, fighting spirit, and dedication. Despite the horror and their rage, they had held to their standards and accomplished the terrible task at hand. *At least we did not give them the satisfaction,* Frye thought grimly. He made a superhuman effort to see the bigger picture of such an experience. He hoped the enemy had seen his men's bravery and that it struck fear into their hearts.

Andrews and Frye were still angry about a number of things. It was the fifth vehicle to be burned in Ameriya; there should have been a fire truck on hand. Both men realized that they probably would not have been able to save the soldiers' lives, but if they had been able to put out the fire faster there would have been more remains to send home to their families. Most of all, Andrews struggled with the fact that the battalion had not put every single asset it could muster into the rescue and recovery. As a noncommissioned officer he felt the highest duty was to show the soldiers that every possible means would be employed to save them and find the perpetrators of attacks on them. "We should have flexed all combat power to the location and started kicking down doors and questioning people about the incident," he later wrote in an e-mail. Andrews believed that the orders to move to the command outpost should have been disobeyed.

Rogers talked over that day's decisions with Andrews, Frye, and others. Rogers was deeply grieved by the loss of the soldiers, but as he reviewed his actions he believed he had made the right call to minimize the number of Alpha Company soldiers at the scene to avoid an "emotional critical mass" that might well have triggered vengeance against the community. But he regretted sending the order over the companywide net. The soldiers would not understand why Rogers wanted to keep them focused on something else. Their lack of violence that day—the absence of any retaliatory action—was, in his view, a major contributor to what would transpire ten days later. He was sorry that some of the soldiers did not and would never accept his reasoning. It was as painful a leadership lesson as an officer could have.

Lt. Col. Kuehl firmly turned aside the appeals from soldiers to lock down Ameriya that night. He was adamant that they would not take actions the population might interpret as taking revenge. If they took out their frustrations on the locals, it would only anger and isolate the very people they were trying to win over. That was exactly what the insurgents wanted to happen. Their ability to react correctly at this juncture would determine whether they ultimately succeeded in their mission.

At the memorial service, Command Sgt. Maj. Gomez overheard one of the soldiers who was saying his final good-byes aboard the aircraft vow to avenge the dead soldiers' deaths. As the senior enlisted man in the unit, Gomez realized he needed to do something to avert any such actions and relieve the soldiers' anger right away. He and Kuehl gathered the men and told them they would continue the fight against the insurgents, but not the people. "Revenge is not a tactic," he told them. "Do not take our fallen soldiers' sacrifices in vain by seeking revenge."

Kuehl knew that the natural desire to retaliate would not dissipate quickly, so in the coming days Chaplain Steve Rindahl sent a daily e-mail and posted copies around the battalion. One of them read:

PSALM 73:2–4

But as for me, my feet came close to stumbling. My steps had almost slipped. For I was envious of the arrogant as I saw the prosperity of the wicked. For there are no pains in their death.

Almighty Father,

It is easy to fall into the trap of wanting to stoop to the terrorists' level. They appear to be able to fight when and where they want with impunity. Lord, keep the Black Knights of the 1-5 Cav dedicated to fighting the good fight. Prevent us from stumbling, maintain our discipline so that we rout out and destroy the enemy but do not take our anger out against those who are caught in the middle.

Amen

Although Kuehl refused to lock down Ameriya, he had no intention of remaining passive. After he went to check on the Delta Company casualties, he called Sheikh Walid and let him have it. Kuehl described what had happened and told the sheikh that he had to do more to help. He had never yelled at the sheikh like he did that night. Kuehl's excellent interpreter, Natalya, a young Iraqi American woman from Detroit, was speaking into the handset, but the raised voice of the officer next to her was clearly audible. Walid said he was very sorry for their losses and would do everything he could to help.

The next day, Col. Burton called Kuehl. Burton wanted to pull the battalion out of Ameriya. The pattern was too similar to what he had seen happen in Adhamiya. He feared the effect on the battalion of losing so many men at once. Kuehl argued adamantly. "Sir, you can't do it. Not right now. I feel we are on the turning point, and we've paid for it too dearly." Burton relented.

Kuehl's sense that they were at a turning point—even after the worst day of his career and possibly his life—was due to several developments. He had been cultivating the imams at the mosques and asking them for help. Even though the violence continued, he felt he was getting somewhere with at least three of them. Second, the population-security groundwork had been laid: they knew the neighborhood and were moving in to stay. Third, they had instituted measures to control the movement of insurgents and materiel in and out of Ameriya. Just maybe, this was the storm before the calm.

While the clearing operations were under way and the preparations were made to move into combat outposts, Ameriya was also being surrounded with a twelve-foot concrete wall. Residents could come and go, but through limited access points that were aimed at keeping car bombs and insurgents out, just as in Adhamiya across the river. This was part of a broader effort that Burton's brigade was undertaking in west Baghdad to cut the primary routes and ratlines the Al-Qaeda-linked insurgents were using to bring fighters, materiel, and car bombs into the city from Anbar province to the west. A double row of barriers was installed along both sides of the expressway that ran from Fallujah into western Baghdad. Insurgents would turn off the expressway north into Ghazaliya or south into Ameriya and hide there or assemble their car bombs.

Throughout April, all night long, cranes hoisted T-walls into place around southern Ghazaliya, Ameriya, and Khadra. The walls were also intended to protect the Sunni civilian population inside from attacks by the Shia militias that were pressing south from the JAM stronghold of Shula, northern Ghazaliya, Kadhimiya, and Hurriya. The latter had been purged of Sunnis over the past two years.

In addition to the walls, a ban on vehicular traffic was imposed to stop car bombs. Residents could drive within Ameriya but had to walk in and out of the neighborhood. Those who worked or had business to conduct outside the neighborhood took taxis or left their cars at the checkpoint. Many Ameriyans remained hunkered down inside their homes, scurrying out to get food from the few local shops that opened at odd hours.

Now that Ameriya was bottled up, a showdown began in the neighborhood. As in Adhamiya, the immediate effect of the measures was to intensify violence inside the walls. The attacks on the battalion escalated dramatically as the cornered insurgents shifted their sights from

Baghdad's civilians to the Americans bearing down on them. The pressures and fissures within the various insurgent groups and those who supported them also began to come to a head.

Ameriyans had been most closely allied with the nationalist Sunni insurgency, made up of former regime members who had lost their jobs and positions, but over the past year they had opened the door to Al-Qaeda. The Al-Qaeda organization had made inroads in Ameriya through some of the imams but also through alliances of convenience with some of the nationalist insurgent groups who were primarily composed of members of the former Iraqi army, which had been dissolved in 2003.

Neither Ameriyans nor the nationalist insurgents had bargained for the harsh measures Al-Qaeda extremists began to impose on the local population, or the degree to which they were willing to target Iraqi civilians to enforce them. The strictures alienated a population that, although Muslim, was modern and western in most of its habits. The Al-Qaeda insurgents started imposing edicts, enforced under threat of violence, that were reminiscent of the Taliban rule in Afghanistan. Women were forbidden to wear brightly colored clothing, and simple pleasures like buying fruit ices from the sidewalk stand were banned. The Al-Qaeda-affiliated insurgents attacked a dozen or more women who were out in Ameriya's streets without *hijabs,* or headscarves, and burned their faces with acid. They threw boiling water on women whose legs were not covered. The attacks against the population steadily increased. They kidnapped some of the local residents, some for money and some to force into action as suicide bombers. In one case a $65,000 ransom was paid. One man was handcuffed to the steering wheel of an explosives-packed car. The breaking point was reached when two prominent Ameriyans were kidnapped at the end of May and a house was blown up.

AT MIDNIGHT ON MAY 29, Dale Kuehl was awakened by a call from Sheikh Walid at the Firdas mosque. Sheikh Walid told Kuehl that a group of Iraqis was going to go after the Al-Qaeda fighters who had kidnapped the two Ameriyans. They did not want any help from the Americans; they just wanted to alert them so they would not interfere. Kuehl tried to convince Walid to provide the intelligence so the Americans could go after Al-Qaeda, but Walid said no. Kuehl tried to persuade him with various approaches, but still the sheikh refused. Finally, after about fifteen minutes of arguing, it was obvious that the Iraqis were going to act no matter what.

Kuehl had just moved his battalion staff back to Camp Liberty because it had proved too difficult to command and control the entire battalion from the JSS Khadra, which lacked the communications and other infrastructure. The police there were not supporting the mission and it was under constant threat. Sick with a stomach flu, he went outside his trailer to sit on the railing between the living quarters and small cinder-block battalion headquarters to discuss the situation with his executive officer, Maj. Rogers, and Maj. Chip Daniels, the operations officer.

After pondering the various possible consequences, Kuehl called the sheikh back and told him through his interpreter, "I'm not allowed to let you do this."

"We're not asking for permission," the sheikh replied.

"Be careful," Kuehl said.

The next day, May 30, Kuehl ordered his troops to stay on the periphery. He knew he was taking a big chance, but his brigade commander, Col. Burton, had agreed that it was a gamble worth taking. Rogers's reaction to the news that Ameriyans were taking matters into their own hands was unequivocal. "It's about fucking time," he told Daniels.

Throughout the day, Sheikh Walid called Kuehl with frequent updates as intense fighting broke out in the streets. It would go on for three days. The fighters announced their uprising against Al-Qaeda, which had declared Ameriya its capital, and set an ambush. They painted graffiti on a wall declaring that Al-Qaeda was no longer welcome in the neighborhood. When the Al-Qaeda fighters came to paint over it, a bomb was detonated, killing them. The mystery fighters also attacked the Maluki mosque and killed three prominent Al-Qaeda leaders who had taken refuge there while the imam was in detention.

The next day, Thursday, May 31, Al-Qaeda counterattacked. Some of them drove a Land Cruiser into a crowded intersection and began wildly firing a machine gun. Then they attacked the mosques with rocket-propelled grenades and machine guns. The fighting moved from the Abbas mosque to the Firdas mosque, where the anti-Al-Qaeda fighters were surrounded. The sheikh called frantically to see if Kuehl's soldiers could help.

Kuehl was inclined to say yes, but he knew he would be out on a limb. He would be collaborating with an illegal group of armed men, some of whom until very recently had been insurgents fighting the Iraqi and U.S. forces. He called Burton to discuss it.

"Absolutely," Burton replied without hesitation. "Let's get this thing going. We have local Iraqis willing to take charge of their own situation against a common enemy. Why the heck not? Let's embrace these guys."

The legal authority for Burton's approval was tenuous, but he was willing to take risks and would stand behind his subordinates even if the venture went south. Still, it was Kuehl's ass on the line since he had no written orders—known as leaning forward in the foxhole. Burton and Kuehl would do it repeatedly in the coming months—with full support from Petraeus, if not from all their superiors.

Kuehl sent two companies to help the Iraqi fighters who were pinned down in the mosque. One was his own Alpha Company, led by Capt. Mike Ernst, and the other was the Stryker Alpha Company from 1-23 that Van Smiley had left behind to help secure the neighborhood's southeastern quadrant, where the mosque was located. The Stryker unit was the first to reach the mosque. Its commander, Capt. Kevin Salge, radioed the battalion headquarters to tell Kuehl what he saw.

"There's a guy here in a ski mask with a PKC [machine gun]," Salge told him over the radio. "He's coming up to the vehicle. I'm a little uncomfortable, but let's see how it plays out."

The soldiers could not distinguish which of the Iraqis shooting at each other in the streets and buildings around the mosque belonged to which group. For all they knew, all of these guys, who had been shooting at *them* a few days before, could turn around and shoot them as easily as the Iraqis they were now aiming at. The man who approached Salge's vehicle did not shoot but instead asked if the soldiers could help defend their perimeter. He also said they had wounded men inside the mosque who needed help.

Platoon leader Frye arrived on the scene with his soldiers from 1-5 CAV's Alpha Company. "It was a shock to see all these guys running around with AK-47s. It was an infantryman's dream," he said with a grin. Normally Iraqis with AKs would be his targets. Now they were "friend-lies." "It was weird," Frye said of the overnight transformation of foe into friend. But he and his men had their orders. They positioned their Bradleys around the mosque to provide protection for those inside.

Frye did not like the fact that the Iraqis were using a mosque as their command post. He would not want anyone bringing weapons inside his church. But he had a job to do, and he was ready to unleash the Bradley's 25 mm chain guns on whatever target was provided to him. His driver hit the switch to lower the rear ramp. Frye and his men ran down the ramp, guns at the ready. They ran into the mosque with their medic. Looking around, Frye asked, through his interpreter, "Who's in charge?" The Iraqis pointed in the direction of a slender Iraqi carrying an AK-47, who was bending over a fighter who had been shot and killed. The Americans bandaged other wounded Iraqis and then called for a medevac.

"What's your plan?" Frye asked the slender Iraqi. "We need to coordi-nate a counterattack to push them back," he replied. "Then we're going to their mosque." Frye first concentrated on getting the wounded Iraqis out safely. The three most seriously wounded were flown to Balad, but one died. Frye then arrayed his men in support of the Iraqis. During the day's battle, an American soldier from the Stryker company was also killed. Sgt. Chad Domino, twenty-three, was shot by a sniper as he en-tered the mosque. Frye, thirty-one, could tell that the Iraqi in charge had military experience from the way he talked, moved, and ordered his men about. The Iraqi said his name was Abu Abid.

Kuehl wanted to play out the emerging relationship to see if their new Iraqi partners were for real. Reports of the new partnership and the on-going battle in Ameriya rocketed up the chain of command to Petraeus's desk. Although Sunnis had turned against Al-Qaeda in Anbar, this was the first time it had happened in Baghdad. What no one knew at the time was that Abu Abid had recently arrived in Ameriya to catalyze the uprising after having done the same in Anbar's Zadran district. Abu Abid found a welcome among Ameriyans ready to turn on the extremists. Petraeus decided the risk was worth it—this was the essence of what he and British Lt. Gen. Graeme Lamb had been discussing for months—and encouraged Kuehl to continue the unorthodox alliance to see how it would evolve.

Sheikh Khaled had previously told Kuehl, "There's someone you need to meet at Firdas mosque." Kuehl had wanted to forge an open alliance with Khaled but he had demurred. In fact, during the violent months of April and May, he would meet with Kuehl only at night. At times they spoke only by phone because Khaled knew he was being watched. Sheikh Walid was also targeted by Al-Qaeda and left the neighborhood. He later asked Kuehl's help in reestablishing his credibility with residents, who felt he had abandoned them. Despite the threats, Khaled was willing to be the channel to those who were ready to push the extremists out of their neighborhood—or at least to try. Kuehl thought it was an effort worth supporting. "Nothing else has worked up to now," he said. Khaled set up Kuehl's first meeting with Abu Abid.

Kuehl laid down certain conditions for cooperation to continue. All the Iraqis' operations had to be carried out jointly with Kuehl's battalion. They were to tell the Americans what they were doing at all times. The Iraqis were also to coordinate their actions with the Iraqi army battalion. They were to submit to biometric scans, fingerprinting, and photographs so the Americans could develop a full registry to positively identify all their members. Finally, they were not to carry PKC machine guns, rocket-propelled grenades, or other crew-served weapons.

The following day, Kuehl's operations officer, Maj. Daniels, joined the group at the Firdas mosque. He was invited in to help plan the next series of raids. Iraqi men milled around in track suits and ski masks with AK-47s slung over their shoulders. They shooed him away from the windows. A sniper had been taking shots at them earlier. One of the Iraqis went up to Daniels's intelligence sergeant with a big smile on his face. "I know you," he said. "You arrested me!"

In the first week of the new alliance, the Iraqis killed ten Al-Qaeda fighters and captured fifteen others. Sgt. Frye's platoon was directed to go on several missions with the Iraqis, as was the Stryker unit. Another

1-23 soldier, Spc. Romel Catalan, was killed on June 2 when a bomb was detonated near his Stryker.

Even though Frye had never trained to work with a band of guerrillas, the confident sergeant instinctively knew how to establish a relationship. Rather than assert his military expertise at the outset, he asked Abu Abid's opinion of how he wanted to conduct the mission and followed his suggestions. He explained how the Bradleys were best used, and they planned their operations jointly. The fighters used their own trucks, and some climbed on the outside of the Bradleys. When they arrived at a target, Abu Abid would point out to Frye which Iraqis were Al-Qaeda affiliates. Frye also helped Abu Abid stay in touch with his wounded men, who were recuperating in the hospital at Balad.

These gestures paid off when Abu Abid's men caught two Al-Qaeda high-value targets. Abu Abid did not want to release them into American custody, but Frye struck a deal with him. Abu Abid would talk to the prisoners for two hours and then hand them over. "He's a trip," Frye said of his Iraqi ally. "But he's a good guy." The platoon sergeant had no illusions about the group's ability to change agendas, however. "They're working with us—for now at least," he said. Lt. Gregg Caravella, Frye's new platoon leader, observed that Frye and the Iraqi got along well because they were both charismatic leaders. Caravella, who had arrived in Iraq fresh out of the officers course in late summer, knew he had one of the best platoon sergeants in the battalion and relied on his experience. Frye took care of his soldiers, but he also made them toe the line. "He can either be your worst enemy or your best friend in the world," Caravella said.

The Americans were impressed by the Iraqi volunteers' knowledge of the neighborhood and their intelligence skills, which were far better than anything they'd seen in the Iraqi army. Abu Abid worked eighteen to twenty hours a day. He was also a strict disciplinarian—at times too strict with his corporal punishment, some of the Americans felt. The volunteers functioned as kind of a SWAT team. They had good light infantry skills. Over time, the Americans sorted out who was who within the group. About 40 percent had been in the nationalist insurgent groups, the Islamic Army of Iraq, or the 1920s Revolution Brigade.

Others were recruits from the neighborhood. Twenty or thirty men formed the core group around Abu Abid.

Abu Abid was a forty-year-old former captain who had served eighteen years in the Iraqi army as an intelligence officer. His real name was Saif Sa'ad Ahmed al-Ubaydi. He was a youthful-looking man, perhaps because unlike many Iraqis he did not smoke, with a ready smile and an equally quick frown for misbehaving subordinates. He was the son of an Iraqi air force general and a Sunni Kurd mother from Sulaimaniya. Three of his four brothers had followed the family profession and joined the military. The two oldest, a general and a captain, had been killed during the Iran-Iraq war in the 1980s. The other two had been killed during the holy month of Ramadan in October 2006 when the sectarian bloodbath was raging out of control. Their bodies were found dumped near the Iranian border. Holes had been drilled in them, nails had been shot through the hands of one brother, and the tops of their heads had been sliced off.

Sitting in Abu Abid's house in southeast Ameriya one night on her first visit to see him in a year, his elderly mother wailed, "He is my last son. The rest were all killed by the Iranians." She lived scarcely two miles away in the neighborhood of Iskan but had been afraid to leave her block. She said her husband offered yogurt drinks to American soldiers when they came to their street. Abu Abid explained that his mother called the Jaish al-Mahdi "Iranians." Abu Abid shared his mother's antipathy for the JAM extremists. He said he did not want revenge, but later he said with a smile, "When we finish with Al-Qaeda, we will take on the Jaish al-Mahdi."

Although Abu Abid had been unknown to Kuehl before the "battle of Ameriya," the sharp-eyed Iraqi had already had contact with Americans. In an interview at the militia headquarters in southeast Ameriya, Abu Abid recounted the path that had led him to Ameriya and the alliance with Kuehl's battalion. His family's business was bakeries, but he had helped U.S. intelligence during 2005 in the town of Tarmiya, north of Baghdad. He gathered information on Jaish al-Mahdi targets in the area. Then, he said, he had lived in Anbar province. The militia leader said he and his followers had moved to Ameriya recently and found a welcome reception among residents who had grown tired of Al-Qaeda's repression. "This is a cosmopolitan country," he said. "People are against Sharia law, beatings, and torture." They were also dismayed that Ameriya's main street, once lined with nice shops, was now full of rubble.

Soon after he arrived in Ameriya, Abu Abid had approached a U.S. patrol to tell them where a bomb was buried. He asked them to handcuff him and take him away so that any insurgents who might be watching would not suspect that he was giving the soldiers information. The Al-Qaeda insurgents in the neighborhood nonetheless learned that he was organizing the neighborhood against them. Shortly before the May 30 showdown, he said, one of the Al-Qaeda militants confronted him in the street and pulled a gun on him. "It misfired," Abu Abid said, "so here I am." He said he then drew his pistol from his waistband and killed his attacker.

On June 8, Petraeus invited the 1-5 battalion operations officer, Maj. Daniels, out to Camp Victory for a run. It was his typical method for getting information from and imparting direction to junior officers. As they started off on the loop around the man-made lake at 6:30 a.m., Petraeus got right to the point. "What is happening in Ameriya?" he asked Daniels. He told the general that every day the "Baghdad Patriots," as they had named themselves, were riding with the battalion's soldiers to identify Al-Qaeda safe houses and fighters in the neighborhood. The battalion was supplying their new partners with fuel and food, and evacuating their wounded, but not giving them weapons or ammunition. They seemed to be well supplied. "We've killed or captured more AQ in this last week than in all the weeks *combined* since we arrived," Daniels told him.

Petraeus nodded and gave him a thumbs-up as they rounded the bend by the airport. "Kuehl has made the boldest decision I have seen a commander make in my fourteen years in the army," Daniels added, noting that many of the officers and soldiers were both skeptical and nervous over the risks Kuehl was taking.

Petraeus turned his head sharply and stared right into Daniel's eyes. "Do *not* stop! Do not stop what you are doing," he said. "You are doing the right thing and now is the time to take risks!" Petraeus went on to give him two specific admonitions. "Do not let our army stop you," he said, knowing that the risk-averse institution would think first of the dangers and downsides and not of the war-winning potential gains. He knew there were plenty of people who would not agree or understand. Second, he said, "Do not let the Iraqi government stop you." He knew the Iraqi government was already nervous about the initiative and would seek to block it.

Daniels was struck by how much Petraeus was willing to risk in order to win. He saw that the general truly believed in the population-security counterinsurgency approach rather than turning over responsibility to the Iraqis. He was intent upon changing the dynamic in Iraq. Daniels was also relieved that he could go back to Kuehl and assure him that he had strong "top cover" from the top commander. Kuehl was struggling with the doubts of his men and worried that he would expend more of their lives. It was reassuring to know Petraeus thought they were doing the right thing.

After meeting Abu Abid, Kuehl learned about his previous help supplying information on JAM to Americans, but his arrival in Ameriya was not the result of a coalition force plan. Abu Abid's network was based on family and army ties, and he maintained a fiercely independent stance, even from Iraqi political parties. He had Iraqi Shiites in his inner circle and his own security detail. Kuehl believed that Iraqi leaders in Ameriya, including Khaled, had recruited him to come to the neighborhood to help throw out Al-Qaeda. As Kuehl got to know the Iraqi, he was impressed by his qualities. He was neither a stooge nor sectarian. He was anti-JAM, but not anti-Shia. But above all, Abu Abid was validated in Kuehl's eyes by the results he helped deliver.

Over the coming weeks Abu Abid and his men helped 1-5 CAV find dozens of IEDs and individuals the battalion was looking for. On June 27 Sgt. Frye's platoon found an arms cache inside a house on Street Two of Ameriya. As they came out, a sniper shot Pfc. Timothy Waite through both legs. The platoon had to shoot its way out of the street and back to base. The private lost a lot of blood and was close to dying. The attacker was from a group of Al-Qaeda insurgents who had been meeting one block south. Within two hours Abu Abid and his militia had identified the sniper as Abu Harith and gone after him. They shot Abu Harith twice but he escaped.

Even with their new allies' help, the fighting was still intense. One day in July Frye's Bradley was struck by a massive, deep-buried IED near the intersection of Market Street and Screaming Lady. The platoon leader, Lt. Caravella, was watching through his Bradley's sights when Frye's Bradley, which was directly in front of him, was engulfed in a cloud of smoke. Frye's side of the Bradley tilted up and almost flipped over, then slammed down into the crater made by the blast. Caravella radioed Frye but heard no answer. Caravella feared the worst.

Frye and his gunner had been knocked out by the blast. When Frye came to, he could not see. Fine dirt and smoke from the explosion swirled around him. He reached around the turret with both hands until he felt his gunner, who had regained consciousness. Frye was speaking but he could not hear himself. He thought he'd lost his hearing. Then he realized that his helmet and headphones had been thrown off his head. When he found them, he first called the driver, who had his own compartment on the left side of the Bradley. His hatch had been blown off but he was unhurt. Then Frye opened the inner turret door and called down into the well to check on the men in the passenger compartment. They were shaken but unhurt. They had been thrown about when the Bradley reared up, but the blast's main impact had been directly under Frye. They were all very lucky to be alive. Frye then radioed Caravella and the track in front of him. "Are we damaged?" he asked them.

"Your right wheels are gone, but your track is still on," came the answer. The reactive armor tiles on the right side had also been blown off in the explosion. Frye's driver started up the engine and it came to life. They sputtered out of the hole and down the road for a few blocks before the Bradley died. The thirty-five-ton vehicle was totaled. Frye and his men got out and took cover inside a house until the quick reaction force arrived. As the initial adrenaline surge subsided, Frye felt the pain. The tough thirteen-year army veteran had broken his tailbone in the blast. He knew it would be a cause for mirth in the platoon. The doctor told him it would take six weeks to mend.

For the first two months of their alliance, the battalion paid Abu Abid and his men rewards for valid information, as the military did to individual citizens. The going rate was $2,500 for IEDs and $10,000 for an Al-Qaeda foreign fighter. But Abu Abid was eager for his militia to be recognized as a legitimate force. He wanted them to be incorporated into the army. In late August the battalion signed a ninety-day contract to hire them as a local guard force, using money from the CERP (Commander's Emergency Response Fund) and the CIA.

On the first payday, Abu Abid's headquarters were thronged by dozens of Iraqi men. Most were young; some were middle-aged. Most carried AK-47s. One burly Iraqi in a knit watch cap named Omar carried a PKC machine gun and a knife in a leg holster; a pair of metal handcuffs dangled from his vest. The battalion's liaison to the militia, Capt. Eric Cosper, drove up in his Humvee convoy. A team of soldiers, headed by Cosper, had been culled from the battalion to provide a constant link to Abu Abid and his men. Cosper entered the building, lugging a heavy army backpack stuffed full of cash for the 227 militia members who had been hired under the contract. Each one was paid $200 a month.

"What *are* we doing here?" he said with an ironic laugh as he walked past the motley crew of rifle-toting Iraqis. It was still a surreal experience for the American soldiers, who knew they had probably been trading shots with this band of guerrillas in the spring. "Is Abu Omar here?" Cosper called out in a deep baritone. He was seeking a former lieutenant colonel who had been a personnel officer in Saddam Hussein's army and was once again playing the same role. Abu Omar appeared in dress slacks and a polo shirt and proceeded to set up the payroll on a desk in one of the rooms. Each militia member was to come in single file, show his photo ID card, and receive an envelope with cash. Cosper left the Iraqis to run the show and sat down in another room. "I told them to stagger the paydays, but it looks like everyone has shown up at once," he said. "Too excited on the first payday." Maybe they wanted to make sure they would get their share.

In addition to the payments, the battalion had also supplied radios and ordered uniforms—blue shirts with a shoulder patch—to make them easier to identify. The volunteers had tried out different names over the past two months, including Baghdad Patriots, Ameriya Freedom Fighters, then Ameriya Revolutionaries, but the latter name also raised concerns that it would be interpreted as a group that aimed to overthrow the Maliki government. Finally, they settled on Forsan al-Rafidan, or the Knights Between Two Rivers. The nickname of their American partners, the 1-5 CAV, was the Black Knights.

The militia set up several outposts around the neighborhood. There were no police in Ameriya, so Abu Abid's men filled that void. The militia was supposed to coordinate with the Iraqi army, but an Iraqi army detachment a few blocks away kept its distance from the compound. They would go out with the Americans on joint patrols. Burton had also secured permission from the ministry of defense for the Iraqi brigade to resupply the volunteers with ammunition. Abu Abid knew that the developing relationship required his men to behave as professionally as possible, even though it was essentially a guerrilla band. Abu Abid told a community meeting earlier that week, "This is the last chance we have. You should cooperate with the Americans." Capt. Cosper had made up his own mind about the unusual alliance as well as the character of Abu Abid. "He lives by a warrior code. When we are with him we are under his protection," he said. "I trust him with my life every day." A senior captain, Cosper was on his third deployment in five years. "I'm the cynic of all cynics. But this right here is giving me hope," he said. In his view, the Sunni had begun to see the Americans as honest brokers in the conflict starting in the latter part of 2006. They were seeking an alliance with the Americans against the extremists on both sides. Like other soldiers based in Sunni neighborhoods, Cosper saw the evolving balance of power in Iraq as favoring the Shia majority, who controlled the government and security forces, over the disenfranchised Sunnis. "If we pull out of here, their chances of survival are limited," he said.

THE STATISTICS OVER THE SUMMER convinced Kuehl that forging the alliance with Abu Abid had been the right thing to do. The monthly rate of IED attacks plummeted from thirty-five in May to two in August.

After August the battalion was never attacked again, and Iraqi civilian deaths in Ameriya would steadily decline from a monthly average of 26 to 0.6 by year's end. There were undoubtedly still Al-Qaeda fighters in Ameriya, but they killed or captured dozens, and many others had left. Most important, he felt that people were beginning to shake off their fear and the neighborhood was beginning to revive. They would continue to hunt Al-Qaeda suspects, but it was now time to emphasize nonlethal operations to rebuild the infrastructure, restart economic activity, and try to revive local political representation. There was only one representative on the neighborhood advisory council; the rest had been killed, quit, or fled the area.

The next step was to restore some normalcy to Ameriya, insofar as the battalion could pry loose city services or otherwise supply what was needed if the Iraqi government proved unwilling or unable. They had to answer residents' demands and reopen the neighborhood to traffic. First they reinforced the checkpoint at the Market Street entrance on the north side of Ameriya with a sandbagged guardpost and more concrete barriers. Iraqi soldiers and the militia were posted at the checkpoint to search cars as they entered. This gate would likely be targeted by insurgents, so they prepared to defend it and minimize civilian casualties. They hoped this controlled access would prevent Ameriya from reverting to its former safe-haven status. The local advisory council did not want the controls to be dismantled, for fear that the bomb-makers would return.

A business sprang up to transport goods by handcart from the checkpoints to the stores on Market and Jordan streets. About 120 stores were now open.

Kuehl was itching for a fight with the Iraqi government over providing services to Ameriya; trash pickup, food and fuel delivery, and water and sewage services were virtually nonexistent. The battalion used its CERP funds to hire locals and jump-start the process. Orange-suited construction workers began to appear on the streets of Ameriya. New cement blocks were laid to replace curbs that had been crushed by Bradleys or blown up by bombs. Eventually the battalion persuaded the city to take over garbage collection, and the ministry of electricity began to repair transformers and power lines. Propane delivery, however, appeared to be snagged in a Mafia-like arrangement between Shia contractors and city officials.

Reconstruction projects created opportunities for graft, so as the battalion poured CERP funds into Ameriya, it monitored the projects closely to ensure that the contractors were not extorted. The 1-5 CAV soldier responsible for shepherding all these projects was the battalion's effects officer, who had worked at the World Bank after attending graduate school. A boisterous and talkative New Yorker, he had been motivated to join the army by the 9/11 attacks. The battalion also received advice and assistance from the brigade's Enhanced Provincial Reconstruction Team, whose head was a retired ambassador, John Bennett, with experience in the Balkans and elsewhere. They debated the best ways to bring functioning local government to Ameriya.

The most important determinant of Ameriya's near-term future would be the fate of Abu Abid and his militia. Would it continue to be a force for stability in the neighborhood and would the national government accept its utility as the Americans had? The U.S. military hoped to persuade the government to incorporate Abu Abid's men and other volunteers into the Iraqi police force. Ameriya, like many Sunni areas, had no police presence. But the government feared that Abu Abid and his men could use a consolidated base in Ameriya to attack them, if that was their ultimate intent. Abu Abid said his goal was for his men to be accepted into the police and army. He said acceptance, not overthrow, was their aim.

From Kuehl's standpoint the incorporation of Abu Abid's men into a police force that would secure Ameriya was an ideal solution. It was clear that the locals preferred the protection of Abu Abid and his militia to that of the Iraqi army. One of the imams proposed that the Iraqi army be withdrawn from Ameriya and that the Knights Between Two Rivers provide all the security. Distrust of Lt. Col. Sabah, the local Iraqi army commander, and his men ran deep in the neighborhood, but he would tell anyone who listened that he had been responsible for bringing calm to Ameriya and Khadra. The immediate U.S. goal was to get the two entities to work together, although in the long run the local security role would belong to the police so the army could shift to its traditional mission of national defense.

Sabah was intensely jealous of Abu Abid's relationship with the battalion, and of the mounting publicity surrounding his volunteers. Petraeus came to visit on August 15, along with the defense minister and Barham Salih, the Kurdish deputy prime minister. Kuehl escorted the large delegation around Ameriya in Strykers. Petraeus sized up Abu Abid during their conversation: it was clear the former officer was well versed in small-unit tactics. He was struck by Abu Abid's leadership presence and his men's obvious esteem for him. In Abu Abid's office, Petraeus asked him if he was willing to invite Shia families back to Ameriya, which Abu Abid did on the spot in front of the U.S. and Iraqi television cameras. Petraeus praised Kuehl's efforts. The top commander's validation was critical, since Kuehl had been improvising without formal written guidance. He had been encouraged to go forth and reconcile, and he had. And by bringing top Iraqi officials, Petraeus hoped to put pressure on Prime Minister Maliki to accept Abu Abid.

As part of the campaign to persuade the Iraqi government to allow Abu Abid's men to be vetted and admitted to the police academy, Kuehl arranged a meeting with the prime minister's National Reconciliation Committee. He took Abu Abid along so he could make his case directly to Bassima al-Jaidri, the committee member closest to Maliki in the Office of the Commander in Chief. Al-Jaidri's strict observance of Islamic custom was evident in her appearance. Her hair was covered and the sleeves of her long dress were closed tightly around her wrists. Kuehl was surprised by her somewhat flirtatious manner with Abu Abid. "I have wanted to meet you," she said to him. "I've heard a lot about you." Abu Abid said his men wanted to be professionals and serve in the security force. He felt that she was toying with him, but he presented his case. His men were disciplined and eager to be part of Iraq's security forces.

As Kuehl and Abu Abid had agreed beforehand, Abu Abid also brought up another matter in the meeting. Parents in Ameriya were concerned, he said, that high school students who had graduated the previous spring still had not received their test results. Students elsewhere in

Baghdad had long since received theirs. If the results were not released, the students would not be able to attend college. For the upper-middle-class families who remained in Ameriya, this was of great concern. They expected their children to go to university and pursue professional careers. Al-Jaidri frowned. This meeting was to discuss security matters. She was not prepared to address it. Kuehl then joined in, not wanting to let the issue drop. She grew angry.

Abu Abid backed off. Kuehl could see that he felt it was best not to antagonize her. After all, she held his fate, and that of all his men, in her hands. In an effort to convince the government of their sincerity, Abu Abid had allowed Kuehl to share the identities of the volunteers with the committee. They could easily track them all down if this venture failed. The meeting ended inconclusively, but the committee agreed to hold regular meetings with Abu Abid until they decided what to do with his band.

To show his gratitude to 1-5 CAV, Abu Abid invited Kuehl and his staff over to his house for a traditional *meskouf* dinner of grilled carp in late August. At 8:30 p.m. Kuehl and the other soldiers climbed into their Humvees at Camp Liberty and set off for Abu Abid's house. They parked at the nearby Combat Outpost Bushmaster, which sat next to a bombed-out building in the middle of powder-fine, shin-deep dirt, and walked in the dark a half dozen blocks to a large stone house. Out of the darkness Omar appeared in a brown dishdasha, his ever-present PKC machine gun slung over his shoulder. He held it against his stomach. "Omar even sleeps with his gun," teased Abu Risha, a hyperactive militia member who trotted alongside him with his AK-47. Kuehl had relaxed the supposed ban on heavy crew-served weapons to allow the militia this one machine gun.

In the courtyard of Abu Abid's house, fighters mingled in front of fires that were roasting a dozen or more giant carp. A short man tended the Iraqi delicacy, swabbing a marinade on each one. Kuehl's security detail stayed outside with the men while his sergeant major, Capt. Cosper, and Natalya, his Iraqi American interpreter, went into the house. Abu Abid greeted them in a crisp white dishdasha. His wife, Khulida, came out from the back room in a long, close-fitting gray coat that buttoned all the way down. She was a pretty, short woman with tasteful makeup. She excused herself after the introductions but left her daughter and son to play in the room and compete for their father's attention. Like those in most Iraqi homes, the front room was lined with couches and easy chairs, and Abu Abid invited the soldiers to sit. They peeled off their body armor and helmets, stowed their rifles in corners, and sat while Abu Abid set up a large dining table in the room's center and passed chocolates to his guests.

The table was soon stacked with plates of massive grilled fish and many side dishes of vegetables, hummus, baba ghanoush, and ground-meat kebabs. Hot pita bread was passed and all the men stood around the table. For some of the soldiers it was their first introduction to *meskouf* and to eating with their hands. After a few moments' hesitation, they dug into the steaming flesh with their fingers or with a piece of bread. Faces registered pleasant surprise at the tasty dish, and fingers navigated the fish bones out of mouths. When the plates and table were cleared away, Iraqi chai tea was served along with bowls of fruit.

Abu Abid then made a speech thanking Kuehl and 1-5 CAV for all they had done to bring peace to Ameriya, and recognizing the soldiers' lives that had been lost. He presented gift after gift to the battalion commander, with the abundant generosity characteristic of Iraqi hospitality. He gave him a necklace and bracelet for his wife and a complete outfit of traditional Iraqi clothing for men: a sparkling white dishdasha, with short and long cotton bottoms to wear underneath the "man dress"; a red-and-white checked headcloth with a black coil to hold it on; and brown leather sandals. To complete Kuehl's transformation into Lawrence of Arabia, Abu Abid bestowed upon him a replica of a wooden Mauser rifle. "A shot has never been fired from it," his host promised.

Kuehl thanked Abu Abid for the gifts. Army regulations would require Kuehl to pay for the gifts or return them, but he was not about to ruin the camaraderie of the evening by mentioning this fact. "How can I repay you for these gifts?" Kuehl said. "How about a Bradley?" joked Abu Abid.

In the rear room, separated from the reception and dining room by a curtain, Abu Abid's wife and the women of the house were eager to talk.

Khulida was a schoolteacher but had been too afraid to teach in Ameriya while the violence of the past year had raged. She had been pregnant with their third child when her husband's two brothers were killed in October 2006, and had miscarried. "One of the brothers had nothing to do with the military or the war, and he was still killed," she lamented. The vivacious woman was beside herself with fear. She had seen women attacked in the street for not covering their faces or wearing brightly colored clothing. She dared not go out shopping for groceries, so her sister-in-law brought them from next-door Mansour. Khulida fetched a portrait of her and Abu Abid's 1999 wedding, as if to show that they had led a normal life once. She looked at the fine white gown and her husband in his tuxedo, and burst into tears. Her young daughter clung to her with wide eyes. Khulida's sister-in-law played with her toddler daughter. Seated next to them were two young teenage girls, who talked shyly about going to school; they were daughters of two of the slain brothers. "Can you tell us how we might get visas to go to the United States?" Khulida begged. "Do you know anyone at the embassy who can help us?"

Both Abu Abid's wife and his mother were convinced that he would not survive. They were traumatized by the violence they had lived through, and their only hope was to leave the country. Their bleak outlook reflected the reality that Iraq had become. Abu Abid and 1-5 CAV were trying to create a new reality, and it took a leap of faith to believe it could happen. They were trying to carve out a survivable Sunni enclave in Baghdad and keep both Shia and Sunni extremists out of it. It would not survive if the Iraqi government did not want it to survive. Kuehl had been receiving a fairly steady trickle of reports of abuses allegedly carried out by Abu Abid or his men, and he checked out each one. In one staff meeting he sent the battalion's tactical human intelligence team back to verify every basic fact of a shooting that had occurred in Ameriya. He was not going to cover for any bad behavior on the part of the militia, but he strongly suspected a disinformation campaign was under way to discredit Abu Abid and provide grounds for denying his fighters admission to the police academy.

Kuehl and his battalion had accomplished an amazing turnabout in Ameriya. They had implemented the full gamut of counterinsurgency tactics, including skillful diplomacy that had won the confidence of the local leaders and population and cemented an alliance with indigenous fighters. They had exploited all of this for intelligence to target and diminish the enemy forces, and had begun to revive the neighborhood's economic, political, and social life. The battalions and brigades had created facts on the ground that could be used as levers to move the national leaders forward. But it remained to be seen whether their local success would hold, and whether it would help catalyze wider progress.

Officers like Maj. Chris Rogers and future classes of the U.S. School for Advanced Military Studies very likely would puzzle over these problems for the rest of their careers. Chris, whose young wife was suffering from symptoms they feared might be Parkinson's disease on top of the diabetes she already had been diagnosed with, would change his career path to military planner after this tour. But, as he had for many long days in the battalion ops center, he would continue to ponder the transcendent question posed by their experience in Ameriya. "Is it possible to link our tactical success here to a strategic endstate for Iraq?" he wondered. The answer to that question would determine how the war would finally end.

10

The Sons of Iraq

Petraeus had seized on the emergence of the Knights of Ameriya because it was just the opportunity he was seeking to encourage local accommodation in Baghdad. This is what the "puzzle diagram" of his campaign plan called for, it was what the long discussions at Maud House had been about, it was what had worked in Anbar. It would be far trickier to implement in the fraught and diverse mosaic of Baghdad, but its Sunni neighborhoods were key havens of the insurgency.

Petraeus was so convinced that Ameriya represented the way forward in Baghdad that he wrote about it in his weekly letter to Defense Secretary Robert Gates on June 2, 2007, when Kuehl's battalion and Abu Abid's men were fighting their very first battle together against Al-Qaeda. That same day, June 2, he urged his other commanders, gathered at Camp Victory for one of their periodic meetings with him, to adopt the same approach in their sectors. "Tribal engagement and local reconciliation work! Encourage it!" he told the officers.

Battalion commanders all over the city made it a priority to cultivate tribal sheikhs, imams at mosques, and other influential locals while the strategic engagement cell contacted insurgent leaders. Petraeus's counterinsurgency adviser David Kilcullen and Multi-National Corps-Iraq drew up a menu of ways in which Iraqis could be recruited and put to work, and by late June the various templates were sent to all the units. Sunnis who were willing to pledge alliance to the government were hired as security guards at checkpoints and key infrastructure for ten dollars a day. Kilcullen worked to get extra money from the CIA to supplement the military's CERP fund.

Many Sunnis responded. By the end of August, seven thousand Iraqis had come forward in Baghdad and eight thousand more in the surrounding "belts" from Yusufiyah to Tarmiya. Iraqis were ready to turn to the Americans as protectors and allies for several reasons. Many had been alienated by the jihadist groups' rhetoric, strictures, and extreme tactics. They were also afraid of the Shia militia violence that had been unleashed against them in the past two years, and they could see a day coming when the Americans would no longer be there. The Americans were now offering them a new option instead of treating them as the enemy. Many of them belonged to nationalist insurgent groups, such as the 1920 Revolution Brigades or the Islamic Army; others had been supporters but not fighters; and still others were merely Sunnis who saw this as their last hope for securing their families and their neighborhoods.

The carrot of reconciliation was also accompanied by a nonstop offensive against those who were still fighting, particularly the numerically smaller but more lethal Al-Qaeda in Iraq. The operations were beginning to have a cumulative effect. "I think we've clobbered them up there in the Diyala River Valley," Petraeus said in late August. "They're very much on the run." This twin approach of recruiting the reconcilables and grinding down the irreconcilables could, Petraeus hoped, end the Sunni insurgency. Instead of seeking to defeat the insurgency by military means alone, he added a pragmatic approach of flipping all those who could be flipped.

The initiative was greeted by criticism and skepticism. Many observers decried it as a program of "guns for hire" and doubted that the Sunni fighters were permanently giving up the armed struggle against the government. They believed Petraeus was merely organizing the next stage of the Sunni-Shia civil war. One U.S. critic, Andrew Bacevich, a military historian and war opponent who, tragically, had just lost his soldier son in Iraq, compared the initiative to arming the Crips to fight the Bloods. He and others argued that the U.S. military was empowering rogue militias that would sooner or later attack the government and lead to an ever more balkanized Iraq.

Petraeus and his subordinates did not deny the risks in forging the expedient alliances, but he explained that it was only the first step. The Sunnis were being moved from the enemy column to the U.S. ally column. For now they were valuable allies in the fight against Al-Qaeda who provided intelligence and helped secure areas that had little or no police presence. "Our long-term concept was to figure out how, over time, to establish a relationship between them and the Iraqi government," he said.

By exhorting the U.S. military to recruit and hire thousands of volunteers, Petraeus resorted to one of his favorite tactics of creating situations that would move the Iraqi government in the direction he felt it needed to go. He did not ask the government to accept a rogue, autonomous force, however, but to accept those who would pledge allegiance with appropriate checks and safeguards. He was trying to get both sides to move, using the Americans as a bridge.

Prime Minister Maliki had agreed to allow Sunnis from the "awakening" movement to join the police and military in Anbar, but he viewed that province as strategically inconsequential and in any case entirely populated by Sunnis. It was an entirely different matter to embrace that formula in the capital and the mixed, densely populated central region of the country. The idea of bringing large numbers of former opponents back into the government, particularly under arms, set off all the alarm bells of the Shia politicians who lay awake nights fearing the return of a repressive Sunni-dominated regime. Many of them preferred a predominantly Shia security force.

A multipronged effort began to persuade the Iraqi government to embrace the volunteers and to devise a detailed plan for institutionalizing the hodgepodge of groups, who eventually became known as the Sons of Iraq. The American plan to incorporate the volunteers into the local Iraqi police was called Operation Blue Shield. The six-stage process began with the vetting of volunteers at the local level in each of the ten Baghdad security districts. This vetting would be conducted by the coalition forces, the Iraqi security forces, and the neighborhood advisory councils. Criminals and those on most-wanted lists would be excluded. All volunteers had already been registered with fingerprints, biometric scans, and photographs. The ministry of interior would then put each candidate through four tests: a medical exam, a physical fitness test, a literacy test, and a criminal-records check. The ministry would verify that the candidate had been endorsed by some combination of the local city council, tribes and/or coalition forces, but it would not conduct its own political litmus test. This was designed to avoid selection by the highly politicized ministry of interior, which was still full of partisan Shiite militia members. Then the ministry would schedule the accepted candidates in the police training course.

The goal was to persuade Iraq's government to accept 12,671 volunteers for police training within six months. Acceptance of a substantial number of volunteers would convince many Sunnis that there was a place for them in the system, and the many safeguards would reassure the government. Thus, the Americans hoped to lessen the paranoia on both sides step by step.

Brig. Gen. John Campbell, who had shepherded the Baghdad security plan from its inception, played a key role in pushing Operation Blue Shield forward. He hoped to persuade the head of the Baghdad Operations Command, Lt. Gen. Abboud Qanbar, to endorse the plan. The prime minister had pledged to support Abboud with all the resources he asked for. If Abboud said he needed the volunteers to help the Baghdad security plan succeed, that was a powerful argument coming from the man the prime minister had personally chosen. Petraeus, meanwhile, worked on Maliki and took his reconciliation committee and cabinet ministers around to meet volunteer leaders.

Abboud and Campbell had developed a close relationship. Abboud called him "my dear friend," and Campbell billed himself as the Iraqi's deputy. Campbell's view was that if he could help Abboud succeed, the U.S. military would be able to go home. Campbell never gave press conferences, so his central role remained unknown. Behind closed doors, he used humor and bluntness to prod the Iraqi generals, who tended to procrastinate, to use the authority the prime minister had given them. For example, he pressed them to disband the National Police Unity Brigade, formerly the notorious Wolf Brigade. The United States had withheld all support and advisers from it. "This is 608 men who are using body armor and helmets that other units could use," he said at a Baghdad Operations Command meeting one day. Abboud shifted his bulk uncomfortably in his chair and shook his jowly chin. "This is a decision the National Police commander must take," he said. "Then let's get Gen. Hussein [the police commander] to the next meeting and ask him to make the decision," Campbell suggested.

Campbell's strategy for winning Abboud's support for Operation Blue Shield was to take him around greater Baghdad to meet all of the volunteer leaders so he could judge for himself their utility and sincerity. Over the past year Campbell had introduced Abboud to the concept of battlefield circulations. Iraqi military tradition held that subordinates pay calls on their superiors, not the reverse. The former inspector general came to realize that visiting troops in the field gave him a surer sense of the decisions that needed to be made, and also boosted the troops' morale.

Campbell crisscrossed the city nearly every day, even as temperatures rose over 110 degrees and sent most Iraqis into indoor hibernation. His peripatetic ways were wreaking havoc on his painfully inflamed knee. He had returned to Fort Hood, Texas, earlier in the summer to have it operated on for the fourth time, though he lacked time for rehabilitation. His knee had gone the way of many burly soldiers' knees after years of daily fitness runs and four tours in the 82nd Airborne Division, where he had made hundreds of parachute jumps with bone-jarring landings. Hopping in and out of his helicopter all over Baghdad every day with his full battle-rattle on, the 194-pound man had ground away what little cartilage remained in the joint. By the end of each day, he could barely stand on his throbbing knee.

Campbell and Abboud visited volunteers all over greater Baghdad—Ameriya, Ghazaliya, Taji, Adhamiya, Ghartan, and Radwaniya. One day in late August they flew in Campbell's helicopter to Ghartan and Radwaniya, on Baghdad's southern rural fringe. The area had been a major ratline into the city. Despite many combat sweeps, bombing campaigns, and clearing operations over the years, the Americans had never been able to shut down this ratline into Dora.

Campbell and Abboud landed on a gravel patch at Combat Outpost Ellis, a lonely walled outpost in a field named for a deceased soldier. The battalion commander, Lt. Col. George Glaze, and his company commander, Capt. Rob Summers, stood waiting in the already-broiling morning sun next to their armored Humvees. Summers lived in the tiny Ellis compound, and Glaze was based at Forward Operating Base Falcon, the large headquarters for the brigade overseeing all of south Baghdad a few miles northeast.

Glaze's operations officer gave the two generals a hood-top briefing with a color PowerPoint handout. He outlined the day's planned route and described the latest activities of their unit, 1st Battalion, 18th Regiment. They had signed up 1,131 volunteers who were manning twenty-six checkpoints in five neighborhoods. The volunteers had helped the battalion find over a hundred pounds of homemade explosive powder in various stages of being "baked," mortars, bomb triggers, artillery rounds, ammunition, and video cameras. In one house they found two explosively formed penetrators (EFPs) and fifteen copper discs for making more. The battalion had also organized elections for vacant seats in the neighborhood council and solicited grant applications from local small businesses.

The soldiers loaded their guests into a convoy of Humvees with a Bradley at either end. As the Humvee lurched down the bumpy dirt road, Lt. Col. Glaze commented, "Two months ago I would not have wanted to drive down these roads." He had lost men to deep-buried bombs, but they had not come under attack since the volunteers started manning the checkpoints. These men may have once helped plant those bombs, but they were now targets of Al-Qaeda in Iraq for having switched sides. At the first checkpoint, men wearing T-shirts and orange reflective sashes stood guard. A Coleman cooler sat inside the sand-bagged hut, which was stacked with AK-47s. The volunteers used their own weapons, but since the Americans paid them, the distinction was somewhat moot.

Lt. Gen. Abboud was approached by an older man in dress pants and a collared shirt who kissed him on both cheeks, Arab style. The two chatted while Abboud inspected the checkpoint. It turned out that Abboud knew the man, who oversaw the volunteers at that checkpoint. He was a fellow former officer in the army until it had been disbanded after the invasion.

After inspecting the second checkpoint, the convoy arrived at the walled, large one-story white stucco home of Sheikh Thair Turqi Tal'al of the Ghartan clan. In a reception room lined with velour couches and chairs, Lt. Gen. Campbell introduced the Sheikh Thair, age thirty, to Abboud and explained that the sheikh had recruited 600 volunteers, all of whom wanted to become official policemen. Thair, resplendent in a spotless, ironed white dishdasha and a black-and-white checked head-scarf, politely corrected Campbell and said he had 650 volunteers. He had met with a senior official of the interior ministry about the application for the first 50 to join the police, he said, but had received no answer.

Campbell told Thair the prime minister's office was now involved in the approval process and that Lt. Gen. Abboud would be making rec-ommendations to him. He hoped the decision would be made soon and said that in the meantime they could remain on contract with Glaze's battalion. He reiterated the three conditions: that all volunteers pledge allegiance to Iraq, that they work locally, and that they accept the com-mand and control of Iraqi security forces. There was another problem, but no one was ready to address it yet. The official formula the ministry of interior had adopted for manning its police force was one policeman per 133 inhabitants, which in Thair's rural area would mean only sixty policemen would be hired.

Thair's tall, slender older brother, Nahad, sat quietly by his side; he had been detained by U.S. forces earlier in the year on suspicion of aiding insurgents, but he had been released. During his detention the idea of switching sides was discussed with him, a tactic recommended by the strategic engagement cell. Sheikh Thair was running the wealthy clan's businesses and farms since his father had fled to Jordan two years earlier. "The Ghartanis have been here since the Ottoman empire," Thair said proudly. But, he said, the family had shut its stores in the Dora market because it was not safe to travel to them. "This area used to be controlled by Al-Qaeda," said the young Iraqi. After a couple of his clansmen were killed, he began recruiting tribes to stand up to the jihadists.

Glaze's company commander, Capt. Summers, had developed the initial relationships with the locals. After he got to know the clan leaders, they reached an agreement to refrain from attacking U.S. forces in exchange for generators and infrastructure projects. One clan leader offered fifty people to guard a bridge and keep bombs from being planted there. At that time, Thair, leader of the largest clan, remained behind the scenes even as he recruited two dozen smaller clans to join into the effort.

Glaze had no doubt about the utility of the new partnership. Neither his troops nor Iraqi troops had been attacked since it began. "I cannot tell you if the government wants a nonsectarian security force," the battalion commander said. "But I can tell you that it is safer at the grassroots." Capt. Summers said the hatred he witnessed between Sunni and Shia ran very deep, and he acknowledged that the two sides might well resume fighting at some point. "These sheikhs can see the logic of our nonsectarian arguments," he said. "But that doesn't mean they will behave in that way."

Several times during the discussion, a short, middle-aged man in business clothes seated next to Thair passed him notes from a tablet he was scribbling on. While tables were brought in for lunch, he introduced himself as Col. Nasser, a former officer in Saddam Hussein's army, who had been ejected by the 2003 decree. He was the sheikh's security adviser and he, too, had known Abboud when he was inspector general of the army. Everyone stood to eat as younger relatives carried in three large steaming trays of rice topped by roasted goat. Militia members stacked their rifles outside and joined the feast.

Thair made a good impression on Abboud. "Because he is the leader of a large tribe and known to all there, he could be a very positive influence," the general said the next day in his office in Adnan palace, which was furnished in the rococo style and pastels the former regime favored. His office was entirely pink, from the tasseled shades and silk curtains to the gilded couches and marble tables. "These people can be helpful to us, and we should look into bringing some of them into the forces." He believed that former army officers, like himself, should not have been dismissed from service unless they were accused of committing crimes, so he was prepared to welcome back such colleagues.

At the next meeting of the Baghdad Operations Command, Abboud spoke in favor of the volunteers. They knew their areas well, he said, and the government was short of forces, particularly police, who were essential for the Baghdad security plan to succeed. He knew the military was also short of officers, and there was no quicker way to meet the need than to reincorporate qualified former officers.

As a first test case, U.S. officials aimed to persuade Maliki to admit volunteers from the rural Abu Ghraib area west of Baghdad to the police academy. Since it was next to Anbar and all Sunni, it seemed a logical first step. Long an insurgent haven, Abu Ghraib lay astride the western highway from Anbar and was an area where military convoys were attacked. It had no police and few Iraqi army troops. It had grown quiet since the U.S. battalion commander had hired a group of volunteers led by Abu Azzam. Campbell, Abboud, and Petraeus all met Abu Azzam. Petraeus found him an intelligent, educated, and well-organized man and took Maliki's reconciliation committee to meet him.

They presented the case to Maliki at the regular weekly meeting of all the top Iraqi and U.S. defense officials, including the prime minister, his national security adviser, and the ministers of defense and interior. Abboud spoke in favor of the volunteers and backed the incorporation of Abu Azzam's men into the police. Petraeus then chimed in to support Abboud's endorsement.

Maliki was not persuaded. He believed the volunteers were insurgents who wanted to overthrow his government. The Americans were wrong to believe their pledges of support and were expanding the groups too rapidly. Maj. Gen. Abdul Ameer denied knowing anything about the Ghazaliya Guardians, even though he had met their leader. Abboud had persuaded the defense minister to allow the army units to interact with the volunteers, but Maliki's advisers believed Abboud had grown too close to the Americans. They were hearing reports from other sources that volunteers were pushing Shia out of their homes. Petraeus asked for specifics so they could investigate the allegations. He was still convinced that incorporating Sunnis was the path to peace.

Successive meetings and phone calls failed to sway Maliki. As the September hearings drew near, Petraeus grew increasingly anxious. He requested a meeting with Prime Minister Maliki at his gated, palm-shrouded residence in the Green Zone, next to the Council of Ministers building. The general began by acknowledging that Maliki had legitimate concerns and outlined the steps they were taking to address them. They had no intention of allowing rogue forces to run rampant. By bringing them into the police, the Iraqi government would exert direct control over them through the chain of command and through its purse strings. He then presented what he thought was the strongest argument. The initiative was designed to defeat Maliki's archenemy, the Al-Qaeda in Iraq (AQI) insurgents. These volunteers were helping to capture AQI fighters. "Bringing these Sons of Iraq into the security services is essential to progress against AQI," Petraeus said, as Sadi Othman translated.

Maliki did not relent, but Petraeus was determined to extract an affirmative answer. Petraeus had learned over the past year that he would occasionally have to show the "full range of emotion, something other than an even temperament," to prevail in such disagreements. At times he feigned anger to convince Iraqi officials to do what he felt was necessary —particularly when he suspected a sectarian agenda was at work. Other times, the vein in his temple stood out and his emotion was authentic. This was one of the latter moments.

"It's make or break time. These guys used to point their guns at us and you. Now they are pointing their guns at AQI," he said, turning up the emotional pitch. "Do you want them to point their guns back at us, to shoot and kill our soldiers and yours?" Petraeus felt like "a four-star action officer," a full general doing the work of a staff aide. But it took the commander of all U.S. forces in Iraq to overcome the prime minister's dogged resistance; no one else could budge him.

Maliki finally agreed to admit Abu Ghraib volunteers to the police academy. Even after Petraeus's showdown with Maliki, that was not the end of it. Iraqi army checkpoints east of Abu Ghraib were attacked, and the Iraqi army commander for the area, Lt. Col. Nasser, alleged that Abu Azzam's men were responsible. He detained fifty volunteers. Campbell and Abboud flew out to investigate. The local American battalion commander had video feed from an unmanned aerial vehicle that showed that the attackers had not come from Abu Ghraib. Petraeus assured Maliki that Abu Azzam's men had remained at their own checkpoints.

The next obstacle came from the interior ministry, which balked at accepting the volunteers. Although 1,738 had been approved, there was room for only 1,500. Then the volunteers themselves expressed concerns about traveling to the training academy in east Baghdad because they would have to pass through Nasser's area. The officer's frequent roundups of Sunnis had convinced Campbell that he had to be replaced. "The people there hate him," he said. "We've got to replace him." But Nasser was one of Maliki's favorites. The prime minister's office often called him directly with instructions rather than going through the chain of command. Abboud agreed that Nasser's posting to this neighborhood was a problem, but he was reluctant to go up against the prime minister.

Finally, Campbell came up with a solution for the Abu Ghraib trainees. He proposed bringing police trainers to an American forward operation base near Abu Ghraib, which could accommodate 1,000 trainees. Campbell would supply helicopters to fly the rest of the recruits across town for the four-week course at the Baghdad Police College. The proposal was accepted, and finally the first class of volunteers was trained and deployed just days before Petraeus left for Washington.

Operation Blue Shield was a perfect example of how change occurred in the country: slowly, with great expenditure of time, effort, and talk, and always with a high possibility of setbacks. It had taken six months to get the first class of volunteers accepted for police training. That inchworm progress would be the standard for measuring the success of Operation Blue Shield—and much else in Iraq.

THE TROOPS IN BAGHDAD HAD BEEN at work on many initiatives in addition to the Sons of Iraq. As the time for the September report and testimony drew near, the units around the city were required to report on the progress they had made. Some parts of the city were markedly more peaceful, but many troubled areas remained.

In west Baghdad, Col. J. B. Burton, who was in charge of thirty-six square miles inhabited by one million Iraqis, had undertaken a major effort to stop what he concluded was a bid "to establish a pure Shia constituency in this area." When he arrived in late 2006 the JAM militia, with help from the Shia army and police, was moving from its Kadhimiya and Shula strongholds into the city's largest remaining Sunni areas of Mansour, Ghazaliya, and surrounding neighborhoods.

So many unsubstantiated allegations of official complicity with JAM swirled around the Iraqi government that Burton's first step was to set up a massive intelligence operation, which traced sectarian actors all the way up to the prime minister's office. This ongoing effort became known as Seventh Veil. The police chief in Ghazaliya, Lt. Col. Musa Abdul Karim, was detained and sent to Camp Cropper, the U.S. military detention center. An Iraqi army major was pulled out of his bedroom one night after being implicated in an attack on U.S. soldiers. Most often, Burton found it far more effective to sit down with Iraqi officials and share the information they had collected. "We'd say, 'Look here, son of a bitch, this is what we've got on you,'" he said, which tended to bring them around quickly. The colonel had the perfect personality for this conversation. Tony Soprano had come to Baghdad and his name was J. B. Burton

Before Burton arrived, there were no U.S. units in Kadhimiya, a bustling Shia hub and home to the city's principal Shia mosque. The imam at the mosque was deeply involved in JAM activities, but he was politically untouchable. One of the Iraqi officers Burton trusted most, Col. Fallah Hassan Kinbar, narrowly survived an assassination attempt after leaving a meeting at the mosque. "That kind of puts the itch on the back of your neck," Burton said. Still, Maliki refused permission to detain the imam. Burton did succeed in replacing an Iraqi army battalion responsible for heavy-handed roundups of Sunnis with a good one.

Also, after bombs were repeatedly found planted in plain sight of the Khadra police station, Burton had the entire unit disbanded. In poor, fetid Shula, his troops had some luck turning young JAM militants against criminal and sectarian leaders and bomb-making cells.

"I would characterize this as a campaign of exhaustion by both kinetic and nonkinetic means being waged against the Sunni population of northwest Baghdad," he said. By September, Burton believed the kinetic, or armed, campaign against Sunnis had been more or less halted in western Baghdad by the joint security stations, walls, volunteers, arrests, and other measures his soldiers had implemented, but the nonkinetic campaign continued as Sunni areas were denied basic city services including power, water, sewage, and food deliveries. He deemed that about 60 percent of his area was in the "control" phase and about 35 percent was still being cleared. Other areas, like Shula, had still not been cleared.

In central Baghdad, the Karkh security district was relatively calm after January's fierce battles along Haifa Street, its main artery. It was a once-wealthy area dotted with high-rise apartments, museums, and government buildings that had become a way station for insurgents. U.S. troops partnered with a National Police brigade whose commander ran twenty-four-hour-a-day patrols and was deemed an effective leader. Attacks had dropped 60 percent since January. Many Sunnis had fled the area, and the remaining population mix was roughly half Sunni and half Shia. U.S. soldiers hired Karkh residents and contractors to clean out sewer lines and repair the local water treatment plant.

Across the river in east Baghdad, Rusafa had been relieved of the scourge of car bombs, at least momentarily. The area was home to Baghdad's most famous gathering spots, Abu Nuwas Street, a riverside promenade that was once frequented by Iraqi families and couples who picnicked on the park's lush carpet of grass or visited its nightclubs and restaurants. The 1st Battalion, 504th Parachute Infantry Regiment brought Abu Nuwas Street back to life. The soldiers enlisted the help of the district advisory council chairman and handed out 150 microgrants of $2,500 to $10,000 to help shopowners get started again. Young Iraqis painted murals depicting Mesopotamian temples and other ancient

Iraqi icons on the twelve-foot blast walls, which were pulled back to the sidewalk to allow traffic to flow again. Thousands of other barricades were removed, and new sidewalks and curbs were laid. Trash was cleared from the park, benches installed, swing sets painted, and grass planted on the bare soil.

Seven meskouf restaurants lining the waterfront were completely rebuilt. Ali Mehdi reopened his restaurant, Asmak Baghdad, in late August. Live fish swam in the ceramic tank and a fire for grilling them burned in the large hearth. Ali stood next to a table of men who sat drinking beer and smoking a hookah. "My father and grandfather ran this restaurant before me," he said. He lamented that so few customers had dared to come out, saying, "I hope more people will come when they decide it is safe." A coffeehouse in the middle of the park, reputed to be seven hundred years old, was being painstakingly renovated according to the original plans soldiers found at city hall. Old men with their heads swathed in turbans carefully laid down new tiles on the floors and walls. Also, antiques dealers and booksellers on the famous Mutanabi Street had begun to recover from a bombing in March.

These were small oases of hope on a landscape still dominated by fear and wreckage. Just north of Abu Nuwas, on the other side of Jumhuriya bridge, Rashid Street was still littered with trash, and broken windows stared from most buildings. The bus station and nearby markets had been the target of numerous bombs. All over central Baghdad, streets remained littered with the rubble of war, and buildings with bullet holes stood as reminders of the violence that had ravaged the city and might yet return. Navigating the city was a tortuous affair, with long waits at gas stations and numerous checkpoints and frightening encounters with careening convoys full of armed guards.

A young Iraqi doctor named Salwa paused while fixing her makeup in the bathroom of an Iraqi restaurant to recount her daily two-hour journey to work. She welcomed the respite from the violence but said in lightly accented English, "It is too soon to know if this is for real." When asked if she would like the U.S. troops to leave, she drew back in horror. "That would be a catastrophe for us!" she exclaimed. "The Iraqi forces cannot do it. Too many still are dying."

In east Baghdad, Col. Jeff Bannister, of the 2nd Brigade, 2nd Infantry Division, was in charge of Rusafa and the heavily Shia districts of Karrada and New Baghdad. Karrada was now relatively quiet, but New Baghdad continued to be the scene of JAM attacks on U.S. troops. Attacks in Bannister's area had declined 69 percent between January and October, and Iraqi army and police had taken the lead in securing much of the area.

Among the trouble spots, Sadr City had not been subject to any full-scale clearing operations. Sadr City was one of two security districts assigned to the 2nd Brigade, 82nd Airborne Division. A joint security station had been opened on its outskirts, joint patrols were conducted, and reconstruction projects funded. U.S. officials were still hoping to channel Sadr's movement into peaceful politics and find a way to demobilize its thousands of militia members without a head-on confrontation. Sadr City also posed a continuing problem for security in other parts of the city. JAM used it as a base from which to lob mortars and rockets into the Green Zone, U.S. military bases, and other targets, using more accurate and powerful weaponry that U.S. officials said the militia was receiving from Iran, including 240 mm and 107 mm rockets and RPG-29 rocket-propelled grenades.

The situation in Adhamiya also remained difficult. Gen. Campbell had always wanted to conduct a house-by-house clearing operation there, which had not been done because the Strykers were sent to Diyala. In surrounding neighborhoods, 740 Sunnis had responded to recruitment efforts in late August, but the local Iraqi army battalion commander arrested some of them. The U.S. battalion commander suspected that his counterpart was involved with the local JAM militia, including an EFP cell that had killed American soldiers.

The large neighborhoods of Shaab and Ur east of Adhamiya were still essentially under JAM control. The smaller neighborhoods of Rabi, Basateen, and Tunis north of Adhamiya had been more tranquil, and the 82nd Airborne's 2-319 Field Artillery Regiment commanded by Lt. Col. Al Shoffner had quickly made progress there. His five hundred troops lived in Combat Outpost War Eagle, where they trained Iraqi sergeants and police in a four-day course on troop-leading procedures,

marksmanship, and checkpoints, using the best Iraqi sergeants as trainers. Each course used eight thousand rounds for marksmanship practice
on AK-47s and PKC machine guns, versus the eighty bullets a year each
Iraqi usually fired in training. Shoffner was also using the "Katusa"
method of embedding Iraqi squads into U.S. units for two months of
on-the-job training.

One of Shoffner's young officers, Lt. Josh Rowan, and his platoon
took to population-based counterinsurgency like fish to water. Their
daily foot patrols determined that most trouble came from the fish market area. A friendly vendor gave them free bread and led them to a
sniper. They also unraveled a kidnapping ring. The soldiers established
cordial relations with the Sunni Endowment Council and the local Sadr
representatives and met regularly with the neighborhood advisory
council. "The only job of the platoon leaders is to network," Shoffner
said. Rowan held a master's degree in defense studies and had read
counterinsurgency works by David Galula and David Kilcullen before
deploying.

In southern Baghdad, Col. Ricky Gibbs, commander of the 4th
Brigade, 1st Infantry Division, was wrestling with one of the most con-
flicted areas of the city. Gibbs estimated that the 700,000 people in his
two districts, East and West Rashid, were about half Sunni and half Shia.
He had opened twenty combat outposts and five joint security stations,
and over half of his troops were focused on the violent Al-Qaeda
stronghold of Dora, where intense battles were fought throughout the
spring and summer. In West Rashid, JAM militias were on a rampage,
pushing Sunnis out of the Saidiya and Bayaa neighborhoods.

In the northern belt around Baghdad, Col. Paul Funk, commander of
the 1st Brigade, 1st Cavalry Division, oversaw a mostly Sunni population of two million spread over nine hundred square miles from
Tarmiya to Saba al Bor. His troops were partnered with three Iraqi army
brigades. The joint security station at Tarmiya was attacked in April in
one of the few successful attempts to overrun the stations. Insurgents
attacked with an explosives-packed car, rockets mounted on a truck,
and small-arms fire, killing two Americans and wounding seventeen.
Saba al Bor, a festering sore, had come under repeated attack from both

Sunni and Shia armed groups, and the Iraqi forces had not been able to secure it. A town of both Sunni and Shia, it had dwindled in size until the late summer of 2007, when families began to return.

The southern belt around Baghdad belonged to Col. Michael Kershaw, commander of the 2nd Brigade, 10th Mountain Division, whose 330-square-mile area spanned the Sunni insurgent zone known as the Triangle of Death. The largest city was Mahmudiya, which was 70 percent Sunni and 30 percent Shia, but Yusufiya, Latifiya, and the rest of the area was mostly Sunni. The area had been home to the Medina division of Saddam Hussein's Republican Guard and to a large weapons and munitions industry. When all of these Sunnis were thrown out of work in 2003, they quickly shifted to insurgent activity. With no U.S. troop presence in the area, it became a safe haven, ambush site, and source of many attacks in Baghdad via the Hilla highway and other ratlines. Under Multi-National Division-Center command, Kershaw's unit saw heavy combat, alongside its partners from Maj. Gen. Abdul Ameer's 6th Division's. Fifty-four of Kershaw's soldiers were killed and 270 wounded.

Kershaw's troops then turned to the engagement approach and eventually registered 16,000 military age males. Some 8,800 were hired as security guards for about $10 a day, and the U.S. deemed 5,800 of those acceptable candidates for the police or military. As of November 2007, however, none had been admitted. Kershaw's brigade also launched grassroots reconciliation initiatives with its provincial reconstruction team, the U.S. Institute of Peace, and the helpful Shia mayor of Mahmudiya, who called for greater employment options and political representation for the Sunni population.

IN ALL OF BAGHDAD, ATTACKS HAD DECREASED by half from the beginning of the surge to September, according to the Multi-National Division-Baghdad (MND-B). The recent dramatic falloff in violence surprised even the soldiers of MND-B, and it was viewed with great skepticism by the media. The rapid growth of the volunteer movement in and around Baghdad remained largely unreported.

An alternative explanation for the decline in violence was advanced, namely, that it was due to the fact that the city was already ethnically cleansed into homogenized neighborhoods and, therefore, there was no further incentive for the two groups to continue killing each other. A great deal of such homogenization had indeed occurred as Sunnis fled to predominantly Sunni neighborhoods and Shia did the same. In addition, hundreds of thousands of Iraqis fled the city entirely. An estimated 2 million Iraqis had left the country and 2.2 million more were internally displaced, according to the United Nations. Yet even after that dramatic exodus, many Sunnis remained and could have been targets for removal.

Despite the sectarian cleansing there were still many Sunnis in Baghdad, and many mixed neighborhoods. It was difficult to determine precisely how many, however, because no current official census data existed either before or after the sectarian violence of 2005–2006. But a U.S. military intelligence official in Baghdad noted that "the Baghdad security plan led to much more accurate [demographic] mapping as the troops fanned out and reported. . . . Now we have much better fidelity on what neighborhoods look like." Soldiers went house to house in many neighborhoods over the course of 2007 and collected basic census data from the residents. Based on these data, the intelligence official believed that the magnitude of the demographic shift had been exaggerated in many media reports. He estimated that Baghdad's population was still somewhere between 30 percent and 40 percent Sunni. That would equal between 1.5 million and 2.8 million Sunnis depending on the total population estimate used. All that could be said with absolute certainty, as Petraeus put it, was that Baghdad was still Iraq's largest Shia city *and* its largest Sunni city.

Many of Baghdad's neighborhoods still were home to both Shia and Sunni. Some areas had always been divided at the level of muhallas (the smallest urban unit containing roughly a dozen blocks) but in places like Mansour, intermarried middle-class families lived next door to each other. One pocket of Shaab had resisted the purging of longtime Sunni residents. While most Sunnis were pushed out of northern Ghazaliya, one part of it resisted the sectarian tide to continue living together as they had for forty-five years. Places like Hurriya and Qahira were indeed cleansed, but Iraqis frequently protested that foreigners made too much of their sectarian differences and too little of their common national and Arab identity.

That plenty of Sunnis and mixed neighborhoods remained in Baghdad underscored the possibility that the sectarian cleansing of 2006 could well resume—or continue, as it was in some areas, such as southern Baghdad. Although the Baghdad security plan had achieved initial successes, the Baghdad division command did not claim that its job was done. Almost half the city was still in "clear" or "disrupt" status, using the categories laid out in the Baghdad security plan of disrupt, clear, control and retain. Some 54 percent of the city's 474 muhallas were in the control or retain phase, while the enemy was still being cleared or disrupted in 46 percent. Violence was still rampant in many parts of the city, and no area was entirely secure. Only 8 percent of the city was being "retained" by Iraqi forces. A U.S. officer closely involved with the Baghdad plan estimated that four more battalions were needed to bring the rest of the city under control: one each for the still-troubled areas of New Baghdad, Adhamiya, and West and East Rashid, and that did not include Sadr City.

No one in the Baghdad division claimed that what they had achieved was sufficient to guarantee success. One Baghdad division officer said his message to the Iraqi government was: "We've bought you time. Now do something with it." Another officer echoed that judgment: "The government has to take advantage of what we have given them. We've done what we said we were going to do. I'm shocked that it worked," he said with a laugh. "But there has been no translation of that into the realm of strategy and policy." In other words, these smart staff officers were asking the obvious question: when and how was a more secure environment going to translate into the political deals that would produce lasting peace?

An opportunity had been created over the first eight months of the Baghdad security plan, and with luck more Sunnis would switch sides. But it was imperative that this effort be leveraged into lasting pacts or at least a sustainable modus vivendi. The volunteers' switch might be a temporary gambit by Sunnis, as many Shia leaders feared. It was equally possible that the Shia-led government intended to wait out the United

States with only minimal concessions, which could be reversed later. The ever-skeptical Baghdad chief of plans, Lt. Col. Doug Ollivant, noted that Iraq's new rulers might not have peace in mind. "Perhaps they are well and faithfully implementing the policy preferences of their constituents," he said. The Sadr movement's growth and consolidation led him to believe that Iraq's democracy might never incorporate the checks and balances that were missing from the 2005 constitution. The United States might have to accept that it had empowered a people who then acted in ways it abhorred. Ollivant noted, "There are twenty-five hundred years of literature on the bad things that democracies tend to do that evidently no one bothered to read."

11

Full-Court Press

Ambassador Ryan Crocker and his team had mounted a full-court press over the summer to try to produce some breakthrough on the national reconciliation agenda by September. They launched a multipronged attack on both the domestic political and diplomatic fronts. Petraeus hoped they would succeed, and lent his support, but he was not holding his breath. He placed more stock in the "bottom-up" accommodations that were spreading in Baghdad and the Sunni provinces of Anbar, Salahuddin, and even Diyala. The prime minister had visited Diyala and Salahuddin as part of the outreach to the Sunni tribes. In Tikrit, Saddam's hometown, Maliki opened up a big suitcase full of Iraqi dinars and passed them out to the sheikhs who had lined up to greet him. It was peacemaking Iraqi-style.

Petraeus's model for converting the "bottom-up" progress into an institutionalized political accommodation was Anbar province, where the Sunni population had turned decisively against Al-Qaeda over the past year. The effort at tribal engagement had actually started before that in several towns by special operations forces under the command of the Combined Joint Special Operations Task Force–Arabian Peninsula. Eleven tribal leaders had risked switching sides in Al Qaim in late 2005, but Al-Qaeda had counterattacked, murdered six of the sheikhs and family members, and dumped their bodies in the desert. That overture was thwarted in the short term, but it contributed to an accumulating disgust among Iraqis. Al-Qaeda's continued attacks on Anbar's traditional leaders, including barbaric killings of their children and relatives, turned the population against the group.

If Al-Qaeda's brutality undermined its own hold on Anbar, its primary safe haven, by attacking its clan structure, the United States had created an opening for Al-Qaeda at the outset by shunning the tribal structure. The United States' alienation of Anbar's largely secular tribes and their subsequent alliance with the religious extremists was a cautionary tale to be plumbed for lessons of what not to do in counterinsurgency. Except for a frustrating and abortive attempt to engage religious and tribal leaders in Fallujah between the two offensives launched against the city in April and November 2004, the approach taken toward the Sunni insurgency and its base had been generally all stick and no carrot. The sheikhs felt disrespected and the population was treated like the enemy for three years, until a joint army-marine force finally turned the province by adopting an entirely different approach.

Col. Sean MacFarland, the brigade commander in Anbar's capital city of Ramadi, began the process in 2006. Ramadi essentially had been taken over by Al-Qaeda, which declared it the capital of the group's proclaimed Islamic State of Iraq. Its police force had been battered and all the stations destroyed. The turning point was the decision of Sheikh Abdul Sattar Bezia al-Rishawi and his clan to turn against Al-Qaeda and then to join forces with MacFarland. Thirty-five tribes and subtribes ultimately joined the Anbar awakening, as it came to be known. The police force expanded from 200 Iraqis who were too frightened to wear their uniforms to 7,400, and thirty police stations and substations were built or rebuilt. When MacFarland's successor, Col. John Charlton of the 1st Brigade, 3rd Infantry Division, arrived in February 2007, attacks averaged between thirty and thirty-five daily in a population of 500,000 and an area of 8,900 square miles, which included Ramadi. He conducted clearing operations in March, and the fighting was fierce, but this time Anbaris helped the U.S. and Iraqi forces. Some 18,000 Anbaris, first paid by Sattar and then hired on CERP contracts, unearthed weapons caches and cleaned the rubble-filled city. By summer, attacks averaged fewer than one a day; on eighty days there were no attacks. In the morning battlefield update in the Multi-National Force-Iraq (MNF-I) amphitheater, Petraeus or another general often would call attention to one of these zero-attack days in Anbar. After so many bad days, months, and years in Iraq, and this province in particular, they could only marvel at the extraordinary turnabout.

Several important steps had been taken to institutionalize the progress in Anbar. These steps constituted the most promising model for the future, in Petraeus's view. First, Prime Minister Nouri al-Maliki had agreed to incorporate large numbers of the Sunni population into the security forces. He had agreed to raise the official quota for Anbar's police force to 21,000, and the province's police academy was reopened. He also made a crucial policy concession that brought Anbaris into the army. The Anbaris had not responded to army recruitment drives for fear that they would be sent to Shia areas elsewhere in the country and killed. The two Iraqi army brigades in Anbar, from the 1st and 7th divisions, were only 60 percent manned and overwhelmingly Shia. Maliki agreed to allow Anbari army recruits to serve in those two brigades, in their home province, for at least their first two years of service. Two recruiting drives produced 1,600 takers, and by the end of the summer one brigade was full and the other approaching full strength.

The second step was to give the Ramadi sheikhs a role in the political process. Sheikh Sattar had petitioned the government to give them seats on the provincial council. With support from the U.S. military, they won twenty nonvoting positions, but at least the tribes had a seat at the table so their views could be heard. Sattar and the other sheikhs lobbied for provincial elections so they could participate and gain real power. Since all resources flowed from the central government to the provincial governments, they wanted to be part of the system to access these funds for their clans. Holding elections would also fully bring the tribes into

the system and mesh the traditional tribal authority structure with formal government.

The third step was for the central government to open the resource
spigot for Anbar, whose provincial government had been largely dysfunctional and where many officials had been assassinated. On rare
occasions when meetings were convened, they were held in Baghdad.
Like most of the country, Anbar had received almost none of its 2006
allocated funding because of the paralysis in forming the Maliki government. Once formed, the ministries were barely functional. To make
matters worse, the provinces were required to go through an extremely
complicated Saddam-era process of submitting project requests to
receive the money. In spring 2007 a State Department contractor, the
Research Triangle Institute, had convened a meeting at the Rashid Hotel
in the Green Zone to help Anbari officials wade through this bureaucratic thicket and submit proposals for 190 projects. As a result, all of
the province's 2006 funds and some of its 2007 funds were disbursed by
the end of the summer.

On the Iraqi government side, the funding flow received crucial im-
petus from indefatigable Deputy Prime Minister Barham Salih. He
shepherded the requests through the government and convened two
conferences in Anbar with Baghdad officials to pledge new resources.
To further sweeten the pot, at the second conference in early September Salih and senior Iraqi officials announced that the central government would provide an additional $120 million in supplemental
funding for reconstruction and to compensate families who lost their
homes in the war. Anbar's governor estimated the war damage at $300
million. A free-trade zone would open in Al Qaim, on the Syrian border, in November, and $5.5 million was pledged to restart Ramadi's
ceramics factory, once a major employer. Japan committed $18 mil-
lion to rehabilitate Ramadi's hospital, and a $30 million microfinance
program to restart small businesses was announced. The soldiers and
marines had already spent $5.5 million over the past four months to
restore about 80 percent of the city's power, remove about half of the
rubble, and repair some of the sewer lines that had been punctured by
buried bombs.

Together these three steps represented the essence of a political solution: Sunnis were granted a role in their own local security, greater political representation, and a substantial share of national resources. In combination, these steps demonstrated a commitment on the part of the central government to enfranchise Sunnis. This was the approach Petraeus believed most viable, and it appealed to the Woodrow Wilson School PhD in him. He described the process: "You see local progress that produces improvements in local security, and then leads to local leaders wanting to connect to the central government because, after all, all resources here flow from the central government." The former insurgents petitioned the government, and in return the government used its power of the purse to control them. "That provides a degree of control that addresses some of the legitimate concerns of the Shia-led government about hiring in some cases former insurgents and in any case Sunni Arabs," Petraeus said.

This solution was the one envisioned in the "puzzle diagram" of the joint campaign plan: a series of political, economic, and security measures that brought peace to one part of Iraq. Anbar was the only province that was virtually all Sunni Arab, so it was far easier for the central government to give Sunnis more control there since Shia groups were not competing there for power, protection, or resources. Anbar also lacked oil or any other major assets, so no one coveted the province; it composed one-third of the country's territory but was mostly hard, rocky desert. But Anbar was a start: if Maliki was willing to share resources and allow local political and security solutions elsewhere, various parts of the country could be pacified. It was, in fact, the way Saddam Hussein had bought the loyalties of the independent clans.

Petraeus envisioned that other pieces of the puzzle would join Anbar over the coming two years. "You have some of the pieces in place in 2008, you get a few more in 2009," he said. "They are not yet all united but at least you get an Iraq that has found ways to live with each other." During that time, Iraqis could begin to resolve some of the big political issues.

He knew that much remained to be done to satisfy demands in Anbar. Sheikhs who did not get political representation or enough resources might return to fighting, but Petraeus considered them unlikely to reunite with Al-Qaeda after being victims of such atrocities as finding the heads of their children delivered in coolers to their doorsteps. Finally, there remained massive war damage, economic privation, and bereavement in a province that had seen some of the war's heaviest fighting. Thousands of Iraqis had died there, along with hundreds of U.S. troops.

Fallujah was representative of the dramatic turnabout in Anbar. Much of the city had been reduced to rubble in November 2004 in the massive Operation Al Fajr. Although Al-Qaeda never reclaimed its former stronghold, many Sunnis were alienated and fighting continued around the heavily guarded city that had once been home to more than 350,000 Anbaris. In 2007, the marines, who had exercised strict control over Fallujah from a large base west of the city, believed they finally hit on the right allies and combination of measures.

In Fallujah and the surrounding area, Col. Richard Simcock was the commander of Regimental Combat Team 6, part of the four thousand additional marines sent to Anbar in 2007. He could have stepped out of a marine recruiting poster, with his close-shaven head, ramrod-straight posture, and clenched jaw. Simcock described the months-long efforts to identify the key sheikhs in each of the surrounding towns and noted that in the past trouble had resulted when Americans empowered clans that did not have the respect or following of the locals. He was aided in this advanced social science experiment by Brig. Gen. John Allen and a red-bearded retired officer named William MacAllister, a self-taught expert in Iraq's 150 tribes.

The tide turned in July, Simcock said, when they identified four key Fallujah-area tribal clans, including the largest federation led by Sheikh Abu Issa Khamis. With more troops and Iraqis flocking into the police force, Simcock finally had enough U.S. and Iraqi manpower to leave in place after operations. "I stopped the whack-a-mole routine," declared Simcock.

One of the clans' sheikhs, Aiffan Sadoun, described their change of heart. "We never attacked the Americans," said the young, mustachioed clansman. "But we closed our eyes." He said Al-Qaeda had killed thirty-seven of his relatives. Now that Fallujah was calm, his father had returned from Jordan. Sadoun wanted to run for mayor, but he said U.S. forces were still needed in Anbar. "Give the American forces the chance to complete the job in Iraq," he said, adding that they should also bring about more balance in the government in Baghdad.

The turnaround was not automatic. Twenty-seven Iraqis were killed by a suicide bomber at a sheikh's funeral in May. The bombing aimed to cause the collapse of the "awakening" movement. All vehicles were banned from the city. A marine officer said the lockdown was also designed to help stop drive-by shootings, since the Humvees were unable to catch the assailants' speeding cars.

The marines later instituted a permit process that allowed Fallujans to take their cars in and out of the city once they had been duly registered. Everyone else had to park outside the city in a large, dusty lot and take a minibus into town. Long lines of cars snaked around a gas station beside the parking lot. Along Fallujah's main east-west street, many storefronts and houses were severely damaged from bombs or heavy-caliber weapons. Many had been reduced to piles of rubble. Concertina wire and low concrete barriers channeled vehicular and foot traffic to certain crossings. A few children played on the streets, and traffic was light. A marine officer estimated that 75 percent of the population had returned, but Fallujah still felt like a ghost town.

By September the marines had turned over security to Iraqi police. No U.S. troops had been killed or wounded in the city since May 18. In ten police precincts scattered across Fallujah, marine companies lived with Iraqis in a tactical overwatch position. The Iraqi police conducted all security operations but were able to call on the marines in the stationhouse if they needed them. At Joint Security Station Khadairy, thirty-five Iraqi policemen were on duty each shift, and Lt. Nick Delong bunked in the two-story building with twenty marines for weeklong stays. "We're here as a QRF, quick reaction force, but we've had no SIGACTS [significant activity involving weapons] for a whole month," he said. Petraeus strolled through the streets with the police chief, Col. Faisal Zaidan. A woman poked her shawl-covered head out of her door to look at Petraeus. "How are things going here?" Petraeus asked her through his interpreter, Sadi Othman. She waved at Zaidan and said, "Very good, thanks to our boys."

Petraeus visited Anbar in early September, not so much to update himself—he was briefed daily on the smallest developments—but to boost the standing of Vice President Tariq al-Hashimi, who accompanied him. Even though many Anbaris did not support his Islamist party, Petraeus hoped that, as the country's top Sunni official, Hashimi would listen to their concerns. Hashimi flew in Petraeus's Black Hawk, along with Dr. Rafaa al-Esawi, a cabinet minister who was a Fallujan physician. After a briefing at the marine base, they piled into MRAPs, the new armored personnel carriers with V-shaped hulls, thick interior padding, and small windows, and drove to the town hall. The mayor and police chief waited outside to greet them and presented Hashimi with an Iraqi flag.

Even though it was 118 degrees, Petraeus led them on a walk down the main street to the market to show Fallujans that he and especially the Iraqi officials were interested in their lives and were not afraid to be there. Dr. Rafaa stopped to introduce Hashimi to shopkeepers and passerby. Petraeus sped ahead at his usual brisk pace, his security detail, a dozen marines, and several journalists forming a bubble around him. Even though the wide commercial street had once been a favorite for snipers, Petraeus wore no body armor and only his soft cap. He stopped at a curbside fruit-drink stand and ordered a round of drinks. Sadi Othman translated as Petraeus chatted with the young man pulverizing fruit and ice in a blender. "Things are much quieter now," the youth said, "but I need more customers."

Like the Pied Piper, Petraeus then led his party into the market, ducking under a low-hanging cloth tarp that covered a warren of stalls. Barrels of grain and tables and crates of fruits and vegetables littered the narrow path, forcing the party to walk single file. It was a perfect place for an ambush, but the security detail was accustomed to its peripatetic boss and managed to envelop him as he darted this way and that. As usual, unmanned aerial vehicles were aloft overhead with their unblinking eyes. The Iraqi vice president followed along, sweating in his dark business suit and wine-colored shirt. He was tired from the all-night negotiating sessions that had taken place in Baghdad over the past week. Dr. Rafaa, a large bear of a man who was also wearing a business suit, mopped his head and ducked into the market. He did not look like he was having fun on this American-style campaign outing.

Fallujah was as peaceful as it had been in the past four years, even if recovery was still a long way off. If the calm continued, Petraeus and his deputy for daily operations in Iraq, Lt. Gen. Raymond Odierno, believed that U.S. forces might be able to depart Anbar soon. It was the one "local accommodation" that was being cemented with support from Iraq's central government. In an obvious attempt to derail Anbar's progress, Sheikh Sattar, the leader of the Ramadi awakening, was killed by a buried bomb outside his house in September.

CROCKER DOGGEDLY CONTINUED his full-court press to extract some shred of "top-down" political progress from Iraq's national leaders. Parliament had recessed without enacting any reconciliation legislation, and Maliki's cabinet was paralyzed. Seventeen of the thirty-seven ministers were boycotting the cabinet, including all the Sunni Tawafuq members except Hashimi, who had remained in his post rather than join the boycott. But he and Maliki rarely spoke. Hashimi said Maliki would have to deliver on a list of eleven Tawafuq demands before the alliance would return to the government. Topping the list was the release of thousands of Iraqis who had been detained without charges or evidence.

Forces were gathering to call a no-confidence vote to topple Maliki's hapless government. Some U.S. officials had come to believe that a change in government was needed. The backers of Shia Vice President Adil Abd al-Mahdi believed a moderate bloc could be formed to vote him in to replace Maliki. Former prime minister Ayad Allawi also positioned himself as an alternative, denouncing the Maliki government in a *New York Times* op-ed. His longtime backers at the Central Intelligence Agency considered the pragmatic strongman a viable replacement, but he would not win any votes from the religious Shia parties that held 128 of the 275 seats in parliament. The Islamists considered Allawi, a secular Shia, a traitor for having once belonged to the Baath Party, and his interim government of 2004–2005 had departed under a cloud of corruption allegations. Allawi might make an eventual comeback, but he did not stand much chance of being elected by the current parliament.

While they too were frustrated with Maliki, neither Petraeus nor Crocker favored his ouster. "When you look at the time and pain it took to form the current government," Crocker said, "I would think those inclined toward change would consider carefully whether you can get what you want in the time frame you want it." Petraeus believed that Maliki could still cobble together enough votes to pass bills. It had taken six months to form Maliki's government. Another such period of drift could very likely send the country back into the chaos of the previous two years. It could also prompt Congress to finally throw up its hands and insist on a troop withdrawal.

Crocker redoubled their efforts to reach some agreement on the political reconciliation agenda, hoping that the calls for Maliki to step down might elicit concessions. Intense negotiations with the second-tier Iraqi officials had been under way since July. Deputy National Security Adviser for Iraq and Afghanistan Meghan O'Sullivan had come to Baghdad for the summer to assist the search for compromises. In mid-August the Americans and the Iraqi deputies presented a set of proposals to Maliki, President Jalal Talabani, vice presidents Mahdi and Hashimi, and Masoud Barzani, the president of the Kurdish region. After a final marathon negotiating session that lasted two days and two nights, the top leaders reached agreement on August 26. The accord was nearly derailed at the last moment when Sunni Vice President Hashimi failed to appear to sign it. He was told that if he defaulted, there would be no release of detainees during the holy month of Ramadan as promised.

Hashimi signed. The accord granted one of the Sunnis' key demands, which was to release detainees who were being held without charge or evidence and to issue pardons according to agreed criteria. Barham Salih pushed for and won agreement on a reform of the entire detainee process that would allow a joint committee of parties to review the detentions and give the process greater transparency. As a first step, 1,700 detainees would be released in the coming month during Ramadan. Petraeus welcomed the agreement on detainee releases; the United States was holding some 26,000 detainees and hoped to reduce that number to 15,000 over the coming year. "We want to pursue detainee initiatives, such as a pledge and guarantor program," he said. In such a program a tribal elder would agree to act as a guarantor to watch over the newly released Iraqis. "This has the potential to produce releases but also a higher probability that they will successfully reintegrate into society," he said.

The five leaders also agreed on two draft laws to be submitted to parliament, on mechanisms to end the government's paralysis, and on the need to negotiate a long-term security accord with the United States. The draft laws revised de-Baathification and defined provincial powers. Agreement on de-Baathification had languished for months, and even now it threatened to unravel before the ink was dry. A week after the accord was announced, Hashimi confided that Tawafuq would not vote for the de-Baathification draft law without additional changes. And, he added, "there are still more demands in order for Tawafuq to come back to the government."

The most important parts of the accord were the mechanisms to remedy the government's dysfunctionality. Maliki agreed to meet regularly with the president and two vice presidents—something he had refused to do since the government's inception—and reach agreements with them. Bylaws would be passed to allow ministers to reach decisions without the votes of all thirty-seven ministers, and deputies would follow through on the agreements the principals reached. The leaders also agreed to shore up party discipline in the parliament to ensure that agreements they reached would be voted on accordingly. By committing the four parties to a more effective working relationship, the accord also reduced Maliki's reliance on the Sadr bloc.

This Government 101 approach would work only if Maliki honored it and began to include Talabani, Mahdi, and Hashimi in the decision-making process. Crocker did not portray it as any more than a beginning. "There will be innumerable political crises in the weeks and months ahead—I can hardly wait," he added with a laugh. Iraqi Ambassador Samir Sumaidaie, who was in Baghdad during this time, had a similar assessment. "Instead of one step forward and two steps back, we are now taking one step forward and maybe one step back."

Crocker saw such torturous negotiations as the only path to a solution. "The future of Iraq lies in the ability of these three communities to work out problems and set policies and courses. They managed to do it, however painfully, and that is the way I think they have to keep going." But he was also critical of the leaders' obstructionist, self-serving behavior. "The political leadership in this country has the responsibility to take actions that benefit the people," he said, instead of treating their ministries as personal fiefdoms. He suggested they join the average Iraqi, who was sleeping on rooftops to escape the suffocating heat and shortage of electricity.

For the United States, the most significant part of the accord was the Iraqis' call for a bilateral accord to replace the U.N. mandate for the Multi-National Force-Iraq Command. Maliki had first raised the possibility of an accord in November 2006 when he met with President Bush in Amman, Jordan. In June 2007, Foreign Minister Hoshyar Zebari visited the White House and proposed that talks begin on such a bilateral agreement, and it was decided that he and O'Sullivan would work on it during her stay in Baghdad over the summer.

Iraq's primary motivation in moving to a bilateral accord was to fully restore its sovereignty and end the U.S.-led coalition's legal basis for its freedom of action in Iraq. The U.N. resolutions that established and extended the Multi-National Force-Iraq Command gave it the right to act, unilaterally if necessary, against threats to international peace and security under the U.N. Charter's Chapter VII authority. A bilateral accord would give the Iraqi government the opportunity to negotiate all the terms under which U.S. forces operated in Iraq and to fully assert its sovereignty. That would include reopening the issue of immunity for U.S. troops and contractors from prosecution in Iraqi courts under Iraqi law, which had been granted since May 2003. The killings of seventeen civilians by Blackwater security personnel in September would greatly inflame this issue. Senior Iraqi officials had also been offended at various times by U.S. troops' searches at checkpoints. Iraqis were eager to gain full control over military operations, including greater control over who would be targeted by U.S. forces.

Zebari, a genial and astute diplomat, saw the accord as a way to put U.S-Iraqi security relations on a stable footing. He had launched into action because U.S. congressional opposition to the administration's policy continued to build: "I was concerned that this [surge] strategy was not going to work, so I said, 'Let us think about an alternative arrangement.'" He met with Vice President Dick Cheney and others to urge talks to begin soon. Although he hoped troop levels would decrease over time, he felt the accord was necessary to define the terms of a continuing presence and reduce the chance of an abrupt withdrawal that could leave Iraq exposed to internal and foreign enemies.

Like other senior Iraqi officials, Zebari did not believe Iraq was ready to defend itself. A U.S. withdrawal would invite further meddling by Iranians, he feared. "If you show them any signs of weakness, they will be more aggressive," Zebari said. "That is how things are interpreted in this part of the world. Now they feel their strategy is working. America is on the run. They follow [the U.S. debate over Iraq] very closely. Syria also shares this view." He and the prime minister had just visited Tehran, and Zebari said he had told senior Iranian officials they were wrong to think their aggression against U.S. forces in Iraq would tie down the United States and make a U.S. confrontation over Iran's nuclear program less likely. "I told them, 'You are wrong; this will only provoke them more,'" said the foreign minister.

A senior U.S. official conceded that negotiating the U.S.-Iraqi agreement would be difficult and that the United States likely would not retain the sweeping authorities it currently enjoyed. But the Iraqi government was determined to regain full sovereignty. "For the Iraqi government, it will signal the real end of occupation," said the official. The accord would include a clause allowing either government to terminate it, but the Bush administration planned to avoid making the foreign-defense commitments in the accord that would trigger the requirement for congressional approval.

Zebari's main partner in bringing the agreement this far was Meghan O'Sullivan, who came to his office to bid him good-bye. She was finally leaving the government to reclaim her life. After the September report was issued and the hearings were concluded, she would belatedly start a fellowship at the Institute of Politics at Harvard's Kennedy School of Government. Friends had counseled her to leave the administration before she was indelibly tied to the controversial history of the Iraq war, but it was far too late for that. She had been a key player for its duration, even though she was unknown to the general public. She had stimulated strongly negative opinions among many of her fellow American officials, some of which were no doubt because she was a tough bureaucratic infighter and wielded the clout of the White House. Middle East experts scorned her lack of experience in the region before 2003, and others seemed to resent her youth and gender. But the main substantive criticism was that she tended to look at Iraq primarily through the lens of the Shia and of the Islamic Supreme Council of Iraq (ISCI) in particular. Perhaps without her realizing it, Shia leaders were also less inclined to compromise because they had her backing, which they took to be the backing of the White House and the president.

She did favor Vice President Mahdi for the prime ministership and viewed Hashimi as a spoiler. A political scientist, O'Sullivan had offered various proposals over the summer for bridging the gaps between the various Iraqi parties' positions on the national reconciliation agenda. In her view, the laws would not be agreed upon until Iraq's disparate visions had been reconciled. The basic divide was between the Sunni (and others') view of a centralized state and the Islamist Shia and Kurd view of a government where powers were devolved to the regions. Since she had helped bring into being a government and constitution that emphasized regionalism, her views tended to support that position. But Sunnis, Sadrists, and nationalists did not support that vision.

Petraeus, who had asked O'Sullivan to come and help with the reconciliation talks, praised her as "exceedingly talented, brilliant writer, quite humble." He knew she was very close to ISCI but did not consider that a liability. ISCI, in his view, had the most sophisticated political machine, although he did not see why they were set upon "ISCI-stan" in southern Iraq. He did admit questions over how beholden the party was to Iran.

There was no way to understand, let alone solve, the Iraqi puzzle without wading into its complexities. Zebari had a favorite way to describe the chronic difficulty that Iraqis had in reaching any agreement of substance. "We have a saying here that the Shia are afraid of the past, the Sunnis are afraid of the future, and the Kurds are afraid of both the past and the future," he said, breaking into a chortle with the last phrase.

THE FULL-COURT PRESS TO ACHIEVE political progress received an unexpected boost just days after the August 26 accord was reached. August 27 was a major Shia holiday to celebrate the birth of Great Imam Mahdi, and thousands of Shia crowded the streets around the Imam Hussein shrine in Karbala. In a somewhat murky incident, JAM militiamen attacked the guards at the Karbala shrine. The clash escalated into a major battle that killed and wounded at least one hundred people and set cars and buildings afire as a million pilgrims made their way into Karbala.

Maliki went ballistic. He was on the phone all night. He ordered a curfew and ordered the pilgrims to leave the city to prevent further bloodshed. His national security adviser, Mowaffak al-Rubaie, badgered the Americans until they let him go to Karbala. He went to the shrine, and at 7:30 the next morning Rubaie called Maliki to tell him it was safe enough for him to come down. He drove down in a fifty-two-vehicle caravan including Iraqi armored cars equipped with heavy machine guns. He had ordered the Iraqi special operations forces to fly down to Karbala in the night to help secure the shrines and stop the fighting in the streets. Lt. Col. Sean Swindell, the U.S. Special Forces officer who was their primary liaison, and the U.S. Special Forces troop that served as their combat advisers went with them. The Iraqi Counter-Terrorist Force, or ICTF, as the Iraq unit was called, had graduated to planning its own missions over the past two years, but the two units normally fought side by side. They joined Karbala's Emergency Response Unit (ERU), a SWAT-type outfit that was advised by another Special Forces team.

Maliki strode into the Karbala provincial council office, a pistol strapped to his side, and personally arrested a council member. He then ordered the immediate launching of a mission to capture the Jaish al-Mahdi militiamen who were believed responsible for the attacks. When the provincial ERU police leader balked at going into a particular neighborhood, Maliki said, "I will go get them myself!" He then took his guards and led all the forces into the neighborhood.

That night, Maliki flew back on one of the special operations helicopters and Swindell heard him praise the Iraqi special operations brigade for the first time. "He called them the golden brigade," said

Swindell. Sadr's attack in Karbala enraged Maliki and appeared to convince him that he had to stop Sadr's violence once and for all. Swindell and other officers believed this was a turning point for Maliki. "Maliki became a leader that day," said one of Petraeus's advisers.

The JAM attack in Karbala was the last straw for Maliki. It was the latest in a string of attacks, including two assassinations, on August 11 and 20, of the governors of Qadisiya and Muthanna provinces in the south, allegedly carried out by Sadr forces. The August 26 accord denounced those killings and hinted at Iranian involvement. JAM had also been behind kidnappings at the oil and finance ministries earlier in the year.

The next day, August 29, Sadr ordered a six-month cease-fire for all Jaish al-Mahdi followers. Sadr seemed to realize that if he did not stand down he would face Dawa and ISCI united against him. Maliki was clearly growing more assertive and more willing to attack his erstwhile Sadrist allies. Sadr then went further and expelled dozens from his movement.

U.S. officials were pleased at Maliki's willingness to rein in JAM violence, but the frictions were not over. "That does not mean he is moving toward our desired position," said a Petraeus adviser who had witnessed Maliki's evolution firsthand. "He's not a horse-trader, not a natural give-and-take politician," said the U.S. officer. If anything, the year's intrigues had made Maliki resolved to gather more power into his hands. This officer no longer saw the sectarianism emanating from Maliki's adviser Bassima al-Jaidri. She was simply Maliki's faithful executor, the U.S. adviser had concluded. "She is totally in sync with Maliki. She reflects him."

Similarly, Sadr's cease-fire was a welcome advance, but it probably did not mean he would end his bid to gain ground against his Shia rivals and to fight the American occupiers. His nationalist message was compromised, however, by his lengthy sojourn in Iran and the Iranian military assistance. He had come to Iraq in May and given a speech calling for Iraqis to unite, but then returned to Iran. Although he still had the power to call masses of poor armed men into action, his absence had weakened his control.

Soon after the cease-fire declaration, Sadrist leader Ahmed Shaibani floated two offers publicly. He suggested letting the Mahdi militia keep the peace in Najaf just as Sunni volunteer groups were doing in Anbar and parts of Baghdad. In return for the same rights in Sadr City, he offered to stop the mortar attacks. Petraeus and the Iraqi government rejected the offers. The ISCI governor of Najaf, with help from the Iraqi special operations forces, had control of Najaf and was not about to hand it over to Sadr. JAM did control several Baghdad neighborhoods, including Sadr City, but the U.S. and Iraqi governments were not prepared to accept that as a permanent state of affairs.

THE FULL-COURT PRESS ALSO INCLUDED several diplomatic initiatives, spearheaded by Iraqi Deputy Prime Minister Salih and Foreign Minister Zebari, to contain Iran and galvanize support from the region and beyond. Iraq was enmeshed in a civil conflict, but it was also the scene of an international chess game. Iran was the key regional player, with the neighboring Arab states lined up on the other side.

"It is in our interest to have good relations with Iran, but the way they are dealing with Iraq is unacceptable," said Salih, bluntly labeling Iran's aim as "expansionism." His solution was a regional balance of power that would contain Iranian ambitions. It would require a U.S. role, he said, noting that Iran "has worked hard to develop equities in Iraq while the U.S. was for many years absent."

At a meeting earlier in the year, Salih had confronted Ali Larijani, a senior Iranian diplomat. "If Iran is seeking the failure of America in Iraq, it is Iraq who will fail," Salih told him. "America will leave and Iraq will fail. Is that what you want?" Larijani, who had been born in Najaf and was considered a pragmatic, albeit conservative, member of the regime, replied, "Absolutely not."

"Iraq has turned into a quagmire for the Americans. It has become a quagmire for the Iraqis," warned Salih. "And you'll be sucked into that quagmire too if you're not careful."

At the Egyptian resort of Sharm el Sheikh in May, Zebari had launched the "neighbors initiative," gathering Iraq's neighbors, the five permanent members of the U.N. Security Council, the Arab League, the G-8, and the Organization of the Islamic Conference. His goal was to persuade the neighboring countries to start acting in constructive ways or at least to stop fueling Iraq's violence. The initiative was envisioned as an ongoing process with working groups to address the specific problems of border security, refugees, and energy.

Europe had been reluctant to help end a war it had staunchly opposed, but new governments in Germany and France were softening that stand. The United Nations, which had lost its envoy and twenty-one employees in a devastating bombing in 2003, was also moving gingerly toward greater support for Iraq. Its small mission in Iraq had agreed to assist and monitor the provincial elections, but U.N. personnel remained concerned that Iraq was still not safe enough to expand the ninety-five-person mission.

A senior Iraqi official acknowledged that it would be hard to persuade other countries to act until Iraq's relationship with Iran was clarified. "The key is what Iran does," said a senior Iraqi official. "It is like a red flag to a bull. Saudi Arabia cannot tolerate an Iraq dominated by Iran. It will do whatever it has to to stop that eventuality." To Sunni countries, it looked like the United States had set up a Shia axis.

A senior U.S. defense official who participated in meetings with Saudi King Abdullah said the monarch openly expressed his loathing for the Maliki government. Abdullah had also harshly criticized both the U.S. presence and the Iraqi government's behavior in an unusual public statement. "In the beloved Iraq, the bloodshed is continuing under an illegal foreign occupation and detestable sectarianism," he said, declining to meet with Maliki as he toured the region in preparation for the May summit. Despite repeated entreaties from Iraq and the United States, Saudi Arabia balked at opening an embassy in Baghdad, though it did forgive some of Iraq's debt. None of Iraq's Sunni neighbors had embassies in Baghdad, for security reasons but also as a silent rejection of the Maliki government.

Saudi Arabia's hostility went beyond rhetoric. The country was a primary source of foreign fighters who were flowing into Iraq, mostly through Syria. As of mid-2007, the United States estimated that fifty to eighty foreign fighters, many of them Saudis, were passing through Syria each month to join Al-Qaeda in Iraq. Eighty percent of the suicide bombers in Iraq were foreign, and half were Saudi youths. The U.S. estimated that in the first half of 2007 alone, 280 suicide bombers had killed or wounded 5,500 Iraqis. Although they were few in number, these foreign fighters caused a disproportionate number of the casualties throughout the war.

The working groups aimed to shut down the flow of foreign fighters through Syria, as well as the flow of arms from Iran. Another objective was to address the hemorrhage of refugees from Iraq into Jordan and Syria, which were struggling under the strain of over two million displaced Iraqis. The United States had high-level meetings with Syria, and Saudi Arabia began to stop issuing one-way tickets to Damascus for Saudi youths. But the administration balked at setting up regular talks with Syria.

In the first direct talks with Iran in twenty-seven years, Crocker held three meetings with Iran's ambassador to Iraq during 2007. On May 28, Crocker presented a dossier summarizing the intelligence from the raids and interrogations of JAM special group leaders, the Hezbollah leader, and Iranian Quds members detained in Iraq. Prime Minister Maliki opened the meeting and then left to let Crocker and Iran's ambassador, Hassan Kazemi Qomi, talk. Crocker requested that Iran halt its weapons trade and destabilization of Iraq.

Iran denied sending arms to Iraq or otherwise destabilizing its neighbor. The two sides both stated that they had a mutual interest in Iraq's stability. For Crocker's part, the main point of the meeting was to lay down a marker. He had shown the Iranians what the United States knew about Iranian involvement in Iraq. Though Iran might deny the activities publicly, it knew that the U.S. knew.

Maliki was not favorably inclined toward Iran. He had lived there briefly before choosing Syria as his home in exile. He had never learned Farsi. And like most Iraqis, who were proud Arabs, he had no desire for Iraq to become the fifty-first state of Persian Iran. Sunni critics called the Maliki government Iranians, but that was not an accurate depiction of Maliki's personal sympathies. Nevertheless, Iran was destined to be a major influence in Iraq. It had already signed major contracts to provide energy, build plants, and trade goods with Iraq.

On July 24 Crocker held a second round of talks in Baghdad with Iran's ambassador. They lasted for seven hours. This time Zebari hosted the talks. There were heated exchanges as Iran continued to deny the evidence that it was arming JAM special groups and, according to further intelligence gathered since the first meeting, some Al-Qaeda-affiliated Sunni groups as well. The outcome of the meeting was a formal statement that Iran pledged not to destabilize Iraq. Iran might not honor it, but there was now a formal pledge to which the government could be held.

Rubaie hosted the third round of talks on August 6. Again Crocker and Kazemi Qomi exchanged their positions, and Crocker demanded that Iran start living up to its commitment not to destabilize Iraq. An additional meeting by a lower-level working group, which had been agreed to in the July talks, was also held to address the details of the security issues and proposals for monitoring mechanisms. The U.S. side was represented by Marcie Ries, the embassy's political-military counselor. In addition to this working group, she led the U.S side in a similar forum with Syria to seek border monitoring and other agreements to stop the flow of foreign fighters from there.

After the August 6 meeting, Crocker and Secretary of State Condoleezza Rice left open the possibility of further talks, but they made clear that they expected action from Iran to justify the continued dialogue. Maliki went to Iran in August, and in September during his visit to New York to address the U.N. General Assembly, he said flatly that Iran was no longer destabilizing Iraq.

That proved to be untrue, but Crocker believed it was worthwhile to keep the door open. He was not opposed to the use of force in Iraq against Iranian agents, to demonstrate that the United States knew what Iran was doing and would stop it with force if necessary. But a more effective mix of sticks and carrots and an overarching diplomatic strategy toward Iran was clearly needed. The administration had decided that it would not hold wider or higher-level talks with Iran until it suspended its uranium enrichment program, but this position limited the options for dealing with the Iran-Iraq problem and Iran's regional activities. U.S. strategy required a long-range view of U.S.-Iranian relations and Iran's place in the Middle East. No one knew whether a combination of sanctions and the promise of normalized relations might dissuade Iran from its quest for nuclear arms and regional hegemony, but a policy of regime change and all out confrontation made many regional players nervous. It would take a sophisticated approach to deal with a wily adversary like the Iranian regime. Crocker fully understood the complexities, but he believed it was possible to reach agreement with both Syria and Iran because "it is in their interest in the long run not to have a radicalized and destabilized Iraq on their borders. But what they will have to overcome is their desire to inflict loss on the U.S., which means coming to the realization that they can't have it both ways."

In the case of Iran, Crocker noted that the long and bloody Iran-Iraq war of the 1980s was a significant factor in Iran's persistent attempts to gain influence and control in Iraq. "We should make clear that we understand the history, we understand what they have suffered out of Iraq, more than any country except Iraq itself, and that they therefore seek outcomes here that will never again permit what Saddam did to them," he said. That did not mean allowing Iran's ambitions to go unchecked, but rather to "see if their whole frame of reference changes into a long, sober look at how Iran's interests are best served."

Given the gulf between Iran and the United States, that was no doubt a years-long task. Crocker, who had been ambassador in Damascus for three years, believed it would be much easier to induce Syria to see where its real interests lay. He noted: "The [radical Sunni foreign fighters] that the Syrians have facilitated are precisely those elements that would like to bring down the Syrian regime. There is heavy unfinished business between the Sunni Islamists and the Shia Alawite regime in Damascus that dates back a quarter century to the annihilation of the Muslim Brotherhood in Hama. They annihilated their fourth-largest city to wipe out the Muslim Brotherhood," the diplomat said. "Syrian Sunnis haven't forgotten that, and Sunni Islamists have definitely not forgotten that. So the extent to which Syria arms, aids, and abets Sunni Islamists is the extent to which they are potentially training the cadres that will come back at them." A full-court press in this quarter might induce some progress rather quickly, if the administration was willing to expend the capital.

12

The September Reckoning

Throughout the summer, political pressure mounted for Petraeus to recommend an end to the surge in September. Since June, he and Lt. Gen. Raymond Odierno had analyzed what they called the "battlefield geometry" in weekly meetings, along with Odierno's chiefs of plans and operations, Col. Bill Rapp and Col. Mike Meese. Rapp kept Petraeus's thoughts on his recommendations compartmentalized in a separate computer file.

Petraeus was determined that no word of his testimony or his recommendations would leak publicly. No one except Rapp saw his testimony statement until September 4 on the flight to Washington, and no one in the administration would see his statement before he delivered it before Congress on September 10. The White House, Secretary of Defense Bob Gates's office, and Central Command (CENTCOM) were clamoring to get advance copies of it, but the general's staff stalled. There was an elaborate plan to send the final presentation electronically as soon as Petraeus delivered his opening statement to the House Armed Services

Committee on Monday morning. As soon as Petraeus finished speaking, his deputy media director, Lt. Col. Joe Yoswa, hit "send" on his computer and e-mailed a copy to all the senior officials in the administration. This was Petraeus's attempt to dispel the allegations that he was being told what to say to Congress and the American public.

The internal battle over the recommendations culminated in late August in a series of meetings with the administration's top officials. The Joint Chiefs of Staff, including its chairman, Gen. Pete Pace, wanted a quick drawdown and transition to noncombat missions. Army chief Gen. George Casey had made his views known on the Hill. The chiefs also had an advocate inside the White House in Lt. Gen. Doug Lute, a likeable and forthright general who had taken Meghan O'Sullivan's place in an elevated position as the Iraq "czar" reporting directly to the president. Lute had been the J-3 chief of operations at the joint staff in the Pentagon and before that the J-3 at CENTCOM, so he came to the job with a knowledge of the war's course from its inception. He had opposed the surge when the joint staff debated the options in late 2006.

Central Command's Adm. William "Fox" Fallon also vociferously advocated a substantial drawdown. He believed the United States was dangerously short of a strategic reserve of forces and equipment to deal with other threats in the Mideast and South Asia, and he was the operational commander for that volatile region. He was also extremely skeptical that the venture in Iraq had any chance of succeeding, and had made it known that he thought a new approach should be adopted.

Secretary of Defense Gates was also personally in favor of a drawdown on a more modest path, but he was not inclined to overrule Petraeus. The views of Petraeus, as the commander on the ground, should carry enormous weight, the secretary believed. But he also believed that CENTCOM and the joint staff should be heard directly by the president, so he constructed a process that allowed each to have his say. Petraeus's superiors had a right to offer their views on Iraq, and it was their responsibility to assess Iraq in light of other regional and global challenges as well as the state of the military services.

The joint staff tried to increase their sway and diminish Petraeus's in the decision-making process. They proposed that Petraeus develop a series of options that they would then evaluate in order to provide a recommendation to the president. Petraeus adamantly opposed the effort to filter his views. He would make his recommendation directly to the president and his superiors would be free to accept or reject it.

In deference to the chain of command, it was decided that Petraeus would brief each of his superiors in turn. On August 25, Petraeus presented his recommendation to Adm. Fallon at the Petraeus's residence at Camp Victory. The two men had clashed from the start. Petraeus had shared his views with him since the spring, at a commanders' conference Fallon convened at As Saliyah base in Qatar, CENTCOM's forward headquarters. The admiral reportedly called him an "ass-kissing little chicken shit" who ingratiated himself with superiors, but Petraeus adamantly denied that Fallon said this to him. "One of the two of us would have been gone," he said. He did say they had "direct exchanges." Another official, a friend of Fallon's, found the derogatory comment entirely plausible. Fallon was far heavier-handed than his predecessor, John Abizaid, ever had been with Gen. Casey. He and Petraeus had gotten off to a sour start when Fallon sent a two-star admiral who had never been to Iraq to travel around Iraq for a week, then present a plan unexpectedly on what Petraeus should do. Petraeus was stunned by the intellectual arrogance of the move, as well as the simplistic briefing, at a time when his Joint Strategic Assessment Team was conducting a rigorous analysis. Petraeus was on his third tour in Iraq, but Fallon was new to the region. Petraeus had been invested with enormous authority by the White House, yet Fallon had landed the job because he was assertive. At age sixty-three, he was not about to change his ways.

On Tuesday, August 28, Petraeus gave his presentation to Secretary Gates, with whom he had talked extensively on several occasions, both in Washington when Petraeus visited in April and on Gates's two trips to Iraq. "He did a very skillful job in fostering the discussion among all of us," Petraeus said.

On Friday, August 31, Petraeus gave his presentation to President Bush. In an unplanned session that was something of a bureaucratic coup, Fallon had flown to Washington and had presented *his* views to the president the night before. He argued that the United States should take on more risk in Iraq to reduce risk elsewhere. He felt Petraeus was being too cautious about the pace of withdrawal and that a mission change would force a faster withdrawal.

The next day, when Petraeus briefed his recommendations to the president, Fallon was sitting at the table along with the chiefs and National Security Council principals Rice, Stephen Hadley, and Gates. Petraeus's attitude, as in the previous sessions, was that he was presenting his views rather than clearing them with his superiors. The president would decide whether to accept or reject them, but his core recommendations were not going to change. In the last ten minutes of the meeting, the president asked Fallon if he had anything else to add. The admiral repeated his view about having a different risk calculus and said he was concerned about other contingencies. At the end of the two hours, the president endorsed Petraeus's recommendations.

The president had also gone to the Pentagon to hear the joint chiefs' views, as Gates had arranged. But in the meeting with the joint chiefs at the Pentagon, in the secure "tank" on the E-ring overlooking the Potomac River, Bush made it clear that he was still very committed to achieving success in Iraq. He did not want to reduce troops to deal with some "totally hypothetical" contingency elsewhere, according to a senior administration official.

A heated public debate had broken out over whether violence in Iraq had indeed declined or whether Petraeus was massaging the facts. *New York Times* columnist Frank Rich questioned Petraeus's character and suggested that he had a history of bending the truth in an optimistic direction, citing the examples of Mosul's descent into violence nine months after his departure and his September 2004 op-ed article in which he touted progress in training the Iraqi security forces. The *Washington Post* ran a front-page article in which an unnamed intelligence official claimed that Petraeus's command counted as sectarian murders only those victims shot in the back of the head, not the front.

The week before Petraeus's testimony, David Walker, head of the Government Accountability Office (GAO), a research arm of Congress that had been tasked to provide an independent report on Iraq, testified about its findings. The GAO had been unable to determine whether sectarian violence had been reduced, he said, "since it is difficult to measure whether the perpetrators' intents were sectarian in nature, and various other measures of population security show differing trends." The report concluded that "the average number of daily attacks against civilians have remained unchanged from February to July 2007." The GAO relied on the same data as MNF-I, but it included data only through July, in order to meet its reporting deadline. The sharp decline in violence dated from August, when the massive volunteer initiative took hold. The GAO report also assessed that only seven of the eighteen benchmarks had been met in full or partially, whereas the administration's July benchmarks report deemed ten to have been met. These differences were partly due to the GAO applying a more rigorous standard of what constituted "satisfactory progress."

This heated debate culminated in a full-page ad, paid for by the antiwar group Moveon.org, which appeared in the *New York Times* on the first day of Petraeus's testimony. Its headline read: GENERAL PETRAEUS OR GENERAL BETRAY US? COOKING THE BOOKS FOR THE WHITE HOUSE. The ad cited the *Post* article and the GAO report, his 2004 op-ed article, and press reports disputing that Iraq's violence had declined. The ad alleged, as others had, that Petraeus was a political general looking for his next promotion rather than a straight shooter who would tell it like it is. Although Petraeus's detractors had used the "Betray-us" pun in private, the incendiary ad caused many critics to recoil. For those in the military community, *betrayal* was a word used to connote treasonous acts and high crimes that were punishable by the severest sanctions. It was, in short, overkill.

When Rapp and Maj. Everett Spain arrived at Petraeus's red-brick home at Fort Myer, on a hill overlooking the Washington monument, to pick him up, Rapp expected that he would be seething over the advertisement. Rapp was angry, but Petraeus did not show any emotion and even seemed upbeat. "Ad hominem attacks are a weak substitute for substantive rebuttals," he said as they crossed the Roosevelt Bridge and drove along the Washington Mall.

Petraeus later acknowledged that he felt "very uncomfortable at being thrust into the political cross-fire that has erupted." He also took solace from a childhood friend who sent him the very apt Rudyard Kipling poem "If." But he was about to give the biggest public performance of his career to date. He put on his game face and would not depart from his planned deadpan demeanor no matter how histrionic the hearings became.

The hearing room on Capitol Hill was packed. After an awkward pause to fix his microphone, which had suddenly gone dead, while Code Pink demonstrators chanted antiwar slogans, Petraeus began with his bottom line: "The military objectives of the surge are, in large measure, being met." He displayed detailed charts showing that violence had declined in eight of the past twelve weeks and that since the height of the sectarian violence in December, civilian deaths of all types had declined by 45 percent. Petraeus's charts gave Americans a chance to look at the trends since October 2004 and decide what to make of them. Violence had declined to about a thousand attacks a week but was still much higher than the six hundred weekly attacks in 2004.

Petraeus credited the gains to "significant blows" dealt to Al Qaeda in Iraq, the disruption of Shia militias, and the application of counterinsurgency practices by "units living among the people they are securing." He also said that Iraqi security forces were taking on more responsibility and continuing to improve, "albeit it slowly and amid continuing concerns about the sectarian tendencies of some elements in their ranks." He gave the most credit to the volunteer phenomenon: "The most significant development in the past six months likely has been the increasing emergence of tribes and local citizens rejecting Al-Qaeda and other extremists," he said.

He did not highlight the Iraqi government's decision to offer jobs or full pensions to 46,800 former members of Saddam's army. These former soldiers had responded to a survey sent out by the prime minister's Office of the Commander in Chief the previous March. The government offered to reinstate 5,000 of the respondents at their former pay and rank, including 270 former generals. It was a huge step toward reversing the Coalition Provisional Authority's Decree 2 and extending an olive branch to former regime members, but what should have been frontpage news was barely a footnote. The September 14 report released by the White House also buried the development on page 8 in half a sentence: "more than 45,000 former army personnel have been granted pensions or reinstated to active duty."

Petraeus next addressed the state of the Iraqi security forces and their readiness to assume the mission of securing Iraq. He said that 95 of 140 units were capable of operating "in the lead." To be capable of independent operations, the Iraqi forces' logistics, personnel, medical, intelligence, and air capacity would all have to increase. Congress had commissioned an independent study of the Iraqi security forces, to be completed before Petraeus's testimony so it would have an expert basis for assessing his judgments. A group of retired U.S. officers and defense officials headed by retired marine Gen. James Jones conducted the study and spent twenty days in Iraq. The report, issued on September 6, concluded that the Iraqi security forces would not be able to operate independently for another twelve to eighteen months. It estimated that adequate logistics capability for the entire force was another two years away.

The study's most sweeping recommendation was to disband the National Police entirely, and it criticized the ministry of interior as sectarian and dysfunctional. There was wide agreement that the police and the ministry were the most problematic of the security apparatus, but Petraeus and other officers in Iraq advocated the continued purging and mentoring of the police and ministry rather than disbanding twenty-seven battalions of needed manpower. The study also recommended that the Office of the Commander in Chief be disbanded and that the practice of the prime minister directing special operations forces outside the military chain of command be ended.

Petraeus concluded by telling the legislators that he had recommended the withdrawal of the first army brigade in December 2007, and the subsequent withdrawal of four brigades and two marine battalions to be completed by July 2008. In addition, a Marine Expeditionary Unit was completing its seven-month tour in Anbar in September and would not be replaced. Those reductions would bring down the U.S. forces level from twenty brigade equivalents to fifteen by July 2008. Petraeus also said "force reductions *will* continue" beyond the summer but that he could not recommend a timetable until the spring. He pledged to do so no later than mid-March 2008.

For the next six hours, legislators grilled Petraeus and Crocker. Many were upset that Petraeus proposed only a five-brigade drawdown over the next ten months. Some disputed his claims of progress. Democratic Rep. Barbara Boxer of California took issue with Petraeus's description of increased security in Iraq. "I ask you to take off your rosy glasses," she said. "You had them on in 2005. I believed you." He would hear the same skepticism the next day, when Democratic Sen. Hillary Clinton of New York said: "Despite what I view as your rather extraordinary efforts in your testimony both yesterday and today, I think that the reports that you provide to us really require the willing suspension of disbelief. In any of the metrics that have been referenced in your many hours of testimony, any fair reading of the advantages and disadvantages accruing post-surge, in my view, end up on the downside."

There had been no major political breakthroughs, and Crocker did not try to sugarcoat the situation. He pointed to the disbursement of oil revenues through the central government's budget to the provinces, the admission of 1,500 Abu Ghraib volunteers to the police academy, and the provisional immunity policy the government had granted to volunteers accepted for police training. Crocker claimed these were all signs that "the seeds of reconciliation are being planted" and described the approach of linking progress at the grassroots level to the central government. "The cumulative trajectory is upwards but the curve is not steep," he concluded modestly. "I cannot guarantee success but I believe it is attainable."

In keeping with his usual practice of flooding the zone to get his message out, Petraeus gave a press conference at the National Press Club on September 12 as well as twenty-three interviews before returning to Iraq. At a roundtable with *USA Today* journalists a reporter asked if he had presidential ambitions. Petraeus asked her to recall the "Shermanesque" response ("If nominated I will not run. If elected I will not serve.") Later he said he was stunned by the question. Having just been thoroughly mauled by Congress and the press, he could imagine nothing less palatable than running for office. Of course, generals had run for office—most recently Wesley Clark—and Colin Powell had actively entertained the notion.

Holly Petraeus was amused by the continual speculation in the media that Petraeus harbored presidential aspirations. "It seems like the Europeans especially are always saying he has presidential ambitions," she said. "It's such a hoot. First of all, he'd be doing it with his second wife." Then she realized she should give an answer that left no doubt: "God, no, he doesn't have presidential ambitions," she exclaimed. Bill Knowlton, Holly's father, agreed that it was hard to imagine Petraeus running for office. "Most generals look upon the rough-and-tumble of campaigns with distaste," he said. Knowlton, who had lectured and advised corporations when he retired, could envision a similar path for his son-in-law. He also thought Petraeus would make a good ambassador to Iraq. When asked if Petraeus might become army chief or even chairman of the Joint Chiefs of Staff, Knowlton said that he had served in the requisite posts, albeit for the minimum time necessary. Knowlton himself had been in the running for army chief, but he had retired after his NATO post. Petraeus had ascended to four-star general, but he had yet to ascend to a higher post than his father-in-law had held.

Knowlton praised Petraeus's stoic demeanor during the hearings. "By keeping his cool, he made those who attacked him look like schmucks," he said. Petraeus's family had been dismayed by the harsh criticism over the summer as the media and congressional leaders accused Petraeus of misleading the public and exaggerating the progress. Holly was equally appalled at those who used her husband as a shield for an unpopular policy. By the *Washington Post*'s count, the president had invoked Petraeus's name 150 times in the past eight months. "I don't appreciate my husband being used by any side," she said, observing that civilian officials make the policy decisions and military officers carry them out. "It is up to his superiors to formulate his mission," she said. But in the bitter wartime debate, Petraeus had inevitably become the defender of the surge and probably just as inevitably had been pegged as "Bush's general."

Nonetheless, Holly's mother, Peggy, noted that the little old ladies in their apartment building did make a distinction between the man and the war: they supported Petraeus but not the Iraq war. Sympathizing with her daughter, she urged her not to watch too much of the news coverage, saying, "You'll drive yourself up the wall." Holly had busied herself settling into their duplex house at Fort Myer, which coincidentally was next door to the one they had lived in when Petraeus worked for Gen. Carl Vuono. She had also taken a job as director of an educational service for military families at the Better Business Bureau, which grew out of her efforts to end predatory lending practices.

The Knowltons were no strangers to being in the middle of a controversial war. During Vietnam, the fact that Holly's father was a top general aroused criticism at the liberal Madeira prep school she attended. She and her mother had worried while her father and brothers were serving on the front lines, especially given Bill Knowlton's penchant for flying to remote hamlets in his lone helicopter. They were glad that soldiers returning from Iraq were not treated as outcasts by the public as Vietnam vets had been.

"We've seen the ugly side of politics," Holly said of the past months, but she was extremely proud of the progress her husband had made in the war "to get it to the point where we can disengage." Her father, who had served in two Middle Eastern countries, believed it would take a long time to sort out Iraq. He hoped the United States would find a way to persevere without wrecking the army. He remembered all too clearly the American departure from Vietnam and the fall of Saigon in 1975, as well as the task of rebuilding the military.

Petraeus missed his family and was grateful for the brief visit with them. He and Holly had flown to Fort Benning, Georgia, just before the hearings to see their son graduate from airborne school. Stephen's transformation from computer geek to paratrooper had astonished Holly, but Petraeus could not have been more pleased as he stood at the edge of Fryar Drop Zone and watched his son leap out of a plane and unfurl his parachute. At the subsequent ceremony, he pinned Knowlton's jump wings on his son's chest, marveling at how much his son resembled him, and announced to the crowd, "I'd like to introduce our latest Airborne trooper."

Stephen had gone off to college, where he changed majors, joined a fraternity, took up martial arts, and then one day announced that he had joined the Reserve Officers' Training Corps. Knowlton was not too surprised. "It's much better when military offspring make their own decisions on their own time," he said. As he had seen during his West Point years, many sons feel pressured to fill their father's shoes. Petraeus had never pushed his son, but he was delighted at his decision.

AS PETRAEUS RETURNED TO IRAQ, in Washington the battle lines that existed before the testimony remained. Petraeus and the White House remained pitted against the military establishment. The White House hoped to preserve its options on the pace of the drawdown after July, but others, including Fallon and Gates, wanted a clear commitment. There were strong arguments on both sides, but to Petraeus's supporters, Casey seemed to be making something of a vendetta out of his opposition to Petraeus and MNF-I. "The army staff has really changed in dynamics since Casey came on board. There is a personal, almost belligerent attitude to what he is doing," said one of Petraeus's advisers. "Casey has been undermining Petraeus," he continued. "He keeps calling senators and talking about the harm the war is doing to the army and the need to be prepared for future contingencies."

There were, however, many signs that the army had reached the breaking point. At Fort Leavenworth Lt. Gen. Bill Caldwell saw that they were short of officer instructors, and classes that should have been filled with captains were not—they were either in Iraq or had left the army. A longtime advocate of shifting to a massively beefed-up advisory effort in Iraq, Caldwell was now overseeing the preparation and training of advisers. Despite the efforts of Lt. Col. John Nagl and others, the system did not put top candidates into those jobs. Caldwell had recommended to Casey that the board that selected lieutenant colonels for battalion command should also pick forty top-notch lieutenant colonels for advisory positions, to guarantee the quality they needed. Too many of the current advisers had not been assigned to troop units for a long time, which limited their effectiveness in the field.

Many of those who argued for a drawdown in Iraq had concluded that the war was already lost and that Iraq's political factions were simply incapable of settling their differences. They argued for a policy of triage and containment to limit the damage done to other U.S. interests. The containment option, advocated notably by former CENTCOM chief Tony Zinni, would be problematic to implement if a raging civil war was under way. Analysts Ken Pollock and Dan Byman had proposed a "catchment basin" notion that would attempt to corral refugees in camps and police the borders. But this option meant tolerating massive killing inside Iraq.

Downsizing to a largely advisory and counterterrorism mission was the primary policy alternative advocated by moderate Democrats, such as Senators Carl Levin and Jack Reed and others. The most detailed version of this alternative policy had been published in June by the Center for a New American Security. In a report titled "Phased Transition: A Responsible Way Forward and Out of Iraq," Jim Miller and Shawn Brimley proposed the immediate initiation of a drawdown to 60,000 troops by January 2009. They would include about 20,000 advisers, another 20,000 quick-reaction forces (8,000 of them in Kuwait), 4,000 air force personnel, and 3,000 special operations forces for counterterrorism missions. The detailed proposal was a plausible blueprint for a *future* security posture, but the three bedrock U.S. security goals in Iraq the authors set out—preventing Al-Qaeda safe haven, regional war, and genocide—could not be accomplished in current conditions with so few troops. Nor did the proposal provide a political strategy to induce the Shia-led Iraqi government to make the necessary concessions to prevent genocide or civil war. Levin believed that setting a timetable to withdraw U.S. troops might extract concessions, but it was a one-shot strategy. Once the United States decided to withdraw, its leverage would diminish very rapidly.

If the United States wanted to affect Iraq's internal dynamics and prevent renewed bloodshed, it would need to remain in the country in substantial numbers. "Congress doesn't understand or doesn't want to understand that counterinsurgency, nation-building, peacekeeping, and peace enforcement all entail being involved with the population," said one of Petraeus's aides. "The idea that you can pull onto a border or go to your bases is going back to Caseyism, which we know didn't work. So why go back to a failed strategy, which is exactly what they are asking for? It is idiocy," he said.

The clock would now tick toward a new deadline in March. The basic question facing the United States was whether it could assist Iraq in finding a political solution that would permit a more substantial drawdown and, if so, what type of military and other resources had to be devoted to that end. In the hearings both Petraeus and Crocker had framed the fight as a competition among ethnic and sectarian communities for power and resources. "This competition *will* take place," Petraeus said, "and its resolution is key to producing long-term stability in the new Iraq." Crocker agreed, saying, "It is the balance of power that has yet to be sorted out." But, as Republican Sen. Richard Lugar of Indiana had observed, a strategy for doing so was still wanting.

13

The Drawdown Begins, and the Cease-Fire Spreads

As the drawdown of U.S. troops began in the fall, Petraeus and Lt. Gen. Raymond Odierno attempted to make it as gradual and seamless as possible. Withdrawal is the trickiest military maneuver of all, and the commanders were determined to minimize the vulnerability of both the departing troops and those left behind. Americans were eager to have all the troops home, but even this reduction from twenty to fifteen brigades entailed large changes in Iraq. It would be felt at every echelon, and most of all for the ground units that would now have twice as much territory to patrol. The commanders did not want to jeopardize the fragile peace that had emerged. Indeed, they were determined to extend it to still-violent areas and use it to push for the elusive "top-down" progress.

During his battlefield circulations, Petraeus told the battalion and company commanders that they would have to "thicken" their presence with increased use of Iraqi army and volunteer forces so the enemy did not spot an opportunity to reenter areas that had been secured. The plan for central Iraq was to "take a little from here, a little from there," Odierno said, rather than to pull out a brigade and leave a gaping hole.

The drawdown scheme was based on the fact that the last army surge brigade would complete its fifteen-month rotation in July 2008. Working backward from that, they plotted one brigade withdrawal every forty-five days. That totaled eight months, meaning the first one would have to come out in December. Petraeus and Odierno had decided that the 3rd Brigade, 1st Cavalry Division in Diyala could be taken out in December. The newly arrived 4-2 Stryker Brigade could spread out to fill the territory. Petraeus did not want to shift troops from the population-security mission too quickly, but the joint chiefs insisted that the new mission statement include an order to begin transitioning troops to an overwatch posture in preparation for subsequent withdrawal.

On the marines' side, a Marine Expeditionary Unit (roughly a brigade equivalent) was sent home from Anbar in September, and two Regimental Combat Teams (roughly battalion equivalents) were moved north to conduct shaping operations to prepare for an offensive against the remaining Al-Qaeda sanctuaries in Ninewa province. Odierno felt vindicated that he had argued for additional marine forces to be sent to Anbar as part of the surge. They had finally been able to cover the entire Euphrates River Valley and secure all the population centers that had harbored Sunni insurgents. He was confident enough of Anbar's progress to plan to reduce the marine battalion equivalents from sixteen to six by April 2008.

Petraeus decided to delay the withdrawal of the second army brigade until March 2008 because the key commands were changing hands at year's end as units completed their fifteen-month tours. This created turbulence and risks as new units and commanders moved in to pick up where their predecessors had left off. In December, the Multi-National Division-Baghdad (MND-B) changed hands from 1st Cavalry Division to the 4th Infantry Division after the customary two weeks' overlap. The relationships forged with Iraqis at every level had been the primary means of effecting change. Among those leaving were Brig. Gen. John Campbell, Col. J. B. Burton, and Lt. Col. Dale Kuehl, who had all been vital to the patchwork peace that had been constructed in Baghdad. Campbell was typically modest but admitted, "You pour your heart and soul into it, so it can be hard to let go. Your legacy is how well you set up your successors for success."

In the highest-level turnover, the Multi-National Corps-Iraq headquarters changed hands in February 2008. Lt. Gen. Odierno and thousands of corps staff completed their fifteen-month tour and handed off the number-two military command in the country to Lt. Gen. Lloyd Austin and the XVIII Airborne Corps from Fort Bragg. Austin had served as deputy commander of U.S. forces in Afghanistan, but this was his first tour in Iraq.

THE MOST DRAMATIC CHANGES in the final months of 2007 occurred in southern Baghdad. The southern Baghdad neighborhood of Dora was the last bastion of Al-Qaeda in the city. It was an ideal insurgent sanctuary because rail lines and roads led from the Sunni towns and former ammunition factories of Yusufiya, Mahmudiya, and Iskandiriya that lay to the south into Dora. East of Dora, in the curve of the Tigris River, lay a swath of date palm groves that were perfect sites in which to hide or launch attacks. From Dora it was a short drive across the river into the heart of the downtown and Shia-populated target areas. Southern Baghdad also included the troubled zones of Saidiya and Bayaa, where sectarian cleansing continued, and Jihad and Amel, which were controlled by Sadr's Jaish al-Mahdi (JAM) militia.

The U.S. officer in charge of this area was Col. Ricky Gibbs, who led the 4th Brigade, 1st Infantry Division. Gibbs knew Petraeus well: he had been his operations officer in the 101st during the first half of its 2003–2004 combat tour. The two men had an open, direct relationship. Petraeus needed someone who would not flinch from the difficult, bloody business of uprooting Al Qaeda from Dora, and Gibbs was such an individual. Repeated clearing operations had failed to uproot Al-Qaeda from Dora, so Gibbs concentrated his available forces there and conducted Operation Dragon Fire from May 1 to the end of June to pinpoint the Al-Qaeda cells. He then launched Dragon Hammer from July to September to detain them and cut the ratline leading into Dora from Arab Jabour while Lt. Col. George Glaze's men dried up the other main ratline through Ghartan with the volunteers they had recruited. That was followed by Dragon Talon 1 and 2 from September to November to rout insurgents from the palm groves.

Gibbs paid dearly during some of the heaviest fighting anywhere in Iraq. He lost 88 killed in action and 170 wounded, one of the highest tolls suffered by any brigade. One of Gibbs's young personal security detail members was medically discharged because he had seen too much violence to sleep or function in his job. "The worst thing was that the very people we were trying to help were the ones blowing us up," he said. One of the National Police units assigned to their area only made matters worse: the largely Shia force would hunker down in barricaded checkpoints and shoot down the street at Sunni residents. The Iraqi unit had no noncommissioned officers and only a half-dozen officers to ride herd on the rank-and-file policemen. A new and better National Police battalion replaced the unit and began to walk the streets with American troops.

By the end of 2007, Gibbs's troops had dismantled fifteen cells of Al-Qaeda-linked insurgents. Five remained, according to their intelligence. Law enforcement advisers had helped train the troops in evidence-collection procedures, and the brigade had detained 221 Iraqis with sufficient evidence to remand three-quarters of them to Camp Cropper.

At the same time they targeted Al-Qaeda cells, Gibbs and his battalion commanders had courted the sheikhs of the dominant Jabouri clan since they arrived in the spring. They had provided some funds to help the sheikhs maintain their date palm groves. Finally in September the attacks began to drop off. Murders of Iraqis fell from 563 in January 2007 to 35 in December, and attacks against U.S. soldiers completely ceased. It was an extraordinary change for soldiers accustomed to being shot at from rooftops and targeted by bombs every day.

Petraeus visited southern Baghdad at the turn of the year to hear in detail about the methods they had used. One of Gibbs's battalion commanders, Lt. Col. Jim Crider, who had also served under Petraeus in the 101st Division, described what they had done. "When we arrived in

June, we inherited zero sources," he said, so his men went door to door to find Iraqis who would be willing to help. They took photographs of every Iraqi they encountered on their street patrols and, one by one, began to identify the insurgents who were hiding in their midst—and sometimes openly greeting the soldiers. Crider rejected the usual practice of offering reconstruction aid to a neighborhood only after it had demonstrated a willingness to help find insurgents. Instead, he dispensed $230,000 in microgrants, which enabled some 120 shops to reopen, installed generators, strung new high- and low-tension wires, and hired sewage-pumping trucks. Tanks of propane were brought in and sold at market rates to undercut the black marketers. They replaced streetlights that had been shot out in years of fighting.

During the briefing, Petraeus peppered Crider with ideas. "Why not give microloans so you can recycle the funds and make them go farther?" "Why not buy streetlights from a company in Baghdad to stimulate the economy?"

One of Crider's most important allies was Dr. Moayad Hamad al-Jabouri, a cardiologist who lived in northeast Dora. His turning point came when he saw a soldier die in front of his house, after his Humvee was blown up by a bomb. He recalled first running to find his young daughter, to make sure she was safe. He then decided to give the names of the two Iraqis he had seen plant the bomb to the soldiers in the combat outpost a few blocks away. Dr. Moayad began to rally his neighbors to do the same and became the unofficial mayor for northeast Dora.

Another ally was Abu Haider, who became the leader of the neighborhood's volunteer movement. Sporting a leather car coat with the collar turned up against the brisk Baghdad winter chill, Abu Haider said he had lived in Dora since 1990. Asked whether he had any experience in the security business, he nodded and said he had been a member of Saddam Hussein's general security directorate. The soldiers put the volunteers to work guarding schools and other fixed installations, such as the new generators that had been installed with steel plates at each end to prevent the transformers from being shot out. To keep tabs on the volunteers, Gibbs's units compiled a registry of their identification cards and their weapons' serial numbers.

Most amazing of all, Ricky Gibbs had managed to crack the code of the National Reconciliation Committee. During a visit to Dora, Petraeus was amazed when Gibbs told him the committee had agreed to admit 5,000 of his volunteers for police training. "I think we'll get all our volunteers in," Gibbs told him. "The MOI [ministry of interior] has authorized 7,600 slots" for Rashid. Gibbs told Petraeus he had an additional 1,250 in training plus 45 already working as bona fide policemen. "How is that possible? The police academy is full of trainees," asked the astonished general, who had fought tooth and nail to get the 1,500 volunteers from Abu Ghraib and one subsequent group of 700 from Mansour into the academy. Gibbs explained that he had worked out a deal for the volunteers to be trained by the National Police in West Rashid.

The colonel shared his secrets for getting on the good side of Bassima al-Jaidri, Maliki's key aide in the Office of the Commander in Chief and the national reconciliation committee. The committee had become the gatekeeper for volunteers to enter the police academy. Gibbs's wife had sent boxes of Russell Stover candy, which he gave to Jaidri as a gift. Chatting with her, he found that like his wife, the committee chairwoman was a statistician by training. He also made a concession in their intense negotiations over volunteers in Saidiya, where JAM was on a rampage. Saidiya was about 70 percent Sunni and 30 percent Shia, but he agreed that the volunteers in that neighborhood would be half Sunni and half Shia. After five months, he had won her over. "You're my favorite colonel," Jaidri told him. The U.S. military needed good relations with her, because the committee's most pragmatic and evenhanded member, Dr. Safa Hussein, had left for Sweden. U.S. officers hoped he would return, but in the meantime they tried to get Jaidri to see the logic of bringing volunteers into the police force.

After Gibbs and Crider had briefed Petraeus, they went for a tour of Crider's neighborhood. It was safer, but still not entirely safe. The day before, a car bomb had blown up in the parking lot of a hospital and on the way into Dora that day, the caravan passed a minibus full of Iraqis that had just been hit by a bomb. Five of its passengers were wounded. Poor visibility had grounded the unmanned aerial vehicles that usually provided surveillance, but Petraeus chose to proceed with the tour. When he reached the neighborhood, his party was joined by a gaggle of Iraqi generals in Dora. A circuslike parade wound down the main street, starting at the concrete blast walls that had been painted with festive murals. Strolling about for over an hour, Petraeus greeted virtually every Iraqi and ducked into shops to buy bread, chocolates, and bananas, handing them off to aides and nibbling on the candy. He chatted with Iraqis, gave a stand-up television interview, and bestowed a soccer ball on a gleeful young boy. A woman watching her children play in a small playground said she was happy that U.S. and Iraqi soldiers were patrolling the streets but said the National Police were "still not welcome."

Petraeus wore no body armor and only his soft cap. Also, he did not carry a gun—unlike George Casey, who usually had his pistol strapped to his side. These choices affected Petraeus's interactions with Iraqi civilians in small but significant ways. He was showing the Iraqi generals his methods of conducting public relations. His bodyguard was always standing nearby, of course, and his security detail always wore protective gear, as regulations required.

Dr. Moayad Hamad was the host for the day's tour. He was eager to show the visitors how peaceful Dora had become. "A year ago this area was full of bodies," he said as they strolled down the main street. Dr. Nada Ibrahim, a Sunni legislator whom Petraeus had invited to join him that day, agreed. "Only a stray dog would walk down this street eighteen months ago," she said. "Dora is like a patient who had a virus of sectarian influence but is now recovering." A doctor, she lived in Adhamiya but had once had a medical clinic in Dora until it became too violent. She wore pants and did not cover her lustrous brown hair. A red-checked *kaffiyeh* scarf was thrown over her caramel-colored woolen coat.

"Now we need the city services to come," Dr. Moayad said. Petraeus agreed that it was now safe enough for the government to begin supplying services and repairing infrastructure. It was his main theme of the day. He had invited the legislator so she would help prod the Iraqi government to bring services to Dora, and to ask her to reopen her clinic.

During an earlier discussion of the topic at Gibb's base, Petraeus's impatience with the Iraqi bureaucracy had boiled over. Turning to Dr.

Nada, he exclaimed, "The government has not spent $8 to $10 billion of its budget this year. That is criminal. All the ministers responsible for this should be put in Cropper [the U.S. detention center]." The general was in his finest irascible form that day. He was kidding when he made that remark, but he hinted at another arm-twisting tactic a few minutes later. Gibbs said he had offered to bring ministry officials to Dora in his brand-new mine-resistant armored vehicles, to no avail. Petraeus snapped, "Tell them that if they want a blue badge to enter the Green Zone, they should get down here to Dora."

At the end of the tour, Dr. Moayad invited the U.S. and Iraqi officers to his house, where his mother's bakery had provided a lavish tableful of cakes, eclairs, baklava, and chocolate-covered strawberries for them. Petraeus presented Moayad with a small plaque and thanked him for helping Dora to rebound. Moayad said he would serve on the local advisory council, but he rejected the idea of running for higher office. "I need to stay here with my people," he said. "When politicians go to the Green Zone, they forget the people."

Petraeus had another motive in inviting Dr. Nada to join him on his visit to Dora. He was blunt in conveying it. "Please tell Saleh al-Mutlak that we are watching his vote on the de-Baathification bill. Your party will vote for it, no?" he urged her. "Tell him Sadi [Othman, Petraeus's cultural adviser] is counting votes for me." Mutlak's party, the National Dialogue Front, was a hard-line Sunni group that had opposed the constitution and was now criticizing the de-Baathification bill. The United States was mounting a campaign for the bill to be passed in early 2008, in order to relax the purge of former Baathists who had not committed crimes. The Sadrists had tabled a number of punitive amendments, which would lead Mutlak's front to vote against the law.

Before he left south Baghdad that day, Petraeus made a brief stop at Combat Outpost Banchee, a three-story building in the middle of a date palm grove. As the wind whipped the dirt into clouds, Petraeus handed out his gold commander coins, embossed with the MNF-I emblem of a winged lion, to soldiers who had been selected for their individual accomplishments, such as the leader of the tactical human intelligence team that had identified the most insurgents. "When I first walked through Dora's streets early this year," Petraeus told them in a short speech, "I wondered why I had come back to command this enterprise." Now, he continued, "you've given hope back to a substantial part of this city. You all get it. You really do understand." For him, Dora symbolized the depths to which Iraq had sunk, so he was especially heartened by its rebound.

Petraeus did not have time that day to visit West Rashid, but he had enthusiastically followed the experiments being conducted there by another protégé, Lt. Col. Pat Frank. Frank, also a veteran of Petraeus's Mosul tour, had achieved the only local cease-fires with the JAM Shia militia forces. He had prepared his 1st Battalion, 28th Infantry Regiment by using his "lessons learned" PowerPoint briefings from Mosul as a training aid. "We had a hard fight from March to July. This place was like Sadr City II," Frank recalled. "We wore JAM down and dismantled its leadership bit by bit." Then one day the militia asked for a cease-fire through intermediaries. Frank began receiving text messages on his cell phone from JAM fighters who wanted to come in from the cold without their cohorts knowing. This first agreement, in the Jihad neighborhood, received a crucial boost from Muqtada al-Sadr's August cease-fire. On September 3, an agreement was signed in Jihad that allowed Frank's unit to conduct operations against those who violated it.

Frank's innovation was to negotiate actual written agreements, which the parties themselves wrote. Two Shia and one Sunni wrote the first one, the Jihad Initiative, which was signed in October by representatives from Jihad and nearby neighborhoods. The Jihad document committed the signatories to ten points, the first of which was "cessation of firing on main streets, markets, and parks." They also agreed to refrain from stealing belongings of people who had been displaced and to repay or resupply those who had lost household goods. Returnees would be resettled with the help of a committee. The signatories also agreed to report all crimes, enemy activity including the emplacement of bombs and breaches of the agreement, and to form a committee of engineers to oversee rebuilding of common buildings such as prayer halls. A committee of three Shia and three Sunnis, elected by the neighborhood, would monitor compliance with the agreement.

Frank then took this template to Amel, where a second accord was negotiated over two months and signed in December, and then to Bayaa, which also had been ravaged by ethnic cleansing. Volunteers were hired, and due to the population mix, the volunteers in Frank's area were recruited from the ranks of the Shia JAM militia as well as Sunnis. His captains rode herd on them and fired any guards who got out of line.

For now at least, this local approach to the Shia violence was probably the most effective. It was difficult to divine who was truly in charge of the Sadrist movement, and it was possible that no one really was. It was also hard to know what Muqtada al-Sadr intended to do. In October 2007, Sadr had signed a truce with the rival Shia Islamic Supreme Council of Iraq party, leading some to hope that he might opt for peaceful political competition for power rather than the fight-and-talk tactics he had used so far.

Sadr's August cease-fire was supposed to last for six months, but at year's end there were rumblings that it might be lifted. Petraeus used his channels to try to find out his intentions. "We do send messages back and forth that are interesting," he said. "I've sent a message twice now saying that we understand you are considering lifting the cease-fire. We just want to confirm that that is not the case. If it is, just let us know, because it will be 'game on' time." Petraeus said the answer came back quickly: "No, the cease-fire is still in effect."

Since the cease-fire Sadr had publicly disavowed by name a large number of individuals associated with the JAM special groups whom the Americans alleged were responsible for atrocities and crimes, but the reality was that the Sadr movement was too amorphous to separate into neat categories. Petraeus said, "I don't know that anybody can speak for the Sadrists right now. They're fragmented." Nonetheless, he said, Maliki "clearly would like to bring the mainstream Sadr political party and its mainstream militia members—although not as a militia— back into the fold, to be part of a constructive partnership in the political arena. They did help elect him, after all."

ONE OF PETRAEUS'S TOP PRIORITIES all over Baghdad, not just in Dora, was to restart municipal services in the Sunni areas that had been deprived of them. Another problem was managing the flow of displaced Iraqis who were beginning to come home as the violence diminished. It was time, Petraeus felt, for the Iraqi government to assume both of these functions. But in many cases, the battalion commanders stepped into the breach. They gathered the locally influential sheikhs they had been relying on to help sort out legitimate housing claims, rental agreements, and alternative lodging for squatters.

In west Baghdad, Col. Bill Hickman—another Petraeus man from the 101st—carried on the work that Col. J. B. Burton had begun. Hickman's orders were to move into tactical overwatch by the end of 2008, which meant handing off all security and service functions to Iraqi entities. If he could not nudge the government into taking on these basic functions, the entire plan would be jeopardized. He also opened the first joint security station in Shula to reduce the Shia extremists' grip on that Shia neighborhood.

In central Baghdad's Karkh neighborhood, much of the economic rebound was occurring spontaneously. As soon as concrete blast walls and electricity generators were put into place, the Alawi market had sprung back to life. The area's unofficial mayor, or *mukhtar,* Khalid Ismael, helped restart the food distribution system and propane delivery so vendors could set up their vegetable stands and fast-food stalls could resume cooking sidewalk meals. Since the detention of a local Sadrist militia leader, Hussein Hany, in late 2007, Ismael said he felt free to drink alcohol again. Iraqis resumed their pastimes: every table in a partly bombed-out tea house was occupied by Iraqi men drinking chai, smoking, and playing dominoes or billiards.

Tough neighborhoods remained. One of them, Ghazaliya, had an energetic new battalion commander, Lt. Col. Kevin Petit, yet another Petraeus protégé. His task was to find ways of mending a neighborhood that had morphed into a Sunni southern half and Shia northern half during the sectarian violence of 2006. Acknowledging the deep gulf between the two sects, Petit thought the two sides might be ready to tolerate each other and cooperate for their own gain. Petit floated some pragmatic proposals to Petraeus during a run at Camp Victory at the end of December. He turned thumbs down on some of them, but Petit knew his old boss was always open to unorthodox approaches to sticky problems.

Petit knew there was another agenda lurking that day. Twelve years earlier, as a company commander in "Doc" Petraeus's brigade, Petit had beaten the colonel by fifty meters in one of their fitness runs that Petraeus always turned into all-out races. Petit had never been to Camp Victory and did not know how far they would run or what the route would be. Petit was not too worried; he had competed in five Ironman triathlons and in 2007 finished in the top ten of the armywide Combatives tournament. After six and a half miles, they hit the homestretch. Petraeus beat Petit by six strides. The younger officer took his defeat in good humor and reissued the challenge for another race.

Ameriya was also at a very delicate juncture, so Petraeus also invited officers from the new unit in charge there out for a talk-and-run. Even though Ameriya's volunteers had been the first in Baghdad, only ninety of some four hundred had been accepted into the police so far. Part of the problem stemmed from the celebrity status of the volunteer leader, Abu Abid. The publicity had given him a rather swelled head; he was a smart man, but he was not inclined to kowtow to the local Iraqi army commander. While Abu Abid sat smoking cigars at night with Lt. Col. Kuehl, the outgoing battalion commander, the Iraqi army commander brooded. Abu Abid's very effectiveness gave the Iraqi government pause.

Kuehl and his soldiers spent their last few days justly celebrating their progress. They attended a farewell dinner with many of the sheikhs, went shopping on Market Street, ate in newly opened sidewalk cafés, and attended the wedding of Abu Omar, the volunteers' intelligence officer. They played soccer with children in the old Body Dump Field, where a playground now stood. They also held a memorial service at the intersection where the six soldiers and their interpreter had died on May 19, to recognize all sixteen service members who had given their lives to pacify Ameriya. Kuehl made a short, heartfelt speech, as Iraqis gathered around.

But within days after Kuehl's battalion left, Ameriya's hard-won peace looked like it might collapse. Abu Abid left to resettle his wife, Khulida, and their two children in Amman, Jordan, with the resident visas Kuehl had been able to secure for them. While Abu Abid was away, Osama bin Laden issued threats against Iraq's volunteers. One of Abu Abid's deputies and his son were bombed and nearly killed. The day after Abu Abid returned, a rocket hit in front of his house. A car bomb was found, and two neighborhood men implicated in graft were shot and killed. The spate of violence alarmed everyone. At the same time, Ameriya residents were frustrated by the slow pace of change. "All the Iraqi people say is '*inshallah, inshallah*'—I hope, I hope, I hope," one irate Ameriyan man said, translating his own sentence into English.

Petraeus gave the new unit the same advice he'd given the last one: "Don't let the Iraqi government bureaucracy stop you—just keep pushing." Abu Abid was restless, but he promised to stay in Ameriya for some months. A new Iraqi army battalion arrived. Another 111 volunteers from Ameriya were accepted for police training, but the Ameriya volunteers remained uncertain about their future. One of Abu Abid's deputies, Hashim Ahmed Ayoub, a former lieutenant colonel who had served twenty-three years in Saddam's army, was sorely disappointed that his name had not appeared on either of the first two lists. A fifty-year-old heavyset volunteer named Mohammed complained that Shias he knew were being hired much more quickly into government jobs. "The problem will come when you guys leave," he fretted. He feared that the government might hunt down the volunteers.

The volunteers' concerns were shared by Ameriya's most influential sheikh, Sheikh Khaled Muhamed Ahmad Mizwid al-Ubaydi, the imam of the Abbas mosque. He wanted the largely Shia army unit in Ameriya to be more balanced in its composition, and he wanted the volunteers to be given leadership positions in the local police force. Given his enormous clout in the neighborhood, Sheikh Khaled would have to be part of any political solution in Ameriya. His demands were not unreasonable, but his utter mistrust and loathing of the government would not be easily assuaged.

In a most intriguing development, Iraq's national security adviser, Mowaffak al-Rubaie, offered Abu Abid a job. Abu Abid weighed the offer. He clearly relished the idea of playing a bigger role in Iraq's future. Yet could he trust the government? For his part, Rubaie knew that Abu

Abid had a great knowledge of the insurgency and would be an enormous asset to their intelligence effort. After all the doubts the government had expressed about the volunteers of Ameriya, it was astonishing that a top official of the government would offer him a senior position. Perhaps, at the end of the day, these mortal enemies might reach accommodations in ways only Iraqis could fathom. Or was it a trap?

THE NUMBER OF VOLUNTEERS had climbed steadily until there were 73,000 Sons of Iraq on U.S. military contracts by the end of the year. Even Petraeus was surprised by the overwhelming response. "This was discovery learning. There wasn't a blueprint for this," he said. "Sunni Arabs took advantage of the opportunity. They came to feel re-liberated over the past year."

But Petraeus and officers below him were still forced to go, hat in hand, to Maliki to seek the admittance of each new tranche of volunteers to the police academy. Those closest to Maliki continued to feed his fears, bringing him reports of volunteers who had attacked Shia or forced them out of their homes. Petraeus was frustrated, though he understood that trust was in short supply. "This is a society that has seen so many conspiracies over the years, and so much plotting, that there is a predisposition to accept outrageous stories as having a kernel of truth," he said. "We spend a fair amount of time confirming or denying that something really bad is going on, and frankly, it is typically *not* going on, although occasionally there is some foundation for some report."

Finally, after a meeting of the ministerial committee of national security was consumed by what Petraeus called "unfounded" rumors, he decided that they had to try to break the logjam in a more definitive way. It was late November. Of the 12,671 volunteers the Baghdad division had hoped to have accepted to the police academy, only 3,000 had been trained—just 1,500 more than the original 1,500 Abu Ghraib volunteers.

He proposed that the top U.S. and Iraqi officials hold a meeting on November 30 to reach a decision. One American and two Iraqis would make presentations. He hoped to find creative ways to resolve the complaints once and for all. He and other generals were spending hours pleading for each class of volunteers to be approved for police training. Odierno was chosen to lay out the arguments for bringing the volunteers into the tent—and the dangers of letting the initiative unravel. Odierno made the case to Maliki. There was a shortfall of Iraqi security forces in Sunni areas. Locally recruited cops were always more acceptable to local residents and were more effective—that had been proven in the United States' own experience. The volunteers as such were intended to be only a temporary force, he said.

To address the prime minister's concerns, the U.S. officials agreed to a list of requirements and conditions. The volunteers would be closely supervised. The United States would not hire more than 103,000. The volunteers would wear tan uniforms and would not use ranks or paramilitary names. The Iraqi government's concern was that the volunteers would constitute themselves into a "third force" that would challenge the Iraqi police and army when the Americans went home. Other conditions were specified: all operations would be conducted jointly with Iraqi forces, no heavy weapons would be allowed, and volunteers hired in mixed neighborhoods would be a balance of Shias and Sunnis. The latter condition was already being met: about one-quarter of the volunteers were Shia. In most heavily Shia neighborhoods there were already ample policemen, so no volunteers were needed or recruited there.

In return, in the key provision of the agreement, Maliki agreed to incorporate 20 percent to 25 percent of the volunteers into the police over the next two years. (Some officials later suggested that some 30 percent of volunteers might become policemen.) The rest of the Sons of Iraq would be offered vocational training or temporary jobs to repair housing and infrastructure. As a good-faith gesture, the ministry of interior cut hiring orders for five thousand volunteers in the week after the meeting. "It was a hugely significant moment," Petraeus said of the breakthrough, which he reported to Bush in their next videoconference.

The agreement would take constant bird-dogging in the months ahead. Indeed, when the ministry of interior sent back the hiring orders for the first 2,000 trainees, the Americans discovered that a number of different names had replaced those of the vetted volunteers. U.S. officers pointed out the discrepancy to the ministry, and the original recruits were returned to the list. There was also a year's backlog of pending requests for badges and equipment, and a shortage of training space. Bureaucratic red tape was both a legitimate problem and an ideal excuse for those who wished to stall: Iraq was the land of the slow roll.

The U.S. commanders asked the Iraqi government to assume financial responsibility for the volunteers. The interior ministry agreed to pay twelve thousand of the volunteers on the CERP (Commander's Emergency Response Program) contracts, who presumably would become police trainees. The Iraqis also agreed to match $155 million in U.S. aid for vocational training of other volunteers in skilled trades. Some of the volunteers were not interested in police work; some did not trust the government enough to want to work for it, and others preferred to go into the army.

The months ahead would reveal whether the agreement would be honored and whether it would prove sufficient. Two outcomes were ultimately required for success of the initiative. Sunni neighborhoods wanted policemen they knew and trusted to secure them. And former insurgents had to be dissuaded in one way or another from resuming armed opposition to the government. Otherwise Iraq's "bottom-up" peace would certainly unravel.

THE GAINS OF 2007 HAD BEEN purchased at a very high price. During the year, 901 members of the U.S. military had died in Iraq—more than any other year since the war began. Thousands of Iraqis had also died. The rate of Iraqi deaths had peaked in the spring and early summer, when the spate of car bombings caused hundreds of deaths in each blast, and then fell off steadily.

The deaths weighed heavily on Petraeus. Reflecting on them, he spoke first of the losses in Adhamiya, and other places where four, five, and six soldiers had been lost in one blow. "There are some people who think that over time a commander gets hardened to losses. I have not found that to be the case," Petraeus said. He attended dozens of memorial services. He flew to their outposts or bases, often sitting alone in the back of his helicopter, with his bodyguard and his aide Maj. Spain in the seats up front. His sergeant major or Bill Rapp accompanied him whenever their duties allowed. Petraeus rarely spoke on these trips, but Rapp wanted to go to keep him company, though he knew he could not share this loneliest of burdens.

Petraeus's mood at year's end was far more brooding than self-congratulatory. He was acutely aware that the positive trends still could be reversed and the fundamental political issues were not resolved. Nonetheless, by now the turnabout in the situation on the ground was indisputable. Attacks were down by more than 60 percent over the past six months, and civilian deaths were 75 percent lower than they had been a year before. In the last week of December, 511 attacks were recorded across Iraq. These levels of violence corresponded with those last seen in the spring of 2005, as the interim government took office and began to chart a sectarian course.

Petraeus was cautious and Americans generally remained skeptical, but at the other end of the spectrum, the attitude in the Iraqi government verged on triumphalism. Offering his own analysis of the year in a lengthy interview, Dr. Rubaie, the national security adviser, recalled how 2007 had begun. "We were in deep shit. There were 150 bodies on the street every day, and six or seven bombs. We were in a civil war," he said. "We got out of it very successfully. This year will be marked as the year that we got out of an impending civil war." He credited primarily the tribal awakening and the volunteers, and then, surprisingly, claimed credit for the initiative. "This has been a government of Iraq [GOI] project since 2005. We said, there is only one way of getting out of the war, and that is for local people to turn around and fight these people, to clean the terrorists out. That's exactly what happened," said the former neurosurgeon. "Some U.S. military leaders I won't name opposed the people's committees, the neighborhood watch groups. It was a GOI initiative. We can claim credit for it." He said it was part of the detailed national reconciliation plan he had composed for Maliki.

Rubaie acknowledged that Petraeus had helped, but the Iraqi also made clear that they had tangled on many occasions. Pausing to choose his words carefully, Rubaie fixed his eyes on his interlocutor as he decided how to elaborate on the general's role. "He is attached emotionally. He cares about the cause. He is taking it as a mission, not as a job." Rubaie had accompanied him to a memorial service for four soldiers in

Diyala. "He was really emotional," he said. "He sees the humongous sacrifices: the blood, sweat, and tears, so he gets upset and irritated by anyone who remotely criticizes the coalition forces. His tolerance for someone who criticizes the coalition is probably zero."

NO SINGLE SILVER BULLET ACCOUNTED FOR the marked decline in violence in the last half of 2007, which reversed the upward trend for the first time since the war began. It was the result of many important innovations in both strategy and tactics that would likely be incorporated into future doctrine—if the army continued to embrace counterinsurgency and stability operations. The measures included the increase in troops, their dispersion, various population control measures, more precise counterterrorism measures enabled by better intelligence, and, most of all, the outreach to the armed antagonists and their constituents.

The addition of thirty thousand U.S. combat troops and enablers to the battlefield was important, as was the addition of one hundred thousand new Iraqi soldiers and policemen. But the way in which the troops were employed was even more important than the numbers. Had the troops been conducting large sweeps and returning to their bases at night they would not have had the same impact. The dispersion of troops into sixty-eight outposts to live with the population they were securing made them a catalyst for much of the grassroots reconciliation and cease-fires that occurred.

Most important, each battalion and company made it a priority to develop relationships and reach out to the "reconcilable" antagonists, their supporters, and the fence-sitters. These were inherently political activities that produced political effects that Petraeus massed rapidly to pressure the Iraqi government to in turn take political action that would affect the war's strategic level. The emphasis on the political line of operations at all echelons stood in stark contrast to past practices, which mostly consisted of sitting at the local advisory council meeting for a long, hot afternoon of debate. Petraeus waded into politics as no general before him had done and directed his troops to do the same.

The measure most directly responsible for reducing violence was the recruitment of the 73,000 volunteers. It literally turned enemies into allies, increasing the numbers of those providing security and intelligence and decreasing the ranks of those fighting against the Americans and the Iraqi government and supporting the insurgency overtly or tacitly. The volunteers' recruitment correlated closely with the decline in violence. The insurgents, many of whom were alienated by the extremists' excesses, made the decision to stop fighting. But the U.S. troops' measures played an important part by setting the conditions for the volunteers to come forward. They would not have done so, at least in such numbers, had the U.S. soldiers not been out meeting with sheikhs, imams, and other intermediaries. They offered paid work but also protection and recognition. The American soldiers placed themselves between the warring parties and absorbed the brunt of the violence until the fighters decided to take a chance and turn their arms in the other direction.

Other tactics, techniques, and procedures that proved effective were those that enabled the soldiers to identify, control, and secure the population. The biometric registry of military-age males and household surveys on a wide scale, using automated systems, allowed for the creation of reliable, shared databases. For the first time in the war, the U.S. military began to develop a comprehensive picture of the human environment that was the battlefield: positive identification of the enemy, the ethnographic composition of the population, and the status of services in a given area. The much-criticized concrete walls around markets, neighborhoods, and key routes, additional checkpoints and X-ray machines, curfews, temporary vehicle bans, and dramatically increased use of unmanned aerial vehicles and sensors all helped separate the fighters from the civilians, catch the former, and protect the later. Technology helped, but just as effective were the soldiers who simply took a notebook computer full of photographs around the neighborhood to learn who was whom. The most precious commodity was the intelligence that came from the population and the volunteers as they began to trust the Americans who lived among them instead of kicking down their doors and leaving.

As a result, combat actions became even more focused and successful in finding valid targets instead of "dry holes" that alienated entire families and even neighborhoods. The rapid fusing of human and technical intelligence enabled continuous operations to dismantle Al-Qaeda cells faster than they could regenerate. Most important, U.S. commanders had finally learned that precision targeting and clearing operations would have only a temporary effect unless U.S. or capable Iraqi forces stayed behind to prevent the remnants of the insurgent and militia groups from returning and rebuilding. Effective counterterrorism operations required more than special operations forces.

All these changes on the ground created a window of opportunity for Iraq that few would have believed possible at the beginning of 2007. Exploiting it would require all the skill Petraeus, Ryan Crocker, and their Iraqi and U.S. allies could muster. The government still had not managed to take any major steps on national reconciliation, and it was to this goal that all efforts were now bent. Without it, the gains bought at such a high price would not last.

14

To the Brink Again

The journey of a pair of two hundred–ton generators from Syria to the Qudas power plant north of Baghdad struck Petraeus as a perfect metaphor for the American experience in Iraq. Day after day, he monitored the creeping advance of the massive machines, which were strapped onto semitrailers. "They're so big that they had to sort of inch across the desert at the rate of five miles per hour," he said. Military engineers reinforced bridges along the way so they could bear the load. Finally the generators arrived, and once connected, they raised electrical production to a record level.

If installing the generators had been a Herculean task, the effort to achieve a political breakthrough was more like the labors of Sisyphus, who pushed the rock up the hill only to watch it roll down again. Prime Minister Nouri al-Maliki had done nothing to implement the August 26 accord by year's end. He had not held even one meeting of the five top Iraqi leaders. Both Secretary of Defense Gates and Secretary of State Rice visited Baghdad in December to tell Maliki he had to start cooperating with his fellow leaders and push the reconciliation legislation through parliament. One official who attended Gates's group meeting said, "He was like a stern father." The secretary was even more forceful in their one-on-one meeting behind closed doors. He urged Maliki to jettison his insular inner circle of sectarian-minded advisers, which one U.S. official enumerated in order of nefariousness as Sami al-Askari, Sadiq al-Rikabi, and Mowaffak al-Rubaie.

Rice was distracted from the mounting crisis over Maliki by other crises. Turkey had finally had its fill of Kurdish PKK (Kurdistan Workers' Party) separatists attacking Turkish targets from their camps in northern Iraq and had begun to hit back. The Iraqi government and Masoud Barzani's Kurdistan Regional Government had turned a blind eye to the PKK provocations. The United States took Turkey's side. Rice also helped to persuade the Kurds to accept postponement of the referendum on the status of Kirkuk, which the constitution had called for by the end of 2007. Since 2003, Kurds had been moving back into Kirkuk, with the ultimate objective of absorbing the city into Kurdistan.

The Iraqi government teetered on the brink of collapse once again when Maliki's fellow leaders issued him an ultimatum at the end of December. In two letters, one signed by Iraqi President Jalal Talabani and Barzani and the other by Tariq al-Hashimi, they criticized Maliki's handling of the political situation, his concentration of power in his own hands, and his inability to work with others. They also accused him of mismanaging oil production, refining, and export; of impeding efforts to stimulate investment; and of mishandling recurrent crises with neighboring countries. If he did not heed their complaints, they would withdraw their support and his government would fall. One of the Iraqi leaders involved said Maliki would have a few weeks to act before the parties called for a vote of no confidence in the parliament. It was not only the Kurdish and Sunni parties who were unhappy with him; the Islamic Supreme Council of Iraq (ISCI) and the Jaafari wing of Dawa were also fed up with his leadership style and his track record.

Maliki received the letters on December 26 and departed for London the following day. The official reason given was to seek medical treatment for exhaustion. Rubaie went with him. Because so many officials and journalists were out of the country for the holidays, news of the ultimatum did not leak out.

When Maliki returned to Iraq, Barham Salih and Hashimi went to see him at home. Salih hoped to convince him to move forward. He told Maliki there was still time to address their concerns, which Maliki said he would take seriously.

Salih had a brief respite from the crisis when his family came for a rare visit. His daughter, Cale, a student at Princeton, showed her tech-hungry father how to chat on his computer so they could stay in touch that way. Salih regretted their long separation. "I'm a terrible father," he said. But Cale did not feel that way. Salih was also ecstatic to see so many Iraqis out attending parties all over Baghdad in celebration of Eid al Adha and the new year. "Did you see the celebrations? It was great!" he exclaimed effusively over a bottle of wine. Could it be that the once-cosmopolitan city was coming back to life? The Sheraton and other hotels downtown hosted celebrations, as did private clubs like the Aliya club in Mansour. The shadow of conservative Islam had fallen over many Shia neighborhoods, but Baghdad's former freewheeling nature was asserting itself at some of the old haunts.

Ambassador Ryan Crocker had been out of the country on holiday leave. For months he had urged Maliki to widen his circle and change how he did business, but upon his return he adamantly told the Kurdish leaders and Hashimi that he opposed any attempt to bring down Maliki. "Don't be thinking in those terms at this time," he told them. "Maliki is simply going to dig in." He repeated the argument he'd made in August. It would not be hard to round up 138 no-confidence votes in the parliament, but months would be lost in the effort to form a new government. Even if they had agreed on Adil Abd al-Mahdi as the new prime minister, prolonged wrangling over how to divide the ministerial pie would certainly ensue. Iran, he feared, would use the delay to prevent a long-term security agreement between Iraq and the United States.

Crocker believed Maliki was a genuine nationalist, not beholden to Iran, and someone who wanted to be seen as a successful leader. "He is not trying to create a Dawa rump state so Sunnis can go off and die in the desert," Crocker said. An ISCI-led government would raise concerns about its ties to Iran and its goal of creating a southern Shia super-region. Crocker believed that the best course was for the United States to continue to work to bring Maliki around. But many senior U.S. officers had concluded that Maliki would not be a bridge builder, whether due to his own sectarianism or that of his aides. He was inscrutable even to those who had met with him regularly over the past year. As one general put it, "Maliki is very hard to read. He has deep-down beliefs that we don't understand."

Mahdi's proponents said he was more pragmatic and willing to horse-trade with Sunni and Kurdish parties. It was unclear how much of ISCI the more moderate Mahdi could bring along, but over the past year ISCI had altered some of its key positions, at least in its public statements. ISCI might be more efficient in governing and adept at striking deals with the Kurds. But that was not necessarily an advance if it meant consolidating the dominance of Islamist Shia political rule, pursuing exclusionary rule, or fragmenting the country.

ISCI policies were determined by Abdul Aziz al-Hakim, who was still the party's power broker despite a battle with lung cancer. Hakim visited Washington in November, where his aides pronounced him well and in need of no further treatment. In two public meetings, Hakim made statements intended to allay doubts about ISCI. The Iraqi constitution did not permit rule by clerics, he said, adding that Iraq's diverse nature made Islamic rule unfeasible. Asked about ISCI's ties to Iran, he said, "There is no financial support, but there are strong relations."

Hakim also indicated that ISCI would not immediately push to form a region out of the nine southern provinces, noting that such a move would have to be endorsed by a referendum in those provinces. Other Shia parties, most notably the Sadrists and Fadhila, opposed the idea. Hakim also voiced his support for the Sunni awakening and for a long-term strategic relationship with the United States, two significant statements he repeated in a major speech in Najaf upon his return. During a lengthy meeting in Washington, Meghan O'Sullivan had encouraged him to do so.

In the end, the Iraqis were walked back from the brink, and the bid to replace Maliki with Mahdi failed. ISCI's leading legislator, Humam

Hamoudi, said, "The conditions in Iraq do not allow for a change of government now. Hopefully he [Mahdi] will be prime minister in the future." Hamoudi also sought to dispel concerns about the party's ties to Iran and position on Islamic rule. With a gentle wave of his right hand, on which he wore a pinky ring with a red stone, Hamoudi described the Islamic Shia clerics' views: "First of all, the *marji'iyya* of Najaf clearly have Iraqi roots. He [Grand Ayatollah Ali al-Sistani] wants to have good relations with Iran . . . but also with Saudi Arabia, because Iraq is first of all an Arab state." ISCI had also tried hard to project a moderate, nationalist image by holding meetings with Sunni sheikhs and Sadrists.

THE SHOWDOWN WITH MALIKI helped to finally end the stalemate on national reconciliation legislation—together with the urgent requests of Rice and Gates and the tenacious labors of the Petraeus-Crocker team. The breakthrough vindicated Petraeus's belief that progress could be made by sheer will, a full-court press, and clever stratagems, but it had been excruciating.

Petraeus had concluded that it was necessary to bring the full resources and leverage of the U.S. military to bear on the task of getting the Council of Representatives to pass reconciliation legislation. He directed the Multi-National Force-Iraq (MNF-I) staff to track the legislative process and the parliamentarians' positions on each significant bill. Like an old-fashioned pol whipping votes, Petraeus had Sadi Othman befriend the parliamentarians and find out how they intended to vote. "We know the legislative process now," Petraeus said. "This is what it takes. This is what we need to do, and the scrutiny that this makes them feel is enormously important to the overall effort."

On January 12, 2008, Iraq's parliament finally passed the Justice and Accountability Act, four and a half years after the Coalition Provisional Authority (CPA) Decree 1 outlawed the Baath Party. Reversing the sweeping purge of the government and army was a key step to knit the country back together. Petraeus recalled how "some of the policies followed by CPA in the first year did take hope away from substantial segments of the population. They were cast out of their jobs, cast out of society, in their minds, disrespected and dispossessed. I remember the impact of the disestablishing of the military and waiting five weeks for the announcement of what would follow. What happened was that hope drained away from certain elements of the population."

The new law's impact would depend on how it was implemented. The guiding principle of the law was that those who committed crimes should be referred to the justice system, and those who had not should be allowed to get on with their lives, but some troubling provisions had been added to the bill. The new law allowed third-tier Baathists to receive pensions, and fourth-tier, or *firqa,* Baath members were now eligible for some government jobs. The latter were banned from senior posts in the security ministries, however, which raised questions about whether more former Baathists would be purged than re-admitted. If so, the new law would not have its hoped-for effect.

On February 13, the Iraqi parliament took another major step forward and passed a provincial-powers law, an amnesty bill, and the 2008 budget in a package deal. After weeks of wrangling, the three measures were bundled so that each main group would get something it dearly wanted. The provincial-powers law called for an elections law to be passed in ninety days and provincial elections to take place by October 1, 2008. It also included a carefully crafted compromise allowing the central government to fire provincial governors under certain circumstances. The deal was almost derailed a few weeks later when Vice President Mahdi vetoed the provincial-powers law, but he was persuaded to retract his veto.

The federalism debate cut to the heart of the power-sharing issue and would likely take years to resolve. Sunnis generally favored a strong central government. Shia and Kurds generally favored strong regional governments, though Shia groups disagreed over the degree of decentralization. National Security Adviser Rubaie proposed forming five regions, only one of which would be predominantly Sunni, composed of Anbar, Salahuddin, and Mosul. Citing Switzerland or Germany as a model, he said, "I'm an ardent federalist."

The problem with such highly federal models was that they tended to harden sectarian divisions, ghettoize the Sunni minority, and discourage nationalist multisectarian and nonsectarian parties and coalitions. Shia voters were a mosaic, not a monolith, and many Iraqis, including Shiites, were disappointed with the performance of the present government and uncomfortable with the Islamization of Iraqi politics and society. Some observers argued that Iraq's intra-Arab puzzle would never be resolved unless the Kurds were taken out of the equation by allowing them to go off on their own, but Turkey's fierce opposition to an independent Kurdistan was an effective veto over that option. Ironically, the now-fractured Shia coalition posed the best prospect for the formation of new alliances that could govern Iraq.

BRINKSMANSHIP WAS ALSO ON DISPLAY as the United States and Iraq set about forging a new relationship based on a bilateral accord that would replace the U.N. mandate. The one certainty about the new relationship was that Iraq would be more assertive. The signs were already there. Even though the Iraqis had assured Crocker and O'Sullivan that the renewal of the U.N. resolution would be handled in a speedy and pro forma matter so they could move on to negotiating the bilateral agreement, that did not happen. Instead, negotiations over the U.N. resolution's renewal turned into yet another exercise in Iraqi brinksmanship replete with all-night bargaining sessions. Maliki's inner circle dominated the process and cut out Foreign Minister Hoshyar Zebari. U.S. officials complained to Maliki about how difficult his aides were to work with, and requested that Rubaie not be part of the team negotiating the bilateral accord. The two countries set out the accord's basic objectives in a November 27 "Declaration of Principles for Friendship and Cooperation," which affirmed the desire of both countries for an "enduring relationship." The United States committed to help secure Iraqi borders and to help train, equip, and arm Iraq's security forces. It also committed to support Iraq's efforts to "combat all terrorist groups regardless of affiliation." U.S. officials had to fight to include language that covered all groups, not just the Sunni ones.

Prime Minister Maliki formally requested that the U.N. Security Council extend the mandate of the MNF-I for one final year on December 7. His letter also requested a review of the need for the MNF-I presence by June 2008 and said Iraq might seek termination of the agreement at any time. This suggested that the Iraqis were prepared to threaten revocation of the U.N. mandate to pressure the United States into accepting its terms for the bilateral accord, which they hoped to reach by July. The Iraqis made clear that they had asked for renewal of the U.N. resolution for the last time. On December 18, the Security Council approved the mandate's extension in Resolution 1790.

The Iraqis played hardball because they always did. They were banking on President Bush's steadfast unwillingness to walk away from Iraq, and perhaps on the unwillingness of any U.S. president to abandon Iraq to Iran and the possible resurgence of Al-Qaeda forces. The Iraqis needed and wanted the United States to continue to provide a security blanket, but they knew the administration was just as eager to stay. Bush's frequent conferences with Maliki worked to the detriment of the U.S. bargaining position. He appeared to be at least as eager as the supposed petitioner to reach the necessary agreements.

What the Iraqi government wanted most was to maximize its control, including over American forces. Crocker took his usual historical long view, noting that Iraq's government needed to gain legitimacy in the eyes of its people and the world. That was the downfall of the British experience in Iraq. "The monarchy never overcame the perception that it was a creature of the British, and that led to the 1958 revolution," he said. "We can't go on operating as an independent military here." But the U.S. military would not allow its troops to be tried in Iraqi courts, and it was wary of becoming a tool in a sectarian agenda.

The United States and Iraq did share common interests in deterring foreign aggression, keeping Al-Qaeda at bay, drawing down U.S. forces, and handing over security to Iraqi forces. The question was under what conditions and timetable, not whether to do it.

It would require some years more for Iraq's security forces to become self-sufficient and capable of deterring potential aggressors. The chief factor constraining the development of any forces, according to Col. Pete Mansoor, whose doctoral dissertation examined the subject, was the size of the officer corps and in this particular case the number of qualified brigade and other midgrade officers.

The Iraqi security forces were growing as quickly as they could. Some 800 army officers were graduating every six months. It was part of an ambitious plan to increase the total armed forces to 580,000 by the end of 2008 and eventually to 640,000. In 2007, the army increased by 55 percent to 200,000 troops. The vice chief of Iraq's armed forces, Gen. Nasir Abadi, said, "We should be in the *Guinness Book of World Records* after the growth we've accomplished this year." But he acknowledged their principal shortfalls: in administrative support; logistics including resupply, medical care, and maintenance; and combat enablers including aircraft, fire support, and intelligence. With the provision of six thousand U.S. uparmored Humvees and other purchases by Iraq, basic soldier equipment had improved, but Iraq still needed attack helicopters and an airplane that could be used both as a trainer and for close air support. Iraq had oil revenues to finance the needed procurement. Abadi, a somber man who had served until 1989 in Saddam's army and spoke English fluently, did not envision rebuilding that war machine. "Iraq's resources should go to rebuilding its infrastructure, developing its oil, and building schools," he said, pointing out that resolving the internal conflict would reduce the demands on the military.

The Iraqi general also noted that Petraeus was progressively turning over more authority to them. "He is getting us ready," Abadi said. A joint operations center had been built at the ministry of defense, and at Petraeus's request Abadi often attended the classified morning briefings. Joint defense and interior command structures had also been formed to coordinate and oversee army and police operations, using the Baghdad Operations Command as a model.

Developing the Iraqi forces was a relatively straightforward issue. The most difficult part was ensuring Iraqi security forces were not used for sectarian or political purposes. A U.S.-style selection board, headed by Abadi, was created to promote officers based on professional criteria. All the senior security officials sat on it. But such processes were still sometimes circumvented.

A bigger problem was that some structures were being used to bypass the military chain of command. The Office of the Commander in Chief and the Counter-Terrorism Bureau had become operational arms rather than advisers. The Counter-Terrorism Bureau, Maliki's link to the Iraqi special operations forces, was originally intended to provide the prime minister the information he needed to sign off on the most sensitive targeting decisions. Maliki now used it to direct operations. Although the September study headed by retired Gen. Jim Jones had zeroed in on this problem and called for abolishing the Office of the Commander in Chief and returning command and control of Iraqi special operations forces to the military chain of command, Petraeus said the decision was not his to make. This was a critical issue, however, since the Iraqi special operations forces were the best-equipped, best-trained, and single most competent unit in the Iraqi arsenal. If Maliki misused them, they could do great damage.

The most widespread problem of politicization remained the Iraqi police and the interior ministry. Col. H. R. McMaster had returned to Iraq at Petraeus's request to study the problems in the ministry of interior and recommend remedies. Over the previous two years, all of the National Police brigade commanders and seventeen of twenty-seven battalion commanders had been replaced. Some eighteen thousand rank-and-file officials had also been purged, but a number of problematic officials remained. One, Gen. Mahdi Gharrawi, was removed from brigade command after his east Baghdad base was found to hold 1,400 mostly Sunni prisoners, many of whom had been tortured. But witnesses withdrew their testimony, and attempts to prosecute him failed. He remained in a ministry job. Others who should have been prosecuted were simply dismissed or transferred to less visible jobs. The opposite problem also persisted: local police commanders who developed close working relationships with the Americans were transferred, as occurred with two east Baghdad police chiefs, who were moved at the end of 2007. The number of U.S. embedded advisers in the Iraqi army and the police remained inadequate, as did training for local police.

Purging the police and interior ministry was not enough. Human rights abuses threatened to make the new regime look frighteningly like the one the United States had removed. Perpetrators had to be held accountable and victims aided. One American official who understood this better than perhaps any other was Ali Khedery, Ambassador

Crocker's aide. He was the only American official who had been in Baghdad, in the inner circle, for the entire five years of the war. The gifted young man had worked in every iteration of the American mission, for Jay Garner, Paul Bremer, and ambassadors John Negroponte, Zalmay Khalilzad, and Crocker. Khedery, who spoke fluent Arabic, traveled with Maliki and knew all the other Iraqi politicians. He had worked with Samir Sumaidaie when he was interior minister, before Bayan Jabr took over and allowed the Badr militia to set up secret prisons in the Jadriya compound. Hundreds of brutally tortured prisoners had been found there in late 2005.

Khedery knew that many human rights travesties had occurred under the new regime. He knew where the metaphorical bodies were buried and many of the actual ones. Many Iraqis called him to find where their family members had been detained. Throughout the years, Khedery had used his contacts and knowledge of the players to ferret out the information and get many Iraqis released. But some trails had gone cold. One Iraqi mother called him regularly. Her son had been taken in 2005 by the Wolf Brigade, the notorious National Police brigade originally known as the Special Commandos. She believed he had been taken to the Jadriya prison. Khedery moved heaven and earth to try to find him. In the summer of 2007, she called him at his desk outside Crocker's office. Her pitiful voice rent him. He was deeply pained that he had not been able to find her son. He hated to admit it, but he knew that the young man was very likely dead. Thin and tired, Khedery finally decided it was time to go back to the United States. He left Iraq in the summer of 2008.

AS THE DEADLINE FOR PETRAEUS'S spring recommendations approached, the fierce jockeying over troop levels resumed. Pressure on him mounted to propose further troop withdrawals. Petraeus aimed to achieve a major victory over Al-Qaeda in Iraq in the coming months, and without it he was reluctant to send more troops home. Operation Phantom Phoenix was launched in January, the first in new offensive to reduce the last redoubts of the Al-Qaeda-linked insurgents in and around Mosul and the surrounding river valleys. Petraeus's intelligence adviser, Derek

Harvey, believed that success was within reach and that it would immeasurably solidify Iraq's tentative peace. "AQ is facing strategic defeat in Iraq, but only if we close the deal," he wrote in an e-mail. "This would have a real impact on Afghanistan and Pakistan." Petraeus was under no illusion that Al-Qaeda insurgents would disappear from Iraq; they would likely continue to operate in small cells for years to come. But if the offensive in the north succeeded, he believed that Iraqi troops aided by special operations forces could prevent a significant regeneration in the future. Petraeus's conversations with Sunnis in the Euphrates River Valley convinced him the Sunni population had definitively rejected jihadism because its extreme methods and practices were fundamentally at odds with their own beliefs. The combination of relentless, precisely focused military pressure and the embrace of Sunnis who turned away from Al-Qaeda had brought him within sight of a momentous achievement.

The Joint Chiefs of Staff asked Petraeus to provide his assessments based on three scenarios of conditions in Iraq—worsening, improving, and staying the same—rather than a recommendation. As they had in the fall, they wanted to use his three assessments to make the recommendation themselves. Petraeus gave them assessments but also insisted on making his own independent recommendation to them and the president. He wanted his view from the ground to be clearly known to all in Washington. The joint staff knew the president was inclined to listen to Petraeus's recommendation.

Army chief Gen. George Casey had become even more vocal about the need to reduce troop levels to reduce the stress on the army, and Adm. Fox Fallon was campaigning openly to have forces for other missions and contingencies in the Middle East. "He wants the forces reduced as much as possible as fast as possible," said a senior Pentagon official. The U.S. commander of NATO forces in Afghanistan had called for two more combat brigades and one more brigade of trainers. Pakistan was in turmoil following Benazir Bhutto's assassination, and the Taliban was resurgent. The Pentagon announced that an additional 3,200 U.S. Marines would be sent to Afghanistan for a one-time, seven-month deployment. NATO allies had been asked to supply the rest of the needed forces but were not likely to do so. Adding to the pressure,

Secretary Gates publicly tipped his own hand a few times by saying he would like to see troop levels reduced to 100,000, or 10 combat brigades, by the end of 2008. Petraeus called Lt. Gen. Pete Chiarelli, Gates's senior military assistant. "Compadre, what are you guys doing to me?" he asked. They all knew how the game was played. The first time, Chiarelli told him Gates had been misquoted. "It would be helpful if he clarified that," Petraeus importuned. Gates then mentioned the ten-brigade figure again, albeit with the qualification that it would depend on conditions on the ground.

In private, Petraeus was adamant. "We are not going down to ten brigades." He fully realized the competing demands for troops, the strain on the force, and the delicate balancing act Gates was trying to perform. "The secretary is trying to find the sweet spot that can keep Congress on board, keep Petraeus in uniform, keep the White House from coming unglued, and keep progress in Iraq," the general said with a laugh as he warmed his hands with a mug of coffee on a chill January day in his ground-floor office at Camp Victory.

President Bush made clear that his priority was maintaining momentum in Iraq when he met with Petraeus and Crocker in Kuwait on January 12. The president reassured Petraeus in private, and after the meeting publicly provided him with the breathing room he sought. "My attitude is, if he didn't want to continue the drawdown, that's fine with me, in order to make sure we succeed," Bush told reporters. "I said to the general, 'If you want to slow her down, fine; it's up to you.'"

Gates endorsed the idea of a brief pause in troop withdrawals after visiting Baghdad in February. The evening Gates arrived in Iraq, Petraeus's intelligence adviser Derek Harvey loitered in the lobby of the Joint Visitors Bureau at Camp Victory where VIP guests were lodged, until Gates appeared, along with his military adviser, Chiarelli. Harvey sought a casual conversation to prepare the ground for the secretary's meeting with Petraeus the next morning. The three men sat in the opulent salon of Saddam-era satin and gilt furniture and talked over cigars. Harvey laid out the arguments for holding force levels steady at fifteen brigades into the fall, previewing the case Petraeus would make the next day.

One of the arguments for keeping fifteen brigades was to provide security for provincial elections, which were to be held in the fall. These elections were of critical importance for three reasons. They would enfranchise the many Sunnis who had boycotted the 2005 provincial elections and give those who had recently stopped fighting a path to peaceful political participation in the new Iraq. Provincial elections would also provide a means to begin sorting out the simmering competition among the Shia groups and channel Shia militia members into the political process. The elections would also provide an important opportunity for new political leaders, groups, and alliances to emerge and establish local constituencies before the national parliamentary elections in 2009. In sum, provincial elections were a key step toward a political solution to Iraq's conflict. The other principal argument was to maintain the offensive against Al-Qaeda, which would likely continue for the rest of the year. Harvey believed more troops might be needed not only for the northern offensive but in the south, where the British were pulling out.

On March 11, Fox Fallon, Petraeus's Central Command (CENTCOM) boss, abruptly resigned after an article appeared in *Esquire* that painted him as the main bulwark against administration hawks lobbying for a military strike on Iran. None of Fallon's remarks quoted in the article were at odds with the stated Bush policy of seeking diplomatic resolution of differences with Tehran, but the tone and manner of the profile, with which Fallon had cooperated, taking its author with him on his travels, was the last straw for the White House. For months the outspoken officer had made no secret of his wish to reduce U.S. forces in Iraq to make more available for Afghanistan and possible contingencies elsewhere. His arguments were entirely legitimate ones for a CENTCOM chief to make. The chairman of the joint chiefs testified that the United States could do no more to meet the Afghanistan commander's request for three more brigades until U.S. troop levels in Iraq began to decline. But the aggressive manner in which Fallon pressed his case ruffled feathers.

The unceremonious departure of a top officer sent ripples through the military establishment, and the perception would persist that Petraeus had outmaneuvered Fallon. "Nobody can corral Petraeus," said one of the joint staff generals, shaking his head. But it was the president's wish that Petraeus and Crocker brief him weekly. The precedent of circumventing CENTCOM had been established earlier, by Secretary of Defense Donald Rumsfeld's frequent direct communications with Casey. Some of the CENTCOM staff was not sorry to see Fallon go. He frequently had left his own key officers behind on his frequent travels and then did not brief them on what had transpired in his meetings with leaders in the Middle East and South Asia.

On March 25, two weeks before Petraeus was due to testify before Congress, Prime Minister Maliki launched a poorly executed offensive in Basra against Sadr's Jaish al-Mahdi militia. U.S. and Iraqi military officials had been developing a plan to launch in June, after weeks of shaping operations. Instead, against Petraeus's advice, Maliki impulsively launched his troops the day after five Iraqi battalions arrived as reinforcements in Basra. He was forced to call on the United States for help. Sadr's militia came out in force, and pitched fighting ensued, not only in Basra but also in several cities around the south and in Baghdad's Sadr City. Sadrists fired dozens of rockets into the Green Zone over several days. One unpublicized reason for the abrupt launching of the offensive was that Sadr's militia had detained Rubaie, Maliki's national security adviser, in February in the principal Shia mosque in Baghdad's Shula neighborhood. Iraqi forces helped rescue him, and the incident reinforced Maliki's determination to bring Sadr's militia under control.

After two days of fighting, just as impetuously as the Basra offensive began, a delegation of Iraqi legislators from the Dawa and ISCI parties went to the Iranian city of Qom to negotiate a cease-fire with Sadr, with help from the Iranian Quds force commander. The blatant Iranian involvement greatly dismayed Petraeus. "The level of their participation, the centrality of their role, should give everyone pause," he said, noting that Iran not only armed the Sadrist special groups but also funded and backed all of the competing Shia Islamist groups. "The degree to which they have their hands on so many levers was revealed very starkly during this episode," he said.

Despite the cease-fire, operations continued to secure the city, the ports at Umm Qasr, and the oil complex at Zubayr. The militias' extortionist control of the ports and oil pumping stations in the Basra area represented a clear threat to Iraq's principal economic lifeline. Some Iraqi units deserted, but two Iraqi battalions did manage to regain control of the ports from the port security services, which were manned by Sadrists. If some two hundred militia leaders in Basra could be detained, a U.S. official estimated, the rest could be dealt with politically. Huge arms caches of weapons and munitions from Iran were found stockpiled around Basra.

Many agendas were at work. The Iraqi government had a legitimate need and reason to stop militia violence. Some also viewed Maliki's offensive in Basra as a bid to crush Sadr's leadership. Dawa also wanted to incorporate Sadrist forces since it was a small party of middle-class intellectuals without much of a grassroots base. The allegiance of some members of the so-called special groups also appeared to be far more fluid than once thought. Some of those in detention claimed their acceptance of Iran's patronage was purely expedient and that they had no desire to promote the Iranian theocratic model. But they detailed the extensive aid that they continued to receive from the Quds Force and the Arabic-speaking Lebanese Hezbollah.

No one could predict the outcome of the intra-Shia conflict or Sadr's role as a future leader. His father's name and legacy were powerful, but Maliki's standing improved with many Iraqis who had grown tired of the Sadr militia's excesses. Maliki had shown himself capable of moving against Shia violence, even if for his own political gain. The one certainty was that the plurality in the Shia community would continue given the clear differences over such issues as Iranian influence, political model, and nationalism versus regionalism.

In testimony to Congress on April 8 and 9, Petraeus announced his recommendation that troop levels remain at fifteen combat brigades (about 140,000 troops including enablers) until mid-September 2008. He would recommend further reductions thereafter as conditions permitted. The next day, after breakfast with Petraeus and Crocker at the White House, President Bush made a brief speech to say that he had accepted Petraeus's recommendations, but he also bowed to concerns over the stress on the U.S. military by ordering that troops' tours of duty be reduced from fifteen months to twelve beginning in August.

At the hearings, most legislators did not dispute that progress had been made, although many feared the gains would prove ephemeral. Violence had declined 70 percent or more since the previous summer, but Petraeus readily acknowledged that the progress was still "fragile and reversible." A rash of suicide bombers in the spring, including several women in flowing black *abayas* who exploded in shrapnel and blood, had reawakened those fears. Daily life in Iraq was still punctuated by grisly acts, such as the kidnapping of the Chaldean archbishop and the delivery of several security contractors' severed fingers to the U.S. military, not as part of a ransom demand but rather as a macabre obituary of men killed months earlier.

Democrats and Republicans alike expressed frustration over three main issues: the war's mounting cost—which now totaled $607 billion—Iraq's failure to make more political progress, and the witnesses' inability to provide a clear picture of the endgame for the war. Many of the legislators were also annoyed that Petraeus could not say when further troop withdrawals would occur.

Democratic senator Barack Obama of Illinois asked Petraeus and Crocker whether their definition of success was unattainably high. Petraeus assured him that they were not holding out for "Jeffersonian democracy." Crocker said, "I think that when Iraq gets to the point that . . . they can drive it forward themselves without significant danger of having the whole thing slip away from them again, then, clearly, our profile, our presence diminishes markedly." But, he added, they were not yet at that point.

Richard Lugar, the ranking Republican on the Senate Foreign Relations Committee, remained troubled that the administration did not know *how* it would reach that point. "Unless the United States is able to convert progress made thus far into a sustainable political accommodation . . . this progress will have limited meaning," he said. The Democratic head of the House Armed Services Committee, Ike Skelton of Missouri, agreed. "We cannot call the surge a strategic success without political reconciliation," he said. "So how can we encourage, if not force, the intransigent political leaders of Iraq to forge a real nation out of their base sectarian instincts?"

The politicians were asking the same question Petraeus had asked five years earlier when he had arrived in Iraq. The war would end, he told them, when the Iraqi competition over power and resources had been resolved. In all probability no one would know that the tipping point had been reached until after the fact. Some important compromises had been struck recently, but they were still uncertain and insufficient. It was an untidy process and the outcome was likely to be imperfect. This answer satisfied no one, but such postmodern endings were part and parcel of this kind of murky war.

15

Tell Me How This Ends

By June 2008 Iraq was calmer than it had been since April 2004. The war was not over, but it clearly had reached a new stage. When Petraeus took command a year and a half earlier, Iraq was on fire. The majority in the United States believed there was no way to avoid an ignominious defeat such as America had not suffered in a quarter-century. The U.S. military faced mounting pressure to depart and leave a strategic country in the Middle East at the mercy of its own turmoil and a wider regional conflict.

Petraeus, with the help of many others, pulled Iraq back from the brink of civil war and created an opportunity for the next administration to bring the war to a soft landing. Accomplishing that will not be easy, but what had seemed inconceivable to most onlookers in 2006 is now distinctly possible—if the forty-fourth American president has the fortitude and wisdom to capitalize on what has been achieved.

Since early 2008 Petraeus had been contemplating his own departure from Iraq. Considering that his legacy would be closely tied with the fate of Iraq, it was surprising that he wanted to leave. But he knew the job in

Iraq would not be done anytime soon, and he was ready to go for two reasons. He was tired. Few could imagine what an excruciatingly difficult job it was to shepherd this complex war, go to the mat daily with the Iraqis, and keep up the punishing pace needed to maintain forward momentum. He had given the effort his all, and Iraq had exacted a toll even on this famously energetic general. By the fall of 2008 he would have been deployed abroad for a total of five years since 2001. Like every soldier, he missed his family.

The second reason was that if he stayed until the end of the Bush administration in January 2009, he believed his career might well be over. Even though he had exceeded all expectations—and accomplished a historic feat of turning around the war—it was Bush's war, and Petraeus had perhaps inevitably been tagged as Bush's general for assuming leadership of it. A new administration led by Democrats might decide that the military would benefit from his leadership and promote him, but given the partisan rancor over Iraq, there was no certainty that it would. President Bush was prepared to promote him to one of the coveted combatant command jobs before he left office. Over several discussions it was agreed that Petraeus would stay in Iraq until the fall to solidify the progress.

Petraeus told the president he thought he could do a good job at NATO, where he had been assigned twice before. His wife, Holly, spoke three of the continent's languages and would be an asset. Her father had been posted there as a four-star general, and Jack Galvin, Matthew Ridgway, and other heroes of Petraeus's had served as the dual-hatted commander of NATO forces and U.S. forces in Europe. It was the most prestigious of the combatant commands, and it would take him out of the political firing line of the unpopular Iraq war. He had felt like his teeth had been kicked in by critics in Congress and elsewhere over the past year, and he was ready for a break.

Fox Fallon's abrupt resignation changed the calculus. The White House wanted to keep Petraeus in the region, and he reluctantly agreed. Petraeus was nominated to succeed Fallon at Central Command, and Petraeus's former subordinate, Lt. Gen. Ray Odierno, was given a fourth star and named to replace him in Iraq in the fall. Odierno had to be talked into the job; his nomination as the army's vice chief of staff had already been announced. He had been deployed to Iraq twice already and had been home for barely six months. His son Tony had lost an arm on his tour. Others who were in the running included Lt. Gen. Stan McChrystal and Lt. Gen. Pete Chiarelli. But in the end the White House decided on Odierno, with Petraeus's endorsement, because it provided the most continuity. Chiarelli became the army vice.

Before Petraeus left Iraq in September he would recommend further drawdowns, assuming the favorable trends of 2008 continued. If the offensive in the north and the nationwide provincial elections went reasonably well, troop levels might be reduced from fifteen to thirteen combat brigades in the remaining months of the administration.

Petraeus's presence at Central Command meant that he was available to help stop any unraveling that might occur after his departure from Baghdad. While his new purview would expand dramatically to twenty-seven countries and many looming threats, one of them was Iraq. He intended to let Odierno and Ryan Crocker carry on the strategy they had helped forge, but he would keep tabs on Iraq and lend a hand if they needed him.

Petraeus would not have stayed in Iraq indefinitely, but departing at that time did increase the risks. The last quarter of 2008 was a crucial window since the U.N. mandate would expire in December. He had opted to reach for the next rung on the career ladder when faced with an apparent choice between mission and career, and the danger existed that the gains would unravel without his hands-on approach. But the White House decision mitigated the risk: by putting him at CENTCOM, given his good working relationship with Odierno, Petraeus could see the Iraq project through into the next administration.

PETRAEUS'S LEADERSHIP AND LEGACY IN IRAQ. Over the past eighteen months, the war in Iraq had turned around by the combined efforts of 170,000 troops, as well as Crocker and thousands of American civilians, and equal numbers of Iraqis who wanted to save their country. But without a doubt Petraeus had been the instrumental figure in obtaining the successes. He brought three crucial traits to the job, which were largely responsible for his success and the legacy he left in Iraq.

First, his intellectual rigor led him to mount a sustained effort to understand the problem. He called upon the best minds he could find to define the problem honestly and shape an approach that employed not only the military but all available levers of influence. He remained open and ready to make the needed adjustments. His previous study of the problems of limited war, his tours in Iraq, and the extended exercise of framing the counterinsurgency manual and refining the army's education and training process were all invaluable preparation for this task.

Second, he did what generals are supposed to do: he led. He used a variety of leadership techniques to communicate with his subordinates, his civilian counterparts, and his Iraqi partners to ensure that they understood what he was trying to achieve with his campaign plan and how they were expected to proceed. His methods included granting a high degree of autonomy to battalion and company commanders.

Finally, Petraeus's temperament was uniquely suited to the demands of the mission. He possessed energy and tenacity in abundance, and Iraq required inordinate quantities of both. During his first tour in Mosul, Petraeus had learned the finer points of Iraqi bargaining tactics and conversational styles. He was willing to bang tables and tell a roomful of Iraqis "I've had it!" or to invoke their sense of honor in order to corral, dragoon, and cajole agreement from fractious marathon meetings. He was willing to feign anger—and to get angry—to get things done, but also deft enough to gauge his impact and adjust his tactics.

Petraeus's intellect, leadership, and relentless nature were critical in turning around the war. The conflict was complicated and intractable, but he had proven that it was not a hopeless situation. His peers might still grumble about him not being a team player, and Iraqi leaders' feathers might have been ruffled on more than one occasion when he refused to acquiesce to their designs, but he had delivered far better results than anyone had expected. His flaws and the frictions would matter little over the long run if the results he achieved in 2007–2008 were leveraged into a lasting peace.

The perseverance demonstrated by Petraeus was matched by that of his "wingman" Ryan Crocker and some equally valiant Iraqis. Such perseverance would still be needed in abundance for the hard road that lay ahead. Crocker was as worn out and ready to leave as Petraeus, and he joked that he woke up some mornings wishing that he had committed an error so egregious that he would be recalled to Washington and fired. He maintained a cautious attitude toward the future. "No one can ever accuse me of being an optimist about Iraq," he said. With luck, their successors would display the same stamina and partnership.

Petraeus and Crocker's main achievement was that they identified the right goal—political accommodation among Iraqis—and then bent all their efforts to that task. They forged the first true political-military strategy of the war and implemented it at the campaign level. Counterinsurgency principles, which are fundamentally about the political nature of war, had previously been applied primarily at the tactical level. Areas that had been impervious to that tactical application of counterinsurgency registered fundamental changes during 2007–2008. While Petraeus and Crocker did not have the authority to determine policy or override White House decisions, they did demand adequate resources and coordinate their application in a way that produced results on a national scale. One had the sense, after eighteen months of observing their partnership, that the hydra-headed U.S. effort in Iraq was finally focused on the right things and indisputably moving in the right direction.

Petraeus's positive traits and innovative approaches would be useful at Central Command as well. Among the many problems awaiting attention were Iran, which was on the march around the region, Lebanon, Afghanistan, and Pakistan. All of them would require sophisticated political-military strategies that addressed the root causes of the conflicts. The strategies would require partnerships with the host nations and international alliances to carry them out successfully. The deteriorating situation in Afghanistan and its inextricable linkage to Pakistan, NATO's limitations, and the fragmented command structure all cried out for a sweeping examination and a new approach to put the effort in South Asia on the right track. An independent multidisciplinary study such as the one carried out for Iraq could help frame the problems accurately, bring non-military insights and remedies to bear, and provide the long-term perspective that any strategy would require.

Beyond his CENTCOM-specific responsibilities, Petraeus was also likely to continue advocating military reforms and national security remedies more generally. He was a leading proponent of "whole of government" approaches to these problems, as he had demonstrated in working closely with Crocker. Among other initiatives, he had supported the development of a government-wide counterinsurgency doctrine under the State Department's leadership and the formation of an interagency clearing house, the Consortium for Complex Operations, to unite such efforts.

THE WAY AHEAD IN IRAQ. The next president has the awesome and solemn duty to bring the Iraq war to the best possible conclusion. It is his responsibility to chart a course that will safeguard U.S. interests and mitigate the war's worst effects. While Americans want U.S. troops to come home, most of them also understand that the United States must exercise its power responsibly and that a precipitous withdrawal puts at risk all the blood and treasure expended thus far. If offered a roadmap with an honest appraisal of what is required, Americans will give the new president their support to carry it out.

The new president has the great advantage of starting with a clean slate and no special relationships or past commitments. He can adopt a new policy that builds on the successes achieved in 2007–2008 and provides the critical missing ingredients that can only be supplied by presidential authority. The basic conceptual change needed is to change the paradigm from war-making to peace-making and to make achievement of the elusive political solution the policy's central goal. What this means is that the political goals as well as the political and diplomatic mechanisms must move to the forefront of the policy. So much of the debate has been about troop levels and missions, but these are subsidiary issues that must be determined once the policy objectives are set. Troops will be needed for peacekeeping, advisory, and other mostly noncombat missions, but at lower and declining numbers. A robust regional diplomatic initiative will also be required, and it will have greater prospects for success as the new approach to Iraq is implemented.

What has been lacking is a policy explicitly aimed at achieving a political solution that ends Iraq's conflict. That phrase has been used often, but its terms must be fleshed out in a full-fledged policy. The United States has not used all of its available leverage, and conflicting crosscurrents in the Bush administration prevented the delivery of a clear message to the Iraqi government. The decisions that need to be made about conditions and leverage are ones that only the president can make. The U.S. military support to Iraq must be offered in exchange for certain basic conditions, which the current administration has been unwilling to impose. But the conditions need to be the right ones, and they need to be negotiated in a way that protects the substantial U.S. interests in the region.

The first decision the new president has to make is whether to pursue a political solution to Iraq's conflict—that is, to help Iraq construct a new foundation for the nation—or to settle for the status quo. He must decide whether the central goal of his Iraq policy is a multisectarian Iraq in which all the groups share political, economic, and military power. That outcome would be the most stable one for Iraq internally and for the region. The previous administration was divided over how hard to push for this solution, and that division prevented effective policy formulation and implementation. The alternative is to accept the consolidation of an Islamist Shia sectarian government which may become closely allied with Iran. That outcome is far less likely to produce stability inside Iraq or in the region. The United States loses nothing by attempting to achieve the first outcome, and the upside is enormous.

The issue must be framed starkly because the perception exists in some circles that the apparent defeat of Al-Qaeda in Iraq means that the United States has finished its task in Iraq. The combat task may be largely finished, but to abandon the quest for a stable internal order will almost certainly lead to renewed civil war and regional spillover. These consequences cannot be prevented simply by posting troops on borders or in bases around the region. They can only be prevented by continuing the hard work of constructing a viable new political order in Iraq. Stability in the region cannot be achieved without stability in Iraq. Some headway has been made in channeling the competition for power and resources into the political arena: the legislative package passed by the Iraqi parliament in February, particularly the compromise on provincial powers, was an important step. But the divisions remain deep and the Iraqi factions are unlikely to resolve the most difficult issues on their own.

There is no magic wand that will resolve Iraq's conflict overnight, but now that blood is no longer running in the streets the chances are better than at any time since 2003 to help Iraq's major constituencies begin to resolve their differences.

Three steps will be required to achieve a lasting political solution. The first step is to reach a conditional agreement with the Maliki government to maintain and extend the ceasefire and set up as many hedges to sectarian behavior as possible in return for continued U.S. support. The second step is the most urgent and critical: the United States must do all it can to ensure the conduct of fair and widely participatory national elections in Iraq at the end of 2009—eleven short months after the new U.S. president takes office—in order to enfranchise all Iraqis and create a more broadly representative parliament and government. The current parliament is too fractured and narrowly based to be able to resolve the fundamental issues concerning Iraq's new constitutional and political order—which will almost certainly require significant constitutional revisions. The third step is to appoint a presidential envoy and offer formal consultative mechanisms to help the new Iraqi government reach viable compromises on the bedrock issues of federalism and sharing national power and resources. These three political steps should be supported by a military peacekeeping approach and an intensive regional diplomatic initiative.

The first step the U.S. president should take is to make clear to the Maliki government that continued U.S. assistance will require the government to take a certain minimal set of actions to prevent Iraq from sliding back into civil war. The most important one is to speedily incorporate all of the vetted Sons of Iraq into the Iraqi security forces or other jobs. This is the single best guarantee that the Sunni insurgency will not break out again. More than the previously agreed-upon 25 percent—probably at least half—should be incorporated into the Iraqi police force. The reason is that Iraqis overwhelmingly prefer to have local residents in charge of neighborhood security, and the police force is still heavily Shia. A recent poll showed that 56 percent of Iraqis support the volunteer Sons of Iraq, versus 49 percent who support the government. Those who disparage or marginalize the Sons of Iraq seriously misunderstand their legitimacy and their critical role in maintaining the ceasefire. If they are not incorporated, the entire foundation for a political resolution of the conflict will unravel.

The new president must also ensure that the U.S. military is not put in the position of supporting sectarian actions. U.S. commanders need to have a continuing role in determining valid targets for action by U.S. troops. The two governments should also agree upon mechanisms to ensure that the Iraqi security forces are not used as a sectarian tool of the government. To this end, the Jones commission recommendation to return the Iraqi special operations forces to the Iraqi military chain of command should be adopted. The Maliki government has rightly taken the bold step of combating the armed Sadr militia, which demonstrates Maliki's willingness to target not only Sunni but also Shia armed groups. But it is essential to build and follow institutional procedures that prevent the political use of the armed forces and the politicization of its members.

The other key requirement to ensure that Iraq's civil war does not erupt again is for the Iraqi government to take urgent action and expend its own funds to facilitate the return of the four million Iraqis who have left the country or been displaced internally. Homes for squatters without legitimate leases must be found, rented, or built. Also, much more must be done to restore basic public services and repair infrastructure in areas lacking them, particularly Sunni areas, and Iraq has ample resources to do so. Taking these actions will be among the most meaningful olive branches that can be offered to the Iraqi population.

These are goals that can and must be achieved very early in the new administration to provide stability during the remainder of the Maliki government. Even before the new U.S. president's inauguration, his transition team must be prepared to signal his intentions and, if necessary, join the negotiation of the bilateral accord that is intended to replace the current United Nations mandate, if the accord has not yet been concluded. This accord implies a radical decrease in U.S. leverage, provided by the Chapter VII provision of the U.N. charter, and a concomitant increase in Iraqi autonomy. If the accord has already been concluded, its terms must be reviewed to ensure that it does not commit the new administration in any way that will aid sectarian agendas or inhibit achievement of the above goals. In particular, the procedures for targeting and undertaking any combat actions by U.S. troops must be joint, and the United States must maintain a clear chain of command with regard to its own troops.

The Iraqi government has been quick to resort to brinksmanship in the negotiation of this accord, but the United States has sufficient leverage to achieve these minimum goals. It must refrain from overplaying its hand, however, because it is not in U.S. interests to abandon Iraq to renewed turmoil or the unchecked influence of Iran—and the Iraqis know that. The fundamental reality is that Iraqis want and need U.S. assistance, at least for now. The Maliki government knows it is not yet strong enough to stand on its own, and it wants the United States to serve as a counterweight to Iran. But U.S. leverage is not unlimited and is diminishing, as the threat from Iraq's most lethal enemy—Al-Qaeda in Iraq—recedes and as the Iraqi security forces grow in size and competence. This means that U.S. leverage will have to be used for the right ends and not overplayed. Iraq can always turn to Iran or use its oil wealth to cultivate other alliances. All or nothing demands by the United States, just like fixed timetables, are one-shot tactics.

The United States does possess significant leverage of various sorts. Iraq would like the United States' help in the following specific areas, beginning with the most existential ones: ensuring the personal security and safety of the leaders and their homes in the Green Zone; conducting counterterrorism raids against insurgents; providing vital combat enablers including air support, surveillance and intelligence, and medical evacuation; training and advising Iraqi security forces; supplying U.S. military equipment under the foreign military sales program; and helping defend Iraq and its borders against foreign aggression. In addition, Iraqi leaders no doubt would like to avoid more rigid conditions on U.S.

assistance that could be legislated by the U.S. Congress. They would also be eager to avoid dissemination of information about corruption and misdeeds at the highest levels of the Iraqi government.

The second and equally urgent step the new U.S. administration must undertake as soon as it assumes office is to help Iraq prepare for national elections at the end of 2009 to elect a new parliament, which will in turn form a government to succeed Maliki's. The main focus of the United States must be on the elections because they hold the key to the political solution of the conflict. It is vital that these elections fully enfranchise the Iraqi electorate so the resulting parliament will have the legitimacy and standing to resolve the main outstanding issues about the nature of the Iraqi state and how power and resources will be shared. In this regard, it is necessary to ensure that the four million Iraqis who are displaced or abroad are able to vote because about half of them are Sunnis, a group currently underrepresented in the parliament.

The administration must strive to ensure that certain basic conditions are met in these elections. In order to produce a broadly representative government with support at the local level, an open list or other electoral system should be adopted (instead of closed party lists) so that voters may vote for individuals and new candidates and small parties are not disadvantaged. The formation of new parties and multisectarian or nonsectarian alliances should be encouraged, or at least not impeded by party bosses. The United Nations and international monitors should be asked to support and observe the vote to increase confidence in the results and the legitimacy of the resulting government. To this end, U.S. troops must remain in sufficient numbers to ensure that the elections are conducted in a climate of peace and security.

While it is impossible to predict the outcome of the elections, it is highly likely that the Shia vote will be fractured. That is the key opportunity that makes new combinations possible. The very fissures within the Shia electorate create the opportunity for a variety of multisectarian and nonsectarian alliances. Many Shia are disgusted with the incompetence, corruption, and sectarianism of the current government. The Shia population is not a monolith, as facile analyses from afar have suggested, and it is not clear that a majority of the Shia prefer an Islamist government, or at least one that imposes strict Islamic practices and alienates or excludes non-Shia constituencies. It is worth remembering that the current government was only elected by a plurality, and its support has dwindled since then. Although Sunni extremism is on the wane, the Shia Islamists in the government have remained reluctant to share power with Sunnis. But not all Shia parties take this view, and the election will be a referendum on this key issue, as well as on the balance of power within the federal system.

The elections will open the door to the possibility of new alliances with new parties and constituencies that have entered the system in the provincial elections. The provincial elections provide a critical springboard for the national elections by legitimizing new actors and by providing far more representative local governments than have existed since the start of the war. That is not to say that it will be easy to form a new national government, but the first step is to achieve the most representative parliament possible. That will provide the basis for achieving compromises on the core issues of the conflict. Any effort to tackle the bedrock issues with the current government is unlikely to produce a good outcome since the government has proven to be both weak and intransigent.

Those bedrock issues include, most importantly, the division of power between the central government, the provinces, and the regions—a matter that will most likely require constitutional revisions. According to a February 2008 poll, 67 percent of Iraqis want to have a strong central government, but the current constitution provides for a weak central government and powerful regions. The structure of the government and apportionment of powers will determine whether the Sunni minority is marginalized or given a voice in the country's affairs. The other issue of enormous consequence is how Iraq's vast oil wealth will be developed and managed, as oil is the country's biggest source of revenue. Other key issues are the de-Baathification law, which may need further revision or at least oversight of its implementation, and the troublesome issue of Kirkuk's status, which remains to be resolved.

The third step is to appoint an envoy to assist the new government in reaching agreement on these systemic issues and to discuss the future

U.S. security assistance role. Given the depth of disagreement and complexity of the issues, it is highly unlikely that the new Iraqi government will be able to navigate its way to lasting compromises without some type of mediation or facilitation by outside parties. The United States should appoint a presidential envoy to offer assistance in the search for solutions and to support other conflict resolution efforts. The possible formulas range from U.N. mediation to a U.S.-led Dayton process (as was used in the Balkans conflict), to less intrusive "facilitation" by a Group of Friends. U.N. Secretary General Ban Ki Moon is committed to expanding the United Nations' role in Iraq, and skillful U.N. envoys have succeeded in brokering peace accords elsewhere. These overtures to help resolve Iraq's fundamental internal conflicts should be made to the new government elected in 2009, which will have far more legitimacy and capacity than the present one to reach the necessary compromises.

The U.S. military posture in Iraq should be based on the outcome of these three political steps. The future of the U.S. military presence in Iraq should be negotiated with the new Iraqi government, based on the conditions that exist at the time, the needs of the Iraqi government, and its willingness to meet the basic conditions that the United States would seek in return for its ongoing support. Rather than decide unilaterally what is best for Iraq, the decision should be made with its new government—which is also the best way to leverage that assistance. Creative mechanisms can be designed to reward the Iraqi government for an inclusive approach to resolving the core issues of the conflict. In the meantime, over the course of 2009, it should be possible to continue troop withdrawals at roughly the current pace to about half of the current level. Most of the remaining troops should be able to transition to largely noncombat advisory missions. Troops are already scheduled to step back from frontline roles into overwatch positions, first at local outposts and precincts and then from the larger bases. They have already done so in Anbar. The United States needs to continue the current cautious pace of withdrawal in order to avoid jeopardizing the gains made.

A residual troop presence of 50,000 to 60,000 troops may be needed for some years, depending on the security conditions in Iraq and the progress toward a political settlement. A long-term Balkans-type peacekeeping presence may be needed. Over time, it may be possible to recruit other allies or the United Nations to help with this task. While it represents ongoing cost and risk to the United States, peacekeeping duty is not as hazardous as the current set of missions, and the bulk of troops will not see combat. A small subset of troops will likely remain as combat advisers, combat enablers, and combat troops to conduct counterterrorism missions.

To alleviate nationalist sensitivities and lower its profile, the United States should reduce its large headquarters and move out of the remaining palaces it occupies. Dispersion of troops is still required at the present time to provide a security blanket and to mentor and advise Iraqi troops. Iraq can benefit from having high-level advisers assigned to its top operational commands, as is currently the case. But there is no reason that the large U.S. command structure cannot be reduced. The three-star Multi-National Security Transition Command is the logical nucleus of the U.S. presence as the mission transforms into a traditional security assistance relationship devoted primarily to training, advising, and equipping the Iraqi forces. Special operations task forces for counterterrorism operations can be nested within this command.

The final piece of a new policy should be a robust and inclusive regional diplomatic initiative. No peacemaking and peacekeeping initiative inside Iraq can succeed without a simultaneous and equally concerted effort to establish a regional security framework. The immediate goals should be to induce support for the Iraqi government and to minimize armed intervention by Iran and other actors. The neighboring Arab states and the Gulf Cooperation Council states will become far more supportive if Maliki enacts the minimal conditions this approach recommends. And the next Iraqi government stands to win even more support to the degree that it addresses Iraqi Sunni concerns through further reforms and legislation. This support from the Arab neighbors will in turn help provide the critical counterweight to Iran's hegemonic designs and, in particular, its apparent attempt to "Lebanonize" Iraq by creating armed groups over which it has significant influence.

The regional dialogue begun by the Bush administration should be continued and elevated with more frequent, higher-level meetings and an accelerated agenda. In addition to the focus on foreign fighters, border security, refugees, and resources, the regional process should seek concrete measures to reduce the chances of a wider Sunni-Shia conflict and Kurdish-Turkish conflict. The strongest cards to limit Iranian intervention in Iraq are Iraqi nationalism and a continuing U.S. presence to balance the inevitable Iranian influence. The ultimate goals of a regional pact should be to deter aggression on all sides, prevent the acquisition of destabilizing weapons, and craft a stable balance of power.

This regional process must be coordinated with other likely diplomatic initiatives. Given Iran's apparent quest to become a nuclear power, or at least to keep that option open, multilateral and bilateral diplomacy and sanctions will also be part of the tool kit to address the problems posed by the Iranian regime. The intent should not be to pit Iraq against Iran or to create an anti-Iran alliance—that will only increase the regime's paranoia—but rather to use all diplomatic means to curtail its destabilizing activities.

In addition to the pressing and complex menu of security problems, the regional diplomatic agenda must include support for political reform and representative government. Democracy promotion should be de-linked from the idea of regime change and instead viewed as a means to ensure the long-term viability of Middle Eastern states. The debate has been framed in an unhelpful dichotomy between support for regional autocrats as a way to ensure short-term stability and demands for democratization regardless of the consequences. The lessons of Latin America's successful transition from dictatorship to democracy two decades ago are instructive, since at the time many believed its culture was not hospitable to representative government.

IRAQ AND THE FUTURE. The Iraq war holds many important lessons for the future, and indeed the future is already here demanding answers. The United States is wrestling with the issue of how large its armed forces, particularly its land force, need to be. The stress on the army and Marine Corps is real. Despite offering a $35,000 bonus to captains who reenlisted, the army fell short of its goal by more than 2,000 officers. No matter what happens in Iraq, the United States cannot continue to rotate thirteen to fifteen brigades into that country indefinitely and at the same time increase its troops in Afghanistan by three brigades as the commander there deems necessary, maintain one brigade apiece in Kosovo and Korea—and keep the thirty-eight-brigade active-duty army and eight-regiment Marine Corps from breaking.

The troop demands in Iraq will decline steadily as political solutions are found to the conflict. The solutions in Iraq *are* political ones. They must be supported by a long-term presence to help keep the peace and nurture professional security forces, but this can be done at much lower levels than the present ones. The needed level can be sustained, particularly with multinational partners. The judgment of the current army chief of staff is that a total deployment of fifteen brigades (in Afghanistan and Iraq) can be sustained. The next two years will be difficult, given the additional demands in Afghanistan, until the planned expansion of the army and Marine Corps comes online. The planned growth is needed, but further expansion does not seem necessary given the current global threat assessment. Issues about the ideal forward-basing posture and related questions remain to be addressed.

The U.S. military does not need to be much larger, but it does need to continue to adapt and evolve. This effort will likely be a high priority in an army with Chiarelli and Petraeus as leaders.

Iraq offers important lessons in how the U.S. military can be best employed in population-centric warfare. The singular success that has been achieved against Al-Qaeda in Iraq is based above all on the Iraqi people's rejection of the organization. The U.S. military used a panoply of new tactics to bring the population over to its side and to use the population to find and capture Al-Qaeda.

Iraq also offers an important model for how all elements of national power can be harnessed at the strategic level to change the trajectory of a conflict. It is this lesson that needs to be urgently applied to the foundering effort in Afghanistan.

New ad hoc organizations were formed to address specific needs in Iraq, underlining the necessity for flexible formations and individuals. These structures included brigades that incorporated such disparate elements as civilian provincial reconstruction teams, other units' battalions and companies, and assets from different organizations. At the MNF-I level, fusion cells and interagency groups were set up to address a multitude of specific problems. And conventional and special forces operated in more integrated fashion than in any previous war.

Not all of the counterinsurgency tactics applied worked, and it will be important to study in depth such issues as the proper sequencing of clearance and control operations, for example, and the most appropriate blends of "population-centric" and "enemy-centric" tactics. Most of all it will be important for counterinsurgency and irregular warfare to remain an integral part of the curriculum rather than allowed to languish as happened after Vietnam. Concerns have been voiced recently that the land forces have focused too much on irregular warfare and allowed conventional war-fighting skills to languish, but much of the combat in Iraq has required many of the latter high-intensity skills as well.

One of the niche needs that remains underserved or ill-served is that of U.S. military advisers. Advisory missions to professionalize new armies often take a decade or more. If the United States is to sustain or expand the current advisory effort in Iraq and Afghanistan without help from other countries, it will need a larger and more capable advisory cadre. To attract the most talented personnel, the army decided in June 2008 to reward those who serve as advisers with career incentives. Also, U.S. Special Forces, whose specialty is advising foreign forces, can be used in more creative ways to enable and improve the military's advisory capacity.

Troops were employed in Iraq in an unprecedented capacity as neighborhood diplomats. Battalion and company commanders rose to the challenge with extraordinary skill and intuition, aided by civilian advisers, intelligence officials, and retired trainers. These lessons need to be captured and studied for future use in Afghanistan and elsewhere.

Further development, encouragement, and use of the abundant human capital in the mid-ranks of the U.S. Army is the most powerful step the institution could take to halt attrition and improve its overall competence as an organization. These midgrade personnel are the seed corn and backbone of the future military. Many lieutenant colonels and senior noncommissioned officers are leaving not only because of repeat tours but also out of frustration with an institution that is not suited to the reality of combat in this era, which is bound to be predominantly irregular in nature because the U.S. military has few peer competitiors. The military institution is by nature hierarchical, but it must find a way to become a flatter, networked, agile organization that embraces innovation and attracts and keeps its brightest stars. These soldiers have accomplished extraordinary feats in the field, and the institution will benefit from finding a way to harness that improvisational talent and experience.

The other principal way to relieve stress on the U.S. military is to invest in the nonmilitary institutions that used to carry out many stabilization, reconstruction, and counterinsurgency missions. That includes the State Department, U.S. Agency for International Development, and U.S. Information Agency, all of which played major roles in the counterinsurgencies of the 1960s, 1970s, and 1980s until they were dismantled or dramatically defunded after the cold war. Until they are appropriately funded and staffed, the much-recommended "whole of government" approaches cannot be implemented. They will remain talking points in conference speeches.

This is the single most important change in spending priorities in the national security budget that the next administration could make. Major nonmilitary institutions can be rebuilt for the price of a few fighter jets. It will require forging a constituency and leadership in Congress, as well as presidential commitment.

Beyond funding such a civilian capacity, sustained training and development of the cadre is needed as well, and not only to staff reconstruction teams. The proposal has been made to transform the National Defense University into the National Security University, which would train a professional civilian policy corps such as exists in other countries. National security policymaking would benefit from training a cadre of officials for careers in the civilian national security sector just as the military does now. Finally, the government's national security processes and structures are in need of a systemic overhaul. If Washington cannot forge a competent national security strategy and execute it, the United States cannot hope to be an effective world leader.

Addressing these deficits and incorporating these lessons will be an integral part of concluding the Iraq war and handling the many challenges of the current era. The clock cannot be rewound and the decision to go to war undone, but the country can learn from what has happened and move forward with new purpose.

Petraeus may not have brought the Iraq war to its conclusion, but what he did accomplish will surely be enshrined in the annals of U.S. military history and counterinsurgency warfare. He will no doubt help to shape the war's endgame from Central Command, while tending the many other challenges in this important and tumultuous region. When historians look for parallels to Petraeus's tour in Iraq, they will most likely compare it to Ridgway's in Korea, where he managed to push back the Chinese and stabilize the Korean peninsula. The Korean war did not end on his watch and it did not end in victory. If Iraq does come undone despite all of the toil and sacrifice, then Petraeus will inevitably be compared to Gen. Creighton Abrams, whose efforts and innovations did not ultimately save the United States from defeat in Vietnam.

When all is said and done, however, Iraq's war must be judged on its own significance and merits. The Iraq war was a folly as egregious as Vietnam. But it was a war with far higher stakes, and the consequences of defeat would reverberate throughout the Middle East. Petraeus gave Iraq a chance to climb out of its civil war and America a chance to redeem itself for the errors it made there. The next president can seize that chance to bring the country together after this bitter experience. The opportunity should not be squandered.

Acknowledgments

This book came about through the combined brainstorming of my editor at PublicAffairs, Clive Priddle, and Peter Osnos, the founder of PublicAffairs. I thank them for the opportunity to write about a war that has deeply affected our country. Clive proposed the idea of a book on Gen. Petraeus and the latter phase of the Iraq war, and Peter shared his insights from Vietnam, including the possible parallels between Gen. Creighton Abrams's command of that war in 1968–1972 and Petraeus's tenure in Iraq. I am indebted to Clive for his thoughtful advice and deft editing. Many others helped bring the project to fruition, including Meredith Smith, John Williams, Antoinette Smith, and the entire production, sales, marketing, and publicity team. Flip Brophy, my agent, has been a source of constant encouragement, even when I doubted the wisdom of attempting to write a book about the war's events as they unfolded. Brian Duffy, another dear friend and my former editor at *U.S. News & World Report*, introduced me to the joys of book-writing and allowed me to make lengthy reporting trips to Iraq at regular intervals, beginning with a two-month sojourn at the war's start in March 2003.

I am immensely grateful to Tom Keaney, acting director of the Philip Merrill Center for Strategic Studies at the Johns Hopkins School for Advanced International Studies, for providing me a berth as author in residence during the final stages of writing and editing the book. The sharp and lively students of the program provided welcome stimulus. I am also grateful for the love and support of my sister, Denise, and her husband, Scott, my brother, Greg, and his wife, Robin, and my father and mother, Bill and Marion, as well as the many friends and colleagues who promised to still be there once I reemerged from this project. Most of all, I thank my dear husband and soul mate, Scott, who supported me with unstinting love, humor, and encouragement, even though the project literally consumed our lives, took me away from home for extended periods, and left him wondering what dangerous spot I might be in at any given moment.

This book would not have been possible without Gen. David Petraeus's agreement to provide extended access to him and all of Multi-National Force-Iraq. The same is true of Ambassador Ryan Crocker and his country team, as well as his predecessor, Ambassador Zalmay Khalilzad, all of whom spent a great deal of time discussing the mind-bending complexities of Iraqi politics with me. Of the many Iraqis who gave generously of their time to help me understand their perspectives and their struggles, I wish to thank especially Deputy Prime Minister Barham Salih, Samir Sumaidaie, who is currently Iraq's ambassador to the United States, Gen. Nasir Abadi, Lt. Gen. Abboud Qanbar, Hoshyar Zebari, and National Security Adviser Mowaffak al-Rubaie. I was fortunate to spend months in Iraq reporting on the military and political developments, including repeated visits to several units. The Multi-National Corps-Iraq and echelons below, especially the Multi-National Division-Baghdad, and the Iraqi Baghdad Operations Command provided access to subordinate units. For my research into Gen. Petraeus's background, I am grateful to his family members and many former colleagues who agreed to interviews.

Many people aided my quest to understand this war's complex political and military dynamics. Dozens of those who granted interviews, the primary research tool used for this book, are cited or quoted in the book, but many are not and still others wished to remain anonymous. Other individuals provided referrals, advice, or assistance of other sorts. All of them endured my repeated inquiries, requests, and visits with good humor, and I thank them all, including Dalia Abdullah, Lt. Col. Josslyn Aberle, Lt. Col. Tony Aguto, Muhamad Ahmad, Capt. Andrew Artis, Hashim Ahmed Ayoub, Col. Dan Baggio, David Barno, John Bennett, Maj. Gen. Kevin Bergner, Steve Biddle, Lt. Col. Scott Bleichwehl, Col. Steve Boylan, Lt. Col. Rudy Burwell, Joseph Collins, Col. Chris Conner, Mitch Conway, Jay Cope, Lt. Col. Curtis Carson, Capt. Britton Crafton, Ali al-Dabbagh, Col. Bill Darley, Julie Eadeh, Capt. Mike Ernst, Maj. Gen. Joseph Fil, Mercedes Fitchett, Capt. Tom Fournier, Maj. Frank Garcia, Lt. Col. James Gavrilis, Natalie Gewargis, Abdul Aziz al-Hakim, Humam Hamoudi, Glenn Harned, Naufel al-Hassan, Lt. Col. Abdul Jabar Hassan Thabit, Lawen Hawezy, Maj. Armando Hernandez, Col. Bill Hickman, Shallaw Hussein, Col. James Hutton, Wade Ishimoto, Maj. Anthony Judge, Capt. Aaron Kaufman, Kamran Karadaghi, Ali Khedery, Maj. Steve Lamb, MaryBeth Long, Lt. Gen. Doug Lute, Col. Pete Mansoor, Phebe Marr, Brett McGurk, Col. H. R. McMaster, Tom McNaugher, Col. Mike Meese, Stephanie Miley, Lt. Col. Charlie Miller, Lt. Maria Miller, Dick Millett, Lt. Gen. Tom Metz, Terry Moran, Maj. Matthew Morgan, Karim al Musawi, Lt. Col. John Nagl, Col. Bob Newman, Lt. Col. Steve North, Meghan O'Sullivan, Phyllis Powers, Martha Raddatz, Philip Reeker, Lt. Col. John Reynolds, Sadiq al-Rikabi, Bruno Roeber, Cale Salih, David Satterfield, Margaret Scobey, Gunner Sepp, Dan Serwer, Sarah Sewall, Michael Shaler, Kate Starr, Maj. Joel Stephanson, Barbara Stephenson, Lt. Col. Steve Stover, Marin Strmecki, Dan Sreebny, Qubad Talabany, Mahddy Talat, Col. Ken Tovo, Paul Tiberi, Matt Tueller, Maj. Gen. Bill Troy, Lt. Col. Monty Willoughby, Sgt. Michael Yasutake, and Lt. Col. Joe Yoswa. I apologize for those I may have overlooked who also contributed to my education in Iraq. I would like to extend a special thanks to all the soldiers who made room for me in their vehicles and outposts and who, along with Iraqi civilians, endured the dangers and privations of the war.

None of these individuals or anyone quoted in the text should be held responsible for any errors, which are solely mine. Although they may not agree with my analysis or conclusions, I am nonetheless sincerely thankful for all of my sources' willingness to share their views and experiences.

Notes

As this is above all a work of journalism, virtually all of the quoted remarks and scenes described are based on my reporting and many dozens of interviews conducted in Iraq and the United States. Sources are provided for those quotations not derived from interviews. I also relied on numerous documents, briefing slides, and other unpublished material my sources supplied. The notes below are intended to provide additional documentation to supplement my firsthand reporting.

CHAPTER 1:
THE GENESIS OF A CIVIL WAR

2   Some believed that modern Iraq was fundamentally an unworkable construct One concept that was widely discussed in the United States was soft partition, as the proposal to establish three largely autonomous regions by Senate Foreign Relations Committee chairman Sen. Joe Biden and Council on Foreign Relations President Emeritus Leslie Gelb became known. Their proposal, which drew on Balkans analogies, stimulated enormous interest after it was published as an op-ed, "Unity Through Autonomy in Iraq," in the *New York Times* on May 1, 2006. Another advocate of the idea was Peter Galbraith, an adviser to the Kurdish regional government, former ambassador to Croatia, and author of *The End of Iraq: How American Incompetence Created a War Without End* (New York: Simon & Schuster, 2006). The Biden-Gelb concept envisioned a highly decentralized country where Kurds, Shias, and Sunnis each governed their own regions with a minimalist central government that guaranteed proportional distribution of the country's oil revenues. A great degree of decentralization was enshrined in the 2005 constitution, which provided for the devolution of substantial powers and formation of regional governments out of provinces, as the Kurds had already done in their three northern provinces. The Iraqis who wrote the constitution and participated most fully in the electoral process were those who favored such a highly federal system, such as the Kurds and the Islamic Supreme Council of Iraq, which advocated forming a region from the nine overwhelmingly Shia provinces of the south.

But many other Iraqis opposed this vision, including nationalists, secularists, religious Shia including Muqtada al-Sadr's bloc and the Fadhila party, and most Sunnis. In a poll conducted in February 2008 for ABC News and the BBC, ARD, and NHK networks, 67 percent of Iraqis favored an Iraq ruled by a central government, 23 percent wanted an Iraq of federated states, and 9 percent wanted an Iraq of separate states. (The latter group was primarily Kurds, 52 percent of whom favored a separate state. The full poll results are posted at www.abcnews .go.com/images/PollingUnit/1060a1IraqWhereThingsStand.pdf.)

The provinces where Sunnis predominantly live lack the lucrative oil resources of Shia and Kurdish areas. No census has been conducted in over fifteen years, but it is generally acknowledged that Sunni Arabs constitute the overwhelming majority in the provinces of Anbar and Salahuddin and a simple majority in Ninewa. Substantial numbers of Sunnis also live in Diyala, Tamim, and Baghdad provinces. According to the 2005 constitution, regions can be formed by three or more of Iraq's eighteen provinces, except for Baghdad province.

3   Bremer's first two decisions L. Paul Bremer III with Malcolm McConnell, *My Year in Iraq: The Struggle to Build a Future of Hope* (New York: Threshold Editions, 2006). By his own account, Bremer was very eager to exercise sole authority while in Iraq, but he subsequently sought to share responsibility for the fateful Decrees 1 and 2 with others. In his memoir, Bremer said the de-Baathification decree had been drafted by the office of Undersecretary of Defense for Policy Douglas Feith. He wrote that "the White House, DOD and State all signed off on this [the de-Baathification decree]" before he issued it (p. 41). Bremer also blamed the Iraqi de-Baathification commission, which he charged with implementing the decree, for overly expansive application of the purge. Before the decree was signed, Bremer aide O'Sullivan wrote a memo to Bremer outlining the implications of imple-menting de-Baathification down to the fourth, or firqa, tier of the Baath Party. While noting the complications it would cause, she also recognized that there was pressure from Shia who wanted even more thorough purges and restitution to victims.

The second decree, which dissolved the security forces, had been drawn up by Bremer aide Walter Slocombe, but Bremer said it had also been extensively vetted with Pentagon and other military officials. He wrote that he had "informed" and "briefed" the president shortly before signing it. In 2007 Bremer still felt he was being unfairly saddled with responsibility for these decisions and wrote an op-ed claiming that he had the president's support for the decrees (L. Paul Bremer III, "How I Didn't Dismantle Iraq's Army," *New York Times,* September 6, 2007). In his book *State of Denial* (New York: Simon & Schuster, 2007), Bob Woodward wrote that Hadley, then deputy national security adviser, did not see either decree and that there was no White House approval, although these assertions were not sourced specifically to either Hadley or Rice (see pp. 197–198). Hadley declined several requests to clarify the discrepancy. Stipends were offered to some of Saddam's military five weeks after it was disbanded, but not to thousands of senior officers.

3   Bremer's memoir . . . documents in detail . . . decisions that favored their interests The memoir, *My Year in Iraq,* also includes a memo Bremer wrote to himself (p. 242) and a revealing account of Hakim's meeting with President Bush (p. 283) that illustrates Hakim's willingness to challenge and even implicitly threaten the administration.

11   Shia leaders . . . playing "winner take all" In the brutally honest prologue to his excellent book, Ali Allawi, a close friend of Mowaffak al-Rubaie's and a former Iraqi government minister, indicates that these were their proclivities. He wrote: "The USA may have fallen for the self-serving description of Iraq's Shia as a force that was simply waiting to express its democratic proclivities and its gratitude to its liberators. . . . The weight of the past was too great, and the opportunities to reverse the hand that history had dealt them were too enticing, to fall for the promise of a non-sectarian and liberal Iraq." See Ali Allawi, *The Occupation of Iraq: Winning the War, Losing the Peace* (New Haven, Conn.: Yale University Press, 2007), pp. 10–11.

12   One of the enduring questions of the war Richard H. Kohn of the University of North Carolina-Chapel Hill, a military historian and one of the foremost experts on U.S. civil-military relations, noted in a March 2007 interview that senior military leaders have an obligation to present their best professional advice to their civilian superiors, but while in uniform, they are compelled to obey lawful orders even if they disagree with them. While they may resign or go public with their dissent, the threat of doing so could be interpreted as an attempt to veto policy decisions that are the province of their civilian superiors. See also a commentary that Kohn coauthored with former Chairman of the Joint Chiefs of Staff Richard B. Myers, "The Military's Place,"

Foreign Affairs (September/October 2007): 147–149. Kohn was also the thesis adviser for H. R. McMaster, whose doctoral dissertation examining the issue of military advice to policymakers during the Vietnam War was published under the title *Dereliction of Duty: Lyndon Johnson, Robert McNamara, the Joint Chiefs of Staff, and the Lies that Led to* Vietnam (New York: HarperCollins, 1997).

13   assessment process of the military apparatuses in Iraq and stateside One such officer, Lt. Col. James Gavrilis, served in the Iraq plans office of the joint staff for two years after two tours in Iraq. He was extremely frustrated at the military's myopic focus on two missions, building Iraqi security forces and counterterrorism. Gavrilis lamented the failure to concentrate on institutional development at the local or provincial level until late 2006, and even then inadequate manpower and insecurity inhibited progress. See his article, "The Mayor of Ar Rutbah," *Foreign Policy* (November/December 2005): 28–35.

13   The fault lay at the strategic level To require interagency planning for "complex contingency operations" and to ensure that political-military plans were developed, the Clinton administration issued Presidential Decision Directive 56 in May 1997, but the Bush administration did not adopt the practice. An unclassified white paper describing the directive is posted at www.fas.org/irp/offdocs/pdd56.htm.

18   Chiarelli had advocated in a *Military Review* article that U.S. troops could and should conduct counterinsurgency missions Maj. Gen. Peter W. Chiarelli and Maj. Patrick R. Michaelis, "Winning the Peace: The Requirement for Full-Spectrum Operations," *Military Review* (July/August 2006): 4–17. After his tour as the Multi-National Corps-Iraq commander, Chiarelli also wrote "Learning from Our Modern Wars: The Imperatives of Preparing for a Dangerous Future," *Military Review* (September/October 2007): 2–15.

19   It had not even published a public strategy for the war The National Strategy for Victory in Iraq is posted at www.whitehouse.gov/infocus/iraq/iraq_strategy_nov2005.html.

22   O'Sullivan drafted a memorandum The memorandum is posted at www.nytimes.com/2006/11/29/world/middleeast/29mtext.html?pagewanted =print.

CHAPTER 2:
A FAILING WAR, AND THE DECISION TO SURGE

27   followed by a drawdown to some sixty thousand troops Author interviews with military officials involved in the review. The four options are also outlined in Thomas E. Ricks, "Pentagon May Suggest Short-Term Buildup Leading to Iraq Exit," *Washington Post,* November 20, 2006. Mansoor's book on his first Iraq tour, *Baghdad at Sunrise: A Brigade Commander's War in Iraq,* will be published by Yale University Press in 2008.

35   Keane was one of the most vocal surge proponents Including Linda Robinson, "Getting Out: It Won't Be Quick or Easy," in *U.S. News & World Report,* December 4, 2006, pp. 38–44.

39   Casey had twice proposed and attempted to draw down U.S. troop levels Eric Schmitt, "Military Plans Gradual Cuts in Iraq Forces," *New York Times,* August 7, 2005, described Casey's first drawdown plan as briefed to the Pentagon in July 2005. According to the author's interviews with Lt. Gen. Thomas Metz, the Multi-National Corps-Iraq commander in 2004–2005, the U.S. coalition envisioned Iraqi forces gradually assuming control locally, regionally, and then nationally. The second Casey plan was described by two officials in Iraq who helped develop and implement it.

40   Gen. Peter Schoomaker had repeatedly warned See the author's interview with Gen. Schoomaker, "A Candid General's Parting Shots," *U.S. News & World Report,* March 18, 2007.

43   ". . . capable of providing the security that Baghdad needs" The speech and a description of the New Way Forward are posted at www.white house.gov/news/releases/2007/01/20070110-3.html.

44   the oft-quoted Colin Powell "Pottery Barn" comment Powell's comment is reported in Michael R. Gordon and General Bernard E. Trainor, *Cobra II: The Inside Story of the Invasion and Occupation of Iraq* (New York: Pantheon, 2006), p. 71.

45   losers of wars could expect to experience diminished influence One of the few to contemplate the broad ramifications of defeat was Richard Haass, the president of the Council on Foreign Relations, who argued that losing in Iraq need not have the same effects as the loss in Vietnam. He favored giving Iraq's government an ultimatum and then cutting U.S. losses while shoring up regional partners to withstand any fallout. See Richard N. Haass, "The New Middle East," *Foreign Affairs,* November/December 2006.

CHAPTER 3:

DAVID HOWELL PETRAEUS

This chapter is largely based on interviews with Petraeus, his colleagues at various points in his career, and family members, and relevant documents.

49   He would be compared to Creighton Abrams Lewis Sorley, *A Better War: The Unexamined Victories and Final Tragedy of America's Last Years in Vietnam*" (Orlando: Harcourt, 1999).

51   Bill Carpenter, the famous "Lonely End" football star Unless otherwise noted, quoted statements of Petraeus are from author's interviews with him.

51   Beneath a photo of a handsome young man with a toothy grin *Howitzer* USMA yearbook, Class of 1974, p. 484.

58   Petraeus quoted Secretary of Defense James Schlesinger Bound copy of Petraeus's dissertation, "The American Military and the Lessons of Vietnam: A Study of Military Influence and the Use of Force in the Post-Vietnam Era," p. 314.

58   He cited as well the judgment of Eliot Cohen Ibid., p. 313.

59   Petraeus coauthored an article with Galvin John Rogers Galvin and David Petraeus, "Uncomfortable Wars: Toward a New Paradigm," *Parameters* 16 (Winter 1986): 2–8.

59   He was also quoted in a 1986 *Wall Street Journal* article as an adviser to Galvin Clifford Krauss and Tim Carrington, "Latin Lesson: U.S. Effort to Win 'Hearts and Minds' Gains in El Salvador," *Wall Street Journal,* September 8, 1986.

59   During Petraeus's sojourn in the civilian world His comments are transcribed in Kendall D. Gott et al., eds., *Security Assistance: U.S. and International Historical Perspectives, the Proceedings of the Combat Studies Institute 2006 Military History Symposium* (Fort Leavenworth, Kan.: Combat Studies Institute Press, 2006), p. 27. He also discusses the applicability of his academic experience in "To Ph.D. or Not to Ph.D.," *American Interest,* July/August 2007, p. 5. In it he writes, "I especially recommend it [a PhD] for all young captains who think, to any degree, that they're the stuff—which is to say, every young infantry captain," he wrote.

63   Petraeus and the "Devil Brigade" changed many of the practices The brigade's stunning success at its training exercise at the Joint Readiness Training Command in Fort Polk is described in Tom Clancy, *Airborne: A Guided Tour of an Airborne Task Force* (New York: Berkley, 1997). Using a clever stratagem and scheme of maneuver, Petraeus launched his attack before the hour he published in his attack order, overran the opposition force, and even caught the observers napping.

67   He believed a leader's job was literally to set the pace One of Gen. Petraeus's impromptu pushup contests is recounted in an article at the outset of the Iraq war. See Jim Dwyer, "Threats and Responses: Division Commander; A Ferocious Competitor Pushes His Soldiers, and Himself, Hard," *New*

York Times, March 18, 2003. Dwyer cites the general's time in the Army Ten Miler as 63:46. Willie Stern, "The General Motors," *Runner's World,* December 3, 2007, wrote that the general clocked in at under six minutes a mile in the 5.7-mile run, leaving Stern and all but Martins, Petraeus's aide de camp Maj. Everett Spain, and two others behind. In a conversation with this author at Camp Liberty, Stern said he was put off by the fact that Petraeus was so competitive and could recall his race times from a quarter century before.

67   Instead in mid-April it leapfrogged north The actions of Gen. Petraeus and the 101st Airborne Division in March and April 2003 in Operation Iraqi Freedom are chronicled in Rick Atkinson, *In the Company of Soldiers* (New York: Henry Holt, 2004).

69   This program was then formalized as the Commander's Emergency Response Program The detail on the 101st's program comes from PowerPoint slides provided by Col. Hickman. See also Mark Martins, "No Small Change of Soldiering: The Commander's Emergency Response Program in Iraq and Afghanistan—CERP," *Army Lawyer,* February 2004, p. 8, for description of the genesis of CERP and legal authorities.

69   CERP projects were judged by the U.S. special inspector general The special inspector general for Iraqi reconstruction, Stuart Bowen, testified to the House Oversight and Government Reform Committee on February 15, 2007, that one of his principal conclusions from the years of investigation and oversight was to "pursue the institutionalization of special contracting programs. In Iraq, smaller scale contracting programs, like the CERP and the Commander's Humanitarian Relief and Reconstruction Program, achieved great success. Congress should legislatively institutionalize such programs for easy implementation in future contingency operations." See also his in-depth investigative and quarterly reports to Congress at www.sigir.mil/reports/Default.aspx.

70   Chalabi's commission Petraeus's comments were made in an e-mail exchange with the author, January 31, 2008.

75   vast unsecured stocks of Saddam's army One of the most extraordinary yet common sights in the weeks and months after the major-combat phase ended was the fantastic quantity of shells, rockets, and bombs that lay about every military base in Iraq. The main base outside Kut, for example, was littered with dozens of earthen revetments where finned blue bombs were stacked. Hangars and cement bunkers were packed to the ceilings with millions of shells and rounds of ammunition. A half-dozen semitrailers of guns and munitions of all varieties were dropped off at a Special Forces camp near Nasiriya in early April 2003, almost casually, by an explosive ordnance detachment to fill a request for AK-47s to arm an Iraqi militia, the Free Iraqi Fighting Forces, that had beeen hastily formed by the United States.

76 rogue armed bands accused of criminal and sectarian violence Lt. Gen. Dempsey discussed the problems frankly in several interviews with the author in 2004, 2006, and 2007. See also Walter Pincus, "U.S. Military Urging Iraq to Rein in Guard Force," *Washington Post,* December 25, 2006, p. A11.

76 Petraeus wrote an op-ed "Battling for Iraq," *Washington Post,* September 26, 2004.

77 Petraeus gave numerous speeches and wrote David H. Petraeus, "Learning Counterinsurgency: Observations from Soldiering in Iraq," *Military Review* (January/February 2006): 2–12.

78 legitimacy as the cornerstone for any successful counterinsurgency Eliot Cohen, Conrad Crane, Jan Horvath, and John Nagl, "Principles, Imperatives, Paradoxes of Counterinsurgency," *Military Review* (March/April 2006): 49.

79 They included not only combat or security operations U.S. Army Field Manual 3-24, *Counterinsurgency* (Washington, D.C.: Department of the Army, 2006), p. 5-3–5-17; see especially paragraph 5-18. Also published as *The U.S. Army–Marine Corps Counterinsurgency Field Manual* (Chicago: University of Chicago Press, 2007). The University of Chicago edition includes forewords by Petraeus, Lt. Gen. James F. Amos, and Lt. Col. John A. Nagl, and an introduction by Sarah Sewall that discusses the need to develop an interagency all-government approach to counterinsurgency.

CHAPTER 4:
THE PETRAEUS TEAM LAUNCHES

87 The insurgents had also stepped up attacks against U.S. aircraft Maj. Gen. James Simmons, MNC-I deputy commanding general, cited these statistics in a February 11, 2007, press briefing at the Combined Press Information Center in Baghdad.

98 Creighton Abrams when he arrived in Vietnam *A Better War,* by Lewis Sorley (Orlando: Harcourt, 1999), pp. 123–124.

98 McMaster was also the author H. R. McMaster, *Dereliction of Duty: Lyndon Johnson, Robert McNamara, the Joint Chiefs of Staff, and the Lies that Led to* Vietnam (New York: HarperCollins, 1997).

99 Kilcullen . . . developed ideas for combating Islamic radicalism as a global insurgency. George Packer, "Knowing the Enemy," *New Yorker,* December 18, 2006, is a comprehensive survey of Kilcullen's thinking.

NOTES TO CHAPTER 5

99   practical tactics soldiers could apply "Twenty-Eight Articles: Fundamentals of Company-level Counterinsurgency" in *Military Review* (May 2006): 103–108, and as Appendix A in U.S. Army Field Manual 3-24, *Counterinsurgency* (Washington, D.C.: Department of the Army, 2006).

99   Another key feature of the group The two dozen JSAT members also included Col. John Martin, a classmate of Petraeus's from West Point who had been his political-military deputy at MNSTC-I and who had returned to duty once again at his old friend's request; Col. Mike Meese, who chaired the social sciences department at West Point and had been with him in the Balkans; CIA veteran Regis Matlak; Ylber Bajraktari, a Kosovar Petraeus had met during the Balkans conflict and a recent Woodrow Wilson School graduate; and Steve Biddle, of the Council on Foreign Relations.

100 coalition forces all over Iraq The non-U.S. members of the coalition evolved over time, as did the number of forces they contributed. At the war's peak in 2004, thirty-two countries contributed 25,595 service members. The force shrank to twenty-six countries and 11,755 troops at the end of 2007. After the United States, Britain contributed the most forces throughout this time. (See Joshua Partlow, "List of 'Willing' Allies Shrinks Steadily in Iraq," *Washington* Post, December 8, 2007.) The British contingent based in Basra was due to shrink to 2,500 by spring 2008. Georgia increased its contingent to 2,000 in 2007 and agreed to relocate it to Kut, in southeastern Iraq, to help monitor the border with Iran.

115 starving Sunni areas of resources McMaster had a personal wish to see the government finally deliver a promised $37 million in to Tal Afar, where his hard-won gains were in jeopardy. The provincial government had not disbursed the money to the city and no one in the central government was making it happen. Nor was the moribund U.S. Iraq Reconstruction Management Office (IRMO) doing anything about it. One American general fumed that IRMO had been "criminally negligent" in its duties and that its director had viewed his role as merely that of a "consultant" with no responsibility for making things happen.

CHAPTER 5:

FARDH AL-QANOON, THE BAGHDAD SECURITY PLAN

120 Ollivant experienced how politics affected Karl Vick, "In Najaf, Iraqi Politics Dictate U.S. Tactics," *Washington Post,* August 24, 2004, p. A01.

120 directing it to fire or withhold fire on given targets Ibid.

121 Ollivant collaborated . . . to write an article Lt. Col. Douglas A. Olli-vant and 1st Lt. Eric D. Chewning, "Producing Victory: Rethinking Conventional Forces in COIN Operations," *Military Review* (July/August 2006), pp. 50–59. Ollivant holds a PhD in political science from Indiana University.

121 ". . . should be the basic tactical unit of counterinsurgency (COIN) warfare" Ibid., p. 50.

122 ". . . powering down . . . to implement a Galula-like solution" Ibid., p. 59.

122 moving to . . . overwatch positions Author interviews and e-mail communications with Ollivant.

122 ". . . that does not count for anything unless you hold it afterward" Interview with author, MND-B headquarters, April 2007.

124 The newly released U.S. Army Field Manual 3-24 See briefing slides at www.whitehouse.gov/nsc/iraq/2007/iraq-strategy011007.pdf.

124 recommended a minimum of 20 counterinsurgents per 1,000 inhabitants FM 3-24, 1-67.

124 under that formula for a population of 6 million For a discussion of these issues, see Linda Robinson, "Why More May Not Be Enough," *U.S. News & World Report,* January 14, 2007, pp. 34–36.

124 Petraeus chose to focus . . . on the sectarian "fault lines" See Andrew Krepinevich, "How to Win in Iraq," *Foreign Affairs* (September/October 2005).

CHAPTER 6:

THE POLITICAL PUZZLE

146 Mahdi . . . also had written a proposal for a super region See Ali Allawi, *The Occupation of Iraq: Winning the War, Losing the Peace,* pp. 408–409. Allawi, a Shia and former interim Iraqi prime minister, had made such a suggestion himself in 1992. But it was the SCIRI leader, Abdul Aziz al-Hakim, also head of the UIA, who publicly called for a Shia-ruled region in the south of Iraq in an August 2005 speech in Najaf four days before the deadline for finishing the constitution.

147 Sadr joined forces with Islamic Dawa His uncle had helped form Dawa in the late 1950s to oppose the rise of the secular and socialist Baath Party. The uncle, Muhammed Bakr al-Sadr, was arrested and executed by Saddam Hussein's regime in 1980.

149 Ryan Crocker . . . kept his feelings about the wisdom of the war Crocker and William Burns cowrote a still-classified six-page memo tilled "The Perfect Storm," reported by *Washington Post* writer Karen DeYoung in her book *Soldier: The Life of Colin Powell* (New York: Random House, 2006).

157 After a half-dozen army officers were forced out Joshua Partlow, "Maliki's Office is Seen Behind Purge in Forces," *Washington Post,* April 30, 2007. Specific cases were also discussed in numerous interviews by the author with U.S. and Iraqi officials, including military advisers assigned to Iraqi units.

161 fire-breathing sermons . . . outside Najaf Sadr, or at least some of his armed retinue, was believed to be responsible for the April 2003 killing of another rival cleric, Abdul Majid Al-Khoei, who returned from exile in London and was slain on the steps of the Najaf mosque in Najaf. In April 2004, Bremer closed Sadr's newspaper and an Iraqi judge working for the occupation authority issued a warrant for Sadr's arrest in the Khoei case. The young cleric called for an uprising that swept through Sadr City, a teeming slum of two million in Baghdad, as well as Najaf, Kut, and other southern cities. Soon the throngs of young men were organizing themselves into the Jaish al-Mahdi, or Army of the Faithful, and responding to his every dictate. After years of dictatorship, Iraq was ripe for mob rule. The Shia Grand Ayatollah Sistani defused the crisis with a cease-fire.

165   suspending ISOF raids for four months They were also at times directed by Iraqi civilian officials to attack suspect targets, in which case they requested more adequate intelligence before proceeding. The Iraqi government had authorized raids on a list of targets including the special groups and their secret cells, but it then suspended all ISOF operations for four months after an incident in Sadr City in March 2006. After a nighttime raid, the bodies of dead Iraqis were arranged in a prayer hall, and Sadrists claimed that it was the scene of a massacre. U.S. officials said seventeen militia members had been killed in a firefight. In late summer the special operations unit was allowed to resume, but the Iraqi government frequently protested if the AC-130 gunship had to be called on to return fire. It also forced the U.S. military to release senior JAM figures who had been detained.

167 MNF-I chief spokesman . . . released a number of details about the captures Transcript of press conference with Maj. Gen. Kevin Bergner, MNF-I chief spokesman, posted at: www.mnf-iraq.com.

CHAPTER 7:
DOWNSIZING EXPECTATIONS

169 Congress passed a war funding bill The requirements, conditions and benchmarks are contained in Section 1314 of P.L. 110–28, the U.S. Troop Readiness, Veterans' Care, Katrina Recovery, and Iraq Accountability Act, 2007.

CHAPTER 8:
THE BLUE SPADERS IN THE INFERNO

This chapter was based on multiple visits to Adhamiya, Command Outpost Apache and Old MOD during 2007, extensive interviews and patrols with various members of 1st Battalion, 26th Infantry Regiment at all echelons, and internal documents. The author also interviewed Lt. Col. Sean Swindell, commander of Special Operations Task Force-Central, in 2006 and 2007.

214 John Meyer would be coming back The 1st Battalion, 26th Infantry Regiment was reflagged as 2nd Battalion, 28th Regiment and moved to Grafenwoehr, Germany, after it returned from Iraq in 2007. Its parent unit was reflagged as the 172nd Infantry Brigade.

CHAPTER 9:
THE KNIGHTS OF AMERIYA

This chapter was based primarily on interviews and firsthand reporting in Ameriya with 1st Battalion, 5th Cavalry Regiment, residents of Ameriya, Abu Abid and his family, and other members of the Forsan al-Rafidan, supplemented by interviews with other civilian and military Iraqi and U.S. officials.

233 "There's a guy here in a ski mask with a PKC" See Joshua Partlow, "For U.S. Unit in Baghdad, an Alliance of Last Resort," *Washington Post*, June 9, 2007, p A01. The author relies on this account for Salge's words. In interviews with the author, Lt. Col. Kuehl used slightly different words in recalling his conversations during the uprising of May 31–June 2, but the versions did not differ substantively. Col. Burton's remarks are his own recollections given to the author in an interview.

CHAPTER 10:
THE SONS OF IRAQ

266 In southern Baghdad, Col. Ricky Gibbs These statistics on the Rashid Security District were given in a press briefing by the brigade commander for the area, Col. Ricky Gibbs, on May 25, 2007, available under the media transcripts section at www.defenselink.mil.

268 Based on these data, the intelligence official believed that the magnitude of the demographic shift had been exaggerated in many reports As of August 2007, the Baghdad division had compiled the data gathered by troops, compared it to other available data and reached the following broad estimates. Neighborhoods that were still 75 percent or more Sunni were Adhamiya, Fadl, Mansour, East Rashid (including Dora), and the West Rashid neighborhoods of Saidiya and Bayaa. Zayuna was deemed to be 70 percent Sunni. The mixed neighborhoods which still contained large Sunni minorities were Karkh, Rusafa, North Adhamiya (Rabi, Basateen, Tunis, Suleikh, Qahira, Waziriya, Mustansiriya), and part of West Rashid. One officer noted that the U.S. military had not recognized the methodical displacement of families from Hurriya in 2005–2006 until the formerly Sunni neighborhood next to Kadhimiya became wholly Shia. The same had also occurred in the large districts on either side of Sadr City, Shaab and Ur to the northwest and New Baghdad to the south, and in Karrada and West Rashid. JAM was actively pushing Sunnis out of Saidiya through the summer of 2007.

269 Fil said 54 percent of the city's 474 muhallas were in the control or retain phase These statistics were given in a September 21, 2007, press briefing by Maj. Gen. Joseph Fil, MND-B commander. Transcript is available at www.defenselink.mil/press. Additional information supplied by the command showed that attacks on civilians in Baghdad had declined from 2,455 in January to 1,527 in July and 718 by the third week of August. Iraqi civilians killed in the city went from 423 in November 2006 to 223 in July 2007; civilian casualties went from 1,472 to 736 in the same time; and dead bodies reported declined from 435 to 136.

CHAPTER 11:
FULL-COURT PRESS

272 When MacFarland's successor, Col. John Charlton of the 1st Brigade, 3rd Infantry Division, arrived in February 2007 Charlton gave these statistics in an August 3, 2007, press briefing, posted at www.defenselink .mil.

274 To further sweeten the pot These statistics on aid to Anbar were provided by Petraeus adviser John Martin and Deputy Prime Minister Barham Salih.

CHAPTER 12:
THE SEPTEMBER RECKONING

296 Frank Rich questioned Petraeus's character Frank Rich's *New York Times* column, "Who Really Took Over During that Colonoscopy," appeared on July 29, 2007. Many other columnists and bloggers speculated that Petraeus would present misleading or false testimony (see for example former CIA analyst and antiwar activist Ray McGovern's column, posted at www.antiwar.com/mcgovern/?articleid=11572). Veteran *Newsweek* reporter Rod Nordland recanted his own 2004 cover story, "Can This Man Save Iraq?" which he labeled "fawning." It is posted at www.newsweek.com/id/40417/page/2.

296 sectarian killing only those victims shot in the back of the head In the three-page handout titled "MNF-I Ethnosectarian Violence Methodology," the violent incidents classified as "executions" are described as follows: "Executions: Civilians that show signs of torture, being bound, blindfolded, or shot anywhere in the head; decapitated, strangled, hung, suffocated, mutilated, and/or three or more bodies found together. This does not include three or more bodies found together due to IDF [indirect fire]. We do use Host Nation reporting when identifying executions since they are the best information available from morgues and police stations. We do not include executions against ISF, IP [Iraqi Security Forces, Iraqi Police], or any other government personnel. Not all executions are ethno-sectarian; there are times when executions can be conducted due to intra-sect violence and are therefore not counted as an ethno-sectarian event. Coalition reporting and Host Nation reporting are used for this category." In addition, the document says: "Murder: There will be occasions where a murder will be categorized as ethno-sectarian violence. Coalition reporting and Host Nation reporting are used for this category. Example: An Iraqi was shot or stabbed coming out of a mosque. This gives the suspicion of ethno-sectarian violence although it does not meet the execution criteria and should be counted as suspected ethno-sectarian violence." The way in which deaths were categorized was one source of dispute; the fact that not all deaths were verified by U.S. personnel posed another problem. The MNF-I command in Iraq included Iraqi government death tolls, but the Department of Defense's quarterly 9010 Report included only data reported by U.S. personnel. (These reports from 2005 to 2008 are posted at www.defenselink.mil/home/features/Iraq_Reports/index.html.) The Iraqi data were not unimpeachable. In a press conference on September 12, 2007, Iraqi National Security Adviser Mowaffak al-Rubaie said various Iraqi ministry counts were not coordinated and probably were inflated by an order of magnitude. Given the difficulties of collecting, verifying, and analyzing the data, and the minimal U.S. effort to collect data on Iraq casualties before 2006, officials could not claim to have completely accurate statistics.

297 The GAO relied on the same data as MNF-I Dr. Stephen Biddle, senior fellow at the Council on Foreign Relations, posted his comparative analysis of the various governmental and nongovernmental statistical reports at www.cfr.org/publication/14295.

298 Petraeus delivered his bottom line Petraeus's testimony and the charts, including one showing the Weekly Attack Trends (2004–2007), are posted at: http://foreignaffairs.house.gov/110/pet091007.pdf.

298 The September 14 report released by the White House The full report is posted at www.whitehouse.gov/news/releases/2007/09/20070914.pdf. The quoted portion is on p. 2.

299 Congress had commissioned an independent study Gen. James L. Jones et al., *The Report of the Independent Commission on the Security Forces of Iraq*, September 7, 2007, pp. 12, 14, hereafter referred to as the Jones Commission report.

300 Crocker did not try to sugarcoat the situation A National Intelligence Estimate released in August predicted: "The IC [intelligence community] assesses that the Iraqi Government will become more precarious over the next six to 12 months because of criticism by other members of the major Shia coalition (the Unified Iraqi Alliance, UIA), Grand Ayatollah Sistani, and other Sunni and Kurdish parties. Divisions between Maliki and the Sadrists have increased, and Shia factions have explored alternative coalitions aimed at constraining Maliki." The ten-page document, "Prospects for Iraq's Stability: Some Security Progress but National Reconciliation Elusive," is posted at http://media.washingtonpost.com/wpsrv/world/documents/nie_dni_20070823_release.pdf.

304 The most detailed version of this alternative policy James N. Miller and Shawn W. Brimley, *Phased Transition: A Responsible Way Forward and Out of Iraq*, Center for a New American Security, June 2007. This unofficial analysis of the troop levels required for a postsurge advisory, counterterrorism, and emergency backstop mission estimates that roughly 53,000 troops would be needed in Iraq and another brigade or two in Kuwait (3,500 to 8,000) for a total of up to 61,000.

305 But as Republican Sen. Richard Lugar of Indiana had observed The statement of the ranking member of the Senate Foreign Relations Committee is posted in full at http://lugar.senate.gov/press/record.cfm?id=282219&&.

CHAPTER 13:
THE DRAWDOWN BEGINS, AND THE CEASE-FIRE SPREADS

323 These levels of violence corresponded with those last seen in the spring of 2005 These statistics were provided in an interview with Gen. Petraeus and briefing slides prepared by MNF-I. Total violent incidents peaked in June 2007 at a rate of nearly 1,600 weekly, as the Phantom Phoenix offensive was launched. Civilian casualties were twice as high during the August–September 2006 sectarian violence and the car bombings of February and March 2007, according to the unofficial count maintained by Icasualties.org.

315 The Jihad Reconciliation document committed the signatories Lt. Col. Frank provided a copy of the original signed document and a translation of the ten points.

318 Iraqis gathered around as Kuehl made a short, heartfelt speech He said: "While others have criticized and cowered, these soldiers put on their gear, picked up a weapon and stood up for something bigger than themselves. We who have been here should never forget what it has cost. . . . Peace is not achieved by protesting and pontificating from an ivory tower. It comes on the backs of the men and women who have stepped forward to do something about it. It comes from men and women who have sworn an oath to defend the constitution of the nation. . . . A piece of paper that sets forth ideals. Ideals that I have heard expressed by the people we have come here to protect. People who have served alongside us also as volunteers not content to see their country torn apart . . . who have joined their country's armed forces. . . . We must remember and let others know of the sacrifices that have been made here."

321 Maliki agreed to incorporate 20 percent to 25 percent of them The number of volunteers the Iraqi government agreed to incorporate into the police force as a result of the November 30 meeting was characterized differently by various officials. Lt. Gen. Odierno used the 20–25 percent figure; MNF-I spokesman Maj. Gen. Kevin Bergner cited 20 percent as the agreed figure; Brig. Gen. Campbell cited the first phase as 12,671 and an additional 15,000 to 20,000 over the next two years, according to the ministry of interior's official ratio of one policeman per 133 residents. In an interview on January 7, 2008, National Security Adviser Mowaffak al-Rubaie told the author that there was "no ceiling" on how many volunteers could be incorporated, although obviously not all 100,000. According to the March 7, 2008, Pentagon 9010 Report, the Iraqi government had "supported the integration" of 9,000 volunteers into the security forces from the Baghdad area, though it was not clear whether that meant all the steps had been completed to admit them into police training. In a March 13, 2008, press conference, Dr. Tasheen al-Sheikhly, an Iraqi government spokesman, said: "Those who wanted to apply are 18,000. But only 6,000 were able to apply and work for the security services . . . due to the security background check." (The Department of Defense report is posted at www.defenselink.mil/pubs and the transcript of the press conference is posted at the Multi-National Force-Iraq Web site, www.mnf-iraq.com.)

Chapter 14:
To the Brink Again

332 Sunnis generally favored a strong central government Some White House officials who were interviewed thought Sunnis should see federalism as a way to protect their local interests. In on-the-record remarks at the Council on Foreign Relations on September 17, 2007, Stephen Hadley said: "This notion that there needs to be autonomy is not new. It's in the architecture; it was in the concept; it's in the constitution. What has happened, the Kurds loved it and took it early. The Shi'a were interested in forming a regional administration in the south of the provinces, and they slowed down because it was of concern to the Sunnis. Oddly, the group that one would have thought had the most to gain from autonomy was most opposed to it and viewed federalism as a threat to a unified Iraq."

332 Rubaie proposed forming five regions In a paper titled "Democratic Federalism," which Rubaie wrote in October 2007 and gave to the author, he proposed creating five regions, only one of which Sunnis would control (composed of Ninewa and Anbar). Salahuddin and Diyala provinces would be combined with Baghdad province in another region despite the fact that the current constitution states that Baghdad cannot form a region. Under his proposal, 70 percent of the national revenues would be distributed to the regions, and the central government would execute only the minimum national functions, including foreign affairs and national defense. Rubaie stated the underlying rationale for this model of government for Iraq: "A prime condition for the successful devolution of power is that the balance should be tipped decisively to the regions; and that only through a new political compact between Iraq's main communities will a new Iraq state be born. The central institutions must earn their legitimacy from the power that the main three communities are prepared to give to the center; and not the other way around. A period during which both the main disadvantaged communities—the Shia and the Kurds—rediscover political control over their destinies must be combined with a federalism that will give the Arab Sunni community the sense of security from a 'tyranny of the majority.' A regional political structure for Iraq can allow for the devolution of religious, cultural, and educational policies more suited to the requirements of the population than a one-dimensional centralism." A shortened version of this paper was published as an op-ed article, "Federalism, Not Partition," *Washington Post,* January 18, 2008.

332 The new law's impact would depend on how it was implemented The law's primary change was to reduce the original ban on the top four levels of Baathists to only the top three levels, according to Article 6.5 of the bill. But Article 6.6 also banned former regime officials from top positions in key ministries such as defense, interior, and foreign. Some 13,000 third-tier Baath Party officials, known as *shubah* members, could receive pensions but were not eligible for government jobs. Some 3,500 fourth-tier, or *firqa*, officials might be rehired in certain ministries. The new law might require Lt. Gen. Abboud Qanbar, the head of the Baghdad Operations Command, to resign. National Security Adviser Rubaie noted to this reporter a few weeks before the vote, "He was a *firqa*-level Baathist Party member, you know." Rubaie did not offer any endorsement of Abboud's performance over the past year.

333 On December 7, Prime Minister Maliki formally requested The text of U.N. Security Council Resolution 1790 is posted at www.uniraq.org /FileLib/misc/Resolution1790.pdf, along with Maliki's request for the June review. The November 27 bilateral declaration of principles is posted at www.whitehouse.gov/news/releases/2007/11/20071126-11.html.

335 Iraqi security forces had embarked on an ambitious plan to increase their numbers Statistics cited by Gen. Abadi were also included in testimony by Lt. Gen. James Dubik, head of the MNSTC-I command responsible for security assistance to the Iraqi forces, January 17, 2008, before the House Armed Services Committee.

336 The September study headed by retired Gen. Jim Jones zeroed in on this problem *The Report of the Independent Commission on the Security Forces of Iraq,* led by Gen. James L. Jones, USMC (Ret.), Chairman, September 6, 2007, p. 53. The report said: "In creating the Office of the Commander in Chief, the Counter-Terrorism Bureau, and in claiming command and control over Iraq's highly capable Special Forces, the Prime Minister is perceived to have established a separate chain of command. At the very least, there now exists the appearance that a senior elected official can bypass existing military command structures for sectarian reasons."

CHAPTER 15:
TELL ME HOW THIS ENDS

353 A recent poll showed that 56 percent of Iraqis Poll results and sample information posted at www.abcnews.go.com/images/PollingUnit/1060a1Iraq WhereThingsStand.pdf.

353 formulas range from U.N. mediation to a U.S.-led Dayton process Former U.S. career ambassador and former Undersecretary of State Thomas R. Pickering advocated this option in "Does the U.N. Have a Role in Iraq?" *Survival,* February/March 2008, pp. 133–141. Iraq's former ambassador to the United States, Rend al-Rahim, proposed the Dayton model in "A Dayton Process for Iraq," *Washington Post,* May 10, 2007, p. A23.

356 According to a February 2008 poll, 67 percent of Iraqis See poll cited above conducted by ABC News and other networks, posted at www .abcnews.go.com/images/PollingUnit/1060a1IraqWhereThingsStand.pdf.

357 A long-term Balkans-type peacekeeping presence may be needed For a sober argument for a long-term peacekeeping presence, see Stephen Biddle's April 2, 2008, testimony before the Senate Foreign Relations Committee, posted at http://foreign.senate.gov/testimony/2008/BiddleTestimony 080402p.pdf.

361 If the United States is to sustain or expand the current advisory effort in Iraq Among the advocates for providing such incentives and rewards is Lt. Col. John Nagl. See his "Institutionalizing Adaptation: It's Time for a Permanent Army Advisor Corps," a monograph published in June 2007 by the Center for a New American Security. The army currently opposes forming a standing advisory corps, but on June 17, 2008, Gen. Casey ordered important changes that enhance career prospects for majors and lieutenant colonels who serve on advisory and provincial reconstruction teams. Lt. colonels who lead transition teams will henceforth receive the same credit as those commanding combat battalions. Another model is to use a private company, on the lines of the long-term training of the Saudi National Guard by Vinnell under U.S. government oversight.

362 Finally, the government's national security process and structures are See, for example, the series of "Beyond Goldwater-Nichols" studies published by the Center for Strategic and International Studies, posted at www.csis.org/isp/bgn/. Nonmilitary agencies charged with key roles in preventing and mitigating conflict and assisting the military in stabilization and postwar reconstruction have been underfunded, understaffed, or disbanded (including the State Department, U.S. AID, and USIA). They lack enough qualified personnel trained in the right skills and languages. Despite numerous directives to rebuild civilian stability operations capacity, presidential leadership and a congressional commitment to adequate funding are still lacking. James Dobbins critiques the administration's tendency to place loyalists rather than competent professionals in key civilian policy jobs in "Who Lost Iraq?" *Foreign Affairs* (September/October 2007): 61–74. For an excellent study of the decision-making process during the early stages of the Iraq war, see Joseph J. Collins, "Choosing War: The Decision to Invade Iraq and Its Aftermath," Occasional Paper No. 5, April 2008, National Defense University Institute for National Security Studies. Collins was deputy assistant secretary of defense for stability operations during the time covered in his study. The paper is posted at www.ndu.edu/inss/Occasional_Papers/OP5.pdf.

Selected Bibliography

The following books and monographs were of use during the writing of this book, as were congressional hearings, the congressionally mandated quarterly *9010 Reports* provided by the Department of Defense, and press briefings at the Pentagon and the Combined Press Information Center in Baghdad.

Ajami, Fouad. *The Foreigner's Gift.* New York: Free Press, 2006.

Allawi, Ali. *The Occupation of Iraq: Winning the War, Losing the Peace.* New Haven, Conn.: Yale University Press, 2007.

Atkinson, Rick. *In the Company of Soldiers: A Chronicle of Combat.* New York: Henry Holt, 2004.

Bremer, L. Paul, III with Malcolm McConnell. *My Year in Iraq: The Struggle to Build a Future of Hope.* New York: Threshold Editions, 2006.

Briscoe, Charles H., Kenneth Finlayson, et al. *All Roads Lead to Baghdad: Army Special Operations Forces in Iraq.* Fort Bragg, N.C.: U.S. Army Special Operations Command History Office, 2006.

Byman, Daniel L., and Kenneth M. Pollack. "Things Fall Apart: Containing the Spillover from an Iraqi Civil War." Analysis Paper No. 11, January 2007. Washington, D.C.: Saban Center for Middle East Policy at the Brookings Institution.

Catton, Bruce. *Grant Takes Command.* New York: Little, Brown, 1968.

Chandrasekaran, Rajiv. *Imperial Life in the Emerald City: Inside Iraq's Green Zone.* New York: Knopf, 2006.

Davis, Eric. *Memories of State.* Berkeley: University of California Press, 2005.

Diamond, Larry. *Squandered Victory.* New York: Times Books, 2005.

Draper, Robert. *Dead Certain: The Presidency of George W. Bush.* New York: Free Press, 2007.

Fallows, James. *Blind into Baghdad: America's War in Iraq.* New York: Vintage, 2006.

Fontenot, Col. Gregory, Lt. Col. E. J. Degen, and Lt. Col. David Tohn. *On Point: The United States Army in Operation Iraqi Freedom.* Annapolis, Md.: Naval Institute Press, 2005.

Fuller, J. F. C. *Generalship: Its Diseases and Their Cure.* Harrisburg, Pa.: Military Service Publishing, 1936.

Galbraith, Peter W. *The End of Iraq: How American Incompetence Created a War without End.* New York: Simon & Schuster, 2006.

Galula, David. *Counterinsurgency Warfare: Theory and Practice.* Westport, Conn.: Praeger Paperback, 2006.

Gordon, Michael R., and Gen. Bernard E. Trainor. *Cobra II: The Inside Story of the Invasion and Occupation of Iraq.* New York: Pantheon, 2006.

Gott, Kendall D., ed. *Eyewitness to War, Vol. II, the U.S. Army in Operation AL FAJR: An Oral History.* Fort Leavenworth, Kan.: Combat Studies Institute Press, 2006.

_____, et al., eds. Security Assistance: *U.S. and International Historical Perspectives, The Proceedings of the Combat Studies Institute 2006 Military History Symposium.* Fort Leavenworth, Kan.: Combat Studies Institute Press, 2006.

Iraq Study Group Report: A Way Forward—A New Approach. New York: Vintage, 2006.

Kahl, Colin H., Michèle A. Flournoy, and Shawn W. Brimley. *The Iraq Inheritance.* Washington, D.C.: Center for a New American Security, forthcoming.

Mansoor, Peter. *Baghdad at Sunrise: A Brigade Commander's War in Iraq.* New Haven, Conn.: Yale University Press, 2008.

Marr, Phebe. *Iraq's New Political Map.* Washington, D.C.: U.S. Institute of Peace, January 2007. Special Report No. 179; the latest of several special reports by the same expert. See also Special Report No. 155 and others on the Iraqi constitutional process.

_____. *The Modern History of Iraq.* Boulder: Westview Press, 2003.

McMaster, H. R. *Dereliction of Duty: Lyndon Johnson, Robert McNamara, the Joint Chiefs of Staff, and the Lies that Led to Vietnam.* New York: HarperCollins, 1997.

Metz, Steven. *Learning from Iraq: Counterinsurgency in American Strategy.* Carlisle, Pa.: Strategic Studies Institute, U.S. Army War College, 2007 (monograph).

Miller, James N., and Shawn W. Brimley. *Phased Transition: A Responsible Way Forward and Out of Iraq.* Washington, D.C.: Center for a New American Security, 2007 (monograph). The most detailed unofficial analysis of the troop levels that would be required for a post-surge advisory, counterterrorism, and emergency backstop mission. It estimates that roughly 53,000 troops would be needed in Iraq and another brigade or two in Kuwait (3,500 to 8,000) for a total of up to 61,000.

Nagl, John A. *Learning to Eat Soup with a Knife: Counterinsurgency Lessons from Malaya and Vietnam.* Chicago: University of Chicago Press, 2005. First published in 2002 by Praeger.

Packer, George. *The Assassins' Gate: America in Iraq.* New York: Farrar, Straus and Giroux, 2005.

Raddatz, Martha. *The Long Road Home: A Story of War and Family.* New York: Putnam, 2007.

Ricks, Thomas E. *Fiasco: The American Military Adventure in Iraq.* New York: The Penguin Press, 2006.

Special Edition Counterinsurgency Reader, Military Review, October 2006. Fort Leavenworth, Kan.: U.S. Army Combined Arms Center.

Thompson, Sir Robert. *Defeating Communist Insurgency: Experiences from Malaya and Vietnam.* London: Chatto & Windus, 1967.

U.S. Army–Marine Corps Counterinsurgency Field Manual. Chicago: University of Chicago Press, 2007. Also published as U.S. Army Field Manual 3-24, Marine Corps Warfighting Publication 3-33.5. University of Chicago edition includes forewords by Gen. David H. Petraeus, Lt. Gen. James F. Amos, and Lt. Col. John A. Nagl, and an introduction by Sarah Sewall that discusses the need to develop an interagency all-government approach to counterinsurgency.

Woodward, Bob. *State of Denial: Bush at War, Part III.* New York: Simon & Schuster, 2006.

Index

Steve Hebert

LINDA ROBINSON is author in residence at the Philip Merrill Center for Strategic Studies at the Johns Hopkins School for Advanced International Studies. She covered wars in Iraq, Afghanistan, and Latin America, as well as other national security issues, as a senior writer for *U.S. News & World Report*. She is the author of the *New York Times* best seller *Masters of Chaos: The Secret History of the Special Forces* and articles in *Foreign Affairs, World Policy Journal, Survival,* the *New Republic, Outside,* and *Condé Nast Traveler.* She was a Nieman Fellow at Harvard University and senior editor of *Foreign Affairs.* She is the recipient of the Gerald R. Ford Prize for Reporting on National Defense for 2004 and other journalism awards.

PublicAffairs is a publishing house founded in 1997. It is a tribute to the standards, values, and flair of three persons who have served as mentors to countless reporters, writers, editors, and book people of all kinds, including me.

I. F. STONE, proprietor of *I. F. Stone's Weekly*, combined a commitment to the First Amendment with entrepreneurial zeal and reporting skill and became one of the great independent journalists in American history. At the age of eighty, Izzy published *The Trial of Socrates*, which was a national bestseller. He wrote the book after he taught himself ancient Greek.

BENJAMIN C. BRADLEE was for nearly thirty years the charismatic editorial leader of *The Washington Post*. It was Ben who gave the *Post* the range and courage to pursue such historic issues as Watergate. He supported his reporters with a tenacity that made them fearless and it is no accident that so many became authors of influential, best-selling books.

ROBERT L. BERNSTEIN, the chief executive of Random House for more than a quarter century, guided one of the nation's premier publishing houses. Bob was personally responsible for many books of political dissent and argument that challenged tyranny around the globe. He is also the founder and longtime chair of Human Rights Watch, one of the most respected human rights organizations in the world.

⋅　　⋅　　⋅

For fifty years, the banner of Public Affairs Press was carried by its owner Morris B. Schnapper, who published Gandhi, Nasser, Toynbee, Truman, and about 1,500 other authors. In 1983, Schnapper was described by *The Washington Post* as "a redoubtable gadfly." His legacy will endure in the books to come.

Peter Osnos, *Founder and Editor-at-Large*